Table of Conte

Chapter 1
Meet Your Sony Cyber-shot DSC-RX100 V

Chapter 2
Your Camera Roadmap

Chapter 3
Camera Settings Menu

Chapter 4
Custom Settings Menu

Chapter 5
Wi-Fi and Application Menus

Chapter 6
Playback and Setup Menus

Chapter 7
Shooting Modes and Exposure Control

Chapter 8

Mastering the Mysteries of Autofocus

Chapter 9
Advanced Techniques

Chapter 10
Introduction to Movie Making

Chapter 11
Making Light Work for You

About the Author

With more than 2 million books in print, **David D. Busch** is the world's #1 selling author of camera-specific photography books, and the originator of popular series like *David Busch's Pro Secrets* and *David Busch's Quick Snap Guides*. He has written more than 200 hugely successful photography guides and camera-specific manuals for Canon, Nikon, Sony, Olympus, Pentax, and Panasonic products, including the all-time bestsellers for the many models, as well as many popular books devoted to dSLRs. As a roving photojournalist for more than 20 years, he illustrated his books, magazine articles, and newspaper reports with award-winning images. He's operated his own commercial studio, suffocated in formal dress while shooting weddings-for-hire, and shot sports for a daily newspaper and upstate New York college. His photos and articles have been published in *Popular Photography, Rangefinder, Professional Photographer,* and hundreds of other publications. He's also reviewed dozens of digital cameras for Ziff-Davis online and print publications.

When About.com named its top five books on Beginning Digital Photography, debuting at the #1 and #2 slots were Busch's *Digital Photography All-In-One Desk Reference for Dummies* and *Mastering Digital Photography*. During the past year, he's had as many as five of his books listed in the Top 20 of Amazon.com's Digital Photography Bestseller list -- simultaneously! Busch's 150-plus other books published since 1983 include bestsellers like *David Busch's Quick Snap Guide to Using Digital SLR Lenses*. His advice has been featured on National Public Radio's *All Tech Considered*.

Busch is a member of the Cleveland Photographic Society (www.clevelandphoto.org), which has operated continuously since 1887. Visit his Nikon website at http://www.sonyguides.com. There you'll find news, tips, and an errata page with typo alerts from sharp-eyed readers, along with an E-Mail Me tab you can use to contact him directly.

Preface

In a few short years, Sony has gone from being a Nikon and Canon competitor to an acknowledged innovator with a lineup of cameras that are smaller, lighter, faster to focus, and loaded with cutting-edge features that many of us have been dreaming about. So, it's no wonder you're excited about your new Sony RX100 V, a tiny pocket-sized camera with full-sized features, including a new sensor design that allows shooting rapid-fire snapshots at up to 24 frames a second, lightning-fast phase detect autofocus, slo-mo movies that can be played back at speeds 40X slower than normal, and Ultra High Definition 4K video. With all these features at your disposal, you don't expect to take good pictures with such a camera -- you demand and anticipate *outstanding* photos.

Unfortunately, your gateway to pixel proficiency is dragged down by the limited instructions provided by Sony. Over the years, Sony has reduced the amount of useful information included in its printed guidebooks, often to a scant few pages, and relegated more detailed instructions to online HTML-based guides and PDF versions that are difficult to navigate. And, sad to say, not everything you need to know is included.

What you really need is a guide that explains the purpose and function of the cameras' basic controls, how you should use them, and *why*. That's what I am giving you in this book. If you want a quick introduction to focus controls or which exposure modes are best, this book is for you. If you can't decide on what basic settings to use with your camera because you can't figure out how changing ISO or white balance or focus defaults will affect your pictures, you need this guide.

Introduction

With Sony's latest version of its wildly-popular RX100 cameras, the Mark V, the company has packaged up the most alluring features of advanced digital cameras and stuffed them into an ultra-compact Wi-Fi/NFC-capable body with an amazing array of features. It boasts a relatively fast Zeiss f/1.8-f/2.8 zoom lens, SteadyShot optical image stabilization, 20 megapixels of resolution, an electronic viewfinder, and built-in flash. An innovative "stacked" CMOS Exmor R 1-inch sensor provides fast image capture and processing, making the 4K video, fast continuous shooting, and video frame rates up to 960/1000 fps possible. It has shutter speeds up to 1/32000th second, and the ability to shoot high resolution still photos while recording HD video.

For those who want a digital camera that can be slipped in a pocket – without sacrificing the full control and features found in much larger cameras, the RX100 V fills the bill. Of course, once you've confirmed that you made a wise purchase, the question comes up, *how do I use this thing?* All those cool features can be mind-numbing to learn, if all you have as a guide is the mediocre manual furnished with the camera. Basic functions and options are explained, but there's really very little about *why* you should use particular settings or features, and the organization may make it difficult to find what you need. Multiple cross-references may send you flipping back and forth between two or three sections of the book to find what you want to know. The basic manual is also hobbled by black-and-white line drawings and tiny pictures that aren't very good examples of what you can do.

Help is on the way. I sincerely believe that this book is your best bet for learning how to use your new camera, and for learning how to use it well. I've tried to make *David Busch s Sony Cyber-shot DSC-RX100 V Fast Track Guide* comprehensive, but easy to comprehend. The roadmap sections use large, color pictures to show you where all the buttons and dials are, and the explanations of what they do are longer and more detailed. I've tried to avoid overly general advice, including the checklists you'll find in other manuals on how to take a "sports picture" or a "portrait picture" or a "travel picture." If you want to know where you should stand to take a picture of a quarterback dropping back to unleash a pass, there are plenty of books that will tell you that. This one concentrates on teaching you how to select the best autofocus mode, shutter speed, f/stop, or flash capability to take, say, a great sports picture under any conditions.

What You'll Learn

This book is aimed at Sony veterans as well as newcomers to digital photography. Both groups can be overwhelmed by the options the RX100 V offers, while underwhelmed by the explanations they receive in their user's manual, which some suspect was written by a Sony employee who last threw together instructions on how to operate a camcorder or DVD player.

I will emphasize *still photography*. However, I *will* devote a lot of space to helping you get up to speed on using the RX100 V's video capabilities. After all, even though tiny in size, it is fully capable of shooting awesome, professional-level movies. But detailed advice about choosing between Internal UHD 4K30 and 1080p/120 fps recording, or technical information about S-Log3 gamma, display assist functions, and other pro-level features are beyond the scope of this book. Given that I expect that only a relatively small -- albeit important -- segment of the readers of this book want or require such information, I'm going with Vulcan philosopher Spock Prime's observation early in *The Wrath of Khan* that "Logic clearly dictates that the needs of the many outweigh the needs of the few."

Who Am I?

After spending many years as the world's most successful unknown author, I've become slightly less obscure in the past few years, thanks to a horde of camera guidebooks and other photographically oriented tomes. You may have seen my photography articles in *Popular Photography, Rangefinder, Professional Photographer,* and dozens of other photographic publications. But, first, and foremost, I'm a photojournalist and made my living in the field until I began devoting most of my time to writing books. Although I love writing, I'm happiest when I'm out taking pictures, which is why I spend many winters ensconced in the Florida Keys, dividing my time between writing books and taking photographs. You'll find images of many of these visual treats within the pages of this guide.

Like all my digital photography books, this one was written by someone with an incurable photography bug. I've worked as a sports photographer for an Ohio newspaper and for an upstate New York college. I've operated my own commercial studio and photo lab, cranking out product shots on demand and then printing a few hundred glossy 8 x 10s on a tight deadline for a press kit. I've served as a photo-posing instructor for a modeling agency. People have actually paid me to shoot their weddings and immortalize them with portraits. I even prepared press kits and articles on photography as a PR consultant for a formerly dominant (and now vestigial) Rochester, NY company. My trials and travails with imaging and computer technology have made their way into print in book form an alarming number of times, including hundreds of volumes on photographic topics. I teach classes, and have branched out into online training courses.

Like you, I love photography for its own merits, and I view technology as just another tool to help me get the images I see in my mind's eye. But, also like you, I had to master this technology before I could apply it to my work. This book is the result of what I've learned, and I hope it will help you master your Sony RX100 V.

I'd like to ask a special favor: let me know what you think of this book. If you have any recommendations about how I can make it better, visit my website at www.sonyguides.com, click on the E-Mail Me tab, and send your comments, suggestions on topics that should be explained in more detail, or, especially, any typos. (The latter will be compiled on the Errata page you'll also find on my website.) I really value your ideas, and appreciate it when you take the time to tell me what you think! Some of the content of the book you hold in your hands came from suggestions I received from readers like yourself. If you found this book especially useful, tell others about it.

Your feedback is what spurs me to make each one of these books better than the last, and if enough of you like what I've done, I may be moved to follow up with a new book the next time Sony introduces one of its photographic innovations. Thanks!

Chapter 1

Meet Your Sony Cyber-shot DSC-RX100 V

For such a tiny camera, your Sony Cyber-shot DSC-RX100 V certainly has an ungainly official moniker! But, of course, your tiny camera with the long name also sports a long list of advanced features. My goal in this book is to show you how to take full advantage of those features. So, don't panic if you opened this book to this introductory "Meet and Greet" chapter and realized that you've already taken several hundred or a thousand (or two) photos with your camera. I realize that most of you didn't buy this book at the same time you purchased your camera. As much as I'd like to picture thousands of avid photographers marching out the door of their retailers with an orange-and-black RX100 V box under one arm, and my book in hand, I know that's not going to happen *all* the time.

It's more likely that you happily worked your way through getting the camera revved up and working well enough to take a bunch of pictures without the universe collapsing. This camera can be incredibly easy to use, right out of the box. Just flick the power switch to On; it's located on top of the camera with an ON/OFF label next to it. Set the language, date, and time if asked, and then, rotate the mode dial at the right edge of the top panel to select the green Auto icon. (See **Figure 1.1**.) Frame the subject on the monitor (the rear LCD screen) -- you don't even need to pop up the electronic viewfinder if you're in a hurry -- then press the shutter release button to take your first shot. That's it!

I've framed this chapter with both the semi-experienced and rawest beginner in mind. Whether you're looking to improve your comfort level with the features of this well-designed (yet fully-featured) camera or are looking forward to starting from scratch, you'll find that the advice I'm about to offer useful. You can zip right through the basics, and then dive into learning a few things you probably didn't know about your RX100 V.

ABOUT THAT NAME

Sony has applied the Cyber-shot name to its point-and-shoot digital cameras since 1996, attaching a DSC (Digital Still Camera) prefix followed by the *series* nomenclature for its RX, T, H/HX, and W series cameras. Point-and-shoot cameras aren't necessarily cheap or simple, as you might guess from a retail price approaching $1,000 for the Cyber-shot DSC-RX100 V, and more than $3,200 for the 42MP Cyber-shot DSC-RX1 R II. I'm going to shorten the name of your camera in this book, for the most part, and refer to it only as the RX100 V.

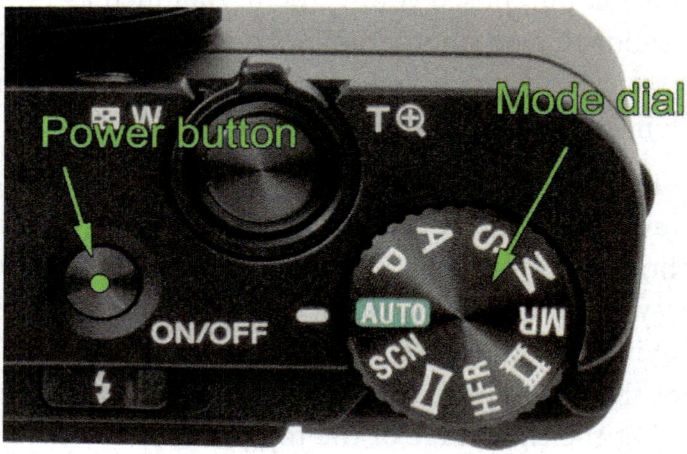

Figure 1.1

Select Auto and take a picture.

Preparing for those steps by charging the battery and inserting a formatted Secure Digital or Memory Stick card isn't exactly rocket science, either. If you rotate the mode dial to any position, such as P, A, or S mode, the camera displays a help screen on the LCD or electronic viewfinder (EVF) indicating the mode's name and purpose. (See **Figure 1.2**.) If you set the mode dial to the SCN position and press the button in the center of the control wheel (located to the immediate right of the LCD monitor), you can then rotate that control wheel to select a scene mode. Press the center button again to confirm your choice, and an icon will appear in the upper-left corner of the LCD monitor screen or EVF to indicate which mode you've selected. The scene modes automatically select all camera settings to make it easy to take excellent shots of people, landscapes, flowers, night scenes, and more.

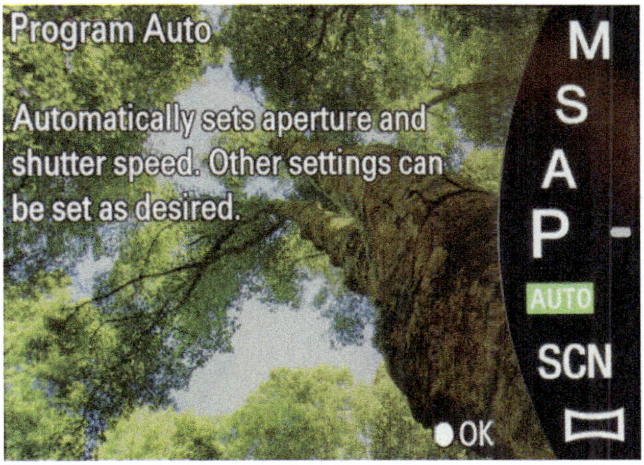

Figure 1.2

A help screen shows each mode's name and typical use.

In practice, though, it's not a bad idea, once you've taken a few orientation pictures with your camera, to go back and review the basic operations of the camera from the beginning, if only to see if you've missed something. This chapter is my opportunity to introduce you to the camera and review the setup procedures for those among you who are already veteran users, and to help ease the more timid into the basic pre-flight checklist that needs to be completed before you really spread your wings and take off. For the uninitiated, as easy as it is to use initially, your Sony RX100 V *does* have some dials, buttons, and menu items that might not make sense at first, but will surely become second nature after you've had a chance to review the instructions in this book.

But don't fret about wading through a manual to find out what you must know to take those first few tentative snaps. I'm going to help you hit the ground running with this chapter (or keep on running if you've already jumped right in). If you *haven't* had the opportunity to use your RX100 V yet, I'll help you set up your camera and begin shooting in minutes. You won't find a lot of operational detail in this chapter. Indeed, I'm going to tell you just what you absolutely *must* understand, accompanied by some interesting tidbits that will help you become acclimated. I'll go into more depth and even repeat some of what I explain here in later chapters, so you don't have to memorize everything you see. Just relax, follow a few easy steps, and then go out and begin taking your best shots -- ever.

Your Out-of-Box Experience

Your Sony RX100 V comes in an attractive box filled with stuff, including a multi-purpose USB/charging cable and AC adapter, a wrist strap, basic instructions, some pamphlets, and a few other items. You'll also need a Secure Digital or Memory Stick card, as one is not included.

The first thing to do is to carefully unpack the camera and double-check the contents. So, check the box at your earliest convenience, and make sure you have (at least) the following:

- **Sony RX100 V camera.** This is hard to miss. The camera is the main reason you laid out the big bucks, and it is tucked away inside a nifty protective envelope you should save for re-use in case the camera needs to be sent in for repair. It almost goes without saying that you should check out the camera immediately, making sure the color LCD on the back isn't scratched or cracked, the battery compartment and connection port doors open properly, and, when a charged battery is inserted and lens mounted, the camera powers up and reports for duty. Out-of-the-box defects in these areas are rare, but they can happen. It's probably more common that your dealer played with the camera or, perhaps, it was a customer return. That's why it's best to buy your camera from a retailer you trust to supply a factory-fresh camera.
- **NP-BX1 lithium ion battery.** The power source for your Sony camera is packaged separately. It should be charged as soon as possible (as described next) and inserted in the camera.
- **My recommendation:** The electronic viewfinder (EVF) and LCD monitor are the culprits that drain the most power from the RX100 V's 1,240 mAh (milli-ampere hour) battery, although the Wi-Fi/NFC feature is a significant drain when activated. You can expect 220 still images when using the LCD monitor to preview your images, or about 210 shots when working with the viewfinder, according to CIPA standards. Although tiny in size, this camera gulps power, and, even with

the generous standards Sony cites in its literature, your battery is likely to last for no more than a few hundred stills or roughly 65 minutes of video. If you are a heavy user of the LCD monitor for review or take many flash pictures, expect even less longevity. Buy *more* batteries, and stick to Sony-brand products; third-party batteries have been known to fail quickly, sometimes in potentially destructive ways.

- **Micro B USB 2.0 cable.** Use this cable to link your Sony to a computer when you need to transfer pictures but don't have an optional card reader accessory handy. While the camera is connected with the cable, the battery inside the body will also be charging. The USB cable can also be connected to the included AC adapter if you want to charge the battery using household power, and will provide a connection to your computer when you upgrade the RX100 V's internal software (*firmware*) from time to time.
- **My recommendation:** Sony stuck with USB 2.0 instead of the faster USB 3.0 protocol because the latter wouldn't allow charging the battery through the USB cable. Use an external charger (described later), instead, and copy images to your computer with any USB card reader, rather than a slow cable connection.
- **AC Adapter AC-UB10.** This is the device that you'll use to charge the battery with household power while it's in the camera (see Figure 1.3, left.) The USB cable plugs into it and the adapter plugs into a wall socket. The cable can also be plugged into a computer's USB port to revitalize your battery.

  My recommendation: The AC adapter is especially useful while traveling, as it eliminates the need to have a computer or laptop powered up to charge the battery.
- **Sony BC-TRX external charger (optional extra).** This handy device (see **Figure 1.3**, center) allows you to recharge one battery while another is ensconced in your camera as you continue shooting. It also includes a USB port and a switch to toggle between charging a battery that's been inserted into the

charger, or directing the power to the USB port so you can charge a battery in the camera (or recharge your smart phone, tablet, or other device). Effectively, this charger is a total replacement for the AC adapter included with your camera.

My recommendation: I strongly prefer this external charger ($49, but frequently available for $30 or less) to the alternative USB cable charging method. Sony uses the X-series batteries in a number of its products, and offers several different compatible chargers. For example, I also own the Sony BC-CXB charger (you can never own too many battery chargers), which can be a little difficult to find in the US (I got mine from Japan). It's smaller, but lacks the status lights and USB ports, so it's strictly a backup in my kit.

- **Application software.** Sony no longer includes a software CD in the package. The first time you power up the camera, it will display the current URL for your country where you can download imaging software for the RX100 V, such as the PlayMemories utility.
- **Printed instruction manual.** The camera comes with a Wi-Fi/One Touch (NFC) connection guide and a brief printed instruction booklet; a longer guide to the camera's operation can be accessed from Sony's esupport.sony.com website. There will also be assorted pamphlets listing available accessories as well as warranty and registration information.
- **Wrist strap and strap adapter.** Sony furnishes a sturdy wrist strap, which you'll want to attach as a safety measure. I purchased an even lighter-weight wrist strap with a quick-release snap, which makes the RX100 V even more pocketable. I'll send you one for a couple bucks (visit www.sonyguides.com.)

Initial Setup

The initial setup of your Sony is fast and easy. You just need to charge the battery and insert a memory card. I'll address each of these steps separately, but if you already feel you can manage these setup tasks without further instructions, feel free to skip this section entirely. You should probably at least skim its contents, however, because I'm going to list a few options that you might not be aware of.

Battery Included

Your Sony RX100 V is a sophisticated hunk of machinery and electronics, but it needs a charged battery to function, so rejuvenating the NP-BX1 lithium-ion battery pack should be your first step. A fully charged power source should be good for as many as 220 shots or up to 65 minutes of video under normal temperature conditions. However, I frequently (always) deplete my batteries more quickly. Sony's estimates are based on standard tests defined by the Camera & Imaging Products Association (CIPA). If you often use the camera's Wi-Fi/NFC feature (discussed later), you can expect to take fewer shots before it's time for a recharge.

All rechargeable batteries undergo some degree of self-discharge just sitting idle in the camera or in the original packaging. Lithium-ion power packs of this type typically lose a small amount of their charge every day, even when the camera isn't turned on. Li-ion cells lose their power through a chemical reaction that continues when the camera is switched off. So, it's very likely that the battery purchased with your camera, even if charged at the factory, has begun to poop out after the long sea voyage on a banana boat (or, more likely, a trip by jet plane followed by a sojourn in a warehouse), so you'll want to revive it before going out for some serious shooting.

My recommendation: As I mentioned earlier, I own several NP-BX1 batteries, and I keep one in the camera at all times. Nevertheless, I always check battery status before I go out to shoot, as some juice may have been siphoned off while the camera sat idle. I go to the Wireless 1 menu and turn Airplane Mode on (as described in Chapter 5) when I don't need Wi-Fi features. While my RX100 V typically lives in my pocket and I leave a camera bag behind most of the time, if I'm going to be out shooting for a full day or more, I always find a place to stash a couple extra batteries.

Charging the Battery

You can charge the battery while it's in the camera, or remove it and use the optional BC-TRX external charger. Depending on which method you choose, either make sure the battery is inserted into the camera or remove it. To extract the battery, press the blue lever in the battery compartment that prevents the pack from slipping out when the door is opened; then, ease the battery out. The battery can only be seated in the camera one way, as shown in **Figure 1.3**, right. (It will fit several *incorrect* ways, but it doesn't "click" into place unless you have the three contacts oriented toward the interior and the label with the X icon facing the front of the camera.) The battery does not need to be fully depleted to be charged; I tend to rejuvenate my batteries before I go out to shoot.

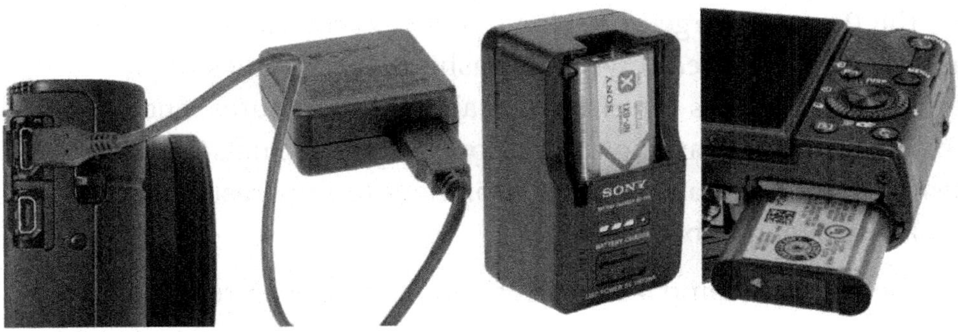

Figure 1.3

AC adapter (left), Sony BC-TRX charger (center); inserting the battery (right.)

Charging in the Camera

To charge the battery in the camera, turn the camera Off. Then, plug one end of the USB cable (with the smaller connector) into the top port under the top door in the right end of the RX100 V (as you hold the camera, see **Figure 1.5**, right). It will fit only when in the proper orientation. Plug the other end (with the familiar USB connector) into the AC adapter and plug that into a wall socket. The AC adapter supplied in the US and Canada has wall plug prongs already attached; in other countries, the adapter is supplied with a power cord with a plug suitable for your country. As discussed earlier, you can also connect the camera to a computer's USB port.

Whether you charge from household power or a computer's USB port, the Power/Charge light glows yellow in the center of the power button (instead of green) without flashing. It continues to glow until the battery completes the charge, in about 230 minutes, and the lamp turns off. Plan for charging time before your shooting sessions; it takes several hours in a warm environment to fully restore a completely depleted battery.

If the charging lamp *flashes* after you insert the battery into the camera, that indicates an error condition. Fast flashing that can't be stopped by re-inserting the battery indicates a problem with the battery. Slow flashing (about 1.5 seconds between flashes) means the ambient temperature is too high or low for charging to take place. Try another battery, or allow the camera to reach room temperature.

External Charging

Charging the battery with the optional BC-TRX external charger is even easier; just slide the battery in, connect to AC power, and the round Charge light will begin to glow. Three status indicator LEDs illuminate in succession to indicate charging progress. One lights up when the charge is 30 to 60 percent complete; two indicate 60 to 90 percent charge; all three show that charging is between 90 and 99 percent complete. When the battery is fully charged, the three status indicator LEDs and Charge light turn off. If you insert the battery and the lights fail to illuminate, the battery is already fully charged.

The BC-TRX charger is quite versatile. A sliding switch on the front allows you to toggle between charging a battery that has been inserted into its compartment, or directing its 5V 1,500 mAh current to its USB port. The USB port can be used with a cable to charge a battery that's in the camera, or some other device, but not both at the same time. If you own other Sony devices, this charger can be adjusted to suit X- and G-type batteries (the RX100 V uses the X type), or, by flipping a lever in the battery compartment, set for N-, D-, T-, R-, or K-type batteries used with other Sony products.

Final Steps

Your Sony RX100 V is almost ready to fire up and shoot. You'll need to power up the camera, pop up the EVF (if you decide to use it), adjust it for your eyesight, and insert a memory card. Each of these steps is easy.

Turn on the Power

There are three ways to turn on the RX100 V, each oriented toward a different type of use. Just choose one of these options:

- **To review images.** Press the Playback button, located just southwest of the control wheel, and marked with a right-pointing triangle. The camera will power up and a green LED in the center of the ON/OFF button will illuminate, but the lens will not extend and the last photo taken will appear on the rear LCD monitor. You can then rotate the control wheel to advance/back up among your shots quickly, leaving the lens safely tucked away.

  In this mode you can press the MENU button to access menu-oriented features. The lens will extend and the camera will display the Playback menu (which I'll describe in Chapter 6). You can use the control wheel to navigate to different menu tabs. I'll show you how later.

- **To take photos using the LCD monitor.** Think of this as a point-and-shoot mode (although the full range of the RX100 V's features are available). Just press the ON/OFF button. The lens will extend and the green LED in the button will illuminate. (If you decide to use the EVF, you can always elevate it, as described next.) I like taking photos with the EVF tucked away, because it is quick and can be used to take an impromptu shot without a lot of fuss.
- **To take photos using the electronic viewfinder.** Press the Finder switch on the left side of the camera (as you hold it in picture-taking position). The EVF will pop up (see **Figure 1.4**, left), the camera will power up, and the lens will extend. Then grab the front part of the component (marked with a white triangle in the figure) and pull it toward the back of the camera (see **Figure 1.4**).

If you forget to perform this last step, the image in the EVF will be severely out of focus. You can now preview your image through the EVF or on the LCD monitor. (When you bring camera to your eye, or anything else comes close to the EVF's sensor, the LCD monitor will turn off automatically.) As I noted, you can always elevate/extend the EVF at any time regardless of how you powered up the camera.

Tucking the viewfinder back into the camera can, at your option, turn the camera off, or allow it to remain powered up. (Use the Function for VF Close entry options Power Off or Not Power Off in the Setup 2 menu, as I'll show you in Chapter 6.)

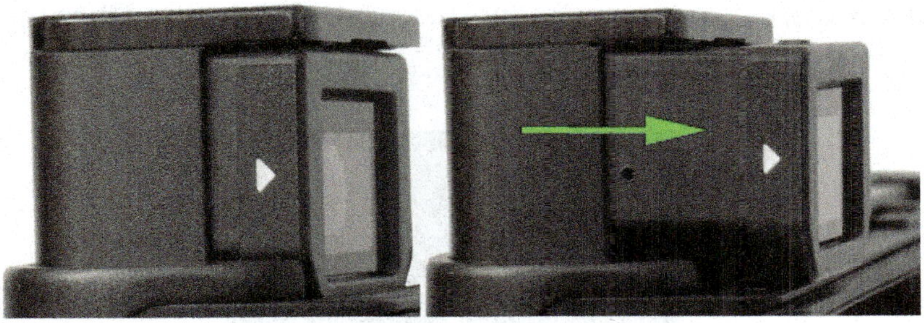

Figure 1.4

Pop up the electronic viewfinder and pull it toward the back of the camera.

If you find the constant switching from viewfinder to monitor is annoying, you can disable this automatic switching using the FINDER/MONITOR setting within the Custom Settings 3menu, as I'll describe in Chapter 4. After one minute of idling (the default), the RX100 V goes into the standby mode to save battery power. Just tap the shutter release button to bring it back to life. (You can select a longer time before power-save mode kicks in through the menu system, as I discuss in Chapter 4.)

When the camera first powers up, you may be asked to set the date and time. The procedure is fairly self-explanatory (although I'll explain it in detail in Chapter 4). You can use the left/right direction buttons to navigate among the date, year, time, date format, and daylight savings time indicator, and use the up/down buttons to enter the correct settings. When finished, *press the control wheel center button* to confirm the settings and return to the menu system.

QUICK CONTROLS

Press the MENU button (highlighted in green at upper right in **Figure 1.5**) to access menus. Use the directional buttons (yellow arrows) to move up/down/left/right, or, rotate the control wheel (blue highlighting). Press the center button (purple highlight) to confirm a selection. Note: color highlighting does not appear on your camera! I'll explain all the controls in Chapter 2, and menu navigation in Chapter 3.

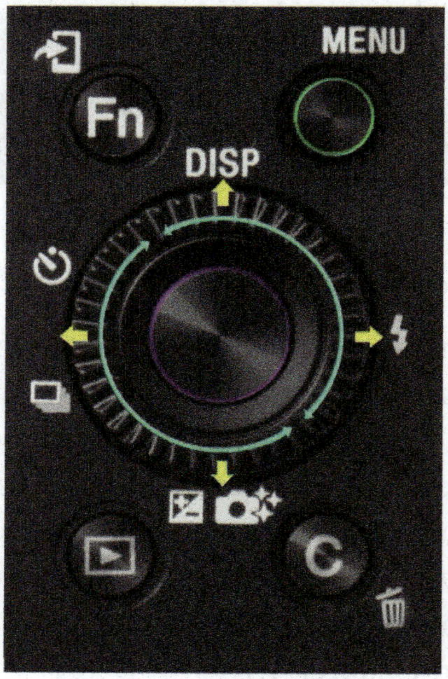

Figure 1.5

Directional buttons (yellow), control wheel (blue), center button (purple), MENU button (green).

Once the RX100 V is satisfied that it knows what time it is, you will be viewing a live view of the scene in front of the lens -- on the LCD screen or in the viewfinder when that is held up to your eye -- whenever you turn the camera on. The view is superimposed with many items of data over the display; these provide a quick method for checking many current camera settings, including current shutter speed and aperture (f/stop), shooting mode, ISO sensitivity, and other parameters.

Adjusting the Diopter Setting

The electronic viewfinder/EVF is a small high-resolution OLED (organic light-emitting diode) screen that can be used instead of the LCD screen for framing your photos or movies. A sensor detects your eye at the viewfinder and shuts off power to the LCD when you are using the EVF. Usually, when you're learning to use the camera's many features, you'll rely on the LCD screen's display, but when you're actually taking photos, you'll sometimes want to use the EVF instead. You can also use it to review your photos or video clips and navigate menu selections.

If you wear glasses and want to use the EVF without them, or if you find the viewfinder needs a bit of correction, rotate the diopter adjustment lever located on the top surface of the EVF house, as shown in **Figure 1.6**. Adjust the dial while looking through the viewfinder until the image appears sharpest.

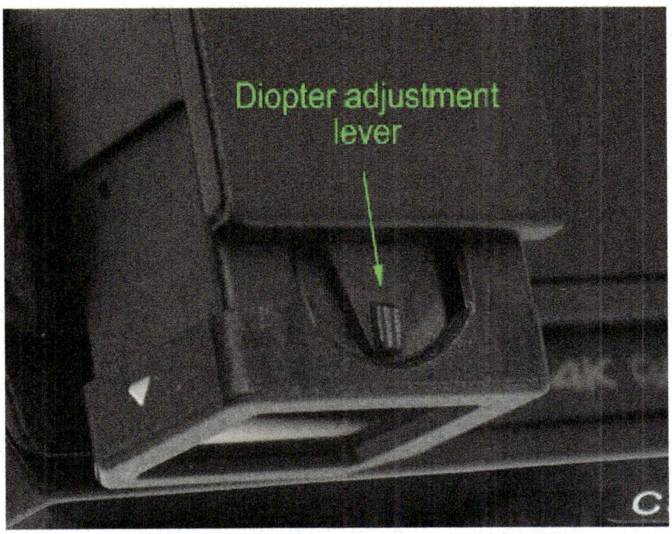

Figure 1.6

Diopter adjustment lever

Inserting a Memory Card

You can't take actual photos without a memory card inserted in your Sony camera. If you don't have a card installed, the camera will sound as if it's taking a photo and it will display that "photo." However, the image is only in temporary memory and not actually stored; you'll get a reminder about that with a flashing orange NO CARD warning at the upper left of the LCD. If you go back later and try to view that image, it will not be there. So, be sure you have inserted a compatible card with adequate capacity before you start shooting stills or videos.

The RX100 V accepts Secure Digital (SD), Secure Digital High Capacity (SDHC), Secure Digital Extra Capacity (SDXC), and Sony Memory Stick Pro Duo (or Memory Stick Pro-HG Duo) cards. The newest type of SD card, the super-high capacity (and super-fast) SDXC type, at this writing, is available in capacities as high as 256GB. The SDXC cards are more expensive and absolutely mandatory to access 4K video and the highest frame rate features, including slow-motion video. Speedy SDHC cards (with capacity up to 32GB) are quite affordable if you don't plan on shooting 4K video and the other advanced modes. I've standardized on Lexar Professional 1000x 128GB SDXC cards, although I still have quite a few of my older 64GB Lexar cards.

Whichever card you decide on, it fits in the single slot underneath the door on the underside of the camera, next to the battery. You should remove the memory card only when the camera is switched off. A blinking red card access light under the door will alert you if the camera is still writing images to the card. Insert an SD card with the label facing toward the back side of the camera (as shown in **Figure 1.7**), or toward the front if inserting any type of Memory Stick Pro card. In either case, the metal contacts go into the slot first; the card will not fit into the slot if it is incorrectly oriented.

Close the door, and your pre-flight checklist is done! (When you want to remove the memory card later, just press down on the card edge that protrudes from the slot, and the card will pop right out.)

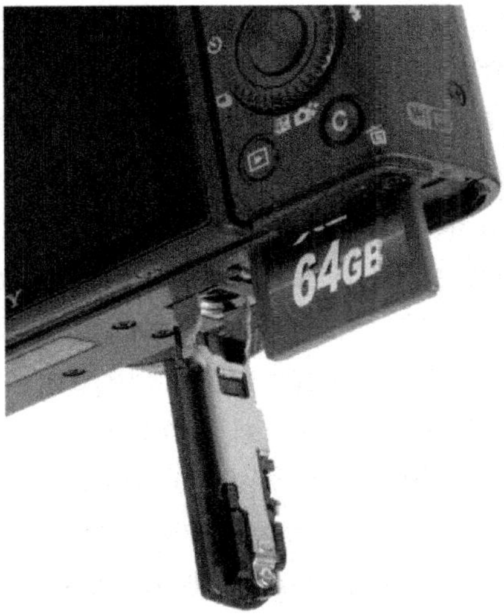

Figure 1.7

The memory card is inserted in the slot on the bottom of the camera.

Formatting a Memory Card

There are three ways to create a blank SD or Memory Stick Pro card for your Sony RX100 V, and two of them are at least partially wrong. Here are your options, both correct and incorrect:

- **Transfer (move) files to your computer.** You'll sometimes decide to transfer (rather than copy) all the image files to your computer from the memory card (either using a direct cable transfer or with a card reader and appropriate software, as described later in this chapter). When you do so, the image files on the card can be erased leaving the card blank. Theoretically. This method does *not* remove files that you've labeled as Protected (by choosing Protect from the Playback menu during review), nor does it identify and lock out parts of your card that have become corrupted or unusable since the last time you formatted the card. Therefore, I recommend always formatting the card, rather than simply moving the image files. The only exception is when you *want* to leave the protected/unerased images on the card for a while longer, say, to share with friends, family, and colleagues.

- **(Don't) Format in your computer.** With the memory card inserted in a card reader or card slot in your computer, you can use Windows or Mac OS to reformat the memory card. Don't even think of doing this! The operating system won't necessarily arrange the structure of the card the way the camera likes to see it (in computer terms, an incorrect *file system* may be installed). In particular, cards larger than 32GB must be initialized using the exFAT format, and while your computer may offer exFAT as an option, it may default to a different scheme. The only way to ensure that the card has been properly formatted for your camera is to perform the format *in the camera itself*. The only exception to this rule is when you have a seriously corrupted memory card that your camera refuses to format. Sometimes it is possible to revive such a corrupted card by allowing the operating system to reformat it first, then trying again in the camera to restore the proper exFAT system.
- **Setup menu format.** Use the recommended method to format a memory card in the camera, as described next.

To format a memory card, just follow these steps:

1. **Press the MENU button.** The RX100 V's "Tile" menu screen may appear (it's off by default, but may have been enabled). You can disable this useless feature as described in Chapter 6. (See **Figure 1.8**, left.)
2. **Select Setup.** If the tile menu is visible, use the left/right directional buttons (the left/right edges of the control wheel) or rotate the control wheel to navigate to the Setup menu (a wrench/toolbox icon), and press the center button (located in the middle of the control wheel) to open up the menu. (If you've disabled the Tile menu, the conventional menu system will appear immediately, without the intermediate Step 2.)

3. **Navigate to the Setup 5 tab.** Once in the conventional menu, use the directional buttons or control wheel to move to the Setup icon (a toolbox) at the far right of the menu tabs. Then, press the down button to move into the Setup tab, followed by the left/right buttons to select Setup 5. (See **Figure 1.8**.)
4. **Choose Format.** Rotate the control wheel on the back of the camera to highlight Format and press the center button.
5. **Confirm.** A display will appear asking if you want to delete all data. If you're sure you want to do so, press up/down to choose OK, and press the center button to confirm your choice. This will begin the formatting process.

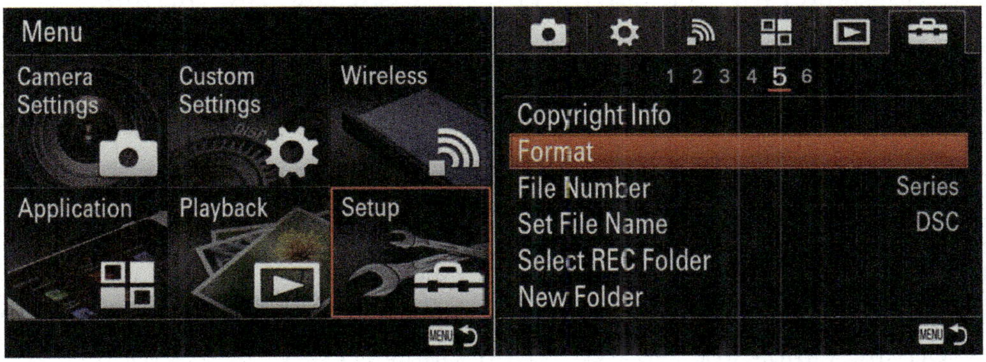

Figure 1.8

Choose Settings in the Tile menu (if enabled) (left), or navigate to the Setup 5 menu (right.)

Selecting a Shooting Mode

When it comes time to select the shooting mode and other settings on the RX100 V camera, you may start to fully experience the "feel" of the user interface. Thanks to the mode dial shown earlier in **Figure 1.1**, it's simple and quick to set a shooting mode. Just rotate the dial to the position you want, such as P (Program Auto). If you've enabled the Mode Dial Guide in the Setup 2 menu, a screen (pictured in **Figure 1.2**) appears with a brief summary as to how that mode works. (You probably won't need the Mode Dial Guide after you've been using your camera for a few days, but I'll show you how to activate it in Chapter 6.)

When you rotate the dial to the SCN position (for the fully automatic scene modes), a brief description appears about Scene Selection, but now you get another option (see **Figure 1.9**, left). Press the control wheel center button and the Scene Selection screen appears (see **Figure 1.9**, right). If you later turn the camera on while it's set for SCN, rotate the control wheel to reveal the screen that shows the available scene modes.

Use the control wheel to reveal the various available scene modes (Portrait, Landscape, Sports Action, Sunset, etc.). Stop scrolling when the scene mode you want appears, and press the center button to activate it. This scene mode will now be the one that's active when you touch the shutter release button. Two specialized scene modes are particularly worth noting: Anti Motion Blur and Hand-held Twilight; they differ in some aspects but both can produce surprisingly fine JPEGs in low light when a high ISO level is used.

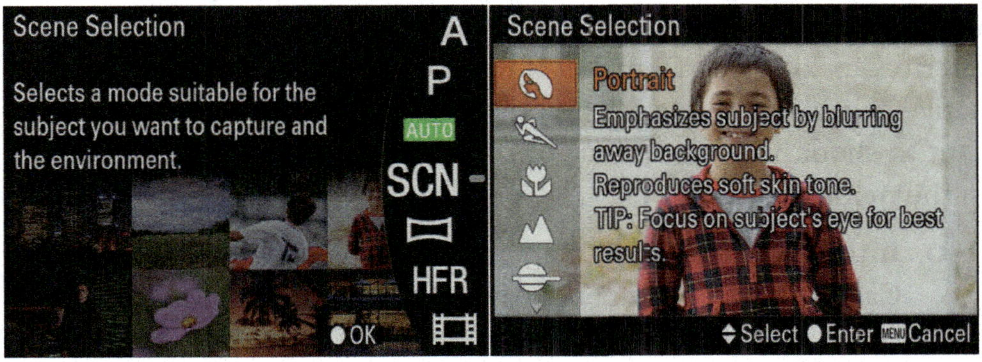

Figure 1.9

Rotate the mode dial to the SCN position (left). Select a scene mode (right).

There is a fully automatic shooting mode, Auto, which includes two options: Intelligent Auto and Superior Auto, in addition to scene modes. In all of these, the camera makes most of the decisions for you (except when to press the shutter). You'll also find three semi-automatic modes (Program, Aperture Priority, and Shutter Priority), which allow you to provide more input over the exposure and settings the camera uses. Sony also provided a fully Manual mode, and a High Frame Rate (HFR) mode for ultra-high-speed slow-motion photography. The final mode that you can select with the dial is Sweep Panorama (an automatic mode that allows you to make an ultra-wide image assembled from a set of photos). You'll find a complete description of the various shooting modes in Chapter 7. MR (Memory Recall) is not a shooting mode, but, rather, is a storage "slot" you can use to save a group of camera settings and recall them instantly by rotating the mode dial to the MR position.

INSTANT HELP

The RX100 V will display information about each of the modes when a mode is selected with the mode dial. You can turn this help off using the Setup 2 menu entry Mode Dial Guide, as I'll explain in Chapter 6.

If you're very new to digital photography, you might want to set the camera to the green Auto setting and start snapping away. The Auto setting invokes one of two Auto modes (you can select which), described next, that will make all the appropriate settings for you for many shooting situations. If you have a specific type of picture you want to shoot, you can try one of the scene modes instead, indicated on the mode dial by SCN.

- **Intelligent Auto.** In Chapter 3 I'll show you how to use the Camera Setting 7 menu's Auto Mode entry to specify whether you want the RX100 V to shift into this Intelligent Auto mode or the Superior Auto (described next) when the mode dial is set to the green Auto position. In Intelligent Auto mode, the RX100 V makes the settings of aperture and shutter speed for you. You still can make some decisions on your own, though, such as whether to use single shots or continuous shooting through a drive mode setting, whether to use the flash, and whether to use autofocus or manual focus.
- **Superior Auto.** If you opt for Superior Auto instead, this mode provides an extra benefit. In scenes that include extremely bright areas as well as shadow areas, the camera can activate its Auto HDR (high dynamic range) feature to provide more shadow detail. I'll discuss this feature in Chapter 6. In very dark locations, it can activate the Anti Motion Blur feature to create a photo with minimal digital noise.
- **Scene Selection.** The SCN position on the dial lets you choose any of thirteen different scene modes, each suited for a different type of subject or lighting condition. In scene modes, you do not get to control any aspect of the camera, except for the choice of autofocus or manual focus and flash. An external flash will not fire when certain scene modes are in use. Here's a brief summary of the options.
- **Portrait.** This is the first of the nine scene modes, selected as sub-choices under the SCN heading on the mode dial. With the Portrait setting, the camera uses settings to blur the background and sharpen the view of the subject, while using

soft skin tones. The internal flash will fire in low light if you have elevated it.

- **Sports Action.** Use this mode to freeze fast-moving subjects. The camera uses a fast shutter speed if possible; in a dark arena, for example, it simply won't be able to set a fast shutter speed so it will not be able to freeze the motion. The camera will fire continuously while the shutter button is held down. External flash will never fire in this mode.
- **Macro.** This mode is helpful when you are shooting close-up pictures of a subject such as a flower, insect, or other small object. External flash will fire in low light if you have popped it into the up position, but the flash may be too bright for a subject that's very close to the camera.
- **Landscape.** Select this scene mode when you want a maximum range of sharpness (instead of a blurred background) as well as vivid colors of distant scenes. External flash will never fire in this mode.
- **Sunset.** This is a great mode to accentuate the warm (red/orange) colors of a sunrise or sunset. External flash will never fire in this mode.
- **Night Scene.** This mode uses slower shutter speeds to provide a useful exposure, but without using flash. You should use a tripod to avoid the effects of camera shake that can be problematic with a slow shutter speed.
- **Hand-held Twilight.** This special mode is designed for use in low light. The camera will set a high ISO (sensitivity) level to enable it to use a fast shutter speed to minimize the risk of blurring caused by camera shake. (In extremely dark conditions however, the shutter speed may still be quite long.) When you press the shutter release button, the camera takes six shots in succession. The processor then composites them into one after discarding most of the digital noise (graininess) that is common in conventional photos made at high ISO. It provides one image that's of surprisingly fine quality. External flash is never fired in this mode.

- **Night Portrait.** Choose this mode when you want to illuminate a subject in the foreground with flash, but still allow the background to be exposed properly by the available light. Be prepared to use a tripod or to rely on the SteadyShot feature to reduce the effects of camera shake. If there is no foreground subject that needs to be illuminated by the flash, you may do better by using the Night View mode, discussed next. Remember that you must elevate the flash before taking a shot if you want the flash to fire.
- **Anti Motion Blur.** Similar to Hand-held Twilight, this mode is also designed for use indoors or in low lighting, but it's more effective at reducing blurring that might be caused by a subject's motion or by a shaky camera. That's because the camera sets an even higher ISO level to be able to use an even faster shutter speed so you should not need to use a tripod. (Of course, in an extremely dark location, the shutter speed may still be a bit long.) It fires six shots and composites them into one with minimal digital noise.
- **Pet.** Provides the best settings for shooting images of small animals and pets.
- **Gourmet.** Produces bright colors and vivid contrast to capture food photos in an appetizing way. S
- **Fireworks.** Instantly gives you the settings you need to capture fireworks. Use of a tripod is recommended.
- **High sensitivity.** Shoot movies and stills in dark locations without auxiliary lighting.
- **Sweep Panorama.** This special mode lets you "sweep" the camera across a scene that is too wide for a single image. The camera takes multiple pictures while you move it; after taking a series of shots, its processor combines them into a single, wide (or long) panoramic final product.
- **Movie.** Allows shooting movie clips.
- **MR (Memory Recall).** This position on the mode dial, simply marked MR, isn't actually an exposure mode. Instead, it

corresponds to your choice of three different groups of settings that you've previously stored in an internal memory storage "slot" (register) numbered 1, 2, and 3. You can use these memory registers to set up the RX100 V for specific types of shooting scenes, and then retrieve those settings from the mode dial's MR position. I'll show you how to store and recall memory registers in Chapter 6.

If you have more photographic experience, you might want to opt for one of the semi-automatic or manual modes, selecting it from the virtual mode dial. These, too, are described in more detail in Chapter 7. These modes, which let you apply more creativity to your camera's settings, are indicated by the letters P, A, S, and M. All overrides are available and flash will always fire if it's elevated in any of the following:

- **P (Program auto).** This mode allows the RX100 V to make the basic exposure settings, but you can still override the camera's settings to fine-tune your image. For example, you can select different combinations of shutter speeds and apertures that produce the same exposure, make your images brighter or darker, change the color balance, and perform other adjustments explained in Chapter 7.
- **A (Aperture Priority).** Choose this mode when you want to use a particular lens opening (called an aperture or f/stop), especially to control how much of your image is in focus. The camera will set the appropriate shutter speed after you have set your desired aperture using the control wheel.
- **S (Shutter Priority).** This mode is useful when you want to use a particular shutter speed to stop action or produce creative blur effects. You dial in your chosen shutter speed with the control wheel, and the camera will set the appropriate aperture (f/stop) for you.
- **M (Manual).** Select this mode when you want full control over the shutter speed and the aperture (lens opening), either for creative effects or because you are using a studio flash or another flash unit not compatible with the camera's automatic

flash metering. You also need to use this mode if you want to use the Bulb setting for a long exposure, as explained in Chapter 6. You select both the aperture and the shutter speed aperture (with the control wheel on the camera back, pressing the down button to switch between the two). There's more about this mode, and the others, in Chapter 7.

Choosing a Metering Mode

You might want to select a particular exposure metering mode for your first shots, although the default high-tech Multi (short for multi-zone or multi-segment) metering is probably the best choice while getting to know your camera. If you want to select a different metering pattern, you must not be using one of the scene modes, Superior Auto, or Intelligent Auto; in these modes, the camera uses Multi metering and that cannot be changed. To change the metering mode, press the MENU button and navigate to the Camera Settings menu (the tab shown earlier in the upper-left corner in Figure 1.8), and thence to the Camera Settings 5 menu to the Metering Mode entry, located fourth from the top. Press the center button, then scroll up/down with the directional buttons to reach Multi, Center (for center weighted), or Spot selections. Press the center button to confirm your choice and return the camera to shooting mode. The three metering options are as follows:

- **Multi metering.** In this standard metering mode, the camera attempts to intelligently classify your image and choose the best exposure based on readings from 1,200 different zones or segments of the scene. You can read about this so-called "evaluative" metering concepts, as well as the other two options, in Chapter 7.
- **Center metering.** The camera meters the entire scene, but gives the most emphasis (or weighting) to the central area of the frame.
- **Spot metering.** The camera considers only the brightness in a very small central spot so the exposure is calculated only based on that area.

OPTION OPTIONS

You'll soon find that your RX100 V gives you multiple ways to select options. In this Quick Start chapter, I'll show you just one of them. For example, you can select a metering mode using the Camera Settings 5 menu, as described, or you can press the Fn button and specify the metering method from the 12-item Function menu that pops up. Alternatively, when the "Quick Navi" screen is shown on the LCD monitor, you can press the Fn button to change the metering mode as well as most of the other shooting settings. I'll show you how to use the other optional methods in Chapter 2.

Choosing a Focus Mode

The Camera Settings menu also has entries to allow you to choose Focus Mode and Focus Area (in the Camera Settings 3 and Camera Settings 4 menus, respective), and are accessed using the same navigation steps described earlier. Focus Mode is the easiest to understand; it determines *when* focus is established.

If you're using a scene mode or one of the two Auto modes, you do not get any options under Autofocus Mode; in fact, it is grayed out since it's not available in these modes. The choices that are available when using P, A, S, or M mode are as follows:

- **Single-shot AF (AF-S).** This mode, sometimes called *single autofocus,* sets focus after you touch the shutter release button and the camera beeps to confirm focus (unless you've turned the beeps off). The active focus point(s) are shown in green on the screen and a green dot appears in the bottom-left corner of the display. The focus will remain locked as long as you maintain contact with the shutter release button, or until you take the picture. If the autofocus system is unable to achieve sharp focus (because the subject is too close to the camera, for example), the focus confirmation circle will blink. This mode is best when your subject is relatively motionless as when you're taking a portrait or landscape photo.
- **Continuous AF (AF-C).** This mode, sometimes called continuous servo or continuous tracking focus by photographers, sets focus when you partially depress the shutter button, but continues to monitor the frame and refocuses if the distance between the camera and the subject changes. (This allows it to continuously focus on a person walking toward you, for example.) No beep sound is provided. A green dot surrounded by two brackets (curved lines) appears to indicate that the camera is not having a problem achieving and maintaining focus. The brackets disappear when focus is achieved, leaving only the green dot. If the camera should fail to acquire focus, the green dot disappears and the brackets

remain. Continuous AF is a useful mode for photographing moving subjects.

- **DMF (Direct Manual Focus).** Allows you to manually adjust focus after autofocus has been confirmed, using the control ring on the lens.
- **Manual Focus.** Focus by rotating the control ring on the lens. The RX100 V offers magnification and Focus Peaking as aids to manual focus. I'll describe their use in Chapter 3.

Selecting a Focus Area

The Sony RX100 V is equipped with an autofocus system that I'll explain in detail in Chapter 8. In scene modes, the focus area that will be used to achieve focus is selected automatically by the camera; in other words, the AF system decides which part of the scene will be in sharpest focus. In the semi-automatic P, A, and S mode, and in the manual M mode, you can allow the camera to select the focus point automatically, or you can specify which focus point should be used with the Focus Area feature.

Set the camera to one of the four semi-automatic exposure modes (P, A, S, or M) and select Focus Area from the Camera Settings 4 menu. By default, it will be set to Wide (multi-point autofocus). Scroll up/down until you reach the option you want to use and press the center button to confirm your selection. There are four autofocus area options, described in Chapter 8. Once you're in the Camera Settings menu, navigate to the Focus Area selection in the Camera Settings 4 tab, then press the center button, and select one of these choices. Press the center button again to confirm. Here's a brief overview of the options.

- **Wide.** The RX100 V automatically chooses the appropriate focus area or areas; often several subjects will be the same distance from the camera as the primary subject. The active AF area or areas are then displayed in green on the LCD or in the viewfinder, depending on which display you're using.

- **Center.** The camera always uses the focus area in the center of the frame, so it will focus on the subject that's closest to the center in your composition.
- **Flexible Spot.** After you select this option from Focus Area, you can use the left/right direction buttons to specify Small, Medium, or Large focus areas. Then, while viewing your subject, you can use the directional controls to move the focus frame (rectangle) around the screen to your desired location. Move the frame so it covers the most important subject in the scene; then press the center button to lock it into place. I'll discuss this topic in more detail in Chapter 8, where I'll cover many aspects of autofocus (as well as manual focus), including some not covered in this chapter.
- **Expand Flexible Spot.** If the camera is unable to lock in focus using the selected focus point, it will also use the eight adjacent points to try to achieve focus.
- **Lock-On AF.** In this mode, the camera locks focus onto the subject area that is under the selected focus spot when the shutter button is depressed halfway. Then, if the subject moves (or you change the framing in the camera), the camera will continue to refocus *on that subject*. You can select this mode only when the focus mode is set to Continuous AF (AF-C). You can activate it for any of the five focus area options described above. That is, once you've highlighted Lock-On AF on the selection screen, you can then press the left-right directional button and choose Wide, Zone, Center, Flexible Spot, or Expand Flexible Spot.

Other Settings

There are a few other settings you can make if you're feeling ambitious, but don't feel bad if you postpone using these features until you've racked up a little more experience with your Sony RX100 V. By default, these camera features will be at Auto so the camera will make a suitable setting.

Adjusting White Balance and ISO

If you like, you can custom-tailor your white balance (overall color balance) and the ISO level (sensitivity) as long as you're not using one of the Auto or SCN modes. To start out, it's best to leave the white balance (WB) at Auto, and to set the ISO to ISO 200 for daylight photos or to ISO 400 for pictures on a dark, overcast day or indoors when you'll be shooting with an external flash. You can adjust white balance and ISO with the White Balance and ISO entries in the Camera Settings 5. After accessing either feature, navigate (scroll) to make the desired setting with the direction buttons; that is the most convenient method, but you can also scroll by rotating the control wheel.

Using the Self-Timer

If you want to have time to get into the photo before the tripod-mounted camera takes the actual shot, the self-timer is what you need. You can get to this feature by pressing the drive mode button (the left direction button of the control wheel) and then scrolling up or down. The drive mode can also be selected from the Camera Settings 3 menu, but it's quicker to use the direct access button.

When the Drive Mode screen is visible, scroll up/down through the various options until you reach the Self-timer: 10 Sec option, which will provide a ten-second delay. Press the center button to confirm your choice and a self-timer icon will appear on the live view display. Press the shutter release to lock focus and exposure and to start the timer. The self-timer lamp will blink and the beeper will sound (unless you've silenced it in the menu) until the final two seconds when the lamp remains on and the beeper beeps more rapidly until the picture is taken.

There are a few options you can select to vary the operation of the self-timer. When the self-timer option is first highlighted, press the left/right keys to choose between 10-second, 5-second, and 2-second options. Also, on the Drive Mode screen, just below self-timer, there is an option labeled C3; scroll to it and you'll see its called Self-timer (Cont.): 10 Sec. 3 Img (or 5 Img). That abbreviation means the camera will take three or five images after the self-timer's 10-second delay has run out. You can also press the left/right buttons and select three or five images to be exposed after 5-second or 2-second delays, as well.

The multiple image option is handy if you are taking family group pictures with a few known inveterate blinkers to be pictured. Note that the self-timer setting is "sticky" and will still be in effect for multiple shots, even if you turn the camera off and power up again. When you're done using the self-timer, reset the camera to one of the other Drive Mode options.

In addition to the Self-timer, Continuous shooting, and Single-shot choices in the Drive menu, there also are exposure/white balance/dynamic range optimization bracketing options, which I'll explain in Chapter 3.

An Introduction to Movie Making

I'm going to talk in more detail about your movie-making options with the RX100 V camera in Chapter 10. For now, though, I'll give you enough information to get started, in case a cinematic subject wanders into your field of view before you get to those chapters. The overrides you have set for certain aspects while shooting still photos will apply to the video clip that you'll record; these include exposure compensation, the White Balance, any Picture Effect, and even the aperture if the camera is in A mode or the shutter speed if it's in S mode. You also get access to the settings for the movie file formats (AVCHD or MP4; the RX100 V has additional XAVC S HD and XAVC S 4K modes we'll explore later in this book) and the resolution in the Record Setting item of the Camera Settings 2 section of the menu.

After you start recording, you can change the aperture or the shutter speed; either step will make your movie brighter or darker as you'll notice while viewing on EVF or LCD while making the adjustments. However, you can also set plus or minus exposure compensation for that purpose while filming. The RX100 V provides an effective Continuous Autofocus in Movie mode and sound is recorded in stereo with the built-in mics located on top of the camera.

Let's save the discussion of those aspects for Chapter 10. For the moment, let's just make a basic movie. With the camera turned on, aim at your subject and locate the red Movie record button in the right-hand corner of the body. (You don't have to switch to Movie mode using the mode dial; the Movie mode position simply gives you access to more movie-shooting controls.)

Compose as you wish and press that button once to start the recording, and again to stop it; don't hold the button down. You can record for up to about 29 minutes consecutively if you have sufficient storage space on your memory card and charge in your battery. The camera will adjust the focus and exposure automatically, and you can zoom while recording, if you have a zoom lens attached to the camera.

After you finish recording a video clip, you can view it by pressing the Playback button at the lower right of the LCD screen. Let's say you have taken some still photos after making a movie; in that case, the movie is not the latest item available to play. In order to play it, you will need to use the index screen; see the last bullet of the section below on "Reviewing the Images You've Taken" for that procedure. While a movie is being played back, certain camera controls act like VCR buttons, including the following options (among others that I'll explain later in this book):

- **Pause/Resume.** Press the center button.
- **Fast-forward.** Press the right direction button, or turn the control wheel to the right.
- **Fast-reverse.** Press the left direction button, or turn the control wheel to the left.
- **Adjust sound volume.** Press the bottom direction button to activate the volume control screen; scroll upward to make it louder or downward for less volume. (You can scroll either by rotating the control wheel or by using the control's top and bottom buttons.)

- **Slow-forward.** While paused, turn the control wheel to the right.
- **Slow-reverse.** While paused, turn the control wheel to the left.

Reviewing the Images You've Taken

The Sony RX100 V has a broad range of playback and image review options. I'll cover them in more detail in Chapter 2. Initially, you'll want to learn just the basics for viewing still photos so I'll assume you have taken only such images. After shooting some JPEG and/or RAW photos, here's how to view them, using controls shown in **Figure 1.10**:

- Press the Playback button to display the most recently taken image. (It's the small button with a > symbol located to the lower right of the LCD monitor screen.)
- Press the left direction button, or rotate the control wheel counterclockwise to view a previous image.
- Press the right direction button, or rotate the control wheel clockwise to view the next image.
- While viewing a photo, press the DISP button (top direction button) repeatedly to cycle among the available displays: views that have no recording data, full recording data (f/stop, shutter speed, image quality/size, etc.), and a thumbnail image with histogram display. (I'll explain all these in Chapter 2.)
- Press the lower-right button, marked with a C (Custom) label and trash can icon, to delete the currently displayed image.
- While the image is displayed, press the MENU button and from the Playback 1 menu, select Rotate, followed by pressing the center button, to rotate the image on the screen 90 degrees. Successive presses of the center button rotate the image 90 degrees each time. (You won't likely need this feature unless you have disabled automatic rotation, which causes the camera to display your vertically oriented pictures

already rotated. I'll explain how to activate/deactivate automatic rotation in Chapter 4.)

- Press the Zoom lever on top of the camera (with a W-T label for Wide-angle and Telephoto) to zoom into (enlarge) and zoom out (reduce) the image view. To exit this screen and return to normal view, press the MENU button.
- While in Playback mode, the pressing Zoom lever toward the W will activate an index screen showing 9 or 25 thumbnail images (select the number using the Image Index option in the Playback 1 menu). Keep scrolling downward to view the thumbnails of the next images (assuming you have shot lots of photos). Scroll to the thumbnail of the photo you want to view and press the center button; the photo will then fill the screen. The RX100 V arranges index images by date shot, and includes a calendar view you can use to look for pictures taken on a specific date. I'll explain those options in more detail in Chapter 6.

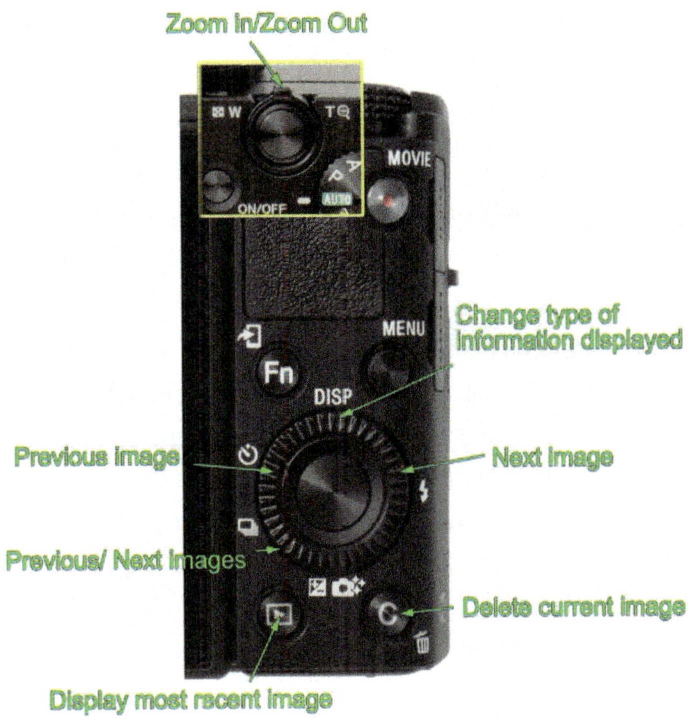

Figure 1.10

Review your images using the pertinent camera controls.

Transferring Files to Your Computer

The final step in your picture-taking session will be to transfer the photos and/or movies you've taken to your computer for printing, further review, or editing. (You can also take your memory card to a retailer for printing if you don't want to go the do-it-yourself route.) Your RX100 V allows you to create print orders right in the camera. It also offers an option for selecting which images to transfer to your computer.

For now, you'll probably want to transfer your images by either using the USB cable from the camera to the computer or by removing the memory card from the RX100 V and transferring the images with a card reader. The latter option is ordinarily the best, because it's usually much faster and doesn't deplete the camera's battery. However, you might need to use a cable transfer when you have the cable and a computer but no card reader. (You might be using the computer at a friend's home or the one at an Internet café, for example.)

Here's how to transfer images from a memory card to the computer using a card reader:

1. Turn off the camera.
2. Slide open the battery compartment door, and press on the card, which causes it to pop up so it can be removed from the slot. (You can see a memory card being removed in **Figure 1.7.**)
3. Insert the memory card into a memory card reader accessory that is plugged into your computer. Your installed software detects the files on the card and offers to transfer them. The card can also appear as a mass storage device on your desktop; in that case, you can open that and then drag and drop the files to your computer.

To transfer images from the camera to a Mac or PC computer using the USB cable:

1. Turn off the camera.
2. Open the port door on the right side of the camera (the upper door) and plug the USB cable furnished with the camera into the USB port (that is also used for charging). (See **Figure 1.3**, shown earlier in this chapter.)
3. Connect the other end of the USB cable to a USB port on your computer.
4. Turn on the camera. From this point on, the method is the same as in entry 3 in the card reader list above.

Wireless File Transfer

Your RX100 V is also equipped with built-in Wi-Fi which provides many options, including a method for wireless transfer of image files to a Mac or Windows computer when connected to a wireless network. This is a multi-faceted topic so I won't begin to discuss it here; instead, you'll find full coverage in Chapter 5.

The camera is also compatible with the Eye-Fi brand memory card that allows for wireless transfer of files to a computer. (It can also be used for wireless transfer to a smart device running a free app.) This card looks and acts exactly like an ordinary SDHC card, but with a big difference. Once you have the card set up with your local Wi-Fi (wireless) network, whenever you take a picture or record a movie with this card in the camera, the card wirelessly connects to your computer over that network and transmits the file to any location you have specified. For example, you might set the Eye-Fi card to send any new JPEG or RAW photos directly to the Pictures folder on your computer and video clips to the Movies folder.

Since the RX100 V already offers a wealth of Wi-Fi features, there's really no need to buy an Eye-Fi card. If you already own one for use with another camera however, it will work well with your Sony too. This will initially preclude the need to learn how to use the camera's own Wi-Fi features, which can seem more complicated because of the sheer number of available options.

Chapter 2

Your Camera Roadmap

The tiny black-and-white drawings in the official Sony manuals -- impaled with dozens of callouts -- can be confusing. At times, looking for information about a specific feature seems a lot like being presented with a world globe when what you really want is to find the capital of Brazil!

In this book, rather than bewilder you with a satellite view, I'm going to give you a street-level map that includes close-up, full-color photos of your RX100 V from several angles, with labels clearly pointing to each individual component, accompanied by a description of exactly what it does. And, I don't force you to flip back and forth among dozens of pages to find out what a particular button or dial does. Each photo is accompanied by a brief description that summarizes the control, so you can begin using it right away. Only when a particular feature deserves a lengthy explanation do I direct you to a more detailed write-up later in the book.

So, if you're wondering what the left direction button on the control wheel does, I'll tell you up front, rather than have you flip to several pages. This book is not a scavenger hunt. But after I explain how to use the drive mode button to select continuous shooting, I *will* provide a cross-reference to a longer explanation later in the book that clarifies the use of the various drive modes, the self-timer, and the several varieties of bracketing. Some readers write and complain about even my minimized cross-reference approach; they'd like to open the book to one page and read *everything* there is to know about bracketing, for example. Unfortunately, it's impossible to understand some features without having a background in what related features do. So, my strategy is to provide you with these introductions in the earlier chapters, covering simple features completely, and relegating some of the really in-depth explanations to later chapters. I think this kind of organization works best for a camera as sophisticated as the Sony RX100 V.

By the time you finish this chapter, you'll have a basic understanding of every control and of the various roles it can take on. I'll provide a lot more information about items in the menus and submenus in Chapters 3, 4, 5, and 6, but the following descriptions should certainly satisfy the button pusher and dial twirler in you.

Front View

When thinking about any given camera, we always imagine the front view. That's the view that your subjects see as you snap away, and the aspect that's shown in product publicity and on the box. The frontal angle is, essentially, the "face" of a camera like the Sony RX100 V. But, not surprisingly, most of the "business" of operating the camera happens *behind* it, where the photographer resides. The front of the camera actually has no significant controls, and few features to worry about. The front view is shown in **Figure 2.1** and described below:

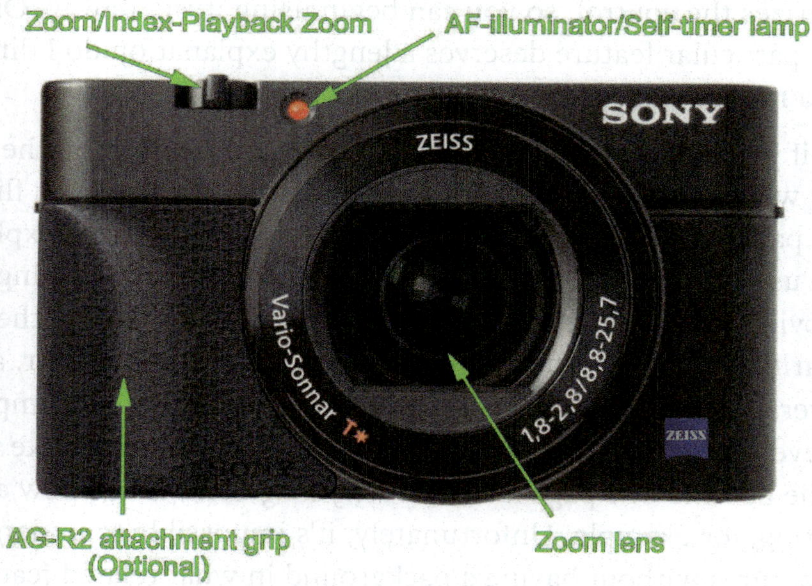

Figure 2.1
The front view of the Sony RX100 V.

- **AF illuminator/Self-timer lamp.** This bright LED flashes while your camera counts down the 2-second, 5-second, or 10-

second self-timer. In 10-second and 5-second mode, the lamp blinks at a measured pace off and on at first, then switches to rapid flashing in the final moments of the countdown. When the self-timer is set to 2 seconds, the lamp flashes quickly throughout the countdown. It also serves as the AF (autofocus) Illuminator, emitting its orange-red glow in dark conditions to help the camera's autofocus system achieve sharp focus.

- **Zoom lever/Index-Playback zoom.** In shooting mode, press this lever toward the T label to power zoom in on your subject in telephoto mode; press in the other direction toward W to zoom out for a wider field of view. When reviewing images in playback mode, pressing in the T direction magnifies the image, as shown in **Figure 2.2**. A navigation box appears showing that the image has been zoomed in centering on the focus point (represented by the orange box within the white-bordered navigation window).

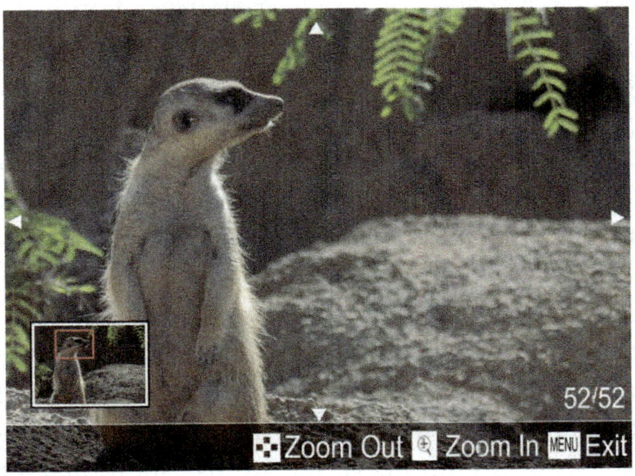

Figure 2.2

Zooming in Playback mode.

Directional triangles simultaneously appear on the screen to indicate you can press the top, bottom, left, and right edges of the control wheel to move the zoomed area around within the frame. Pressing the lever in the W direction reduces the size of a magnified image to full-frame view, and from there to either 9 or 25 thumbnail images (which you can specify using the Image Index entry of the Playback 1 menu, as I'll describe in Chapter 6).

- **Zoom lens.** Your permanently attached Zeiss Vario-Sonnar T* zoom lens is a miracle of optical science, providing you with a power-zoom focal length range equivalent to 24-70mm (compared to a full-frame camera like the Sony a7 II), with large, fast maximum aperture and excellent sharpness, all packaged to retract compactly into your camera's tiny body when not in use. The lens has an internal 0.9-stop neutral-density filter, which provides a 3-stop reduction in exposure. You often won't *need* the filter to compensate for extra bright light, as the camera's 1/32,000-second top shutter speed (when using the electronic shutter, described later) and f/11 smallest aperture alone should do the job, but the filter can come in handy to reduce incoming light when you want to use slower shutter speeds or wider apertures. You'll find more on using ND filters in Chapter 7 and more on using your lens's features in Chapter 9.

Note that the lens does not have a thread for attaching filters or a lens hood. **My recommendation:** Should you have the need for mounting a filter, such as a polarizer, consider the Sony VFA-49R1 Filter Adapter. It's an inelegant solution, at best, but works. The kit comes with an adapter ring that fastens to the front of your lens with an adhesive, and a guide to help you center it. After the adhesive cures for about 24 hours, you can screw in 49mm filters (or, possibly, larger filters through the use of step-up ring adapters). Lensmate (`www.lensmateonline.com`) has additional RX100-series adapters for filters, as described in Chapter 9.

- **Hand grip (optional).** The RX100 V's smooth front surface actually doesn't provide much of a gripping surface for holding the camera securely. **My recommendation:** Spring for the optional Sony AG-R2 attachment grip, a stick-on elastomer and polycarbonate-like aid that affixes to the front surface, while not adding much bulk to the svelte camera.

On the right side of the RX100 V (as seen when you're holding the camera to shoot) are several important components, shown in **Figure 2.3**:

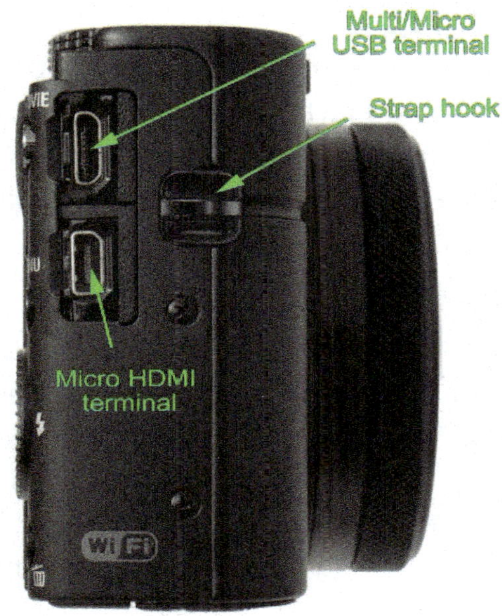

Figure 2.3

The right side of the RX100 V.

- **Multi/Micro USB terminal.** This is the top port that's visible when you peel back its protective cover. Connect the RX100 V to your computer using this port, with the USB cable that's supplied with the camera. That connection can be used to upload images to the computer, to charge the battery while it's in the camera, and to upgrade the firmware to the latest version available for the RX100 V, using a file downloaded from the Sony support website. (esupport.sony.com). The same port serves as a charging port when the USB cable is connected to the included charger, or plugged into a powered USB port.

If you'd like to see the images from your camera on a television screen, you'll need to buy an HDMI cable (not included with the camera) to connect this port to an HDTV set or monitor. You can also link to an external video recorder when using DUAL REC mode to output 4K video to both the memory card and recorder. Be sure to get a Type D cable; it has a male micro-HDMI connector at the camera end and a standard male HDMI connector at the TV end.

Once the cable is connected, you can not only view your stored images on the TV in Playback mode, you can also see what the camera sees by viewing your TV screen. So, in effect, you can use your HDTV set as a large monitor to help with composition, focusing, and the like.

WHAT'S MISSING?

You'll note that the RX100 V does not include jacks for microphones or headphones, so you cannot plug in better quality mics for recording sound, nor monitor your audio as you shoot using headphones. That might seem like a serious omission for a camera with sophisticated video-shooting capabilities, including ultra-high-definition 4K capture. Of course, in Sony's defense, most advanced videographers won't be using this ultra-compact camera to shoot pro video.

But, assuming they *do*, there are several solutions for both omissions. If, for some reason, you want to use the RX100 V for video (instead of a camera with interchangeable lenses, such as the a7 II models, or a Sony E-mount camcorder), you may be working with an outboard video recorder, such as the Atomos Shogun (about $2,000), which has its own 7-inch monitor and can accept HDMI input from the camera, with audio output for monitoring. It's also common to capture video and sound separately, and the Shogun includes two XLR microphone connectors for attaching pro mics, and the ability to sync with the time codes the RX100 V can embed in its video stream. While all this may seem farfetched, it's viable. I'll introduce you to the camera's advanced video features in Chapter 10.

Figure 2.4 provides another view of the camera as seen from the other side. The lens is shown extended, with the pop-up flash and electronic viewfinder in their elevated positions.

Here's what the key components are:

- **Pop-up flash.** Sony says this tiny flash has a range of 1.31 to 33.46 feet at the wide-angle zoom setting, and 1.31 to 21.22 feet at the telephoto setting. Of course, shooting subjects at the greater distances requires ramping up the ISO sensitivity of the sensor, and the largest distances are possible only when ISO sensitivity is set to Auto. I'll explain all your flash options in Chapter 11.

Tip: When the flash is elevated, you can use the index finger of your left hand to point it toward the ceiling in bounce flash mode. If the camera is set to ISO Auto, the RX100 V will automatically increase the ISO sensitivity so you'll get surprisingly good bounce illumination from this tiny flash unit.

- **Pop-up electronic viewfinder/Viewfinder pop-up switch.** The EVF elevates when you press upward on the switch located on the side of the camera. You must then pull out on its slide-out element to use the viewfinder. I'll explain this component in more detail in the next section.
- **NFC indicator.** This isn't a control per se; the label emblazoned on the side of the camera indicates the touch point for connecting the RX100 V with an NFC (Near Field Communication) device, such as an Android smartphone or tablet. When linked, the two devices can communicate directly using short-range wireless technology, as I'll describe in Chapter 5. Although Apple added NFC communications to the iPhone 6/6s and 6+/6s+, it functions only with Apple Pay, so you'll need to use the camera's Wi-Fi capabilities to connect to your iOS device.
- **Control ring.** This is a multi-function control that you can use as-is, or, you can redefine its behavior to suit your preference. If you want to depart from its default "Standard" function, you

can specify one of nine alternate functions in the Custom Key Settings entry located in the Custom Settings 5 menu. I'll explain all your options in Chapter 4, but **Table 2.1** provides a summary. Here are some of your options:

- **Standard.** As you can see from the table, in the default Standard mode, the control *ring* mirrors the behavior of the control *wheel* located on the back of the camera to adjust f/stops and shutter speeds in P, A, S, and M exposure modes.

  However, if you switch from autofocus to manual focus (MF) or direct manual focus (DMF) the control *ring* is used to adjust focus, and it no longer mirrors the control wheel's functions.

Tip: Here's a "gotcha." If you select both manual *focus* and manual *exposure*, the control wheel does double duty. You must use the control *wheel* to set both shutter speed and aperture, and you can switch between the two by pressing the down directional button. Don't panic! I'll explain all the focus options in Chapter 8.

- **Zoom.** When you select this behavior in the Custom Key Settings entry, the control ring zooms in and out, just like the W-T switch, in all modes except for MF and DMF (in which the control ring adjusts focus instead.) When Zoom is chosen, you can also choose from standard, smooth zoom, quick zoom, or zooming in incremental step in the Custom Settings 5 menu.
- **Other options.** You can also select exposure compensation, ISO, white balance, Creative Style, Picture Effect, shutter speed, aperture, or Not Set as functions for the control ring.

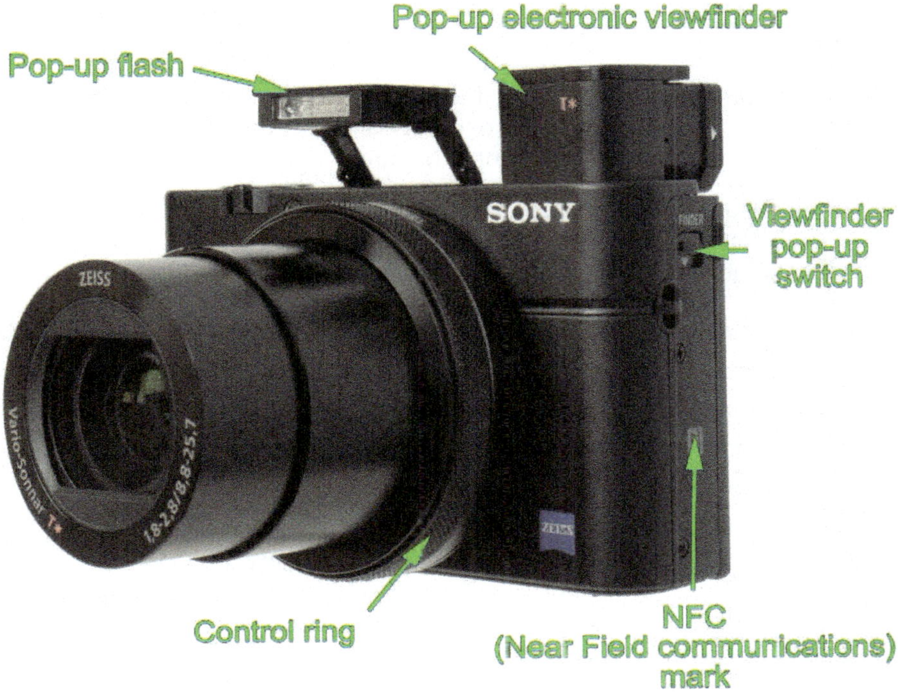

Figure 2.4

The left side of the RX100 V

Table 2.1

Standard Control Ring Function

Exposure Mode	Control Ring Function
Program Mode	Rotate left for smaller aperture/right for a faster shutter speed, while the other value changes to retain equivalent exposure.
Aperture Priority	Adjusts aperture.
Shutter Priority	Adjusts shutter speed.
Manual Exposure	Adjusts aperture while control wheel adjusts shutter speed.
Movie Mode	P mode: No function. A, S, or M modes, as described above. (Exposure mode set with Movie entry in Camera Setting 8 menu.)
High Frame Rate Mode	P mode: No function. A, S, or M modes, as described earlier. (Exposure mode set by pressing center button when mode dial moved to HDR position. Select exposure mode with control wheel or directional buttons.)
Sweep Panorama	Adjusts panorama direction among up, down, left, or right.
Intelligent Auto/Superior Auto	Zooms lens in and out.
Scene Modes	Cycles among scene modes.

The Sony RX100 V's Business End

The back panel of the Sony is where most of the camera's physical controls reside. There aren't that many of them, but, some of them can perform several functions, depending on the context, or custom key definitions you select. The key components labeled in **Figure 2.5** include:

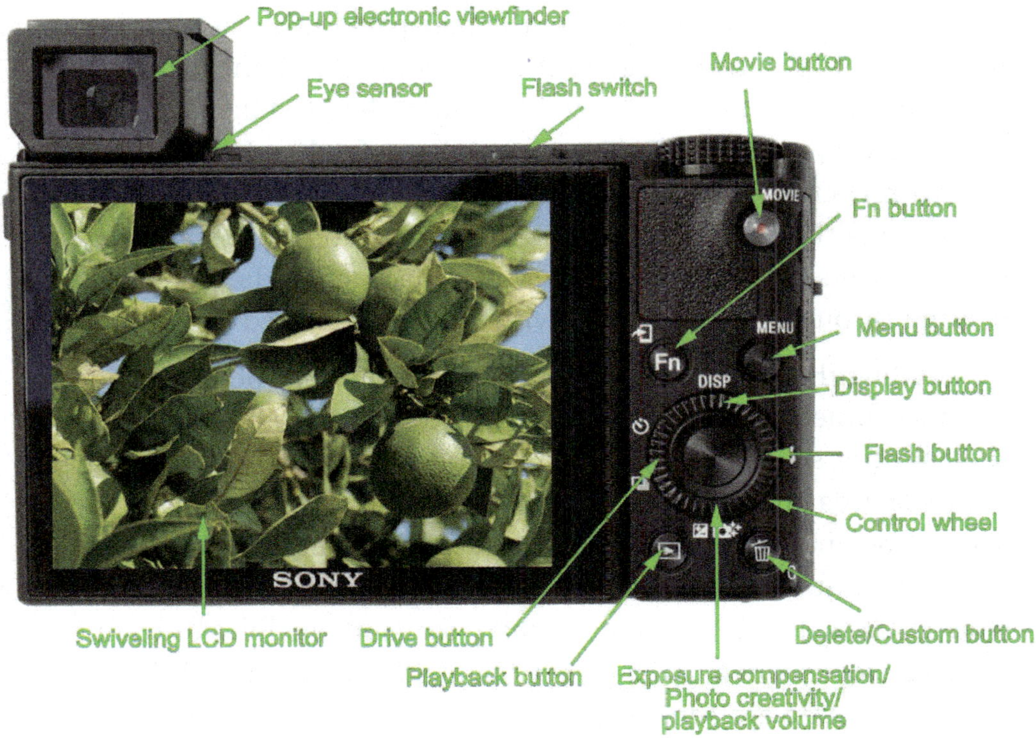

Figure 2.5

The back panel of the RX100 V.

- **MENU button.** Press to enter the multi-tabbed menu system. This button also serves to exit many functions, including menu settings, and playback zoom. A Menu/Exit label will appear in the viewfinder or LCD in that case.
- **Viewfinder window.** Look into this window to activate the eye-level electronic viewfinder (EVF), an internal OLED (organic LED) display with 2.4 million dots of resolution. It

shows 100 percent of the frame at .59X magnification. I especially like this viewfinder when shooting in dim light, when the enhanced view is quite bright. It's not as useful for continuous shooting as the camera may not show the previous image rather than a "live" view. You can frame your composition and see the information on the electronic viewfinder's display.

While some shooters will use the rear-panel LCD monitor for framing their photos instead of the electronic viewfinder, the latter offers some benefits. On sunny days, when the LCD display is often obliterated by glare, the EVF is definitely preferable. It includes Zeiss' T* anti-reflective coating, too. However, if you wear your glasses while using the EVF, bright sunlight approaching from some angles may still cause glare; you're better off adjusting the diopter value and peering through the viewfinder with your uncorrected eyeballs.

Holding the camera pressed up against your face helps provide extra steadiness to reduce camera shake (and image blurring) at very slow shutter speeds. (Even the built-in optical image stabilization is not a panacea and is more effective when the camera is braced and at least somewhat stable.) Both EVF and LCD monitors can be used with the camera's focus peaking and focus magnification features, which makes it easier to achieve sharp focus manually -- or to fine-tune autofocus when using Direct Manual Focus (DMF). The EVF has a solid-state eye sensor next to it that senses when you (or anything else, unfortunately) approach the viewfinder; the camera then triggers a switch that turns off the back-panel LCD, and activates the viewfinder screen. You can set this feature to Auto, or specify full-time viewfinder use with the FINDER/MONITOR entry in the Custom Settings 3 menu, as I'll explain in Chapter 4.

As I mentioned in Chapter 1, if you elevate the EVF when the camera is powered down, the RX100 V will automatically turn on. Tucking the EVF back into the camera body can turn the camera off again, or allow it to remain on.

Choose your preference in the Function for VF Close entry of the Setup 2 menu.

- **Eye sensor.** This tiny sensor, located to the right of the EVF viewing window, detects when your face (or anything else) approaches the viewfinder.
- **Swiveling LCD monitor screen.** This swiveling screen can be used to preview images and to view them afterward, and to display/navigate menus. The LCD monitor has 3:2 proportions, which is perfect for previewing/shooting/reviewing stills. When you're shooting movies or using some aspect ratio other than 3:2, black bars appear at the top and bottom of the screen.

You can set the LCD monitor brightness with an item in the Setup 1 menu, to be discussed in Chapter 6; there's a special feature that provides a super bright display, useful on bright days when the screen would otherwise be difficult to view. The monitor swivels upward or downward to provide a waist-level view (**Figure 2.6**) or, by flipping the camera upside down, shoot images in "periscope" mode with the camera held overhead.

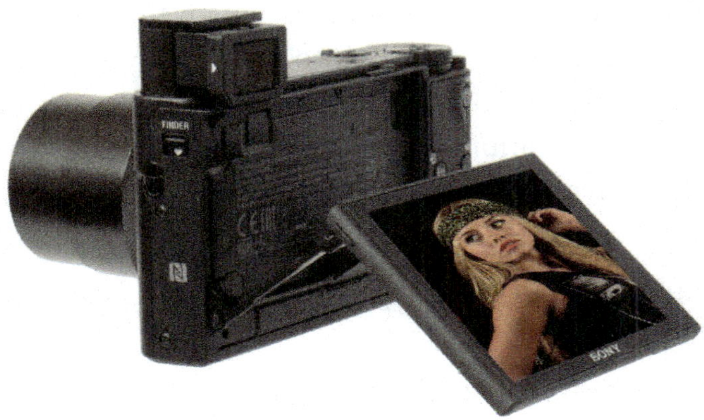

Figure 2.6

The LCD monitor tilts up or down to provide a variety of viewing angles.

The monitor can also be reversed to face you if you decide to grab a selfie. In this configuration, the RX100 V does something very clever: you see a mirror image reverse view of yourself, rather than the view the camera will actually record. You can compose yourself using your familiar visage, rather than wondering why your hair is parted on the wrong side. It will also automatically set a 3-second self-timer that activates when you press the shutter release, allowing you to get composed before the picture is taken. If you're the impatient type, you can de-activate the delay using the Self-portrait/ -timer entry in the Custom Settings 4 menu.

- **Function/Send to Smartphone** button. This button has multiple functions:
- **Playback mode.** Press the Fn button to transmit the picture you are currently viewing, or multiple images to your smartphone. I'll show you how in Chapter 5.
- **Shooting mode.** Press the Fn button to produce a screen with shooting setting options, as seen in **Figure 2.7**. By default, the 12 functions shown are displayed. However, as I'll describe in Chapter 4, you can choose exactly which functions you'd like to display; you aren't locked into twelve. If you prefer, you can define a single row of six favorite functions, or include some other number/combinations of choices. To adjust any of the functions, just follow these steps.
    1. Press the Fn button and use the directional keys to highlight one of the options from the 12 shown on the screen.
    2. When your setting is highlighted:
        - Press the center button to produce an adjustment screen with all the choices shown in a vertical list on the left side of the screen. You might need to do this as you are learning to use your camera and would like to see all your options. Then use the directional buttons to select the option you want. If a choice has multiple options, it will be accompanied by a right-pointing or left-pointing

arrow. For example, when you choose the self-timer, you can press the left/right buttons to select timer durations of 2, 5 or 10 seconds. Press the center button to confirm your choice and exit, or press MENU to cancel.

- Optionally, you can rotate the control wheel *or* the control ring to cycle among the available choices, which will appear one by one as you spin. Just press MENU to confirm your choice and exit. While this is *potentially* a faster method, some of the choices have multiple options in this mode as well, in which case you'll need to press the center button to access them with the left/right buttons as described above.

- **Playback button.** Displays the last picture taken. Thereafter, you can move back and forth among the available images by pressing the left/right direction buttons or spinning the control wheel (on the back of the camera) to advance or backtrack one image at a time. To quit playback, press this button again. The RX100 V also exits Playback mode automatically when you press the shutter release button halfway (so you'll never be prevented from taking a picture on the spur of the moment because you happened to be viewing an image).

- **Control wheel.** This ridged dial, which surrounds the large center button, also has multiple functions, depending on the camera's mode. In both Shooting and Playback modes it can be useful for navigating menu screens to get to the item or option you want to use.

  The control wheel performs several important functions and is the only control on the camera that can be activated in two different ways: you can turn the ridged part of the wheel to perform certain actions (such as navigation or setting exposure controls), and you can press on the various edges at top, bottom, left, and right. In that mode, the edges serve as directional buttons for navigating through menu screens, for example.

- **Playback mode.** When an image is magnified in Playback mode, all four buttons can be used to move the viewing area around within the magnified image and within the index screens during playback. When the image is not magnified, the left/right buttons move to the previous/next image on your memory card in Playback mode.
- **Shooting mode.** When the camera is in Shooting mode, rotating the control wheel is used to adjust shutter speed (in Shutter Priority mode), aperture (in Aperture Priority mode), or both (in Program mode). The four directional buttons are used to make adjustments. For example, when the Autofocus Area is set to Flexible Spot, you can use all four of the direction buttons to move the focus bracket to any of its available positions on the screen. In Manual exposure mode, the control wheel is used to adjust both shutter speed and aperture, switching between them with a press of the down button.
- **Directional buttons.** Each direction button also has a default specific purpose that produces an adjustment screen when pressed. That direct access function is labeled on the area outside the wheel itself. You can also redefine any of these keys using the Custom Keys entry in the Custom Settings 7 menu, as described in Chapter 4. Here's a brief summary of their default definitions:
- **Up key/DISP button.** The up key is labeled as DISP, for Display Contents, and it provides display-oriented functions, which vary depending on your Shooting/Playback mode:
- **Shooting mode**. When the camera is in Shooting mode, press the DISP button repeatedly to cycle among the three screens that display data in the electronic viewfinder display or the six screens that display information about current settings on the LCD screen.

The default display for the LCD is called Display All Info (shown in **Figure 2.8**, later in this chapter). This provides a full information display with a great deal of data overlaid over the live preview to show the settings in effect. The data provided when the camera is in a SCN mode or either Auto mode is quite limited; use P, A, S, or M mode to view all of the available data in each display option. Not all the information shown in the figure will be displayed at all times.

When you keep pressing the DISP button, the camera LCD cycles through other viewing modes, including No Display Info, which actually provides a few bits of data, a Graphic Display that shows the shutter speed and aperture on two related scales along with some recording information, a Display All Info screen filled with data, an Electronic Level display, and a basic display with a histogram in the bottom right of the screen. There is also a For Viewfinder/Quick Navi text information screen that omits the thumbnail and shows only shooting information. When you press the Fn button when the For Viewfinder screen is visible, you can then select and change settings, as I'll describe shortly. You can enable/disable each of these information displays using the DISP Button entry within the Custom Settings 2 menu, as I'll explain in Chapter 4.

- **Playback mode.** In Playback mode, the DISP button offers different display options, as you would expect. When viewing still images during playback, press the DISP button to cycle among the three available playback screens: full recording data; histogram with recording data; and no recording data. When displaying a movie on the screen, the DISP button produces only two screens: with or without recording information. There is no histogram display available.

- **Down button: Exposure compensation/ Photo Creativity.** This button has several functions, which differ depending on the exposure mode you're using.

- **Program, Aperture Priority, Shutter Priority, or Sweep Panorama modes.** Pressing this button reveals the exposure compensation display. Scroll up/down among the plus and minus options by rotating the control dial, the control wheel, or by pressing the direction buttons of the wheel. I'll discuss exposure compensation and other exposure-related topics in Chapter 7.
- **Intelligent Auto and Superior Auto modes.** Pressing the down button reveals a Photo Creativity screen that allows you to adjust parameters. These include Background Defocus (depth-of-field), Brightness, Color (hue), Vividness (saturation or color richness), and Picture Effect. Each of these has an Auto setting, which allows the camera to decide on the adjustment, or you can rotate the control wheel to modify the default values individually for each of the five parameters. You can reset any of them to Auto by pressing the C/Delete button.
- **Scene modes.** This button cycles through the scene modes when the mode dial is set to SCN.
- **Manual exposure mode.** By default, in Manual exposure mode, the control wheel adjusts the shutter speed, and the control ring (on the front of the camera) adjusts the aperture. If you've redefined the control ring to perform some other function, you can use the control wheel to adjust both shutter speed and aperture. Just press the down directional button to toggle between them. Note: if you have not redefined the control ring, the down button sets both the control ring and control wheel for aperture adjustment, which is fairly useless in Manual exposure mode. The LCD monitor and EV will display icons representing the control wheel and control ring with Av (aperture

value) or Tv (time value) next to them to remind you how the controls are set.

- **Left key/Drive mode button.** One press of this button in a compatible shooting mode leads to a vertical list of options at the left side of the screen that let you set the self-timer, enable the camera to shoot one frame at a time or continuously at a fast or very fast rate, or set up bracketing. The latter causes the camera to automatically take a series of shots, varying the exposure for each to ensure you get the best exposure possible.

When you scroll to the self-timer or exposure, white balance, or DRO bracketing options, you can press the left/right key to adjust options for those drive modes, as discussed in Chapter 7.

- **Right key/ISO button.** When not helping you navigate to the right through menus and other screens, this button lets you activate the ISO screen in a compatible shooting mode. You can then scroll up/down among the options by rotating the camera's control wheel or by pressing the wheel's direction buttons. You'll learn more about ISO in Chapter 3.
- **Center/OK button.** The center button functions as the selection button; press it to select or confirm a choice from a menu screen.
- **Delete/Custom button.** This button accesses an In-Camera Guide in Shooting mode. You'll probably want to change it to a more useful function, such as AEL Toggle (to lock exposure) using the Custom Keys feature explained in Chapter 4. In Playback mode, the C button serves as a delete key.

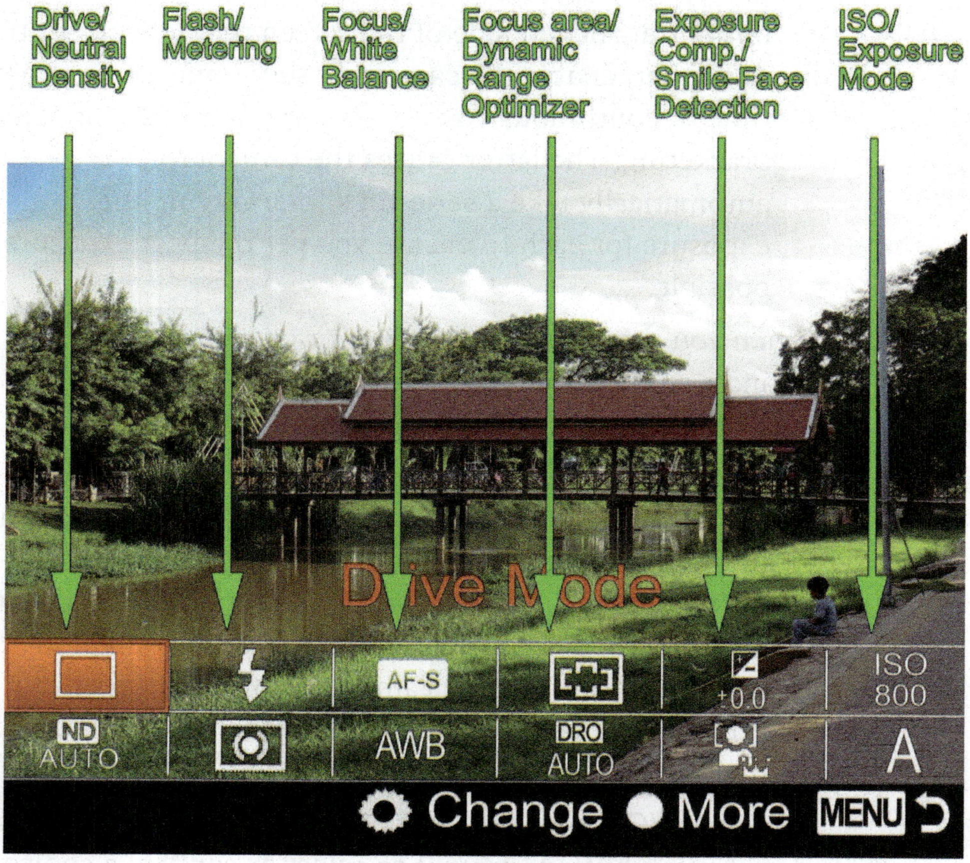

Figure 2.7

Up to 12 user-selectable choices are available in the Function menu. This is the default layout.

LCD Panel Data Displays

The Sony RX100 V provides a tilting and expansive 3-inch color LCD with high resolution to display everything you need to see, from images to a collection of informational data displays. Some of the data is shown only when you are viewing the Display All Info screen, but even then, not every item of data will be available all the time. (See **Figure 2.8.**) As discussed earlier, the electronic viewfinder display options provide much less data in order to avoid cluttering the live preview with numerals and icons during serious photography.

Here's a description of the most important information that the camera can display in the LCD in Display All Info when it's set for P, A, S, or M mode; less data is available in other display modes and when other Shooting modes are being used.

- **Shooting mode.** Shows whether you're using Program Auto, Aperture Priority, Shutter Priority, Manual, Panorama, one of the scene modes, or one of the two Auto modes.
- **Memory card/Uploading status.** Indicates whether a memory card is in the camera. (If you remove the card, a blinking NO CARD indicator will appear instead.) If the camera is connected using Wi-Fi, the indicator will display icons representing the upload status.
- **Exposures remaining.** Shows the approximate number of shots available to be taken on the memory card, assuming current conditions, such as image size and quality. When shooting a movie, the recordable time remaining is shown instead.
- **Aspect ratio/Image Size.** Shows whether the camera is set for the 3:2 aspect ratio or wide-screen 16:9 aspect ratio (the image size icon changes to a "stretched" version when the aspect ratio is set to 16:9) and whether you're shooting Large, Medium, or Small resolution images. When the camera is set to the 16:9 aspect ratio, the display has black bands at the top and the bottom, as you would expect with the longer/narrower

format vs. the 3:2 aspect ratio which is closer to square in shape.

- **Image quality.** Your image quality setting (JPEG Extra Fine, JPEG Fine, JPEG Standard, RAW, or RAW & JPEG) is displayed.
- **Frame rate/Movie recording settings.** These icons show what movie settings are in use such as 60i FH (full HD video at 60i). I'll discuss your movie-making options, including file formats and size, in Chapter 10.
- **NFC active indicator.** Shows when your RX100 V is linked to another device using Near Field Communications.
- **Battery status.** The remaining battery life is indicated by this icon.
- **Metering mode.** The icons represent Multi, Center, or Spot metering. (See Chapter 7 for more detail.)
- **Flash exposure compensation.** This icon is shown whenever the pop-up is active to indicate the level of flash exposure compensation, if any, that you have set.
- **White balance.** Shows current white balance setting. The choices are Auto White Balance, Daylight, Shade, Cloudy, Incandescent, Fluorescent, Flash, Color Temperature, and Custom. I'll discuss white balance settings and adjustments in Chapter 4.
- **Dynamic Range Optimizer/HDR.** Indicates the type of dynamic range optimization (highlight/shadow detail enhancement) in use: Off, Auto DRO, levels 1-5 of DRO, or the special Auto HDR feature, all described in Chapter 9.
- **Creative Style.** Indicates which of the six Creative Style settings (Standard, Vivid, Portrait, Landscape, Sunset, or Black-and-White) is being applied.
- **Picture effect.** Shows which of the special effects, such as Toy Camera, Pop Color, or Posterization is being applied. I'll explain these options in Chapter 3.

- **SteadyShot indicator.** Provides information as to whether the SteadyShot image stabilizer is On or Off, and warns you that the shutter speed will be too long for the stabilizer to fully compensate for camera shake.
- **Flash charge in progress.** This lightning bolt icon appears on the screen when the flash unit is active; a solid orange dot beside it indicates the flash has recycled (charged) and is ready to fire.
- **AF illuminator status.** This icon appears when conditions are dark enough that the AF Illuminator will be needed in order to light up the area so that the autofocus system can operate properly.
- **Flash mode.** Provides flash mode information when the pop-up flash is active. The possible choices are Flash Off, Autoflash, Fill-Flash, Slow Sync, Rear Curtain, and Wireless. Not all of these choices are available at all times.
- **Drive mode.** Shows whether the camera is set for Single-shot, Continuous shooting, Speed Priority Continuous shooting, Self-timer, Self-timer with continuous shooting, or Exposure bracketing. There is one additional option available: Remote Commander, which sets up the camera to be controlled by an infrared remote control.
- **AE Lock.** Appears when autoexposure has been locked at the current setting.
- **ISO setting.** Indicates the sensor ISO sensitivity currently set, either Auto ISO or a numerical value. I'll discuss this camera feature in Chapter 9.
- **Exposure compensation.** This indicator shows the amount of exposure compensation, if any, currently set.
- **Aperture.** Displays the current f/stop set by the camera or, in Manual or Aperture Priority mode, as set by the user. If you're viewing the Graphic display, icons indicate that wider apertures produce less depth-of-field (a "blurry" background)

while smaller apertures provide a greater range of acceptable sharpness (increasing the odds of a more distinct background).

- **Shutter speed.** Shows the current shutter speed, either as set by the camera's autoexposure system or, in Manual or Shutter Priority mode, as set by the user. If the camera's Graphic display is used, the screen illustrates that faster shutter speeds are better for action and slower speeds are fine for scenes with less movement.
- **Focus indicator.** Flashes while focus is underway, and turns a solid green when focus is confirmed.
- **Focus mode.** Shows the currently selected focus mode, such as AF-S, AF-C, DMF (Direct Manual Focus), or MF (Manual Focus), as explained in Chapter 8.
- **Focus area mode.** Displays the active focus area mode, such as Wide, Center, or Flexible Spot, as explained in Chapter 8.
- **Picture Profile.** If you've specified a picture profile image customization setting in the Camera Setting 6 menu, your choice (from PP1 to PP7) is indicated here. I discuss picture profiles in Chapter 3.
- **Zoom.** Shows when digital zoom modes are active.
- **Neutral-Density Filter.** Shows whether the ND filter is enabled.
- **Function of Control Ring/Wheel.** Indicates the functions of the control ring and control wheel, as these may change depending on your current mode and how you have defined the controls using the Custom Keys options.
- **Setting Effect.** Indicates whether the LCD shows the effects of any adjustments, including exposure, white balance, or Picture Effects in Shooting mode.
- **Database indicator.** This warning appears when your memory card's image database is full or has errors.
- **Audio recording.** Shows whether sound recording is enabled/disabled for movie shooting.

- **Airplane mode.** Appears when Airplane mode has disabled Wi-Fi and NFC communications.

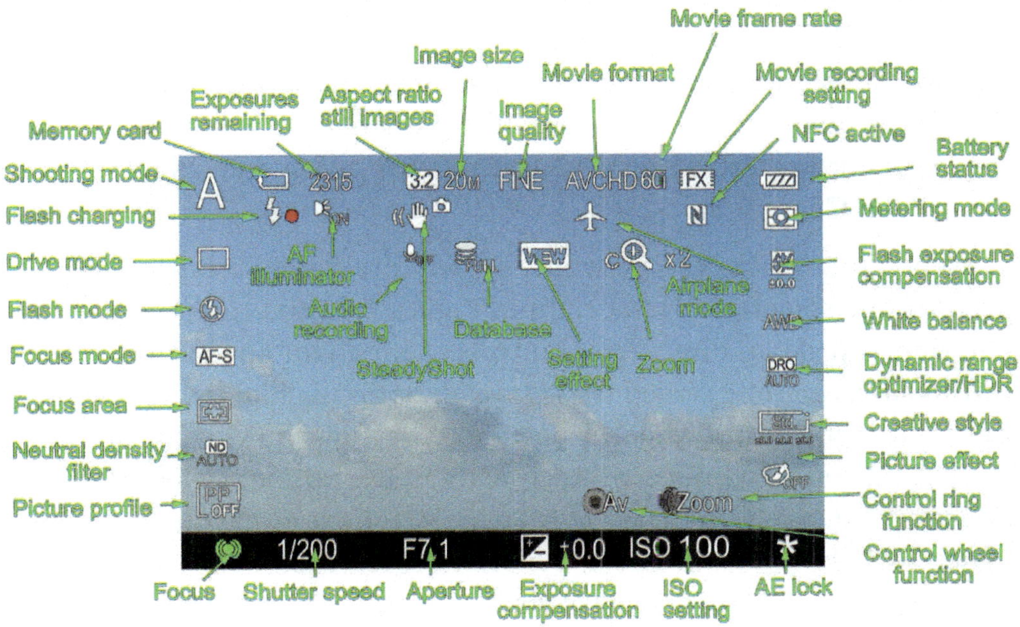

Figure 2.8

The Display All Info screen on the LCD.

Some of the same items of data are also available when other display options are selected with the DISP button, as discussed earlier in this chapter. When the Graphic Display option is used, the camera provides an illustration of the value of a small or wide aperture, and a fast or slow shutter speed, as discussed in the previous section.

Using the Quick Navi Function Menu

If you select the Quick Navi screen by pressing the DISP button until it appears, the LCD monitor shows the For Viewfinder/Quick Navi display, with only the data and no live view of the scene, as you can see in **Figure 2.9**, left. The For Viewfinder/Quick Navi text-only displays are shown only on the LCD monitor and not in the viewfinder, and must be activated, like the other LCD displays, using the DISP button setting in the Custom Settings 2 menu, as I'll describe in Chapter 3.

When the Quick Navi screen is shown, press the Fn button to produce the screen shown at right in Figure 2.9. You can then use the left/right/up/down directional buttons to highlight any of the settings that are not grayed out. Once an option is highlighted, you can rotate the control wheel to change its settings quickly, or press the OK button to produce a screen with all the options. Use the directional buttons and OK button to select the option you want. The Quick Navi screen is, in effect, a more fully featured Function menu. When the Quick Navi display is visible on the LCD monitor, you must compose images using the electronic viewfinder.

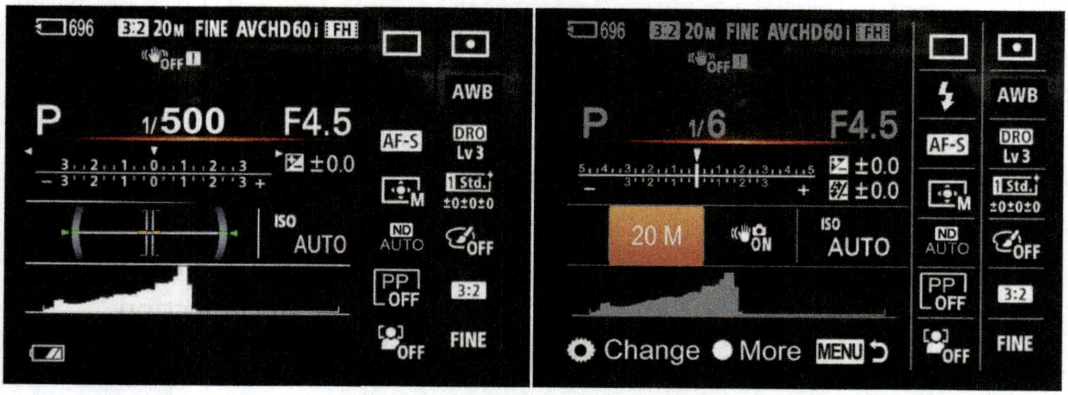

Figure 2.9

The For Viewfinder/Quick Navi information screen is available only for the LCD monitor and is not shown in the viewfinder.

Going Topside

The top surface of the RX100 V has several frequently accessed controls of its own. They are labeled in **Figure 2.10**:

- **Stereo microphones.** A pair of microphones on the top panel of the camera can capture stereophonic audio while making movies.
- **Mode dial.** Rotate this dial to select Shooting modes including Manual exposure, Shutter Priority, Aperture Priority, Program Auto, Auto (either Superior Auto or Intelligent Auto, as you specify in the Auto Mode setting of the Camera Settings 7 menu), scene modes, Panorama, HFR (high frame rate), Movie mode, and the Memory Recall (MR) positions (which allow you to choose from up to three predefined groups of settings).
- **Control ring.** Don't confuse this with the control wheel on the back of the camera. It's used, often in conjunction with the control wheel, to provide additional options. For example, in Manual exposure mode, by default the control ring adjusts the aperture, while the control wheel sets the shutter speed.
- **On/Off button.** Press to turn the camera on or off; a green LED will glow to indicate the camera is powered up.
- **Zoom lever.** This lever has different functions in shooting and playback modes:
- **Shooting mode.** Press the Zoom lever on top of the camera (with a W-T label for Wide-angle and Telephoto) to zoom into (enlarge) and zoom out (reduce) the image view.
- **Playback mode.** Pressing the Zoom lever toward the W will zoom out to full-frame view and then activate an index screen showing 9 or 25 thumbnail images (select the number using the Image Index option in the Playback 1 menu), and thence to Calendar view, which collects pictures by the date you shot them. (Press the center button to view the images taken on a highlighted date.)
- Use the directional buttons to navigate among index thumbnails. Scroll to the thumbnail of the photo you want to

view and press the center button; the photo will then fill the screen. The RX100 V arranges index images by date shot, and includes this calendar view to help you search for pictures taken on a specific date. I'll explain those options in more detail in Chapter 6.

- **Pop-up electronic viewfinder.** Press the Finder button on the side of the camera to elevate the EVF, then pull the eyepiece toward the back of the camera to ready the RX100 V for viewing.
- **Flash pop-up switch.** Press the Flash pop-up switch to elevate the flash. Press it down to tuck the flash back into the camera. You'll learn more about using this flash in Chapter 11.
- **Shutter release button.** Partially depress this button to lock in exposure and focus. Press it all the way to take the picture. Hold this button down to take a continuous stream of images when the drive mode is set for Continuous shooting. Tapping the shutter release when the camera's power save feature has turned off the autoexposure and autofocus mechanisms reactivates both. When a review image or menu screen is displayed on the LCD, tapping this button removes that display, returning the camera to the standard view and reactivating the autoexposure and autofocus mechanisms.

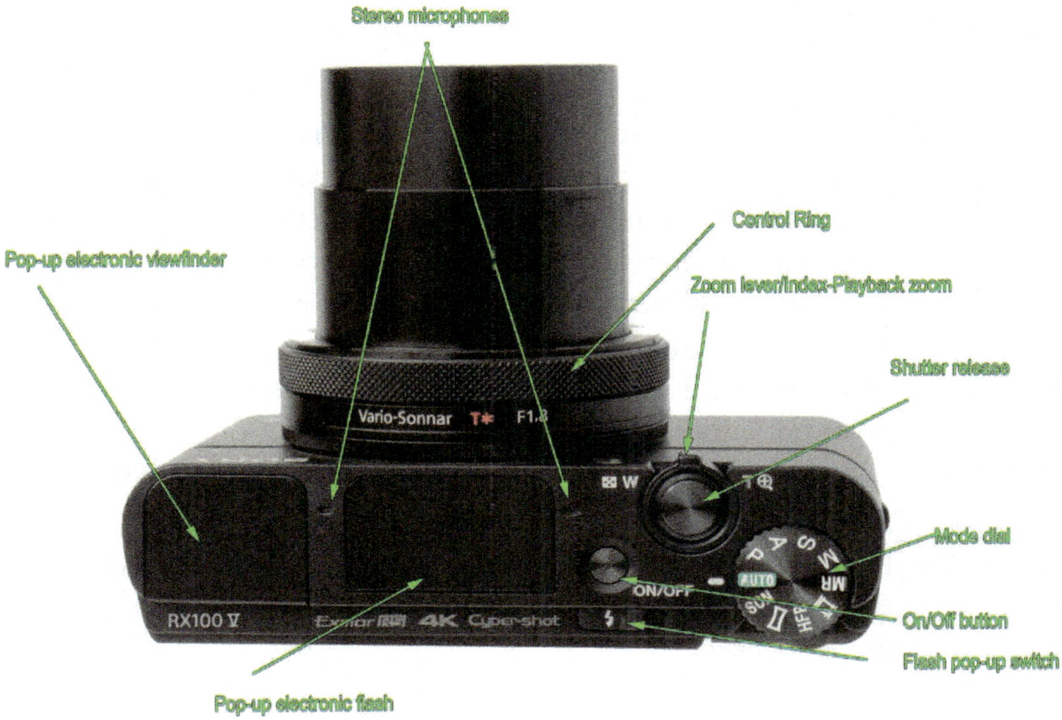

Figure 2.10

The top of your RX100 V.

Underneath Your Sony RX100 V

The bottom panel of your RX100 V has only a few components, illustrated in **Figure 2.11**.

- **Tripod socket.** Attach the camera to a flash bracket, tripod, monopod, or other support using this standard receptacle. The socket is positioned roughly behind the optical center of the lens, a decent location when using a tripod with a pan (side rotating) movement, compared to an off-center orientation. For most accurate panning, the socket would ideally be placed a little forward (actually in *front* of the camera body) so the pivot point is located *under* the optical center of the lens, but you can't have everything. There are special attachments you can use to accomplish this if you like.
- **Battery compartment door/memory card cover/latch.** Slide the latch to open the door and gain access to the battery and memory card.
- **Speaker.** Sounds emanating from your camera are produced by this tiny speaker.
- **Memory card access lamp.** Flashes red while the memory card is being written to. This lamp's location on the underside of the camera is not ideal. (I like to view the access lamp as a confirmation that a camera is actually taking pictures and saving them to the memory card.) However, it is underneath the battery/memory card cover door you must open before removing a memory card, so you should notice its red glow *before* you make the mistake of changing cards before the current image(s) are safely stored on your card.

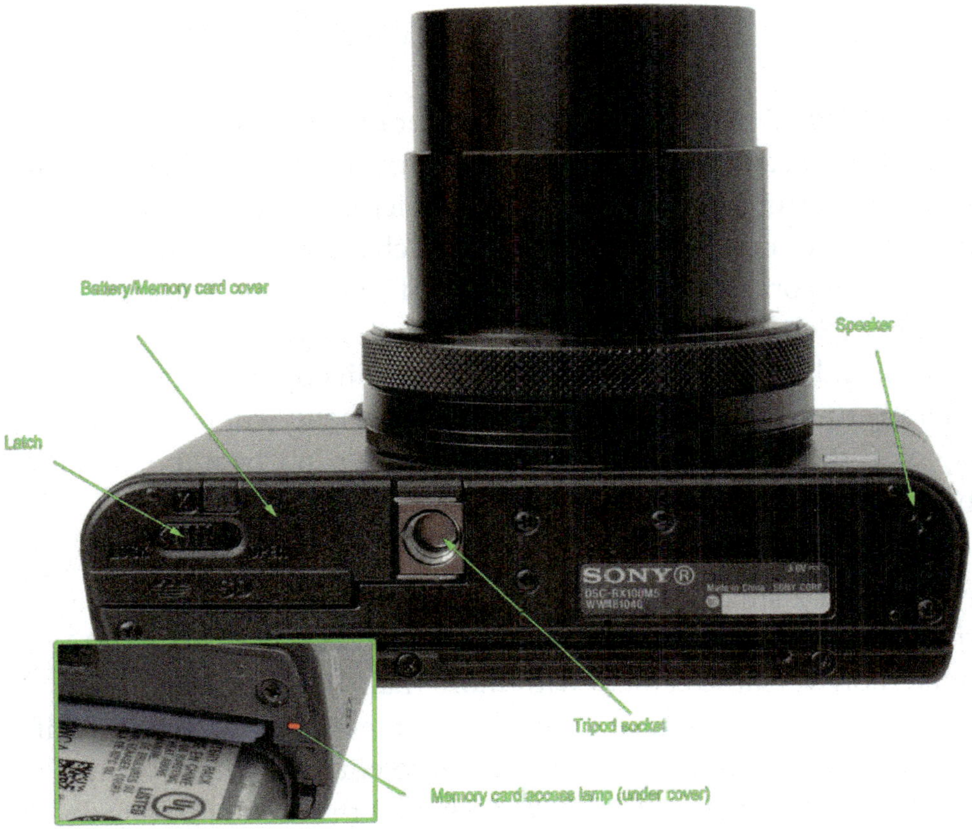

Figure 2.11

The bottom panel of the RX100 V.

Chapter 3

Camera Settings Menu

The RX100 V has a remarkable number of features and options you can use to customize the way your camera operates. Not only can you change settings used at the time the picture is taken, but you can adjust the way your camera behaves. This chapter and the next three will help you sort out the settings for all of the menus. These include the Camera Settings, Custom Settings, Wireless, Application, Playback, and Setup menus. This chapter details options with the Camera Settings menu; the Custom Settings menu will be covered in Chapter 4; the Wireless and Application menus in Chapter 5; and the Playback and Setup menus will be addressed in Chapter 6.

Why four entire chapters just on the menus, when other sources may have just a single chapter with a line or two about each menu entry explaining what they do? As you're discovering, the RX100 V is an incredibly versatile camera with more than 130 different menu entries, many of which have submenus and multiple options. Even if you're a Sony veteran or an advanced photo enthusiast, you want more than just a brief explanation of what all the menu options do. You also need to know what they *don't* do, *when* to use each one, and, most importantly, when *not* to use them.

And, I'll bet, you purchased this book because you also wanted to know *my* personal preferences for settings and how I use these features. When I share what I know in person at workshops and other sessions with groups of photographers, I always tell them my informal motto: *I make terrible mistakes, so you don't have to!* I like to push cameras to their limits -- or beyond -- and, in the process, discover exactly what they can do, and what they can't. The RX100 V is small, but mighty, and has a surprising number of advanced capabilities worth exploring.

I'm not going to waste a lot of space on some of the more obvious menu choices in these chapters, especially those with only On/Off or

Enable/Disable options. Instead, I'll concentrate on the more complex aspects of setup, such as autofocus. I'll start with an overview of using the camera's menus themselves.

Anatomy of the Menus

The menu system is quite easy to navigate. Press the MENU button to enter Menuland. Six tabs are arrayed across the top, representing the Camera Settings, Custom Settings, Wireless, Application, Playback, and Setup menus. If a menu tab is active, but no entry within that tab has been selected, the tab will be highlighted in orange. You can press the left/right directional buttons to move from one orange-highlighted tab to the next.

Press the down directional button or rotate the control wheel to move highlighting from the tab down to the entries within that menu tab. When working within a menu tab, the currently selected menu tab will be highlighted in black, as you can see in the figure, and the other tabs are given a gray background. The number of that menu's tab is underlined in orange, as you can see in **Figure 3.1**.

TILE MENU

The vestigial Tile menu, with picture icons for each of the six main menu headings, is disabled by default, as it is essentially useless. (It was shown in Figure 1.8 in Chapter 1.) The only thing you can do with this leftover from Sony's NEX camera era is move to the conventional menu system. If it has been enabled on your camera, I recommend you immediately eliminate the extra step, using the Setup 2 menu's Tile Menu setting to disable it, described in Chapter 6.

You can choose any item in the displayed tab, and press the center button to produce a screen where you can adjust the options within the highlighted entry. While navigating any menu tab, use the left/right directional buttons to move to the next tab in that menu group, and then to wrap around to the first tab in the next group.

For example, if you are using the Camera Settings menu, the right button will take you from Camera Settings 1 to Camera Settings 2, and thence onward to the Camera Settings 3 to 10 tabs. Note that each of the main tabs may have several pages or subtabs: the Camera Settings menu has tabs 1 to 10; the Custom Settings menu has tabs 1 to 6; the Wireless menu has two tabs, 1 and 2; the Application menu has just one tab; the Playback menu has three tabs, 1, 2, and 2; and the Setup menu boasts tabs 1 to 6. The advantage to having so many menu tabs is that all the entries for a given page can be shown on a single screen.

NO MENUS REQUIRED

Of course, not everything has to be set using these menus. The RX100 V has some convenient direct setting controls, such as the buttons of the control wheel that provide quick access to the drive modes, display information, ISO, and exposure compensation options. These and other buttons can be assigned other direct access functions -- more than 50 different functions in all if you include Not Set. These control features allow you to bypass the multi-tabbed menus for many of the most commonly used camera functions.

There is also a Function menu that appears when you press the Fn button, with a set of shooting setting options, as I described in Chapter 2. Although the Fn menu has a default set of 12 functions, you can redefine those entries as well. Your RX100 V offers a remarkable degree of customization.

At times you will notice that some entries on various menu screens are "grayed out;" you cannot select them given the current camera settings. For example, if you decide to shoot a panorama photo, you may find that the Panorama: Size and Panorama: Direction choices in the Camera Settings 2 menu are grayed out. Want to know why? Scroll to the grayed out item and press the center button. The camera then displays a screen that explains why this feature is not available: for this example, it's because the feature is not available when Shutter Priority mode is active. Unfortunately, that's not very helpful. The screen *should* have instead told you that the Panorama settings are not available when the shooting mode is anything *other* than Sweep Panorama. Given the incomplete information (and lacking this book), you might have spent several frustrating minutes switching to other shooting modes, still to find that no Panorama settings are possible. Thanks, Sony!

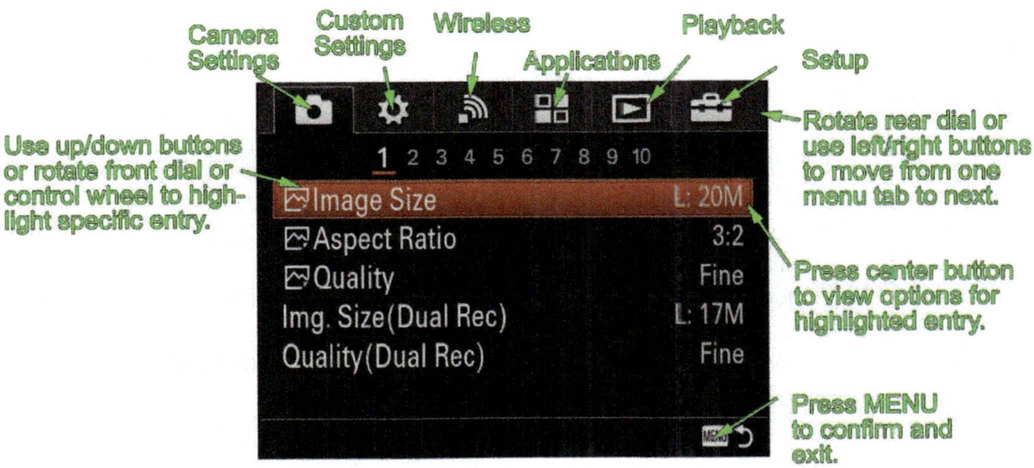

Figure 3.1

Press MENU to jump directly to the camera's conventional menu system.

ABOUT THOSE ICONS

Menu entries are largely text, but some are preceded by an icon, such as the "mountain" icon shown next to the Image Size, Aspect Ratio, and Quality entries in **Figure 3.1**. A mountain icon indicates that the particular menu entry applies *only* to still photography; an icon resembling a film frame shows that the menu entry applies *only* to movie making. Presumably, entries without any icon can be used with both. The Enlarge entry in the Playback menu, and Language entry in the Setup menu are preceded by magnifying glass and text icons, respectively, and are apparently used just for decorative purposes.

Camera Settings Menu

Figure 3.1, earlier, shows the first screen of the Camera Settings menu. As you can see, at most only a half dozen items are displayed at one time.

The items found in this menu include:

- Image Size (Still Image)
- Aspect Ratio (Still Image)
- Quality (Still Image)
- Image Size (Dual Record)
- Quality (Dual Record)
- File Format (Movie)
- Record Setting (Movie)
- Dual Video REC
- HFR Settings
- Panorama: Size
- Panorama: Direction
- Drive Mode
- Bracket Settings
- Flash Mode
- Flash Compensation
- Red Eye Reduction
- Focus Mode
- Focus Area
- AF Illuminator (Still Image)
- AF Drive Speed (Movies)
- AF Track Sensitivity (Movies)
- Exposure Compensation
- ISO
- ISO Auto Minimum Shutter Speed
- ND Filter
- Metering Mode
- White Balance
- DRO/Auto HDR
- Creative Style
- Picture Effect
- Picture Profile
- Focus Magnifier
- Long Exposure Noise Reduction (Still Image)
- High ISO Noise Reduction (Still Image)
- Center Lock-on AF
- Smile/Face Detection
- Auto Dual Recording
- Soft Skin Effect (Still Image)
- Auto Object Framing (Still Image)
- Auto Mode
- Scene Selection
- High Frame Rate
- Movie
- SteadyShot (Still Image)
- SteadyShot (Movie)
- Color Space (Still Image)
- Auto Slow Shutter (Movie)
- Audio Recording
- Micref Level
- Wind Noise Reduction
- Memory Recall
- Memory

Image Size

- **Options:** L, M, S
- **Default:** L
- **My preference:** L

Here you can choose between the RX100 V's Large, Medium, and Small settings for JPEG still pictures. The larger the size that's selected, the higher the resolution: as resolution increases, the images are composed of more pixels.

As you scroll among the options, you'll note that the size for Large, Medium, and Small is shown in megapixels, as you can see in **Table 3.1**. The number of pixels will vary, depending on which of the four available *aspect ratios* (image proportions) you've chosen. For example, you'll get 20.1 MP in Large mode using the 3:2 aspect ratio, and 17 MP in Large mode using the 16:9 aspect ratio.

Table 3.1

Image Sizes Available

	Large (L)	Medium (M)	Small (S)	VGA
Aspect Ratio: 3:2	20 MP: 5472 x 3648 pixels	10 MP: 3888 x 2592 pixels	5 MP: 2736 x 1824 pixels	N/A
Aspect Ratio: 4:3	18 MP: 4864 x 3648 pixels	10 MP: 3648 x 2736 pixels	5 MP: 2592 x 1944 pixels	0.3 MP: 640 x 480 pixels
Aspect Ratio: 16:9	17 MP: 5472 x 3080 pixels	7.5 MP: 3648 x 2056 pixels	4.2 MP: 2720 x 1528 pixels	N/A
Aspect Ratio: 1:1	13 MP: 3648 x 3648 pixels	6.5 MP: 2544 x 2544 pixels	3.7 MP: 1920 x 1920 pixels	N/A

Navigate to this Image Size menu item, press the center button, and scroll to the desired option: L, M, or S. Then press the center button to confirm your choice. As I noted, the actual size of the images depends on the aspect ratio you have chosen in the subsequent menu item, either the standard 3:2 or optional 4:3, wide-screen 16:9, and square 1:1 formats. When you're using the 4:3 aspect ratio, one additional image size, the 640 x 480-pixel VGA resolution, can be chosen if you want truly tiny image files, suitable for uploading to your smartphone and thence to your contacts by e-mail, Instagram, or some other destination. Additional image sizes also are available when you are using Sweep Panorama, which I'll explain later in this chapter.

Except for social networking applications, there are few reasons to use a size other than Large with this camera, even if reduced resolution is sufficient for your application, such as photo ID cards or web display. Starting with a full-size image gives you greater freedom for cropping and fixing problems with your image editor. An 800 x 600-pixel web image created from a full-resolution (large) original often ends up better than one that started out as a small JPEG.

Of course, the Medium and Small settings make it possible to squeeze more pictures onto your memory card. The smaller image sizes might come in handy in situations where your memory cards are almost full and/or you don't have the opportunity to offload the pictures you've taken to your computer. For example, if you're on vacation and plan to make only 4 x 6-inch snapshot prints of the photos you shoot, setting a lower resolution will stretch your memory card's capacity. Even then, it makes more sense to simply buy and carry memory cards with higher capacity and use your RX100 V camera at its maximum resolution.

This setting affects *only* JPEG images. Indeed, if you select RAW for Quality, you'll find that the Image Size option is grayed out, because the camera will always shoot Large photos in RAW. With the RAW & JPEG quality setting, the RX100 V captures full-size, Large RAW images as well as a JPEG image in the size you specify here.

Tip: When traveling you might decide to capture only Small JPEG images to e-mail or post on social media, while retaining Large RAW images to work with in your image editor when you return home. Select Small here, and choose RAW & JPEG under Image Quality. If you want the smallest possible JPEG images, first set the Aspect Ratio (as described next) to 4:3, choose VGA here for Image Size, and select RAW & JPEG under Image Quality. You'll end up with full-size RAW images and tiny 640 x 480-pixel snapshots you can e-mail with ease.

Aspect Ratio

- **Options:** 3:2, 4:3, 16:9, and 1:1 aspect ratios
- **Default:** 3:2
- **My preference:** 3.2; you can always crop to other sizes in your image editor

The aspect ratio is simply the proportions of your image as stored in your image file. The standard aspect ratio for digital photography is approximately 3:2; the image is two-thirds as tall as it is wide, as shown by the outer green rectangle in **Figure 3.3**. These proportions conform to those of the most common snapshot size in the USA, 4 x 6 inches. Of course, if you want to make a standard 8 x 10-inch enlargement, you'll need to trim some of the length of the image area since this format is closer to square; you (or a lab) would need 8 x 12-inch paper to print the full image area. The 3:2 aspect ratio was also the norm in photography with 35mm film. Your RX100 V's sensor has 3:2 proportions; if you select any other aspect ratio, some pixels are trimmed off the top, bottom, or (with the 1:1 aspect ratio) sides.

The 4:3 aspect ratio happens to be the same proportions used by Micro Four Thirds cameras, such as those produced by Olympus and Panasonic. That same aspect ratio has been used in the past for standard definition television broadcasts and motion pictures before the widescreen era. Some like these proportions for presentations. You can use the 4:3 aspect ratio when you know you will need photos in that format (and don't want to crop a whole batch manually in an image editor) or when you want access to the VGA image size.

If you're looking for images that will "fit" a widescreen computer display or a high-definition television screen, you can use this menu item to switch to a 16:9 aspect ratio, which is much wider than it is tall. The camera performs this magic by cutting off the pixels at the top and bottom of the frame, and storing a reduced resolution image (as shown in **Table 3.1**). Your 20.1 MP image becomes a 17 MP shot if you set the camera to shoot in 16:9 aspect ratio instead of using the default 3:2 option. If you need the widescreen look, this menu option will save you some time in image editing, but you can achieve the same proportions (or any other aspect ratio) by trimming a full-resolution image with your software. The 16:9 option and other aspect ratios are most useful if you plan to take a *lot* of photos that will work best in that particular format.

When you set the RX100 V to shoot in an aspect ratio other than 3:2, black bars appear in the live view image on the LCD monitor and EVF to show you the exact area that will be captured in the JPEG file. (See **Figure 3.2**.)

Note: For all aspect ratios other than 3:2, the camera trims *only* the JPEG version. Your RAW images are still captured at full size using the 3:2 proportions, but your desired aspect ratio is noted in the image file. Many image editors, including Sony's Image Data Converter, will honor your setting and either crop during import or highlight the portion of the image you specified. You can still revert to a full-size 3:2 image if you like.

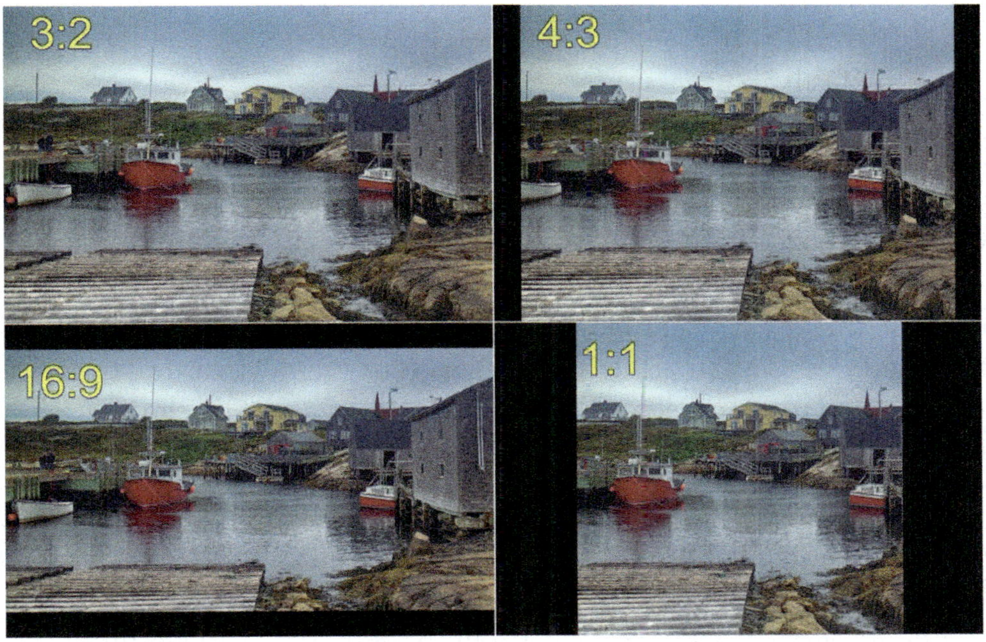

Figure 3.2

Available aspect ratios and the image areas each represents.

Quality

- **Options:** RAW, RAW & JPEG, Extra Fine, Fine, Standard
- **Default**: Fine
- **My preference**: Extra Fine

This menu item lets you choose the image quality settings that will be used by the RX100 V to store its still photo files. In this case, "quality" doesn't refer to the *resolution* of the image (that's taken care of by the Image Size parameter), but, rather, by how much *compression* is applied to the photo as it is stored on your memory card. Extra compression produces smaller files, but at the cost of discarding some image information and lower overall quality.

The *number* of pixels in your photo remains the same, but adjacent pixels with similar tones are stored using a compromise value, so fine distinctions between them are lost. Additional compression techniques are used to store those values using the smallest number of bits. The amount of squeezing that can take place varies depending on the type of scene, so file *sizes* can vary. You may not visually notice that information has been discarded.

Here, you have five options: RAW, RAW & JPEG, Extra Fine, Fine, and Standard. In truth, RAW is a file format and not a quality specification at all, but nearly all cameras include this option in the Quality section of their menus. (The Extra Fine, Fine, and Standard options are relevant only to JPEGs.) Here's what you need to know to choose intelligently:

- **JPEG compression.** As I noted, to reduce the size of your image files and allow more photos to be stored on a given memory card, the camera's processor uses JPEG compression to squeeze the images down to a smaller size. This compacting reduces the image quality a little, so you're offered your choice of Extra Fine, Fine, and Standard compression. Standard compression is quite aggressive; the camera discards a lot of data. While Fine is, well, just fine, you'll find that Extra Fine provides even better results so it should really be your *standard* when shooting JPEG photos.

- **JPEG, RAW, or both.** You can elect to store only JPEG versions of the images you shoot (Extra Fine, Fine, or Standard), or you can save your photos as "unprocessed" RAW files. These consume several times as much space on your memory card. Or, you can store both file types at once as you shoot.

Many photographers elect to shoot *both* a JPEG and a RAW file (RAW & JPEG). I do that myself, so I'll have a JPEG version that might be usable as-is, as well as the original "digital negative" RAW file in case I later want to make some serious editing of the photo with imaging software for reasons discussed shortly. If you use the RAW & JPEG option, the camera will save two different versions of the same file to the memory card: one with a .JPG extension, and one with the .ARW (Alpha RAW) extension that signifies Sony's proprietary RAW format.

As I noted under Image Size, there are some limited advantages to using the Medium and Small resolution settings, and similar space-saving benefits accrue to the Standard JPEG compression setting. All of these options help stretch the capacity of your memory card so you can shoehorn quite a few more pictures onto a single card. That can be useful when you're away from home and are running out of storage, or when you're shooting non-critical work that doesn't require full resolution (such as photos taken for real estate listings, web page display, photo ID cards, or similar applications).

But for most work, using lower resolution and extra compression is false economy. You never know when you might actually need that extra bit of picture detail. Your best bet is to have enough memory cards to handle all the shooting you want to do until you have the chance to transfer your photos to your computer or a personal storage device.

JPEG vs. RAW

You'll sometimes be told that RAW files are the "unprocessed" image information your camera produces, before it's been modified. That's nonsense. RAW files are no more unprocessed than camera film is after it's been through the chemicals to produce a negative or transparency. A lot can happen in the developer that can affect the quality of a film image -- positively and negatively -- and, similarly, your digital image undergoes a significant amount of processing before it is saved as a RAW file. Sony even applies a name (BIONZ X) to the digital image processor used to perform this magic in Sony cameras.

A RAW file is closer in concept to a film camera's processed negative. It contains all the information, with no compression, no sharpening, no application of any special filters or other settings you might have specified when you took the picture. Those settings are stored with the RAW file so they can be applied when the image is converted to JPEG, TIF, or another format compatible with your favorite image editor. However, using RAW converter software such as Adobe Camera Raw (in Photoshop, Photoshop Elements, or Lightroom) or Sony's Image Data Converter (available for download from various Sony websites worldwide), you can override a RAW photo's settings (such as White Balance and Saturation) by applying other settings in the software. You can make essentially the same changes there that you might have specified in your camera before taking a photo.

Making changes to settings such as White Balance is a non-destructive process in a RAW converter since the changes are made before the photo is fully processed by the software program. Making a change in settings does not affect image quality, except for changes to exposure, highlight or shadow detail, and saturation; the loss of quality is minimal however, unless the changes you make for these aspects are significant. The RAW format exists because sometimes we want to have access to all the information captured by the camera, before the camera's internal logic has processed it and converted the image to a standard file format.

A RAW photo does take up more space than a JPEG and, in uncompressed mode, preserves all the information captured by your camera after it's been converted from analog to digital form. Since we can make changes to settings after the fact while retaining optimal image quality, errors in the settings we made in-camera are much less of a concern than in JPEG capture. When you shoot JPEGs, any modification you make in software is a destructive process; there is always some loss of image quality, although that can be minimal if you make only small changes or are skilled with the use of adjustment layers.

JPEG provides smaller files by compressing the information in a way that loses some image data. The lost data is reconstructed when you open a JPEG in a computer, but this is not a perfect process. If you shoot JPEGs at the highest quality (Extra Fine) level, compression (and loss of data) are minimal; you might not be able to tell the difference between a photo made with RAW capture and a Large/Fine JPEG. If you use the lower-quality level, you'll usually notice a quality loss when making big enlargements or after cropping your image extensively.

RAW Always?

So, why don't we always use RAW? Although some photographers do save only in RAW format, it's more common to use either RAW plus the JPEG option or to just shoot JPEG and eschew RAW altogether. While RAW is overwhelmingly helpful when an image needs to be modified, working with a RAW file can slow you down significantly. The RAW images take longer to store on the memory card so you cannot shoot as many in a single burst. Also, after you shoot a series, the camera must pause to write them to the memory card so you may not be able to take additional shots for a while (or only one or two at a time) until the RAW files have been written to the memory card. When you come home from a trip with numerous RAW files, you'll find they require more post-processing time and effort in the RAW converter, whether you elect to go with the default settings in force when the picture was taken or make minor adjustments.

Those who often shoot many photos in one session, or those who want to spend less time at a computer, may prefer JPEG over RAW. Wedding photographers, for example, might expose several thousand photos during a bridal affair and offer hundreds to clients as electronic proofs on a DVD disc. Wedding shooters take the time to make sure that their in-camera settings are correct, minimizing the need to post-process photos after the event. Given that their JPEGs are so good, there is little need for them to get bogged down working with RAW files in a computer. Sports photographers also avoid RAW files because of the extra time required for the camera to record a series of shots to a memory card and because they don't want to spend hours in extra post-processing. As a bonus, JPEG files consume a lot loss memory in a hard drive.

My recommendation: As I mentioned earlier, when shooting sports, I'll switch to shooting Large/Extra Fine JPEGs (with no RAW file) to minimize the time it takes for the camera to write a series of photos to the card; it's great to be able to take another burst of photos at any time, with little or no delay. I also appreciate the fact that I won't need to wade through long series of photos taken in RAW format.

In most situations however, I shoot virtually everything as RAW & JPEG. Most of the time, I'm not concerned about filling up my memory cards, as I usually carry at least three 128GB memory cards with me. If I know I may fill up all those cards (say, on a long trip), I'll also carry notebook computer and an external 2 terabyte hard drive to back up my files.

Image Size (Dual Rec)

- **Options:** L:17M, M:7.5M, S:4.2M
- **Default**: L:17M
- **My preference**: L:17M

This option specifies the image size (resolution) of JPEG still photos taken when you're shooting video. There's no reason to sacrifice the ability to snap off a still photo while movie shooting is underway. Just press the shutter button to take a *high resolution* still picture using the image size you select here. (Other cameras may limit you to saving a video frame, typically a 2 megapixel 1920 x 1080 snapshot.) The photos taken in this mode are cropped to the same 16:9 aspect ratio used to capture video, but are otherwise saved in your choice of Large (17 megapixels), Medium (7.5 megapixels) or Small (4.2 megapixel) image sizes. (You can view the pixel dimensions of each in **Table 3.1** within the Aspect Ratio: 16:9 row.)

You can also set the camera to take still photos automatically, as I'll explain later in this chapter under the discussion of Auto Dual Record in the Camera Settings 7 menu.

The Dual Record features provide JPEG images only (no RAW), and are available *only* when using one of the following video modes:

- **XAVC S.** 30p/25p 50M (NTSC/PAL), 24p 50M (NTSC only)
- **AVCHD.** 60i/50i 24M, 60i/50i 17M, 24p/25p 24M, 24p/25p 17M (NTSC/PAL)
- **MP4.** 30p/25p 16M (NTSC/PAL)

Quality (Dual Rec)

- **Options:** Extra Fine, Fine, Standard
- **Default:** Extra Fine
- **My preference:** Extra Fine

You can specify the image quality for snapshots taken during movie shooting using this entry. It is separate from the Image Quality option explained earlier, and has no effect on JPEG images captured when you are *not* shooting movies.

File Format (Movie)

- **Options:** XAVC S 4K, XAVC S HD, AVCHD, MP4
- **Default**: AVCHD
- **My preference**: MP4 for beginners; XAVC S HD for enthusiasts.

This is the first entry on Camera Settings 2 menu (see **Figure 3.3**). The RX100 V offers full HD (high-definition) video recording in the AVCHD format in addition to MP4 format. Advanced video shooters can also choose from the XAVC S 4K or XAVC S HD, which support faster recording speeds for improved quality, as I'll explain in detail in Chapter 10.

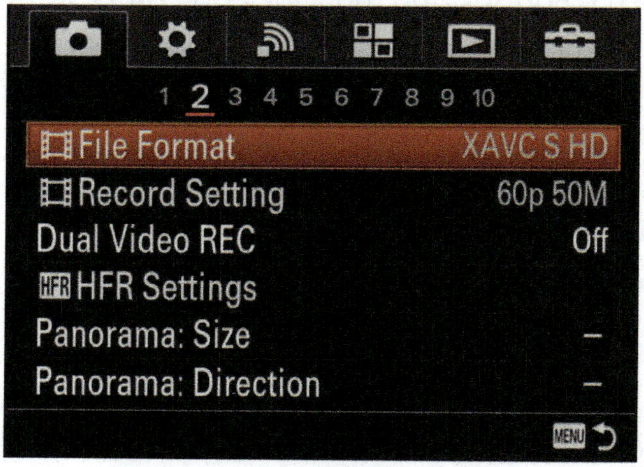

Figure 3.3

File Format is the first entry in the Camera Settings 2 menu.

By default, movies are recorded in AVCHD, but this menu item allows you to switch to XAVC S 4K/XAVC S HD or MP4. The latter is a format that you can edit with many software programs and is more likely to be supported by older computers than AVCHD or either XAVC S choice. The MP4 format is also more "upload friendly;" in other words, it's the format you'll want to use if you plan to post video clips on a website. I prefer it for those just getting into movie making. If you're a more advanced video shooter with software that can handle XAVC S HD, that's a more versatile choice.

XAVC S 4K and XAVC S HD are high-resolution formats you'll want to use for your enthusiast/pro-level video. In either case, you'll need a fast memory card of at least 64GB capacity to support the higher frame rates possible with these formats. (The camera disables both formats if a 64GB SDXC card is not present.) The XAVC S 4K format, in particular, is especially demanding because of its ultra-high 3840 x 2160-pixel resolution (roughly four times that of full HD). Note that, because of these demands, certain features such as HDMI Info. Display, Smile/Face Detection, and Center Lock-on AF (all discussed later) are disabled. You'll find more on choosing movie file formats in Chapter 10.

Record Setting (Movie)

- **Options**: Varies (17 choices)
- **Default**: AVCHD: 60i (FX) 24M
- **My preference**: I prefer to use XAVC S at 60p/50M. For "quickie" videos for editing with Windows Movie Maker or iMovie, my choice is MP4 at 1920 x 1080/60p/28M.

This item allows you to choose from various options if you are using AVCHD, XAVC S, or MP4. Your choices are shown in the left-hand column of each of the tables that follow. Note that the frame rates apply to countries using the NTSC system, such as the US, Japan, and some other countries. For countries that use the PAL system, 25, 50, and 100 frame rates replace 30, 60, and 120 fps respectively. I'll explain frame rates, scanning, and bit rates in Chapter 10, which details all of the terminology and concepts and other aspects of movie making. See **Tables 10.1** to **10.4** in Chapter 10 for a detailed listing of the resolution, frame rate, and bit rate of each Record Setting option.

Dual Video Record

- **Options**: On, Off
- **Default**: Off
- **My preference**: Off

When switched On, the camera will record a low-quality MP4 format version of your video at the same time it captures the AVCHD or XAVC S video (as specified in the File Format entry above). It cannot be chosen if your selected File Format is MP4, or any Record Setting of 60p or faster, other than 60i. Because of the extra processing time required, it is not compatible with the RX100 V's electronic image stabilization feature Intelligent Active SteadyShot.

You might want a lower-quality MP4 version for quick review, rough editing, or some other purpose, and still have a high-quality AVCHD or XAVC S version for final editing. Note that the MP4 video produced using this setting is *much* lower in quality than either MP4 format selected under File Format (above). Use this option *only* when you truly will accept a highly compressed, reduced resolution version of your video. You'll need to use a large, fast memory card when capturing two versions of a video simultaneously. (If you're shooting XAVC S, the camera *requires* such a card, in any case.)

HFR Settings

- **Options:** Record Setting, Frame Rate, Priority Setting, Record Timing
- **Default**: N/A
- **My preference**: N/A

High frame rate photography (HFR) allows you to capture video of either 2-second (higher quality) or 4-second (lower quality) duration at frame rates of up to 960/1000 frames per second (NTSC/PAL). When played back at conventional frame rates, these clips produce smooth slow-motion video that is up to 40X slower. I'll explain this feature in detail in Chapter 10, but the four parameters (shown in **Figure 3.4**) include:

- **Record Setting.** Your choice of 60p, 30p, or 24p. All three use 50 megabits/second transfer rates.
- **Frame Rate.** Select 240, 480, or 960 frames per second (NTSC); or 250, 500, 100 frames per second (PAL).
- **Priority Setting.** Your choice of a 2-second high quality clip, or 4-second reduced quality clip.
- **Record Timing.** Choose whether the clip is captured when you press the shutter release down all the way, or whether pressing the shutter release causes the camera to capture the 2- or 4-second sequence that immediately *preceded* the "trigger."

Tip: As you increase frame rates, the image area is reduced, producing a "crop factor" that alters the field of view dramatically. I'll show you exactly how your image is cropped with an illustration in Chapter 10.

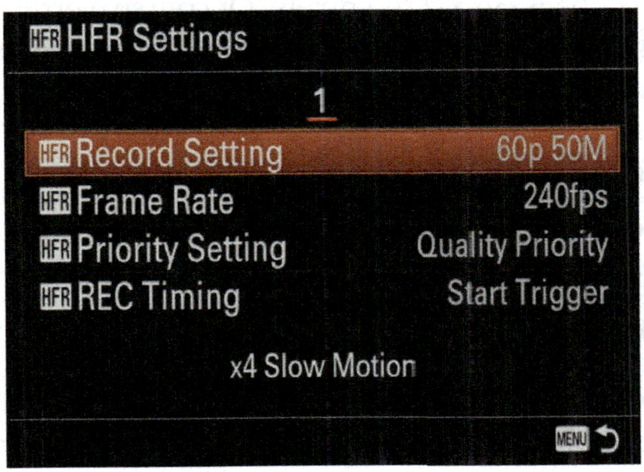

Figure 3.4
HFR Settings.

Panorama: Size

- **Options:** Standard, Wide
- **Default:** Standard
- **My preference:** Wide! If you're shooting panoramas, go for it.

This item is available only when the shooting mode is set to Sweep Panorama mode (usually abbreviated as Panorama). This item offers only two options: the default Standard and the optional Wide, which can produce a longer/taller panorama photo.

With the Standard setting, if you are shooting a horizontal panorama, the size of your images will be 8192 x 1856 pixels. If your Standard panorama photos are vertical, the size will be 3872 x 2160 pixels. (The options for panorama direction are covered in the next section.) If you activate the Wide option instead, horizontal panoramas will be at a size of 12416 x 1856 pixels, and vertical panoramas will be 5536 x 2160 pixels. Of course, vertically panned panorama photos are actually "tall" rather than wide regardless of the option you select.

Panorama: Direction

- **Options:** Right, Left, Up, Down
- **Default:** Right
- **My preference:** Right

When the shooting mode is set to Sweep Panorama, this menu item gives you four options for the direction in which the camera will prompt you to pan: right, left, up, or down. Note that when the live view screen is displayed on the LCD or EVF, you can cycle among the four shooting directions by rotating the control ring.

The camera actually is processing the image pieces you have already captured *as you continue to shoot,* so you have to select one of these directions so the camera will know ahead of time how to perform this processing of the many JPEGs you'll shoot while panning. Within seconds of finishing the capture, all your shots will be aligned and stitched together into the final panorama photo. The default direction (right), is probably the most natural way to sweep the camera horizontally, at least for those of us who read from left to right. Of course, you may have occasions to use the other options, depending on the scene to be photographed; for a panorama photo of a very tall building, for example, you'd want to use one of the vertical options (up or down).

Table 3.2 shows the size and resolution of Wide and Standard panoramas in both horizontal and vertical camera orientations.

Table 3.2

Sweep Panorama Image Sizes Available

Format	Megapixels	Resolution
Standard Panorama -- Horizontal	15 MP	8192 x 1856
Wide Panorama -- Horizontal	23 MP	12416 x 1856
Standard Panorama -- Vertical	8.4 MP	2160 x 3872
Wide Panorama -- Vertical	12 MP	2160 x 5536

With the camera held in the horizontal (landscape) orientation and panned left to right or right to left, the resulting panorama proportions are shown in **Figure 3.5** for Standard (top) and Wide (bottom) options. Both versions are 1856 pixels tall, but measure 8192 and 12416 pixels wide, respectively.

If you hold the camera in the horizontal orientation and pan up or down, different proportions result, as seen in **Figure 3.6**. Standard and Wide versions are each 2160 pixels wide, but measure 3872 and 5536 pixels tall, respectively. In practice, your RX100 V gives you four different panorama proportions.

Vertical Orientation for Horizontal or Vertical Pans

There are actually two more techniques for shooting panoramas. You can rotate your camera to the *vertical* (portrait) orientation and pan left or right, or up or down. I find the former technique most useful: vertical camera orientation, but left/right horizontal pan. Because each of the frames that are captured have a 2:3 aspect ratio, rather than the standard 3:2 aspect ratio, you'll end up with a pano that's less wide, and encompasses more of the scene vertically. Simply set Panorama: Direction to Down and pan left to right, or Up and pan right to left when the camera has been rotated 90 degrees counterclockwise. You'll end up with a different aspect ratio that is less widescreen in appearance, as you can see in **Figure 3.7**, which compares the normal Standard pan with the camera held horizontally and the Standard pan with the camera rotated vertically.

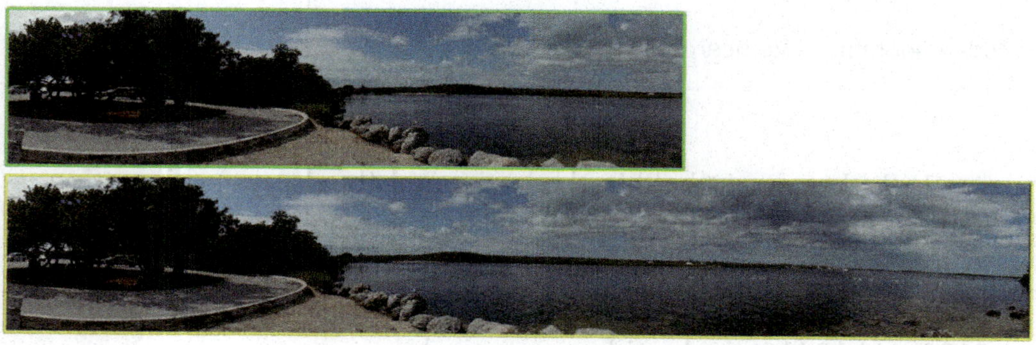

Figure 3.5

Horizontal standard format (green box) and wide format (yellow box), produced by panning left or right.

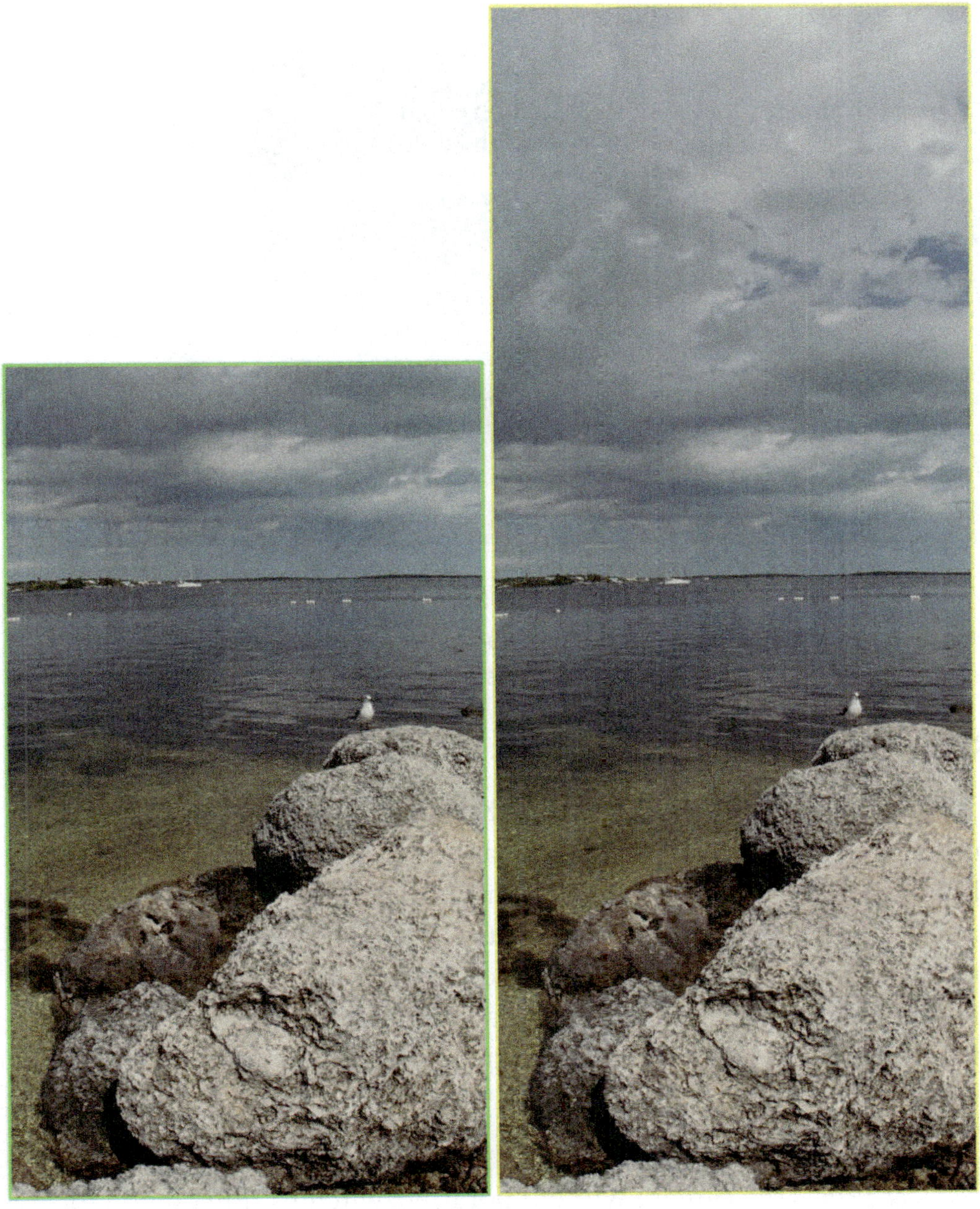

Figure 3.6

Vertical standard format (green box) and wide format (yellow box), produced by panning up or down.

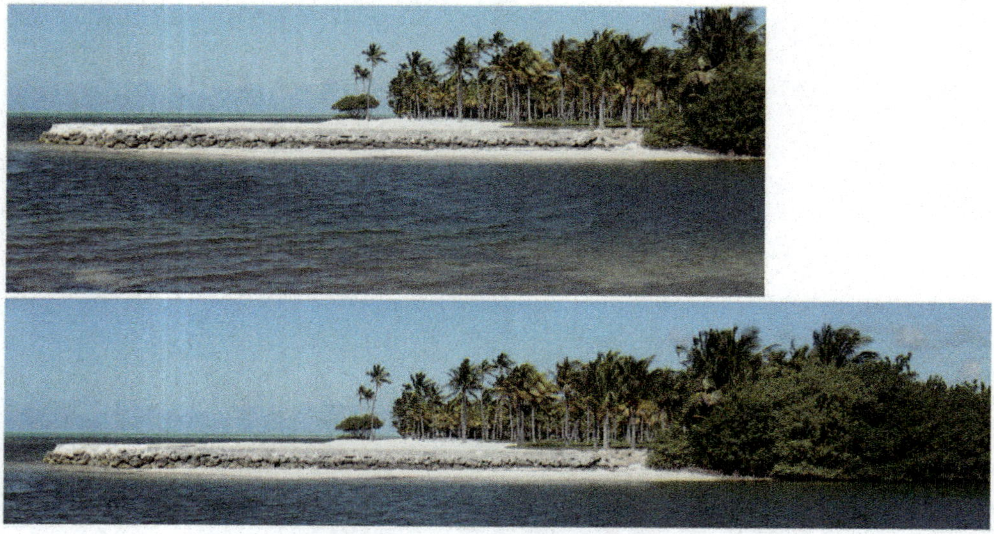

Figure 3.7

Horizontal panorama with the camera rotated to vertical orientation, and Panorama: Size set to Standard (top); at bottom is a Standard horizontal panorama.

Shooting Panoramas

I spent last winter in the Florida Keys and expended a lot of time taking panoramas with this camera, as you can see from the illustrations. While the process is simple in concept, it can be frustrating in execution, chiefly because it's easy for your "sweeping" motion to be too fast or too slow, and you may be 80 percent through the process when the camera informs you that your movement was at the wrong pace. Here's a procedure that will help you minimize the frustration.

1. **JPEG only.** Know that if your camera is set to RAW or RAW & JPEG, the camera will temporarily switch to JPEG mode for the panorama (panos cannot be shot using RAW format), but will restore your original setting when you rotate the mode dial out of the Panorama position.
2. **Rotate carefully.** Your "wide" panorama will encompass roughly 220 degrees, so plant your feet firmly such that the center of your picture is straight in front of you. Keep the

camera as near to your body as possible (use the EVF -- please don't shoot panos with the LCD monitor!) so that the rotation point as your body twists is as close as possible to the sensor plane. Technically, the pivot point should be located underneath the center point of the lens, but it's easier to use the back of the camera as a reference.

3. **Fix focus and exposure.** Lock focus and exposure before you start shooting, as the camera doesn't adjust once capture begins. Moreover, you can't zoom during a pan.
4. **Twist your body.** With your feet securely anchored, twist your body as far as you can toward the angle you'll use for the beginning of the exposure. That is, if you choose Right, twist as far as you can to the right.
5. **Untwist while shooting.** While viewing through the electronic viewfinder, begin shooting, slowly "untwisting" to pan the camera until you're facing forward again.
6. **Keep speed constant.** Continue twisting smoothly toward the finish position. It's important to keep a constant speed.
7. **Watch progress in viewfinder.** As you shoot, the camera will provide a highlighted view of the area currently being captured as it takes overlapping shots. An arrow is shown on the screen to indicate the direction you should be moving.
8. **Too slow/too fast.** If you rotate too slowly or too quickly, a message that the camera could not shoot the panorama will appear, advising you to move more slowly or more quickly.
9. **Wait while camera assembles your pano.** You'll finish twisted all the way in the opposite direction from your initial position. When you have successfully captured a panorama, the screen will blank for a few seconds while the camera stitches your exposures together. It will then display your finished shot.
10. **View entire panorama.** The preview shows a reduced-size version of the entire panorama; press the center button to see a scrolling display of the entire shot.

There are a few aspects of panorama shooting that you might not have considered:

- **"Multiple" exposures.** Panoramas are best rendered with subjects that do not move. If something is in motion as you sweep the camera, you may get multiple renditions of that subject.
- **Collateral "damage" from cropping.** Avoid including very important information at the very top and bottom of your frames (when shooting in left/right mode, for example). Because you probably won't hold the camera perfectly level as you pan, the camera will automatically try to align your images as they are stitched together, and there will often be some "excess" image above and/or below that is cropped out to produce a seamless image.
- **Quick control.** If you shoot lots of panos, you can redefine the control ring around the lens to quickly adjust the panorama direction. Just redefine it with that function using the Custom Keys options described in Chapter 4.

Drive Mode

- **Options:** Single Shooting, Cont. Shooting (3.5/10/24 fps), Self-timer (2/5/10 seconds), Self-timer Continuous (3 or 5 shots), Continuous Bracket (3 or 5 images at 0.3/0.7/1.0/2.0/3.0 increments), Single Bracket (3 or 5 images at 0.3/0.7/1.0/2.0/3.0 increments), White Balance Bracket (Lo/Hi), DRO Bracket (Lo/Hi)
- **Default**: Single Shooting
- **My preference**: N/A

This is the first entry on the third page of the Camera Settings menu. (See **Figure 3.8**.) Just as with the drive (left) button on the back of the camera, there are several choices available through this single menu item. Your choices include:

- **Single shooting.** Takes one shot each time you press the shutter release button.
- **Continuous Shooting.** Captures images, at rates of 3.5, 10, and 24 frames per second using Lo, Medium and High settings selected by pressing the left/right buttons when Continuous Shooting is highlighted.

  The RX100 V's electronic shutter must be used, so this setting is not available when Shutter Type is set to Mechanical. While Continuous Shooting mode tries to maintains autofocus, you can set Focus Mode to Continuous AF and AEL w/Shutter to Off or Auto and focus and exposure are locked at the settings for the first image in a sequence. You can find a longer discussion of continuous shooting in Chapter 9.
- Continuous shooting is disabled if the shooting mode is set to Sweep Panorama or a scene mode (other than Sports Action), and when Picture Effect is set to Soft Focus, HDR Painting, Rich-Tone Mono, Miniature, Watercolor, or Illustration. It's also unavailable when using Auto HDR, Multi Frame Noise Reduction, Smile Shutter, or Silent Shooting (all discussed later in this chapter).
- **Self Timer (2 sec./5 sec./10 sec.).** Takes a single picture after two, five, or ten seconds have elapsed. When this choice is highlighted, press the left/right buttons to toggle between the durations. The self-timer is unavailable when you're using the Sports Action scene mode, Smile Shutter, or Sweep Panorama. Use longer settings when you want to get in the picture yourself; the 2-second option is useful when you're only interested in avoiding vibration when the RX100 V is mounted on a tripod, and would rather not wait for a longer period before the picture is taken.
- **Self-Timer Continuous.** The self-timer counts down wither 5 seconds or 10 seconds (your choice), and then takes either 3 or 5 images. The left/right buttons cycle among the various options. You can cancel the timer by pressing the Drive button

and selecting Single Shooting, or by tapping the shutter button a second time.

- **Continuous Bracket (BRK C).** Captures three, five, or nine images in one burst when the shutter release is held down, bracketing them 0.3, 0.7, 1.0, 2.0, or 3.0 stops apart. (However, 9 images at the 2 EV and 3 EV settings are not available; all other combinations are valid.)

  The left/right buttons are used to select the increment and number of shots. In Manual exposure mode (when ISO Auto is disabled), or in Aperture Priority mode, the shutter speed will change. If ISO Auto is set in Manual exposure mode, the bracketed set will be created by changing the ISO setting. In Shutter Priority mode, the aperture will change.

  My recommendation: Use continuous mode when you want all the images in the set to be framed as similarly as possible, say, when you will be using them for manually assembled high dynamic range (HDR) photos. I often use continuous bracketing with a fairly large increment (2 or 3 stops) when I am experimenting: deliberately under- or overexposing an image can produce dramatically different results from "normal" exposure.

  You can use the flash when continuous bracketing is active, but, because of the time required for the flash to recycle, you'll need to press the shutter button each time to take subsequent images (effectively switching the camera into Single Bracket mode, described next).

  Only the last shot in the set is displayed when using Auto Review. With all types of bracketing, the exposure/bracket scale at the bottom of the EVF or LCD monitor (in Display All Info mode) will display indicators showing the number of images shot and the relative amount of under/overexposure. Don't forget that you can dial in exposure compensation, and *that* will affect the amount of over/underexposure applied while bracketing. Continuous bracketing (and Single

Bracketing) is disabled when using Superior Auto, scene modes, or Sweep Panorama.

- **Single Bracket (BRK S).** Captures one bracketed image in a set of three, five, or nine shots each time you press the shutter release, bracketing them 0.3, 0.7, 1.0, 2.0, or 3.0 stops apart. The left/right buttons are used to select the increment and number of shots. In this mode, you can separate each image by an interval of your choice. You might want to use this variation when you want the individual images to be captured at slightly different times, say, to produce a set of images that will be combined in some artistic way.
- **White Balance Bracket (BRK WB).** Shoots three image adjustments to the color temperature. While you can't specify which direction the color bias is tilted, you can select Lo (the default) for small changes, or Hi, for larger changes using the left/right buttons. Only the last shot taken is displayed during Auto Review.
- **DRO Bracket.** Shoots three image adjustments to the dynamic range optimization. While you can't specify the amount of optimization, you can select Lo (the default) for small changes, or Hi, for larger changes, using the left/right buttons. Again, only the last shot taken is displayed during Auto Review.

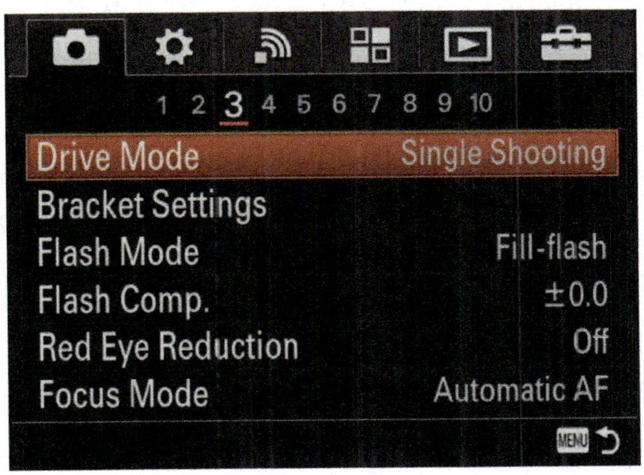

Figure 3.8
The third page of the Camera Settings menu.

Bracket Settings

- **Options:** Self-timer During Bracketing: Off, 2 sec., 5 sec., 10 sec.; Bracket **Order**: 0-+, -0+
- **Default**: Off; 0-+
- **My preference**: Off; -0+ for HDR, 0-+ for all other

This item has two entries that let you customize how bracketing is applied.

- **Self-timer during bracketing.** You can choose delays of 2, 5, or 10 seconds before bracketing begins, or disable the self-timer during bracketing. This clever option solves a problem: how to use the self-timer (say, to avoid shaking a camera mounted on a tripod) when bracketing (which resides in the same Drive menu). With continuous bracketing, all exposures will be taken after the self-timer delay; if you're using single bracketing, the delay takes place before each shot in the bracket set is exposed.
- **Bracket order.** The default is metered exposure > under exposure > over exposure. This works well for most subjects, especially action, because the first (normal) exposure will often be the best shot, while the subsequent (bracketed) exposures may not picture the peak moment. However, if you're shooting photos that will later be manually assembled into an HDR photo, you might find it more convenient to expose in order of progressively more exposure: under exposure > metered exposure > overexposure. The order you choose here will also be applied to white balance bracketing.

Flash Mode

- **Options:** Flash Off, Autoflash, Fill-Flash, Slow Sync., Rear Sync.
- **Default**: Depends on shooting mode
- **My preference**: N/A

This entry offers options for the several flash modes that are available. Not all of the modes can be selected at all times, as shown in **Table 3.3**. Flash Off, for example, works only when using an auto/scene mode, because the flash might otherwise pop up automatically. I'll describe the use of flash in detail in Chapter 11.

Table 3.3 Flash Modes

Exposure Mode	Flash Off	Auto Flash	Fill Flash	Slow Sync.	Rear Sync.	Flash Exposure Compen-sation	Red-Eye Reduction
Intelligent Auto	Yes	Yes	Yes	No	No	No	Yes
Superior Auto	Yes	Yes	Yes	No	No	No	Yes
Program Auto	No	No	Yes	Yes	Yes	Yes	Yes
Aperture Priority	No	No	Yes	Yes	Yes	Yes	Yes
Shutter Priority	No	No	Yes	Yes	Yes	Yes	Yes
Manual Exposure	No	No	Yes	Yes	Yes	Yes	Yes
Sports, Pets, Gourmet, Landscape, Sunset	Yes	No	No	No	No	No	No
Macro	Yes	Yes	Yes	No	No	No	No

Flash Compensation

- **Options:** -3 to +3 in 1/3 or 1/2 EV steps
- **Default:** 0.0
- **My preference:** N/A

This feature controls the flash output. It allows you to dial in plus compensation for a brighter flash effect or minus compensation for a subtler flash effect. If you take a flash photo and it's too dark or too light, access this menu item. Scroll up/down to set a value that will increase flash intensity (plus setting) or reduce the flash output (minus setting) by up to three EV (exposure value) steps. You can select between 1/3 EV and 1/2 EV increments in the Exposure Step entry described later in this chapter. Flash compensation is "sticky" so be sure to set it back to zero after you finish shooting. This feature is not available when you're using Intelligent Auto, Superior Auto, Scene, or Sweep Panorama modes. I'll discuss this and many other flash-related topics in detail in Chapter 11.

Red Eye Reduction

- **Options**: On, Off
- **Default**: Off
- **My preference**: Off

When flash is used in a dark location, red-eye is common in pictures of people, and especially of animals. Unfortunately, your camera is unable, on its own, to totally *eliminate* the red-eye effects that occur when an electronic flash bounces off the retinas of your subject's eyes and into the camera lens. The effect is worst under low-light conditions (exactly when you might be using a flash) as the pupils expand to allow more light to reach the retinas. The best you can hope for with this option is to *reduce* or minimize the red-eye effect. After all, the feature is called red-eye *reduction,* not red-eye *elimination.*

It's fairly easy to remove red-eye effects in an image editor (some image importing programs will do it for you automatically as the pictures are transferred from your camera or memory card to your computer). But, it's better not to have glowing red eyes in your photos in the first place.

To use this feature, you first have to flip up the internal pop-up flash. When Red Eye Reduction is turned on through this menu item, the flash issues a few brief bursts prior to taking the photo, theoretically causing your subjects' pupils to contract, reducing the red-eye syndrome. It works best if your subject is looking toward the flash. Like any such system, its success ratio is not great.

Focus Mode

- **Options:** Single-shot AF (AF-S), Continuous AF (AF-C), DMF (Direct Manual Focus), MF (Manual Focus)
- **Default**: Single-shot AF (AF-S)
- **My preference**: Continuous AF (AF-C)

This menu item can be used to set the way in which the camera focuses. I'll discuss focus options in detail in Chapter 8.

- **Single-shot AF (AF-S).** With this default setting, the camera will set focus and it will keep that focus locked as long as you maintain slight pressure on the shutter release button, as discussed in the previous section; even if the subject moves before you take the photo, the focus will stay where it was set. If you use this setting for still photos and then switch to Movie mode, the camera switches temporarily to AF-C.
- **Continuous AF (AF-C).** The camera will continue to adjust the focus if the camera-to-subject distance changes, as when a cyclist approaches your shooting position. The camera will constantly adjust focus to keep the subject sharply rendered. It uses predictive AF to predict the moving subject's position at the time you'll take the next shot and focusing at that distance. This option is useful when you're photographing sports, active children, animals, or other moving subjects, making it possible to get sharply focused shots.

- **Direct Manual Focus (DMF).** Press the shutter button halfway down to let the camera start the focusing process; then, keeping the button pressed halfway, turn the focusing ring to fine-tune the focus manually. You might want to use DMF when you are focusing from a short distance on a small object, and want to make sure the focus point is exactly where you want it. If you use this setting for still photos and then switch to Movie mode, the camera switches temporarily to AF-C.
- **Manual Focus (MF).** If you select Manual Focus, you turn the focusing ring on the lens to achieve the sharpest possible focus. With both DMF and Manual Focus, the camera will show you an enlarged image to help with the focusing process, if you have the MF Assist option turned on in the Custom Settings 1 menu (described later).

Focus Area

- **Options:** Wide, Center, Flexible Spot, Expand Flexible Spot, Lock-On AF
- **Default:** Wide
- **My preference:** Wide for general use; Lock-On AF Wide for sports and action

This is the first entry on the Camera Settings 4 menu (see **Figure 3.9**.) When the camera is set to Autofocus, use this menu option to specify where in the frame the camera will focus when you compose a scene in still photo mode, using the focus area selection you specify. I'll explain these options, the special requirements, and include illustrations of the focusing areas in Chapter 8.

- **Wide.** The camera uses its own electronic intelligence to determine what part of the scene should be in sharpest focus, providing automatic focus point selection. A green frame is displayed around the area that is in focus. Even if you set one of the other options, Wide is automatically selected in certain shooting modes, including both Auto and all SCN modes.

- **Center.** Choose this option if you want the camera to always focus on the subject in the center of the frame. Center the primary subject (like a friend's face in a wide-angle landscape composition); allow the camera to focus on it; maintain slight pressure on the shutter release button to keep focus locked; and re-frame the scene for a more effective, off-center, composition. Take the photo at any time and your friend (who is now off-center) will be in the sharpest focus. Use this option instead of manually selecting a focus point to quickly lock focus on the center of the frame, then press the defined AF lock button to fix the focus at that point so you can recompose the image as you prefer.
- **Flexible Spot.** This mode allows you to move the camera's focus detection point (focus area) around the scene to any one of multiple locations using the directional buttons. When this option is highlighted, use the left/right directional buttons or control wheel to change the size range of the spot among Small (S), Medium (M), and Large (L).

  This mode can be useful when the camera is mounted on a tripod and you'll be taking photos of the same scene for a long time, while the light is changing, for example. Move the focus area to cover the most important subject, and it will always focus on that point when you later take a photo.
- **Expand Flexible Spot.** If the camera is unable to lock in focus using the selected focus point, it will also use the eight adjacent points to try to achieve focus.
- **Lock-On AF.** In this mode, the camera locks focus onto the subject area that is under the selected focus spot when the shutter button is depressed halfway. Then, if the subject moves (or you change the framing in the camera), the camera will continue to refocus *on that subject*. You can select this mode only when the focus mode is set to Continuous AF (AF-C). Note that Lock-On AF is different from Center Lock-On AF, discussed in Chapter 3, and in more detail in Chapter 8.

This option is especially powerful because you can activate it for any of the five focus area options described above. That is, once you've highlighted Lock-On AF on the selection screen, you can then press the left-right directional button and choose Wide, Zone, Center, Flexible Spot, or Expand Flexible Spot.

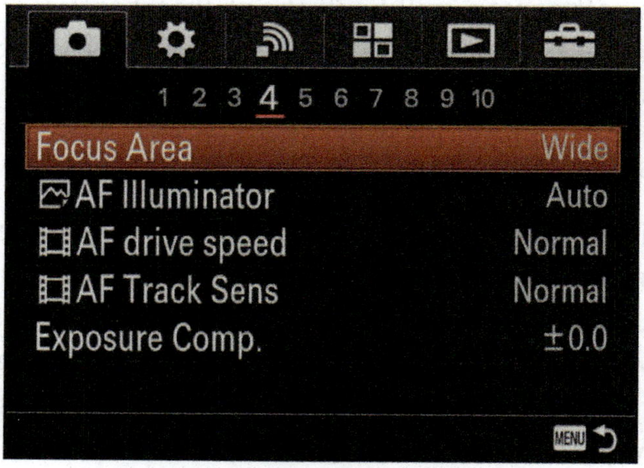

Figure 3.9

Focus Area is the first entry in the Camera Settings 4 menu.

AF Illuminator (Still Image)

- **Options**: Auto, Off
- **Default**: Auto
- **My preference**: Auto

The AF illuminator is a red light activated when there is insufficient light for the camera's autofocus mechanism to zero in on the subject. This light emanates from the same lamp on the front of the camera that provides the indicator for the self-timer and the Smile Shutter feature. The extra blast from the AF illuminator provides a bright target for the AF system to help the camera set focus, and may help close down your subjects' pupils as an anti-red-eye measure when shooting with flash. This menu item is a still-photos-only option, as the illuminator does not operate while shooting movies.

The default setting, Auto, allows the AF illuminator to work any time the camera judges that it is necessary. Turn it off when you would prefer not to use this feature, such as when you don't want to disturb the people around you or call attention to your photographic endeavors. The AF illuminator doesn't work when the camera is set for manual focus or to AF-C (Continuous autofocus), when shooting movies or panoramas, or in certain other shooting modes, including the Landscape, Night View, or Sports Action varieties of SCN mode.

AF Drive Speed (Movies)

- **Options:** Fast, Normal, Slow
- **Default:** Normal
- **My preference:** Normal for most scenes, Fast for sports and action

This entry is a movies-only setting for the RX100 V that is used to adjust how quickly the camera focuses while capturing video. It's used in conjunction with AF Track Duration, described next. Unlike stills, when focus changes while shooting movies it is apparent in the clip, and can be undesirable. Your three options are as follows:

- **Fast.** The camera focuses as quickly as possible, but with slightly less precision. This setting is good for sports, action, photojournalism, and street photography, and any situation where it's important to keep the main subjects in focus as they move around. In such situations, the automatic focus adjustments add to the feeling of following the action; any delay in refocusing would be disconcerting.
- **Normal.** The AF responds smoothly to subject movement by refocusing gradually. With scenes that are not filled with constant action, this mode may be the least noticeable to the viewer.
- **Slow.** Focusing is much less speedy, and is a good choice if your subjects are moving at a constant rate of speed and direction. This setting will allow the a7R II/a7 II to smoothly follow focus. Choose Slow to be on the safe side, in such

situations, particularly when using older lenses that are themselves somewhat pokey in achieving focus.

AF Tracking Sensitivity (Movies)

- **Options:** High, Normal
- **Default**: Normal
- **My preference**: Normal

This is another movies-only setting, which works hand-in-hand with AF Drive Speed just described. The previous option determines how quickly the camera locks in focus; this one determines how quickly the camera unlocks focus from the subject it is currently tracking, and focuses instead on another subject that intervenes. For example, if you're shooting a football game as a running back is breaking through the line and a referee bolts along the sideline in front of you. With this feature set to High, the camera will very quickly switch to the ref, and then should return its attention to the running back -- but often, not quickly enough. A better choice would be to use Normal, so that the camera briefly ignores the referee, who is likely to have moved on in a second or two. Focus tracking will remain on your running back. Your options include:

- **High.** The camera quickly responds to new subjects that cross the frame. This is the best setting to use for fast-moving subjects, such as sports or frenetic children, *as long as you don't expect intervening subjects*. The camera will smoothly follow your subjects, especially if AF Drive Speed has been set to Fast, too.
- **Normal.** Response to movement is a bit slower, so that the camera doesn't constantly refocus as subjects move about the frame. This is the default, and should be used when there is only moderate movement, and especially if the movement is across the width or height of the frame (rather than coming toward you or away from you), and when you're using a small f/stop, because the increased depth-of-field will eliminate the need for most re-focusing.

Exposure Compensation

- **Options:** From +3 to -3
- **Default**: 0.0
- **My preference**: N/A

If you decide to access this item from the menu instead of using the other available access methods (such as the Fn button/Function menu), go into the exposure compensation screen and adjust using the control wheel or the left/right direction buttons. Scroll until you reach the value for the amount of compensation you want to set to make your shots lighter (with positive values) or darker (with negative values). I'll discuss exposure compensation in more detail in Chapter 7.

Remember that any compensation you set will stay in place until you change it, even if the camera has been powered off in the meantime. It's worth developing a habit of checking your display to see if any positive or negative exposure compensation is still in effect; return to 0.0 before you start shooting. Exposure compensation cannot be used when the camera is set to Intelligent Auto, Superior Auto, or one of the SCN modes. If you use exposure compensation a lot, keep in mind that you can redefine the control ring to perform this function using the Custom Keys entry discussed in Chapter 4.

ISO

- **Options:** ISO Auto (with upper/lower limits); Settings from 80 to 12800; Multi Frame Noise Reduction
- **Default**: ISO Auto
- **My preference**: ISO Auto, set to ISO 100 Minimum/ISO 1600 Maximum

This is the first entry on the fifth page of the Camera Settings menu (see **Figure 3.10**). This menu item can also be accessed by pressing the right (ISO) button on the control wheel. It allows you to use the ISO setting (sensor sensitivity) in one of three ways:

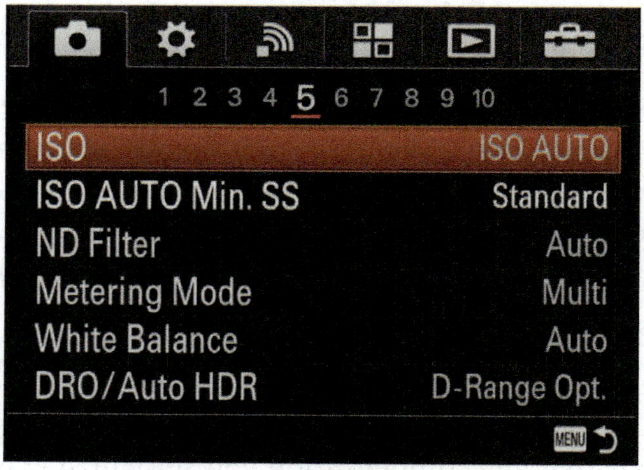

Figure 3.10

The fifth page of the Camera Settings menu.

- **Multi Frame NR (Noise Reduction).** The camera takes 4 or 12 shots and first aligns them (because, hand-held, there is probably some camera movement between shots) and sorts out the image pixels that are common to all the shots (and which remain more or less the same in each individual shot) from the random visual noise pixels (which will be different in each shot, because they are *random*). It then creates an image that (in theory) uses only the image pixels, with much less visual noise. The processing takes a few seconds, so you wouldn't want to use it when you plan to take multiple shots within a short period of time.

  To activate Multi Frame NR, highlight the entry (which is by default confusingly labeled ISO Auto, rather than Multi Frame Noise Reduction). You can then press the right button to highlight the left option at the bottom of the figure (the maximum ISO setting you want to use), and the amount of multi frame noise reduction to be applied (High or Standard). The camera will take and combine 12 shots if you choose High, and 4 shots if you select Standard.

Multi Frame NR can only be used when Image Quality is set to JPEG, and is unavailable when D-Range Optimizer or Auto HDR are activated. Note: the camera also offers a Hand-Held Twilight scene mode, which doesn't let you choose shutter speed, ISO setting, white balance, and other parameters, but produces comparable (or sometimes even better) images. If your image suits the automated settings of the Hand-Held Twilight mode, it's certainly faster and requires fewer decisions from you.

- **Auto ISO.** The true Auto ISO setting is the second entry from the top. After highlighting this entry, you can press the right button and choose a minimum ISO to be used as well as the maximum ISO applied (which prevents the camera from taking a clutch of pictures at, say, ISO 25600, unbeknownst to you). For general shooting, I use ISO 100 and ISO 1600 for my limits and raise the upper end to ISO 3200 or 6400 for indoor subjects (especially sports, which can benefit from faster shutter speeds and/or smaller f/stops). (See Figure **3.12.**)

  If you're using Manual exposure, you probably won't want to use Auto ISO, which may end up correcting your intentional under- or overexposure you've specified to produce a particular effect.

- **Fixed ISO settings.** You can Select ISO settings from 50 to 25600, and the camera will take all its shots at that sensitivity. Strictly speaking, ISO 125 is the lowest real sensitivity the camera can produce; that's the "native" sensitivity of the sensor. The 80/100 settings are "interpolated" and produce slightly higher contrast and lower quality. To remind you of that, they are each shown with white bars above and below them in the selection menu. I recommend using those ersatz values only when you really need a lower sensitivity, say, to use a wider f/stop in very bright conditions, or when you want to use a slower shutter speed to intentionally produce the blur of, perhaps, a waterfall. A neutral-density filter attached to your lens can also reduce the amount of light reaching the sensor. Fixed ISO settings are your best bet when using Manual exposure, for the reason outlined previously.

Your choices are restricted when you're using Panorama mode or fully automatic and scene modes since the camera always uses ISO Auto. Note too that ISO Auto is available in M mode. Settings up to 25600 are available in still mode, and up to 12800 for movies. (If you've selected a higher sensitivity when you switch to movie-making mode, the camera will automatically change to 12800.)

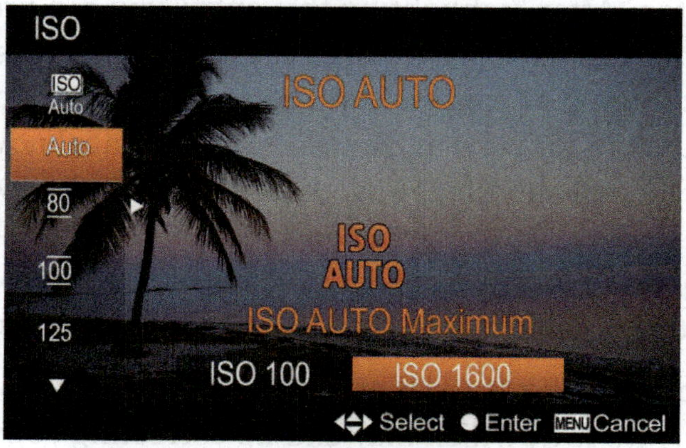

Figure 3.11

ISO Auto allows specifying minimum and maximum ISO sensitivity.

ISO Auto Minimum Shutter Speed

- **Options:** Faster, Fast, STD, Slow, Slower, 1/32000th-30 seconds
- **Default**: STD (Standard)
- **My preference**: STD (Standard)

Use this entry with the RX100 V to specify the shutter speed that activates the ISO Auto feature described above. You'll want to use ISO Auto most frequently to avoid having the camera select a blur-inducing slow shutter speed when using P (Program Auto) or A (Aperture Priority) modes. (*You* always select the shutter speed yourself in S and M modes.) Depending on how well you can hand-hold the camera, or your level of trust for the lens and/or in-body image stabilization, you can choose which shutter speed you deem "too slow," and your RX100 V will boost the ISO sensitivity as required when ISO Auto is active. You can choose from values that the camera calculates, or supply a specific shutter speed, below which Auto ISO will start to do its stuff.

TIP: The ancient rule about using a minimum shutter speed that's the reciprocal of the focal length (that is, 1/60th second with a 60mm zoom setting) continues to be taught, even though it's basically meaningless in this day and age. Different people vary widely in their ability to hand-hold a camera steadily; one person may get nominally sharp images (with a given focal length, subject, and viewing distance of the final image) at 1/60th second, while another may require a shutter speed of 1/250th second to get the same sharpness. Some people are unable to perceive a *difference* in sharpness, anyway, and the rule doesn't take into account either the magnification of the "cropped" image or the anti-shake properties of SteadyShot. You're better off doing your own tests, or, simply, doubling the rule's recommendation (using, for example, 1/250th second at a 60mm zoom setting).

The camera-calculated minimum speeds are very cool because they are based on the focal length of your zoom setting, giving you faster minimum speeds with telephoto settings, and longer minimum speeds with wide angle settings. The Fast and Fastest settings increase the minimum shutter speed by 1 and 2 stops (respectively) from the standard setting for a particular focal length. The Slow and Slower settings lower the minimum shutter speed for that focal length by 1 and 2 stops (respectively).

- **Faster/Fast.** When you highlight this entry, you can press the left/right directional buttons to choose between Faster and Fast, STD (Standard), Slow, or Slower. The RX100 V will activate ISO Auto at shutter speeds that are faster than the "standard" setting (which is calculated individually based on the focal length or zoom setting of your lens). This is a more conservative setting.

- **STD (Standard).** The camera detects the current focal length/zoom setting and selects a minimum shutter speed that takes into account the effect the focal length has in magnifying the degree of blur. That is, a 200mm lens calls for higher shutter speeds than, say, a 50mm lens.
- **Slow/Slower.** This is a more liberal setting that allows slightly slower shutter speeds than specified by STD before ISO Auto kicks in. Use if you have an extraordinarily steady hand.
- **1/32000th-30 seconds.** You can bypass the camera's internal algorithm mumbo-jumbo and directly select a shutter speed that you want to use to activate ISO Auto. If you choose 1/32000th second, ISO Auto will effectively be active all the time (except when 1/32000th second is used as the shutter speed). Select 30 seconds, and ISO Auto will not activate at all.

ND Filter

- **Options:** Auto, On, Off
- **Default:** Auto
- **My preference:** Auto

This setting is used to control a gray filter that can be moved into the light path inside the RX100 V (see **Figure 3.12**). It provides a three-stop reduction in the amount of illumination reaching the sensor, producing the effect (exposure-wise only) of changing from f/11 to the exposure equivalent of f/32, or from 1/125th second to 1/1000th second. Depth-of-field and action-freezing qualities remain the same, but, under existing light conditions, you are able to use an aperture that is three stops larger *or* a shutter speed that is three stops slower and achieve the equivalent exposure. In most cases you won't need to activate the ND filter because a scene is too bright; your camera's 1/32000th second shutter speed can usually handle that. Instead, the filter is useful for creative effects, such as blurring waterfalls, when you *want* to use a particular combination of f/stop and shutter speed. I'll show you some more things you can do with the neutral-density filter in Chapter 9.

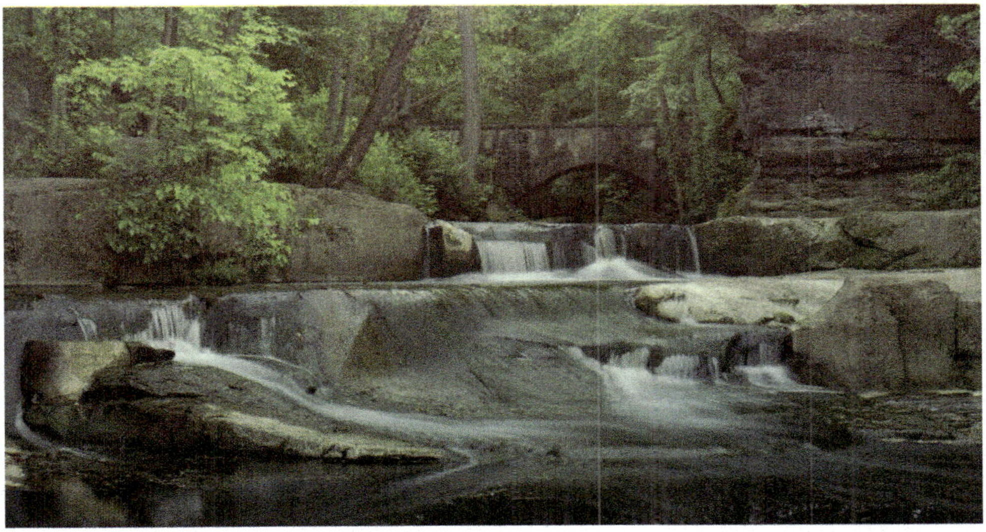

Figure 3.12

The three-stop neutral density filter allows using slower shutter speeds to blur moving subjects when shooting with the camera mounted on a tripod.

Metering Mode

- **Options:** Multi, Center, Spot
- **Default:** Multi
- **My preference:** Multi

The metering mode determines how the camera will calculate the exposure for any scene. The camera is set by default to Multi, which is a multi-zone or multi-segment metering approach. No other options are available in either Auto mode or in SCN modes or when you're using digital zoom or the Smile Shutter.

- **Multi.** Evaluates many segments of the scene using advanced algorithms; often, it will be able to ignore a very bright area or a very dark area that would affect the overall exposure. It's also likely to produce a decent (if not ideal) exposure with a light-toned scene such as a snowy landscape, especially on a sunny day. While it's not foolproof, Multi is the most suitable when you must shoot quickly and don't have time for serious exposure considerations.

- **Center.** Center-weighted metering primarily considers the brightness in a large central area of the scene; this ensures that a bright sky that's high in the frame, for example, will not severely affect the exposure. However, if the central area is very light or very dark in tone, your photo is likely to be too dark or too bright (unless you use exposure compensation).
- **Spot.** When using Spot metering, the camera measures only the brightness in a very small central area of the scene; again, if that area is very light or very dark in tone, your exposure will not be satisfactory; it's important to spot meter an area of a medium tone. You'll learn how metering mode affects exposure in the Chapter 7, which covers exposure topics in detail.

White Balance

- **Options:** Auto WB, Daylight, Shade, Cloudy, Incandescent, Fluorescent (4 options), Flash, C.Temp/Filter, Custom, Custom Setup
- **Default**: Auto (AWB)
- **My preference**: AWB

The various light sources that can illuminate a scene have light that's of different colors. A household lamp using an old-type (not Daylight Balanced) bulb, for example, produces light that's quite amber in color. Sunlight around noon is close to white but it's quite red at sunrise and sunset; on cloudy days, the light has a bluish bias. The light from fluorescents can vary widely, depending on the type of tube or bulb you're using. Some lamps, including sodium vapor and mercury vapor, produce light of unusual colors.

The Auto White Balance feature works well, particularly outdoors and under artificial lighting that's daylight balanced. Even under lamps that produce light with a slight color cast such as green or blue, you should often get a pleasing overall color balance. One advantage of using AWB is that you don't have to worry about changing it for your next shooting session; there's no risk of having the camera set for, say, incandescent light, when you're shooting outdoors on a sunny day.

The RX100 V also lets you choose a specific white balance option -- often called a preset -- that's appropriate for various typical lighting conditions, because the AWB feature does not always succeed in providing an accurate or the most pleasing overall color balance. Your choices include:

- **Daylight.** Sets white balance for average daylight.
- **Shade.** Compensates for the slightly bluer tones encountered in open shade conditions.
- **Cloudy.** Adjusts for the colder tones of a cloudy day.
- **Incandescent.** Indoor illumination is typically much warmer than daylight, so this setting compensates for the excessive red bias.
- **Fluorescent (four types).** You can choose from Warm White, Cool White, Day White, and Daylight fluorescent lighting.
- **Flash.** Suitable for shooting with the RX100 V's flash unit.
- **C.Temp/Filter/Custom/Custom Setup.** These advanced features provide even better results once you've learned how to fine-tune color balance settings, which I'll explain in Chapter 9.

When any of the presets are selected, you can press the right button to produce a screen that allows you to adjust the color along the amber (yellow)/blue axis, the green/magenta axis, or both, to fine-tune color rendition even more precisely. The screen shown in **Figure 3.13** will appear, and you can use the up/down and left/right buttons to move the origin point in the chart shown at lower right to any bias you want. The amount of your amber/blue and/or green/magenta bias is shown numerically above the chart. You'll find more information about white balance in Chapter 9.

My recommendation: If you shoot in RAW capture, though, you don't have to be quite as concerned about white balance, because you can easily adjust it in your software after the fact. Here again, as with ISO and exposure compensation, the white balance item is not available in either Auto mode or in SCN modes; when you use any of those, the camera defaults to Auto White Balance.

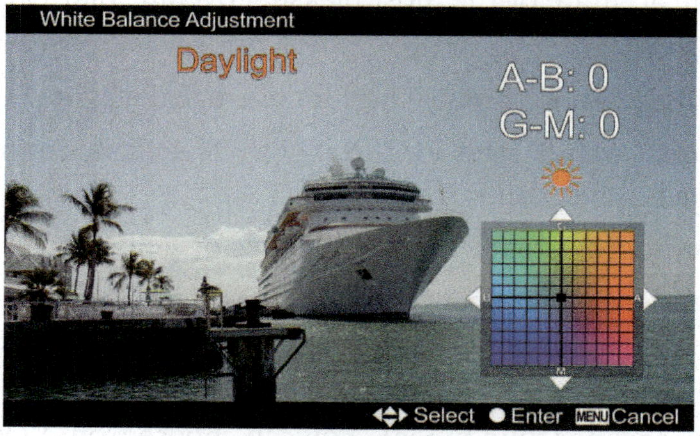

Figure 3.13

Fine-tune the color bias of your images using this screen.

DRO/Auto HDR

- **Options:** DRO Off, DRO Auto, DRO Levels 1-5, AUTO HDR (1-6 EV interval)
- **Default:** DRO Off
- **My preference:** DRO Off

The brightness/darkness range of many images is so broad that the sensor has difficulty capturing detail in both bright highlight areas and dark shadow areas. That's because a sensor has a limited dynamic range. However, the RX100 V is able to expand its dynamic range using extra processing when dynamic range optimization (DRO) is active. It's on by default at the Auto level where the camera evaluates the scene contrast and decides how much extra processing to apply; this is the only available setting in certain automatic camera modes. In other modes, you can turn DRO off, or set it manually to one of five intensity levels. There's also an Auto HDR feature discussed in a moment.

When the DRO Auto option is highlighted, you can press the left/right keys to set the DRO to a specific level of processing, from 1 (weakest) to 5 (strongest). You'll find that DRO can lighten shadow areas; it may darken bright highlight areas too, but not to the same extent. By level 3, the photos you take will exhibit much lighter shadow areas for an obviously wide dynamic range; DRO Auto will never provide such an intense increase in shadow detail.

In addition, you'll find the Auto HDR (High Dynamic Range) feature, available only in the P, A, S, M shooting modes (Program, Aperture Priority, Shutter Priority, and Manual). If you select this option instead of DRO, the camera will take three photos, each at a different exposure level, and it will combine them into one HDR photo with lighter shadow areas and darker highlight areas than in a conventional shot. You can control the intensity of this feature. After scrolling to Auto HDR, press the left/right buttons to choose an exposure increment between shots, from 1.0 EV to 6.0 EV. The one you select will specify the difference in exposure among the three photos it will shoot: 1 EV (minor exposure difference) for a slight HDR effect to 6 EV (a huge exposure difference) for a dramatic high dynamic range effect. If you don't choose a level, the camera selects an HDR level for you. I'll provide tips and examples of DRO and HDR in Chapter 7.

Creative Style

- **Options**: Standard, Vivid, Neutral, Portrait, Landscape, Black & White; adjustable versions of these, plus Clear, Deep, Light, Night Scene, Autumn Leaves, Sepia, and Sunset
- **Default**: Standard
- **My preference**: Standard

This is the first entry in the Camera Settings 6 menu. (See **Figure 3.14**.) It option gives you six basic Creative Styles with fixed combinations of contrast, saturation, and sharpness. They each have a number prefix on the screen: 1: Standard, 2: Vivid, 3: Neutral, 4: Portrait, 5: Landscape, 6: B&W. Each also appears a second time (without the number prefix) and with the addition of Clear, Deep, Light, Night Scene, Autumn Leaves, Sepia, and Sunset. You can adjust the contrast, saturation, and sharpness of the non-numbered versions using the left/right buttons to choose an attribute, and the up/down buttons to adjust that attribute. You can apply Creative Styles when you are using any shooting mode except Superior Auto, Intelligent Auto, or any of the scene modes. I discuss the use of this option in Chapter 9.

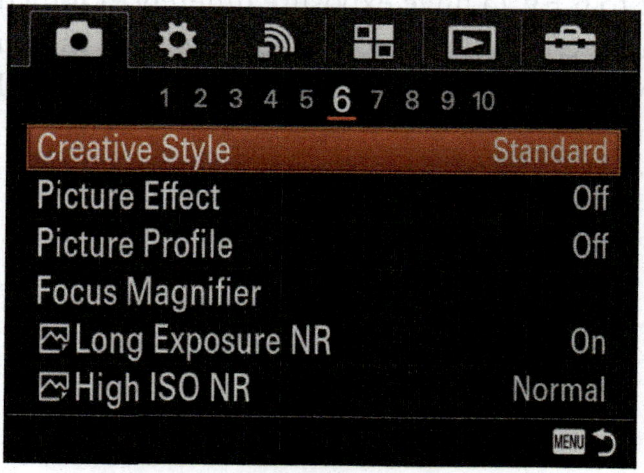

Figure 3.14

Picture Profile is the first entry in the Camera Settings 6 menu.

Picture Effect

- **Options**: Off, Toy Camera, Pop Color, Posterization, Retro Photo, Soft High-key, Partial Color, High Contrast Monochrome, Soft Focus, HDR Painting, Rich Tone Monochrome, Miniature, Watercolor, Illustration
- **Default**: Off
- **My preference**: Off

This camera feature, allows you to create JPEG photos with special effects provided by the camera's processor in JPEG capture mode (but not in RAW or RAW & JPEG) when the camera is in P, A, S, or M mode. It's not available for use when shooting movies. Scroll through the options in this item and watch the change in the preview image display that reflects the effect that each option can provide if you activate it; if you find one that looks interesting, press the center button or touch the shutter release button to confirm your choice and return to shooting mode.

When some effects are highlighted, left/right triangles will appear next to their label, indicating you can press the left/right keys to select an option available for that effect. Not all provide this extra benefit.

- **Toy Camera.** Produces images like you might get with a Diana or Holga "plastic" camera, with vignetted corners, image blurring, and bright, saturated colors. It's at Normal by default, but when you press the left/right buttons you can select Normal, Cool, Warm, Green, or Magenta.
- **Pop Color.** This setting adds a lot of saturation to the colors, making them especially vivid and rich looking. When used with subjects that have a lot of bright colors, the effect can be dramatic. Duller subjects gain a more "normal" appearance; try using this setting on an overcast day to see what I mean.
- **Posterization.** This option produces a vivid, high-contrast image that emphasizes the primary colors (as shown in **Figure 3.14**, upper left) or in black-and-white, with a reduced number

of tones, creating a poster effect. The default rendition is Color, but a monochrome option also appears if you press the left/right keys.

- **Retro Photo.** Adds a faded photo look to the image, with sepia overtones.
- **Soft High-key.** Produces bright images.
- **Partial Color.** Attempts to retain the selected color of an image, while converting other hues to black-and-white. (See **Figure 3.14**, upper right.) It's set at Red by default, indicating that photos will retain red tones, but you can also choose Blue, Green, or Yellow.
- **High Contrast Monochrome.** Converts the image to black-and-white and boosts the contrast to give a stark look to the image. (See **Figure 3.14**, lower left.)
- **Soft Focus.** Creates a soft, blurry effect. It's at Mid by default (for a medium intensity); press the left/right buttons to specify Lo or Hi intensity.
- **HDR Painting.** Produces a painted look by taking three pictures consecutively and then using HDR techniques to enhance color and details. It's at Mid by default (for a medium intensity); press the left/right buttons to specify Lo or Hi intensity. The camera will quickly shoot three photos, at varying exposures, and combine them into one. (This is most suitable for static subjects; do not move the camera until all three shots have been fired.)
- **Rich-tone Monochrome.** Uses the same concept as the one above but creates a long-gradation black-and-white image (by darkening bright areas but keeping dark tones rich) from three consecutive exposures.
- **Miniature.** You select the area to be rendered in sharp focus using the Option button. The effect is similar to the tilt-shift look used to photograph craft models. (See **Figure 3.14**, lower right.) Press the left/right keys to position the blurry area to the left, right, top, bottom, or middle of the image; watch the

preview display while scrolling among them to get a feel for the effect that each one can provide.

- **Watercolor.** Creates a look with blurring and runny colors, as if the image were painted using watercolors.
- **Illustration.** Emphasizes the edges of an image to show the outlines more dramatically. The left/right buttons can be used to adjust the effect from Low, to Mid, or High levels.

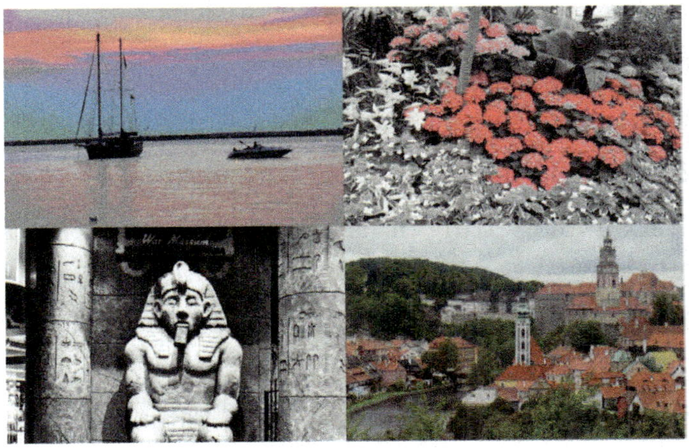

Figure 3.15

Clockwise, from upper left: Posterization, Partial Color, High Contrast Monochrome, Miniature.

Picture Profile

- **Options:** Picture Profiles PP1-PP7, Off
- **Default:** Off
- **My preference:** Off

Picture Profiles are a great tool for advanced movie shooters. You can customize the picture quality, including color and gradation of your movies by defining the parameters included in each of seven different Picture Profiles. To make these adjustments, connect the camera to a TV or monitor using the HDMI port, and use the picture on the screen as a guide while making your changes. After connecting the camera to your HDTV/monitor, navigate to this menu entry and select which Picture Profile you want to modify. Press the right button to access the index screen, then press the up/down buttons to select the parameter to be changed. Then make your adjustments and press the center button to confirm.

Even a short course in how each of the parameters affects video images, and a discussion of how to select the best settings would require a chapter or two of technical discussion, and is thus beyond the scope of this book. I'm going to provide a quick listing of each type of setting for a reminder; your Sony manual provides more information about each of these. The seven Picture Profile presets already have default values:

- **PP1:** Example setting using [Movie] gamma
- **PP2:** Example setting using [Still] gamma
- **PP3:** Example setting of natural color tone using the ITU709 gamma
- **PP4:** Example setting of a color tone faithful to the [ITU709] standard
- **PP5:** Example setting using [Cine1] gamma
- **PP6:** Example setting using [Cine2] gamma
- **PP7:** Example setting using [S-Log2] gamma

The parameters you can adjust include:

- **Black Level.** Sets the black level (-15 to +15). Black level is the level of brightness at which no light is emitted from a screen, resulting in a pure black screen. Adjustment of this parameter ensures that blacks are seen as black, and not a dark shade of graph.
- **Gamma.** Selects a gamma curve, a formula which corrects for the nonlinear relationship between the brightness (*luminance*) captured by a sensor and the brightness of the image as it's displayed on a monitor. In other words, correction is needed to make what you see on a screen more closely resemble what the camera captured in real life. You can choose from nine different gamma curves.

- **Black Gamma.** Corrects gamma in low-intensity areas, using Range and Level controls.
- **Knee.** Sets "knee point" and slope for video signal compression to prevent overexposure by limiting signals in high-intensity areas of the subject to the dynamic range of your camera. In short, a higher knee level produces more detail in the highlights; a lower knee level produces fewer details in the highlights.
- **Mode.** In Auto mode, the knee point and slope are set automatically; in Manual mode, they are set manually.
- **Auto Set.** When Auto is selected, values are automatically chosen by the camera for the maximum knee point, sensitivity, manual settings, and knee slope.
- **Color Mode.** Sets type and level of colors, from among Movie, Still, Cinema, Pro, ITU-709 Matrix, Black & White, and S-Gamut.
- **Saturation.** Sets the color saturation, from -32 to +32 values.
- **Color Phase.** Sets the color phase (-7 to +7).
- **Color Depth.** Sets the color depth for each color phase.
- **Detail.** Sets parameters including Level, and Detail adjustments including Mode, Vertical/Horizontal Balance, B/W Balance, Limit, Crispning (sic), and Hi-Light Detail.
- **Copy.** Copies the settings of the picture profile to another picture profile number.
- **Reset.** Resets the picture profile to the default setting. You cannot reset all picture profile settings at once.

Focus Magnifier

- **Options**: Activate
- **Default**: Off
- **My preference**: N/A

If you like to focus manually, this is a very useful aid, one of several that Sony generously offers to enhance the chore of achieving sharp focus without using autofocus features. It's very similar to the MF Assist feature found in the Custom Settings 1 menu, and, in fact, requires that MF Assist be turned on before the Focus Magnifier can be used. Unlike MF Assist, Focus Magnifier can be used in Movie mode. To use the Focus Magnifier, just follow these steps:

1. **Enable Focus Magnifier.** The automatic function of the Focus Magnifier can be enabled with the MF Assist entry of the Custom Settings 1 menu, described in Chapter 4. When set to On, the magnifier kicks in whenever you are using manual focus.
2. **Switch to manual focus.** When MF Assist is activated, the Focus Magnifier operates automatically when the camera is set to manual focus. You can change to MF using the Function menu, the Quick Navi screen, or the Focus Mode entry of the Camera Settings 4 menu. You can also define a key, such as the C custom key, to switch to manual focus. (Use the Custom Key Settings entry in the Custom Settings 4 menu, as outlined in Chapter 4.)
3. **Invoke Focus Magnifier.** Use this menu entry to activate it. You can also define a key to summon it. I selected Focus Magnifier as my definition for the right directional button using Custom Keys.
4. **Rotate the control ring.** The image is enlarged, and a navigation window appears at lower left showing an orange rectangle that represents the current location of the blown-up section. (See **Figure 3.16**.)

5. **Zoom in/out.** Pressing the center button enlarges the image from 1X to 8.6X and 17.1X.
6. **Adjust the magnified area.** A quartet of triangles surrounds the image, indicating that you can move the enlarged window around with the frame. Use the left/right/up/down keys to move the enlarged area.
7. **Manually focus.** Rotate the control ring to achieve sharp focus. A scale along the bottom of the screen shows the approximate focus distance.
8. **Take picture or exit.** Press the shutter release all the way down to take a photo, or press it halfway to exit from the Focus Magnifier. The magnifier will also time out after 2 seconds or 5 seconds, or may remain on with no limit -- depending on how you've set Focus Magnifier Time in the Custom Settings 1 menu (as described in Chapter 4).
9. **(Optional) Return to autofocus.** Remember to return to autofocus when you no longer want to focus on your subject manually.

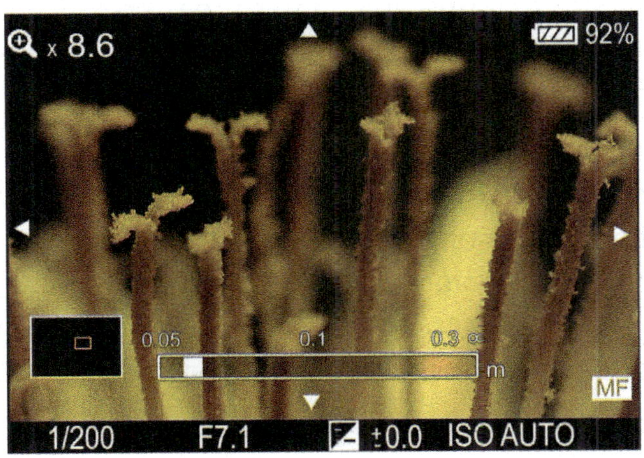

Figure 3.16

The focus magnifier makes manual focusing easier.

Long Exposure NR/High ISO NR (Still Image)

- **Long Exposure NR: Options**: On/Off; **Default**: On
- **High ISO NR: Options**: Normal, Low, Off; **Default**: Normal
- **My preference**: On for Long Exposure NR; Off for High ISO NR

I've grouped these two menu options together because they work together, each under slightly different circumstances. Moreover, the causes and cures for noise involve some overlapping processes. Digital noise is that awful graininess that shows up as multicolored specks in images, and these menu items help you manage it. In some ways, noise is like the excessive grain found in some high-speed photographic films. However, while photographic grain is sometimes used as a special effect, it's rarely desirable in a digital photograph.

The visual noise-producing process is something like listening to a CD in your car, and then rolling down all the windows. You're adding sonic noise to the audio signal, and while increasing the CD player's volume may help a bit, you're still contending with an unfavorable signal to noise ratio that probably mutes tones (especially higher treble notes) that you really want to hear.

The same thing happens when the analog signal is amplified: You're increasing the image information in the signal, but boosting the background fuzziness at the same time. Tune in a very faint or distant AM radio station on your car stereo. Then turn up the volume. After a certain point, turning up the volume further no longer helps you hear better. There's a similar point of diminishing returns for digital sensor ISO increases and signal amplification as well.

Your RX100 V can reduce the amount of grainy visual noise in your photo with noise reduction processing. That's useful for a smoother look, but NR processing does blur some of the very fine detail in an image along with blurring the digital noise pattern. These two menu items let you choose whether or not to apply noise reduction to exposures of longer than one-third second and how much noise reduction to apply (Normal or Low) when shooting at a high ISO level (at roughly ISO 1600 and above).

The RX100 V imposes some restrictions. For example, Long Exposure NR is automatically activated when using scene modes, Intelligent Auto, or Superior Auto. High ISO NR is grayed out when the camera is set to shoot only RAW-format photos. The camera does not use this feature on RAW-format photos since noise reduction -- at the optimum level for any photo -- can be applied in the software you'll use to modify and convert the RAW file to JPEG. (If you shoot in RAW & JPEG, the JPEG images, but not the RAW files, will be affected by this camera feature.) As well, High ISO NR and Long Exposure NR are never applied when the camera is set to Sweep Panorama, or continuous shooting, continuous bracketing, Sports Action, Hand-held Twilight, Anti Motion Blur scene mode, or when the ISO is set to Multi Frame Noise Reduction.

Digital noise is also created during very long exposures. Extended exposure times allow more photons to reach the sensor, but increase the likelihood that some photosites will react randomly even though not struck by a particle of light. Moreover, as the sensor remains switched on for the longer exposure, it heats up, and this heat can be mistakenly recorded as if it were a barrage of photons. To minimize the digital noise that can occur during long exposures, the RX100 V uses a process called "dark frame subtraction." After you take the photo, the camera fires another shot, at the same shutter speed, with the shutter closed to make the so-called dark frame. The processor compares the original photo and the dark frame photo and identifies the colorful noise speckles and "hot" pixels. It then removes (subtracts) them so the final image saved to the memory card will be quite "clean."

Context-Sensitive

The RX100 V has a novel "context-sensitive" noise-reduction algorithm that examines the image to identify smooth tones, subject edges, and textures, and apply different NR to each. This processing works best with areas with continuous tones and subtle gradations, and does a good job of reducing noise while preserving detail. Because the BIONZ X digital processing chip is doing so much work, you may see a message on the screen while NR is underway. You cannot take another photo until the processing is done and the message disappears. If you want to give greater priority to shooting, set both Long Exposure NR and High ISO NR to Off.

Long Exposure NR works well, but it causes a delay; roughly the same amount of time as the exposure itself. That would be a long 10 seconds after a 10-second exposure. During this delay the camera locks up so you cannot take another shot. You may want to turn this feature off to eliminate that delay when you need to be able to take a shot at any time.

You might want to turn off noise reduction for long exposures, and set it to a weak level for high ISO photos (or entirely off, as I do) in order to preserve image detail. (NR processing blurs the digital noise pattern, but it can also blur fine details in your images.) Or, you simply may not need NR in some situations. For example, you might be shooting waves crashing into the shore at ISO 200 with the camera mounted on a tripod, using a neutral-density filter and long exposure to cause the pounding water to blur slightly. To maximize detail in the non-moving portions of your photos, you can switch off long exposure noise reduction.

Center Lock-On AF

- **Options:** On, Off
- **Default:** Off
- **My preference:** Off

This setting, the first on the Camera Settings 7 menu, tells the camera to detect a subject positioned in the center of the frame and then adjust focus as the camera tracks its movement. A pair of white boxes appear in the EVF and LCD monitor. Move the camera to center the box on the subject you want to track and press the center button. The camera will then track that object as you reframe, or the subject moves, until you take a picture. Center Lock-On AF is not available at all when focus is set to manual. However, unlike Lock-On AF, it can be used when capturing video.

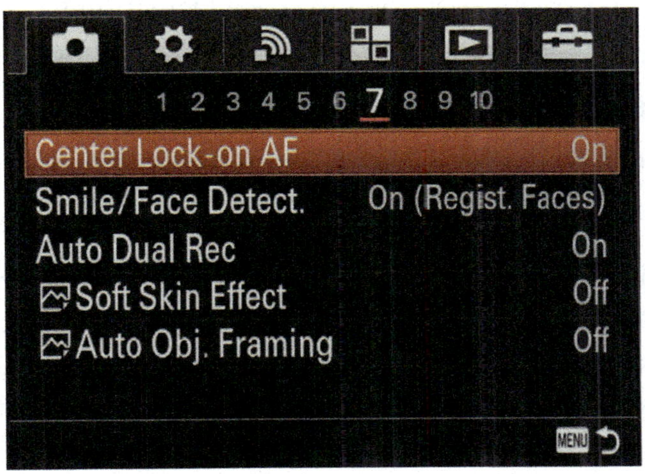

Figure 3.17

The Camera Settings 7 menu.

Like the Focus Magnifier function, this feature isn't "live" all the time once you've set it. It requires a trip to the Camera Settings menu each time you want to use it, unless you define a custom key to summon it. You can use a button that you don't use much while shooting. In my case, that's the Flash (right directional) button.

This feature is different from the Lock-On AF option, described in Chapter 4. They key differences:

- **Menu/Key Access.** Center Lock-On AF must be selected from this menu, or summoned with an assigned custom key. Lock-On AF, when active, can be triggered simply by pressing the shutter release halfway.
- **Fixed Zone.** Center Lock-On AF always uses the center of the frame to lock onto a subject. Lock-On AF can be set for any of the available focus area options, including Wide, Zone, Center, Flexible Spot, and Expand Flexible Spot.
- **Available in Movie mode.** Center Lock-On AF, unlike Lock-On AF, can be used in Movie mode.

Smile/Face Detection

- **Options:** Face Detection Off, Face Detection On (Registered Faces), Face Detection On, Smile Shutter (Normal Smile, Slight Smile, Big Smile)
- **Default:** Off
- **My preference:** On

Your camera can detect faces and zero in its focusing prowess on them. You can also tell the camera to use face detection to identify a face and look for a smile; it takes a photo each time it sees a smile (actually, it's just looking for an array of pearly white teeth). This is an interesting high-tech feature, because the subject's smile acts as a sort of remote control.

With this option activated, the camera will survey the subjects before it and try to determine if it is looking at any human faces. If it decides that it is, it sets focus, flash, exposure, and white balance settings for you. When active, one of six indicators will appear on the LCD or EVF:

- **Gray square.** A face has been detected. The square will turn green when the shutter release is pressed halfway and focus is achieved.

- **Gray square/white square.** Face(s) detected, and priority will be given to the face in the white square. Either or both squares will turn green as the shutter release is pressed halfway and focus is achieved.
- **Multiple gray/white squares.** More than one face has been detected, and priority will be given to the face in the white square, which turns green when the shutter release is pressed halfway and focus is achieved.
- **Magenta square.** A registered face has been detected and will be given priority. Additional faces will be outlined with a white square. The magenta square will turn green when the shutter release is pressed halfway and focus is achieved.
- **Green brackets.** No face has been detected and focus will be achieved using the area(s) outlined with the brackets.
- **Orange squares.** Smile Detection is active and faces outlined will be monitored for smiles.

The four options available with this menu entry include:

- **Face Detection Off.** Disables all face detection.
- **Face Detection On (Registered Faces).** When set to On (Registered Faces), any faces previously logged will be given priority. As you press the shutter button to take the picture, the camera will attempt to set the exposure and white balance using the face it has selected as the main subject. If that result is not what you want, you can start over, or you may want to take control back from the camera by choosing Flexible Spot or Center for the Autofocus Area and placing the focus spot exactly where you want it.

  You'll need to register faces you want to recognize separately using a Face Registration option, and even assign a priority for up to eight faces (ranking them 1 to 8 on your face recognition speed dial). Sony has hidden the registration feature, as you might guess by now, in a completely different menu, specifically the Custom Settings 4 menu. Happy hunting! I'll describe the process in Chapter 4.

- **Face Detection.** In this mode, the camera diligently looks for any human face it can find, and doesn't care who it belongs to. Use this option if you have few friends, or, more than eight that you don't want to offend.
- **Smile Shutter.** Activate this feature, and press the left/right buttons to specify Normal Smile (the default), Big Smile, and Slight Smile. Set Big Smile for example, and the camera won't take a photo when the detected face smiles only slightly; it will wait for a serious toothy grin. You will need to experiment to find out which level to use. The sensitivity of this feature depends on factors such as whether the subject shows his or her teeth when smiling, whether the eyes are covered by sunglasses, and others. I suggest leaving it at Normal Smile, changing it only if that does not work as you had expected. Keep in mind that Smile Shutter uses a lot of power, so you will want to use it sparingly, or as a novelty feature.

There is no limit to the number of smiles and images you can take with this feature; you, or whoever is in front of the camera, can keep smiling repeatedly, and the camera will keep taking more pictures until it runs out of memory storage or battery power. Of course, the main purpose of this feature is not to act as a remote control; it's really intended to make sure your subject is smiling before the photo is taken. Whenever Smile Shutter triggers the shutter release, it also flashes the red light of the AF Illuminator as a signal to the person that a picture is being taken.

Auto Dual Record

- **Options:** Off/On (Standard, High, Low)
- **Default:** Off
- **My preference:** Off

This item is a painless way to capture high resolution still images (rather than 2 MP frame grabs) automatically while shooting video. (See **Figure 3.17.**) As an automatic feature, the RX100 V itself decides when and how often to capture a snapshot. While your video recording is underway, when the camera decides that a scene containing human faces is photo-worthy, it will save a still image using the Image Size (Dual Rec) and Quality (Dual Rec) settings described earlier in this chapter. In other words, you can automatically stockpile images up to 17 MP and Extra Fine quality without having to think about it. The camera may apply the Auto Object Framing feature, described shortly, to crop the image using Rule of Thirds guidelines.

When you select On, you can press the left/right buttons to choose from Standard, High, or Low frequency. I have been unable to tell exactly what these frequencies are, because they depend on how often your video includes what Sony calls an "impressive composition," and, apparently, my own work doesn't make the cut very often. Keep in mind that you can always shoot stills automatically while movie shooting, simply by pressing the shutter release.

Soft Skin Effect (Still Image)

- **Options:** Off/On (Lo, Mid, Hi)
- **Default:** Off
- **My preference:** Off

This item can be used to instruct the camera's processor to minimize blemishes and wrinkles in the detected face, which usually helps produce a more flattering picture. I find it more suitable for photos of women than of men. If you choose On, press the left/right buttons and select the low, middle, or high intensity for skin softening. This effect does not work when shooting movies or in any continuous shooting mode, including bracketing and continuous self-timer, nor when using the Sports Action scene mode, Sweep Panorama, or RAW capture mode.

Auto Object Framing (Still Image)

- **Options**: Off/Auto
- **Default**: Auto
- **My preference**: Off

When this feature is active, the RX100 V analyzes three types of images: close-up shots, images taken using Center Lock-On AF (discussed earlier), and images containing faces (only when Face Detection is activated). When it's On and the camera detects a close-up subject, tracked object, or face, it takes the photo as you composed it but also makes another image and saves that to the memory card as well. This second photo is made after cropping the photo you had composed into one that the camera thinks is a more pleasing composition. If you have Setting Effect On specified in the Live View Display entry of the Custom Settings 2 menu, a white frame appears to show the cropped area before it is stored. The camera's processor uses the Rule of Thirds compositional technique when making its cropping decision so the eyes will not be in the center of the image area, for example.

Since cropping makes the image smaller, the processor adds pixels to ensure that the photo will be full size. It uses Sony's By Pixel Super Resolution Technology for the "up sampling"; this technology maintains very good image quality.

My recommendation: Certainly, Auto Object Framing is a feature intended to attract novices and inveterate snap shooters, but I find it useful at parties when taking quick shots of friends; in most cases, the photo with automatic cropping is preferable to the original (sloppily composed) shot. Of course, both photos are available on the memory card so you can use either of them.

Auto Mode

- **Options:** Intelligent Auto, Superior Auto
- **Default:** Intelligent Auto
- **My preference:** Superior Auto

This entry is the first on the Camera Settings 8 menu. (See **Figure 3.18**.) It allows you to specify which of the camera's two fully auto modes (Intelligent Auto and Superior Auto) is activated when the mode dial is moved to the Auto position. Most users of a camera as sophisticated as this one won't use either one very often, so Sony has uncluttered the mode dial by allowing you to specify which of the two Auto modes you'd like to activate by default. This entry is grayed out (unavailable) if the mode dial is not set to the Auto position.

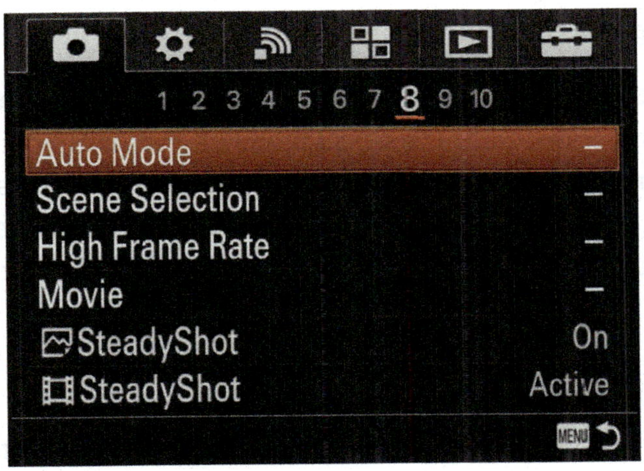

Figure 3.18

The Camera Settings 8 menu.

Scene Selection

- **Options:** Select Scene Modes
- **Default**: None
- **My preference**: N/A

This entry is available *only* when the mode dial is set to SCN. It provides an alternate method for choosing among the available scene modes, described in Chapter 1. Rotate the control wheel, or use the up/down buttons to select the scene mode you would like to use.

High Frame Rate

- **Options:** Program Auto, Aperture Priority, Shutter Priority
- **Default**: Program Auto
- **My preference**: Program Auto

This setting allows you to select the exposure mode used when shooting high frame rate (HFR) video. The menu entry is available only if the mode dial is set to the HFR position. Use this entry in conjunction with the HFR Settings entry described earlier in this chapter. You'll find an extensive discussion of HFR photography in Chapter 10.

Movie

- **Options:** Program Auto, Aperture Priority, Shutter Priority, Manual Exposure
- **Default**: Program Auto
- **My preference**: Program Auto works well for me when shooting movies

This setting is available only when the mode dial is in the Movie position and allows you to specify which exposure mode is used (from among P, S, A, and M options) when shooting movies; the mode you select can be different from the one set for still photography mode.

SteadyShot (Still Image)

- **Options**: On, Off
- **Default**: On
- **My preference**: On

SteadyShot is on by default to help counteract image blur that is caused by camera shake, but you should turn it off when the camera is mounted on a tripod, as the additional anti-shake feature is not needed, and the anti-shake mechanism may be "confused" and make unnecessary corrections. In other situations, however, I recommend leaving SteadyShot turned on at all times.

SteadyShot counters camera movement by shifting lens elements in the opposite direction of the movement, using motion detectors built in the camera. This form of anti-shake is called optical image stabilization.

SteadyShot (Movie)

- **Options:** Intelligent Active, Active, Standard, Off
- **Default**: Standard
- **My preference**: Active

This setting allows the camera to adjust the behavior of SteadyShot, based on the amount of image stabilization typically required at particular focal lengths. That is, telephoto lenses "magnify" camera shake and thus can benefit from more aggressive image stabilization. Indeed, this aspect is one reason why in-lens IS is often touted as superior to in-body stabilization. Your RX100 V gives you three levels of SteadyShot, and the opportunity to turn it off entirely.

SteadyShot for movies uses a combination of optical image stabilization, as described above, and *electronic image stabilization,* which takes advantage of the fact that a movie frame is cropped out of the total available pixels in the 5472 x 3648-pixel sensor. The camera compares successive frames, looking for image areas that don't move between frames (such as background objects), and can, if necessary, rotate and/or shift the next frame to align those non-moving pixels. Because there are pixels located beyond the boundaries of the frame, this shifting can take place without leaving any blank spots in the frame. A slight amount of cropping can be used to ensure that the aligned image displays correctly.

Remember that movies are typically shot at relatively slow shutter speeds (1/30th to 1/125th second), which makes stabilization important; but also keep in mind that we view each frame for only a brief time. A mildly blurry 1/30th-second movie frame may not be as objectionable as a slightly blurry still photo shot at 1/30th second. The SteadyShot modes Sony offers include:

- **Intelligent Active.** This mode is very aggressive in the amount of rotating and shifting it uses to produce a stable image, and may crop the image more than the other modes. Dual Video Recording is disabled during this mode (which is why I use it less than the less-aggressive "Active" mode). Because of the amount of image processing required, three useful movie-making options are not available when Intelligent Active is enabled: 4K capture, High Frame Rate video, and 100/120 frame rates. I use this when capturing video from off-road vehicles on uneven terrain.
- **Active.** This mode also uses electronic image stabilization, but is less aggressive and does not produce the same degree of anti-shake. Unless you feel your camera movements are likely to be especially severe, this may be your best all-around choice for movie making. Dual Video Recording is enabled, but 4K, HFR, and 100/120 fps shooting is disabled.
- **Standard.** This setting uses only optical image stabilization, and provides the least amount of anti-shake, typically two stops worth, or slightly more.
- **Off.** Disables SteadyShot for movies. Use this option when the camera is mounted on a tripod, or when you actually want some blurriness as a creative effect.

Color Space (Still Image)

- **Options:** sRGB, Adobe RGB
- **Default**: sRGB
- **My preference**: Adobe RGB

This menu item is the first entry on Camera Settings 9 menu. (See Figure 3.19.) It gives you the choice of two different color spaces (also called color gamuts). One is named Adobe RGB, an abbreviation for Adobe RGB (1998), so named because it was developed by Adobe Systems in 1998, and the other is sRGB, supposedly because it is the *standard* RGB color space. These two color gamuts define a specific set of colors that can be applied to the images your Alpha captures.

You're probably surprised that the RX100 V doesn't automatically capture all the colors we see. Unfortunately, that's impossible because of the limitations of the sensor and the filters used to capture the fundamental red, green, and blue colors, as well as that of the LEDs used to display those colors on your camera and computer monitors. Nor is it possible to print every color our eyes detect, because the inks or pigments used don't absorb and reflect colors perfectly.

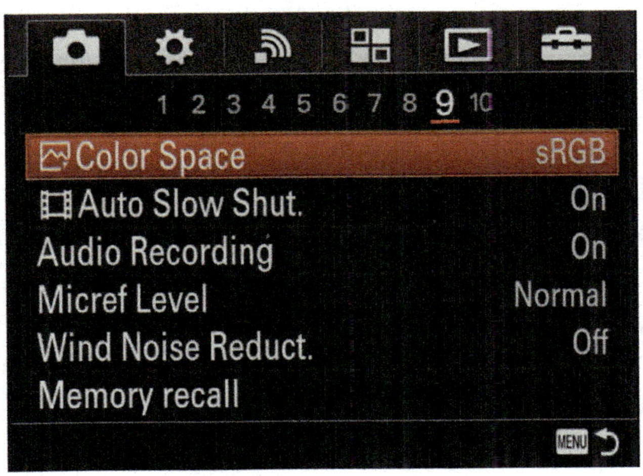

Figure 3.19

The Camera Settings 9 page.

Instead, the colors that can be reproduced by a given device are represented as a color space that exists within the full range of colors we can see. That full range is represented by the odd-shaped splotch of color shown in Figure 3.20, as defined by scientists at an international organization back in 1931. The colors possible with the camera's Adobe RGB option are represented by the larger, black triangle in the figure, while the sRGB gamut is represented by the smaller, white triangle. As the illustration indicates, Adobe RGB (1998) is an expanded color space, because it can reproduce a range of colors that is spread over a wider range of the visual spectrum.

Regardless of which triangle -- or color space -- is used by the Sony RX100 V camera, you end up with 16.8 million different colors that can be used in your photograph. (No one image will contain all 16.8 million!) But, as you can see from the figure, the colors available will be different.

ADOBE RGB vs. sRGB

You might want to use sRGB, which is the default for the Sony camera, as it is well suited for the colors displayed on a computer screen and viewed over the Internet.

(It is possible to buy a specialized and very expensive computer monitor that's specifically designed to display nearly the entire Adobe RGB (1998) color gamut, such as the EIZO SX2762W, which sells for about $1,500 in the US, but I doubt that many readers own a monitor of that type.) As well, images made in sRGB color space are fine for use with inexpensive inkjet printers that use three ink colors in a single cartridge. Note too that most mass market print-making services (including kiosks and online photofinishers) have standardized on sRGB because that is the color space that 95 percent of their customers use.

Adobe RGB's expanded color space is preferable for professional printing. Because it can reproduce a wider range of colors than sRGB, it's definitely a better choice if you own a high-end inkjet photo printer that employs five or more color ink cartridges. Since pro and custom printing labs also use machines of this type, they'll provide the best results in prints made from images in the Adobe color space. You'll get slightly richer cyan-green mid tones, a bit more detail in dark green tones, and more pleasing orange-magenta highlights (as in a sunset photo).

So, if you often make inkjet prints using a high-end machine, or order prints from custom or pro labs, it makes sense to set the camera to Adobe RGB. Later, if you decide to use some of the photos on a website, you can convert them to sRGB in your image-editing software.

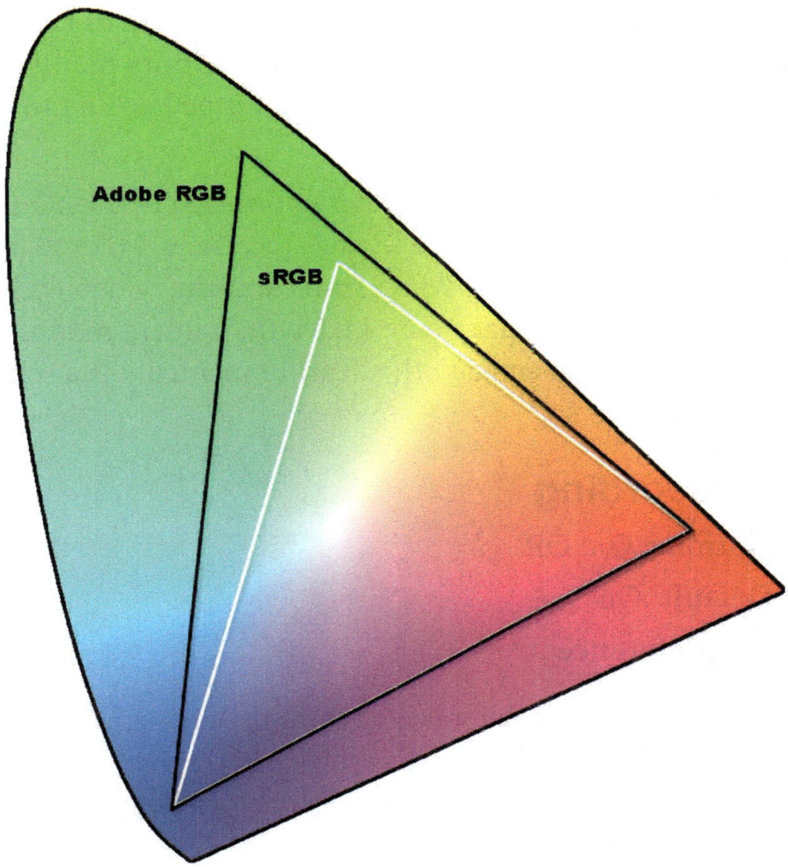

Figure 3.20

The outer figure shows all the colors we can see; the two inner outlines show the boundaries of Adobe RGB (black triangle) and sRGB (white triangle).

Auto Slow Shutter (Movie)

- **Options:** On, Off
- **Default:** On
- **My preference:** Off

When shooting movies in very dark locations, the best way to ensure that the video clips are bright is to use a slow shutter speed. When this menu item is On, the camera can automatically switch to a slower shutter speed than its default. Of course, the RX100 V must be set to Aperture Priority mode to give the camera the ability to change the shutter speed (the shutter speed is fixed at your selection in Shutter Priority mode). Logically, ISO must be set to ISO Auto, because, if the aperture is fixed (in Aperture Priority mode), to use a slower shutter speed the ISO sensitivity must be boosted to compensate.

This is a mildly useful feature; there's no need to use S mode and set a slow shutter speed yourself in dark locations. I like to leave this setting off, however, because when I am capturing video with a slow shutter speed, I want to make sure I have the camera mounted on a tripod, and the need to activate this feature manually is a reminder to me that I need to do so.

Audio Recording

- **Options:** On, Off
- **Default:** On
- **My preference:** On

Use this item to turn off sound recording when you're shooting videos, if desired. In most cases you'll want to leave the setting On, in order to capture as much information as possible; the audio track can be deleted later, if desired, with software. However, there could be occasions when it's useful to disable sound recording for movies, for example, if you know ahead of time that you will be dubbing in other sound, or if you have no need for sound, such as when panning over a vista of the Grand Canyon. At any rate, this option is there if you want to use it.

Micref Level

- **Options:** Normal, Low
- **Default:** Normal
- **My preference:** Normal

This entry tells the RX100 V whether you want quiet parts of your audio recording to be amplified. You can choose Normal or Low.

- **Normal.** The camera attempts to amplify all sounds up to roughly the same level, so that, say, quiet talkers will sound just as loud as more strident speakers. This can be particularly helpful when you're shooting a movie of a group of people, or in situations where the background sounds are especially important. It's usually safe to leave this setting at Normal most of the time.
- **Low.** Quiet sounds are *not* amplified. This would be useful when interviewing someone in a noisy environment. Because the camera's microphones are closer to the speaker than to the background noises, your subject's words will be more prominent and clear.

Wind Noise Reduction

- **Options:** On, Off
- **Default:** Off
- **My preference:** Off

Designed to muffle the howling sound produced by a loud wind passing over the built-in microphones, this item (when On) is for use when recording video. It's off by default because Wind Noise Reduction (provided by the camera's processor) does degrade sound quality, especially bass tones, and the recording volume is reduced. I recommend setting it to On only when shooting in a location with loud wind noises.

Memory Recall

- **Options:** Select register to store settings
- **Default:** None
- **My preference:** N/A

The RX100 V gives you the option of storing up to three different groups of settings in separate registers, and then recalling those settings for use later by rotating the mode dial to the MR position. Note that you can *store* settings when using any shooting modes (using the Memory entry that follows). But to *recall* a set of stored settings, you must rotate the mode dial to the Memory position, marked with MR on the mode dial. I'll explain recalling settings here, and show you how to store them under the next menu entry, Memory.

This item is a powerful and useful tool. It enables you to save almost all of the settings that you use for a particular shooting situation, and then recall them quickly. This function lets you save a pair of distinct sets of camera settings. Each will be a custom-crafted set that you can activate at any time. Simply activate the set that fits your current needs. For example, you might set up Register 1 with the settings you use while shooting volleyball in an indoor arena, Register 2 for use in landscape photography outdoors, and Register 3 for indoor family portraits. Whenever you encounter any of those three types of scenes, activate the memory channel with the suitable settings for that situation. You can then begin shooting immediately.

Here's how to activate saved settings:

1. **Mode dial.** Rotate the mode dial to the MR position and press the center button. You cannot recall any memory settings until the MR mode is chosen.
2. **Review settings.** The screen shown in **Figure 3.21** appears, displaying the first screen of saved settings for the currently orange-highlighted register (1, 2, or 3). Use the up/down direction buttons to see the other screens of settings for that register.

3. **Select register.** Use the left/right buttons or rotate the control wheel to select the register you want to activate.
4. **Confirm.** Press the center button to confirm your choice.

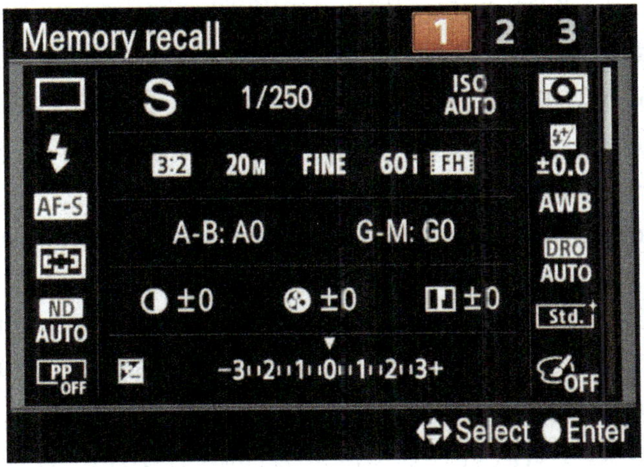

Figure 3.21
Recall settings stored in the 1, 2, or 3 memory slots.

Memory

- **Options:** Store settings on your memory card
- **Default:** None
- **My preference:** N/A

This is the only entry on the Camera Settings 10 menu (so I'm not illustrating that menu with a figure.) The power of the memory feature stems from the fact that so many shooting settings (but not Custom Key settings, unfortunately) can be saved for instant recall in any memory register. The mode dial should *not* be set to the MR position. Instead, before you access the Memory item in the menu, make the desired settings in terms of camera exposure mode, drive mode, ISO, white balance, exposure compensation, metering mode, focus mode, and other settings.

Then, to save your current settings on your memory card in one of the three slots, just follow these steps:

1. **Set up your camera.** Set your camera to the shooting mode, and adjust the camera to use the settings you'd like to store. The register can preserve shooting mode, aperture, shutter speed, and settings from the Camera Settings menu.
2. **Navigate to Memory entry.** Select the Memory entry in the Camera Settings 9 menu, and press the center button.
3. **Review settings.** Use the up/down buttons to scroll through the current settings to make sure they are satisfactory. A great deal more information is available than is shown in the figure (note the scroll bar at right). You can press the up/down buttons to view additional screens with detailed listings of your current settings. Exit and change desired settings, then start again at Step 2.
4. **Choose Register.** Press the left/right buttons to select in which of the memory locations you'd like to store your current settings -- 1, 2, or 3.
5. **Proceed or cancel.** Press the center button to confirm and store your settings, or press the MENU button to cancel.
6. **Activate register.** To use your stored settings, rotate the mode dial to MR, and select register 1, 2, or 3, as described earlier.

Chapter 4

Custom Settings Menu

Additional shooting options are available from the Sony RX100 V's Custom Settings menu. Custom Settings are adjustments that you generally don't make during a particular shooting session, but need to tweak more often than those in the Setup menu, which is described in Chapter 6. This menu has some very cool features, including the ability to assign more than four dozen different behaviors to the camera's C (Custom) key, control ring, and directional buttons.

Custom Settings Menu

These entries are used to adjust a variety of autofocus and manual settings, as well as exposure, display, and other options.

- Zebra
- MF Assist (Still Image)
- Focus Magnifier Time
- Initial Focus Magnification
- Grid Line
- Marker Display (Movie)
- Marker Settings (Movie)
- Auto Review
- DISP Button
- Peaking Level
- Peaking Color
- Exposure Settings Guide
- Live View Display
- AF Auto Area Clear
- Display Continuous AF Area
- Phase Detect Area
- Pre-AF (Still Image)
- Zoom Speed
- Zoom Setting
- FINDER/MONITOR
- Release without Card
- AEL w/Shutter (Still Image)
- Shutter Type (Still Image)
- Self-Portrait Timer
- Face Registration
- Write Date (Still Image)
- Function Menu Set.
- Custom Key (Shooting)
- Custom Key (Playback)
- Zoom Function on Ring
- MOVIE Button
- Wheel Lock

Zebra

- **Options:** OFF, IRE 70, 75, 80, 85, 90, 95, 100, 100+
- **Default:** Off
- **My preference:** 80

This feature, the first entry in the Custom Settings 1 menu (shown in **Figure 4.1**), warns you when highlight levels in your image are brighter than a setting you specify in this menu option. It's somewhat comparable to the flashing "blinkies" that digital cameras have long used during image review to tell us, after the fact, which highlight areas of the image we just took are blown out.

Zebra patterns are a much more useful tool, because you are given an alert *before* you take the picture, and can actually specify exactly how bright *too bright* is. The Zebra feature has been a staple of professional video shooting for a long time, as you might guess from the moniker assigned to the unit used to specify brightness: IRE, a measure of video signal level, which stands for *Institute of Radio Engineers.*

When you want to use Zebra pattern warnings, access this menu entry and specify an IRE value from 70 to 100, and 100+. Once you've been notified, you can adjust your exposure settings to reduce the brightness of the highlights, as I'll describe in Chapter 7.

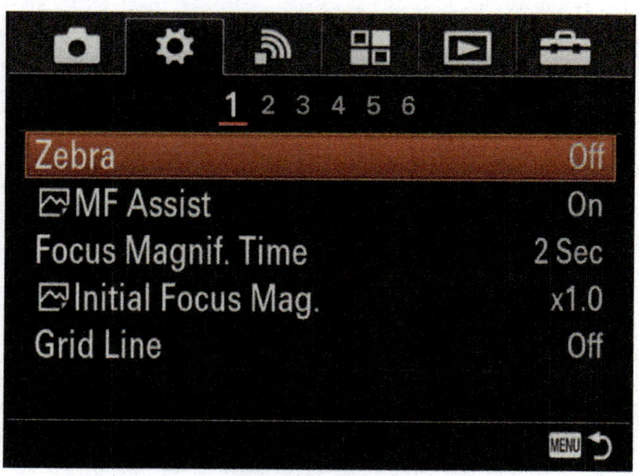

Figure 4.1
Zebra is the first entry in the Custom Settings 1 menu.

So, exactly how bright *is* too bright? A value of 100 IRE indicates pure white, so any Zebra pattern visible when using this setting (or 100+) indicates that your image is extremely overexposed. Any details in the highlights are gone, and cannot be retrieved. Settings from 70 to 90 can be used to make sure facial tones are not overexposed. As a general rule of thumb, Caucasian skin generally falls in the 80 IRE range, with darker skin tones registering as low as 70, and very fair skin or lighter areas of your subject edging closer to 90 IRE. Once you've decided the approximate range of tones that you want to make sure do *not* blow out, you can set the camera's Zebra pattern sensitivity appropriately and receive the flashing striped warning on the LCD of your camera. (See **Figure 4.2**.) The pattern does not appear in your final image, of course -- it's just an aid to keep you from blowing it, so to speak.

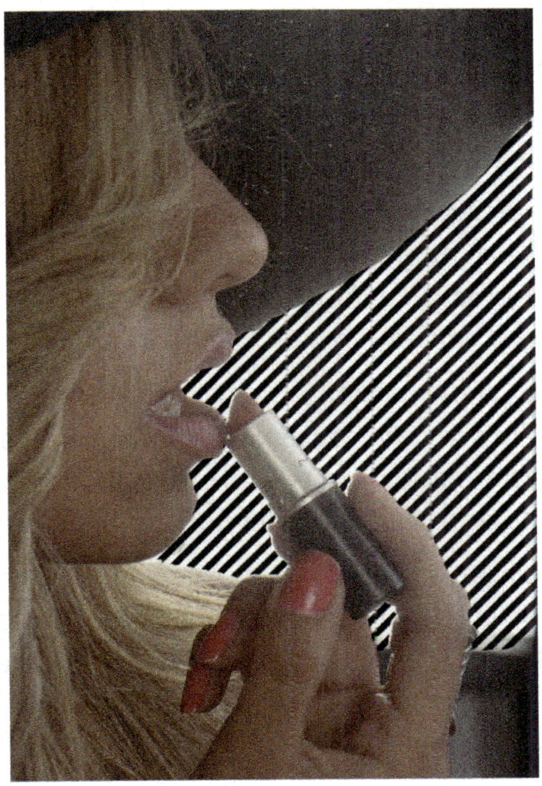

Figure 4.2

The flashing stripes show an area is overexposed.

MF Assist (Still Image)

- **Options**: On, Off
- **Default**: On
- **My preference**: On

When you are using manual focus or manual focus in the DMF mode, the camera enlarges the screen so you can better judge by eye whether the important part of your subject is in sharp focus. This feature is not available in Movie mode. You can turn MF Assist Off if you find that you don't need it. Adjust the magnifier time-out using the entry described next. To use MF Assist, follow these steps:

1. **Begin manual focus.** With the MF focus setting, just rotate the control ring. The Focus Magnifier (described in Chapter 3) will activate automatically. If you're using DMF, you must press the shutter release halfway, which activates *autofocus*. When AF has zeroed in on your subject, you can then adjust focus manually by rotating the control ring while keeping the shutter release halfway down.
2. **Zoom in.** While focusing, the image on the LCD will appear enlarged. You can press the center button to zoom from 8.6X to 17.1X normal size. Note that you must hold the shutter release down halfway to continue using the Focus Magnifier.
3. **Position focusing area.** A pair of rectangles in the lower-left corner of the screen represents the enlarged area, and where it resides in the frame. Use the directional buttons to move your view around within the preview image.
4. **Stop focusing.** When you stop rotating the control ring, or after the focus magnifier time has elapsed (described next), the LCD display will revert back to normal (non-magnified) display so you can see the entire area the camera will record.

Focus Magnifier Time

- **Options:** 2 sec., 5 sec., No Limit
- **Default:** 2 sec.
- **My preference:** 5 sec.

This entry can be used to specify the length of time that the MF Assist feature will magnify the image during manual focusing. If you find that it takes you longer than two seconds to manually focus using MF Assist, you can change the time to five seconds, or to No Limit; the latter, used in MF mode, will cause the image to remain magnified until you tap the shutter release button (you don't need to actually take a picture).

No Limit is not practical in DMF mode, because you must keep the shutter button depressed halfway the whole time, or continue pressing to take a picture. If you take your finger off the shutter release, the next time you press it again, AF is re-activated and changes your focus point. If you want to use the Focus Magnifier in DMF mode, it's better to set the 2 or 5 second elapsed time and keep your finger on the release button until you actually decide to snap off a picture.

Initial Focus Magnification

- **Options:** x1.0, x5.3
- **Default:** x1.0
- **My preference:** x5.3

Specifies the default focus magnification factor when the Focus Magnifier is activated. You can choose x1.0 (no magnification) or x5.3. I prefer to see the image zoomed in, to avoid the extra step of zooming manually after the Focus Magnifier kicks in.

Grid Line

- **Options**: Rule of 3rds Grid, Square Grid, Diag.+Square Grid, Off
- **Default**: Off
- **My preference**: Off

This feature allows you to activate one of three optional grids, so it's superimposed on the LCD or EVF display. The grid pattern can help you with composition while you are shooting architecture or similar subjects. I sometimes use the Rule of Thirds grid to help with composition, but you might want to activate another option when composing images of scenes that include diagonal, horizontal, and perpendicular lines. (See **Figure 4.3**.)

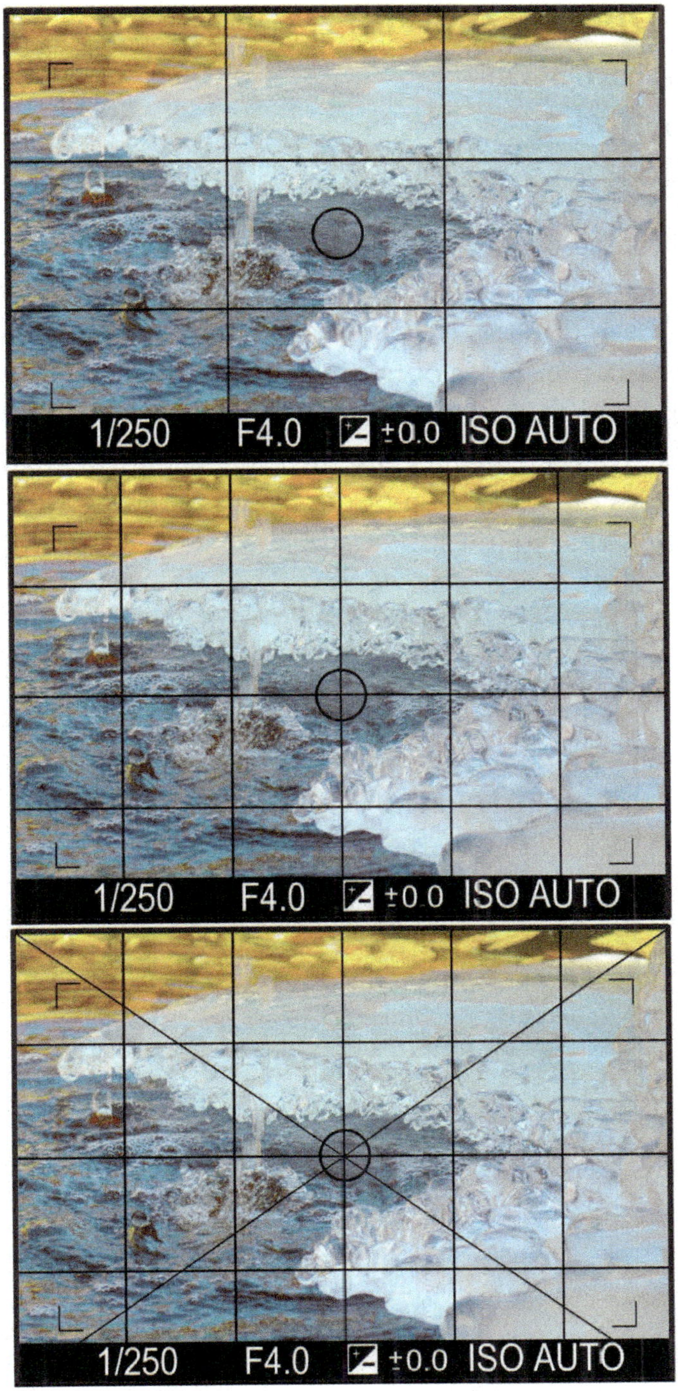

Figure 4.3

Grid lines can help you align your images on the LCD.

Marker Display (Movie)

- **Options**: On, Off
- **Default**: On
- **My preference**: N/A

This is the first entry on the Custom Settings 2 menu. (See **Figure 4.4**.) When shooting video that will end up being displayed in other than HDTV's 16:9 ratio, it's useful to know exactly where the boundaries of other types of frames are, so the image can be composed to keep important subject matter contained within those boundaries. This setting lets you turn the display of any of four different types of markers on or off, as described in the Market Settings entry that follows.

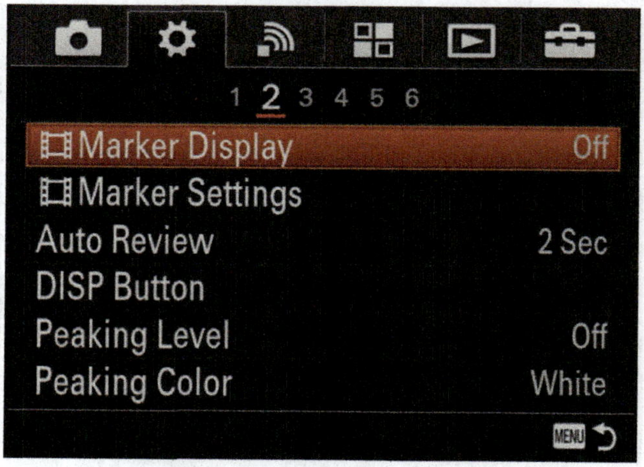

Figure 4.4
Custom Settings 2 menu.

Marker Settings (Movie)

- **Options:** Center, Aspect, Safety Zone, Guideframe
- **Default**: Center
- **My preference**: N/A

This entry allows you to choose which markers are displayed during video capture. You can select any or all of the following, if you like, although using more than one or two markers is likely to be confusing. Your choices (shown in **Figure 4.4**) are as follows:

- **Center -- On/Off.** Whether or not to the center marker is shown in the middle of the shooting screen. The default value is Off.
- **Aspect -- Off / 4:3 / 13:9 / 14:9 / 15:9 / 1.66:1 / 1.85:1 / 2.35:1.** This activates a marker showing your preferred aspect ratio. The default is Off.
- **Safety Zone -- Off / 80% / 90%.** Sets the safety zone display that represents the standard range that can counted on to be visible on a consumer television set, taking into account the frame or bezel that surrounds the screen.
- **Guideframe -- On/Off.** Enables/disables a guideframe that can be used to verify whether a subject is parallel or perpendicular.

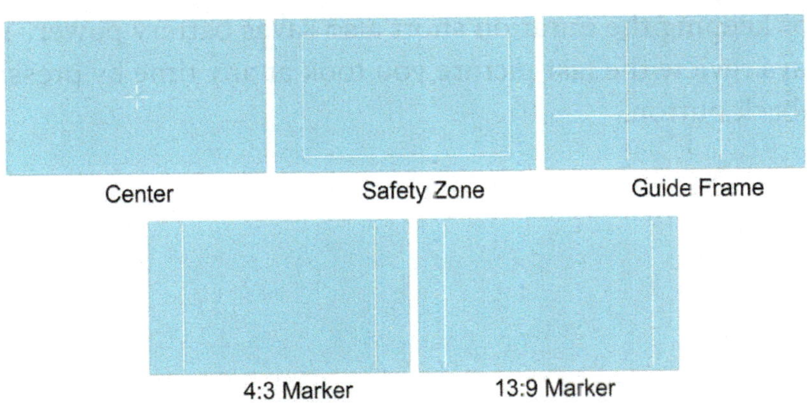

Figure 4.5

Video guide markers.

Auto Review

- **Options:** Off, 2 sec., 5 sec., 10 sec.
- **Default:** 2 sec.
- **My preference:** 10 sec.

When this item is set to 2, 5, or 10 seconds, the camera can display an image on the LCD or viewfinder for your review immediately after the photo is taken. (When you shoot a continuous or bracketed set of images, only the last picture that's been recorded will be shown.) During this display, you can delete a disappointing shot by pressing the Delete button, or cancel picture review by tapping the shutter release button or performing another function. (You'll never be prevented from taking another picture because you were reviewing images.) This option can be used to specify whether the review image appears for 2, 5, or 10 seconds, or not at all.

Depending on how you're working, you might want a brief display or you might prefer to have time for a more leisurely examination (when you're carefully checking compositions). Other times, you might not want to have the review image displayed at all, such as when you're taking photos in a darkened theater or concert venue, and the constant flashing of images might be distracting to others. (I find the silent electronic shutter and disabling image review especially helpful at acoustic concerts and plays.) Turning off picture review or keeping the duration short also saves battery power. You can always review the last picture you took at any time by pressing the Playback button.

DISP Button

- **Options (Monitor):** Graphic Display, Display All Info., No Disp. Info., Level, Histogram, For Viewfinder
- **Options (Viewfinder):** Graphic Display, Display All Info., No Disp. Info., Level, Histogram
- **Default:** Graphic Display, Display All Info., No Disp. Info.
- **My preference:** Activate all but Graphic Display

Use this item to specify which of the available display options will -- and will not -- be available in Shooting mode when you use the LCD or viewfinder and press the DISP button to cycle through the various displays. Choose from Monitor or Viewfinder and mark or unmark the screens you want to enable or disable. The Monitor selection (see **Figure 4.6**, left) includes a For Viewfinder option that displays a text/graphic display of your current settings on the back-panel LCD. (See **Figure 4.7**.)

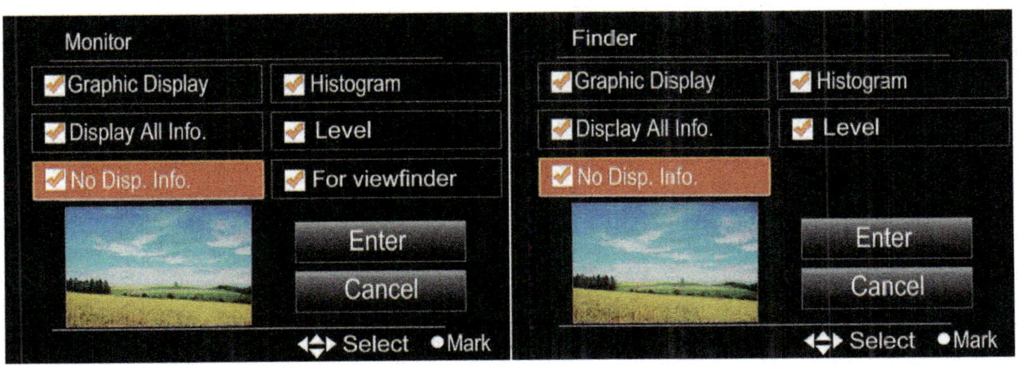

Figure 4.6

Select which display screens are shown on the LCD monitor (left) or viewfinder (right).

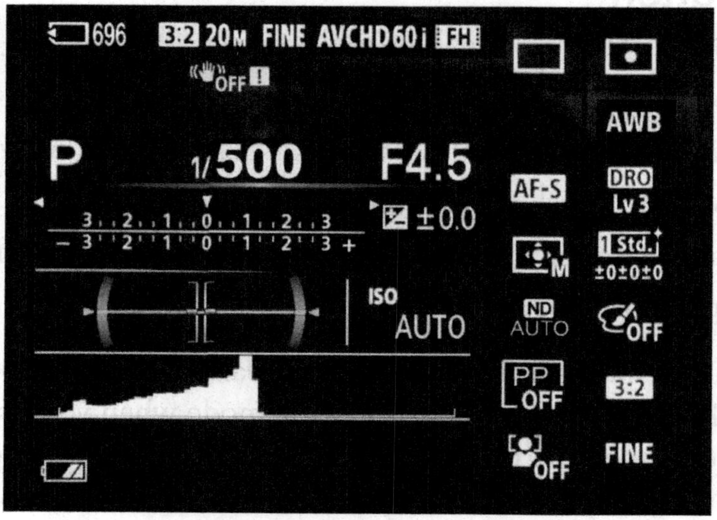

Figure 4.7
For Viewfinder Display.

You can use this menu item to deselect one or more of the display options so it/they will never appear on the LCD when you press the DISP button. To make that change, scroll to an option and press the center button to remove the check mark beside it. Naturally, at least one display option must remain selected. If you de-select all of them, the camera will warn you about this and it will not return to Shooting mode until you add a check mark to one of the options. If you turn the camera off while none are selected, the camera will interpret this as a Cancel command and return to your most recent display settings.

The same screens (other than For Viewfinder) are shown in the electronic viewfinder with slight differences. At the bottom of the viewfinder version is an analog exposure indicator; and the viewfinder/monitor displays can be different. That is, you can choose to view the Graphic Display in the EVF, and Display All Info on the LCD monitor. Here's a recap of the available display options for the monitor.

- **For Viewfinder.** This display can be shown only on the LCD monitor. When visible, you can press the Fn button to produce the Quick Navi screen, which I explained in Chapter 2.

- **Graphic Display.** When selected, this display shows basic shooting information, plus a graphic display of shutter speed and aperture (except when Sweep Panorama is the mode in use). If you learn how to interpret it, you'll note that it indicates that a fast shutter speed will freeze motion, that a small aperture (large f/number) will provide a great range of acceptably sharp focus, and other information of this type. (See **Figure 4.8**, upper left.)
- **Display All Info.** The default screen when you first turn the camera on, this option displays data about current settings for a complete overview of recording information. (See **Figure 4.8**, upper right.) Not all of the information in the figure may be displayed at one time, and there are additional icons not shown because they occupy the same space on the screen as another indicator.
- **No Disp. Info.** In spite of its name, this display option provides the basic shooting information as to settings, in a conventional size. (See **Figure 4.8**, lower left.)
- **Histogram.** Activate this option if you want to be able to view a live luminance histogram to assist you in evaluating the exposure before taking a photo, a feature to be discussed in Chapter 9. The basic shooting data will appear in addition to the histogram. (See **Figure 4.8**, lower right.)
- **Level.** This display shows how much the camera is rotated around the lens axis (horizontal tilt) as well as how far it is tilted forward and backward. When the camera is not perfectly level, orange indicators show the amount of forward/backward and horizontal tilt. (See **Figure 4.9**, left.) When the camera is level in both directions, the indicators turn green. (**Figure 4.9**, right.)

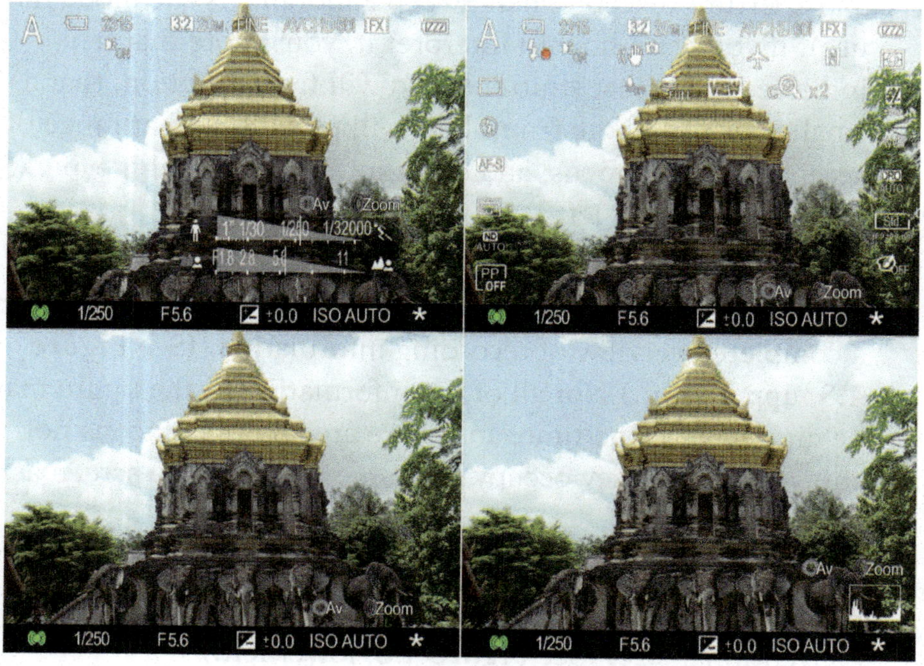

Figure 4.8

Informational displays.

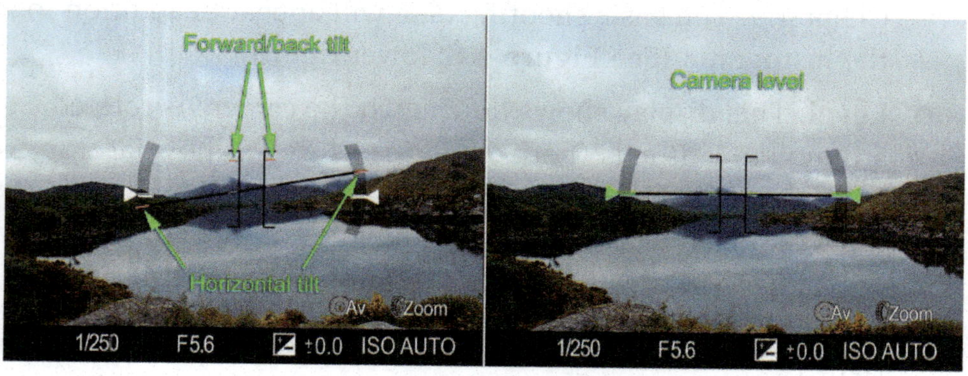

Figure 4.9

Orange indicators show the amount of tilt (left.) When the camera is level, the indicators turn green (right.)

Peaking Level

- **Options:** High, Mid, Low, Off
- **Default:** Off
- **My preference:** High

This is a useful manual focusing aid (available only when focusing in Manual and Direct Manual modes) that's difficult to describe and to illustrate. You're going to have to try this feature for yourself to see exactly what it does. *Focus peaking* is a technique that outlines the area in sharpest focus with a color; as discussed below, that can be red, white, or yellow. The colored area shows you at a glance what will be very sharp if you take the photo at that moment. If you're not satisfied, simply change the focused distance (with manual focus). As the focus gets closer to ideal for a specific part of the image, the color outline develops around hard edges that are in focus. You can choose how much peaking is applied (High, Medium, and Low), or turn the feature off.

Peaking Color

- **Options:** White, Red, Yellow
- **Default:** White
- **My preference:** N/A

Peaking Color allows you to specify which color is used to indicate peaking when you use manual focus. White is the default value, but if that color doesn't provide enough contrast with a similarly hued subject, you can switch to a more contrasting color, such as red or yellow. (See **Figure 4.10** for an example using a snake.)

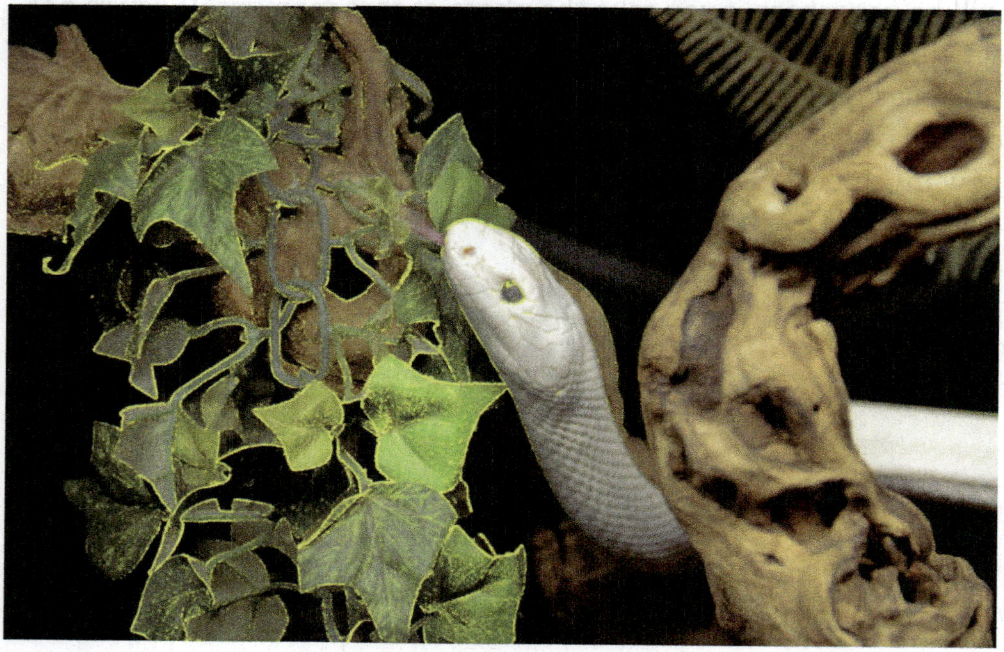

Figure 4.10

You can choose any of three colors for peaking color (for manual focus), but only if you have activated the Peaking Level item. For this white snake, yellow was a better choice than red or white.

Exposure Settings Guide

- **Options:** On, Off
- **Default:** On
- **My preference:** On

This is the first entry in the Custom Settings 3 menu (see **Figure 4.11**). This feature is of most use to those with poor eyesight, but a convenience for all. All it does is show a scrolling scale on the LCD or viewfinder with an enlarged rendition of the current shutter speed or aperture highlighted in orange. It more or less duplicates the display of both that already appears on the bottom line of the screen, but in a larger font and with the next/previous setting flanking the current value. In Aperture Priority mode, the scale shows f/stops. In Shutter Priority mode, you see shutter speeds. In Program mode, both are visible. When using Manual exposure, a single scrolling line appears showing shutter speed *or* aperture. You can toggle between setting shutter speed or aperture by pressing the down directional button. I like to leave it switched on, as the display is a reminder of which parameter I'm fooling with at the moment.

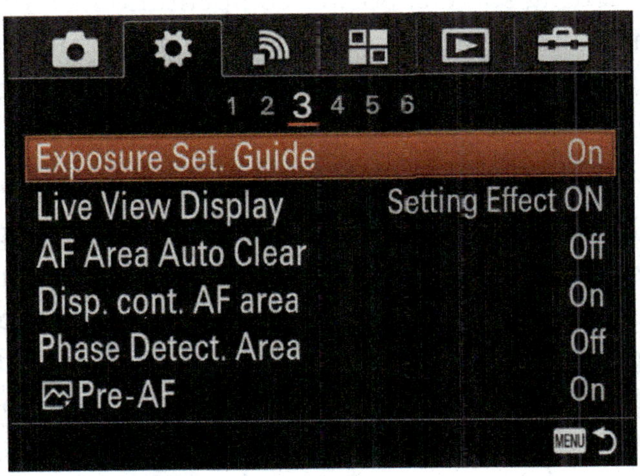

Figure 4.11

The Custom Settings 3 menu.

Live View Display

- **Options:** Setting Effect ON, Setting Effect OFF
- **Default:** Setting Effect ON
- **My preference:** Setting Effect ON

The RX100 V is always in a "live view" mode, showing you what the sensor sees. This entry lets you specify whether the camera should apply any exposure settings or effects that you've selected to the image before presenting it to you as a preview.

When Setting Effects are active, the live view display in the EVF or the LCD reflects the *exact* effects of any camera features that you're using to modify the view, including as exposure compensation and white balance. In that mode, this allows for an accurate evaluation of what the photo will look like and enables you to determine whether the current settings will provide the effects you want.

The ON option can be especially helpful when you're using any of the Picture Effects, because you can preview the exact rendition that the selected effect and its overrides will provide. It's also very useful when you're setting some exposure compensation, as you can visually determine how much lighter or darker each adjustment makes the image. And when you're trying to achieve correct color balance, it's useful to be able to preview the effect of your white balance setting.

I leave this setting On virtually all the time. The only time I turn it off is when I am using the camera's built-in flash to trigger studio strobes set to slave mode, which is a highly unusual scenario, at best, as this camera doesn't have any sort of wireless flash mode. If I do need to trigger a studio flash, I set Flash Compensation to -3, in which case the burst is so feeble it will not contribute to the exposure when "in competition" with the studio flash. Then, I set the optical slave triggers on the studio strobes to their "digital" position, so they activate only when the RX100 V's main flash (not the pre-flash) is emitted, assuming the camera's reduced flash output is strong enough for the slave to detect it and fire. In such situations, I'll be shooting in Manual exposure mode, and will have the aperture set to f/11, possibly with the ND filter enabled (because the studio flash are so bright). In such cases, when Setting Effect is set to ON, the camera will show you a preview based on the ambient light, rather than the flash. The result? Your viewfinder or LCD monitor image is very, very dim. You'll want to select Setting Effect OFF so the camera will boost the electronic image to viewable levels. Most of us with access to studio flash will be using another camera rather than the RX100 V in such situations.

If there is some other reason why you'd like to preview the image without the effect of settings visible, you can set this feature to OFF. Naturally, the display will no longer accurately depict what your photo will look like when it's taken. So, for most users, ON is the most suitable option.

Display Continuous AF Area

- **Options**: On, Off
- **Default**: On
- **My preference**: On

This item determines whether the previewing display on the monitor or EVF shows the active Wide or Zone focus areas when you're using Continuous AF. It has no effect on their display if you're using Center or Flexible Spot in Continuous AF area modes, or autofocus modes other than AF-C.

Sometimes too much information can be distracting. In Wide mode, you may be treated to a dancing array of green rectangles squirming around on your screen as the camera focuses and refocuses in anticipation of you eventually pressing the shutter release all the way down and taking a picture. I think that the constantly shifting focus requires less continual feedback about what focus areas are being used, so you may want to switch the feature off. In my case, I don't mind the display, and I tend to leave it on most of the time, even though it consumes a little more battery power.

Phase Detect. Area

- **Options:** On, Off
- **Default:** On
- **My preference:** On

The RX100 V has 315 phase detection points embedded in its sensor, as I'll describe in detail in Chapter 8. This entry allows you to enable or disable *display* of the phase detect points on the viewing screen. The area is not shown when the camera is shooting movies.

AF Area Auto Clear

- Options: Off, On
- Default: Off
- My preference: On

Determines whether the focus areas are on display full-time, or whether they should vanish automatically after focus is achieved, giving you a clean frame on which to compose your image. I use the DISP. button to hide most of the information anyway, and this option provides an even more unobstructed view of my subject.

Pre-AF (Still Image)

- **Options**: Off, On
- **Default**: Off
- **My preference**: Off

This setting tells the camera to attempt to adjust the focus even before you press the shutter button halfway, giving you a head start that's useful for grab shots. When an image you want to capture appears, you can press the shutter release and take the picture a bit more quickly. However, this pre-focus process uses a lot of juice, depleting your battery more quickly, which is why it is turned off by default. Reserve it for short-term use during quickly unfolding situations where the slight advantage can be useful. I use it for sessions when I am photographing younger children or pets who are in constant movement. Having the camera already calculating focus can be an advantage.

Zoom Speed

- **Options:** Normal, Fast
- **Default**: Normal
- **My preference**: Normal

This entry, the first in the Custom Settings 4 menu (shown in **Figure 4.12**), allows you to specify how quickly the camera will zoom while shooting movies. Zoom speed during still photograph is not affected. That's because how quickly the camera zooms is really relevant only when capturing video. Having to wait an extra second while preparing to shoot a still photograph is no big deal, but when the camera is "rolling" or about to "roll" in a video shoot, the pace of the zoom can be important. For example, if you're zooming in on a landscape scene you might want to use a slow zoom (which is quieter, more subtle, and less abrupt). Use the Normal setting for that. The Fast setting increases your chances of recording the zoom motor's noise during movie making.

On the other hand, if you're shooting a parody of a kung-fu movie, you might want to use a fast zoom to zero in on a fighter's face when he (or she, in this Ronda Rousey era) reacts to an impending spear thrust. The Fast setting can come in handy. In typical Sony fashion, the choice of *type* of zoom is the next entry in the menu, but the setting for determining which physical control *activates* the zoom and *how quickly* it zooms are tucked away in the Custom Settings 5 menu near the end of this chapter.

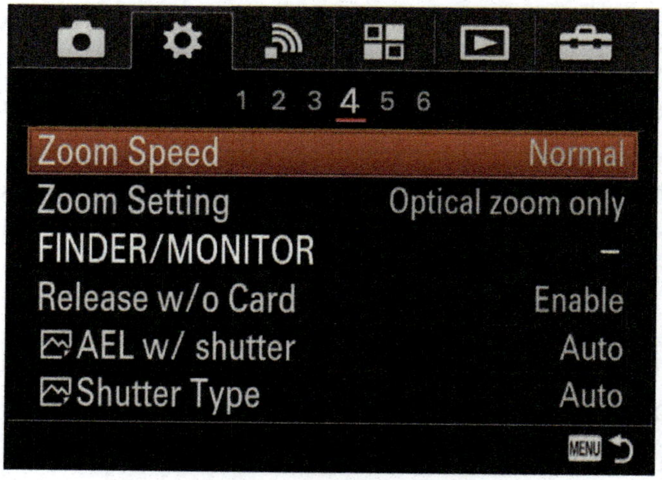

Figure 4.12

Custom Settings 4 menu.

Zoom Setting

- **Options:** Optical Zoom Only, Clear Image Zoom, Digital Zoom
- **Default:** Optical Zoom Only
- **My preference:** Optical Zoom Only

The RX100 V has three different types of zoom settings: Optical Zoom, Clear Image Zoom, and Digital Zoom, and you can choose any *one* of them here. My preference is to stick with optical zoom only, as it provides the best overall results, even though the zoom range is limited to the equivalent of 24-70mm. Neither Clear Image nor Digital Zoom give me the image quality I am looking for. However, if you don't need the best quality for some applications, the two electronic zoom modes are available.

My basic recommendation is to use optical zoom only most of the time for still photographs and then crop to your precise requirements in your image editor. (The Digital Zoom setting does produce results most would find acceptable, however.) Most of us don't have that option when shooting movies, however, and the digital zooming options may indeed be your best choice. As noted elsewhere in this book, each frame of a movie is viewed only for a fraction of a second, so the loss of sharpness caused by digital zoom may not even be noticeable.

ZOOM CONTROLS

The RX100 V has three physical control options that can be used to zoom in and out, as shown in **Figure 4.13**.

- **Control Ring.** The ring around the lens does not zoom by default (except in either Auto mode), but you can use the Custom Keys feature described later in this chapter to redefine it to smoothly zoom in and out as you rotate the ring. You can further refine its operation to zoom more quickly or in step increments, using the Zoom Function on Ring option also described. These options give you greater control over how the zoom behaves.
- **Zoom lever.** The swiveling lever located concentric to the shutter release can be used to zoom from W (wide) to T (tele) using a speed (Normal or Fast) that you specify in the Zoom Speed entry discussed previously.
- **RM-VPR1 remote.** This wired remote comes with two cables, including one that plugs into the RX100 V's multi-terminal port. It has a W/T switch that allows zooming. A key advantage of this control is that it isn't necessary to touch the camera to zoom, to stop/start movie making, or take a still photograph while capturing video. The zoom switch is flanked by a Movie button with the red dot below, and a shutter release button above. If the camera is

mounted on a tripod, the RM-VPR1 remote is an ideal tool for controlling zoom and capture.

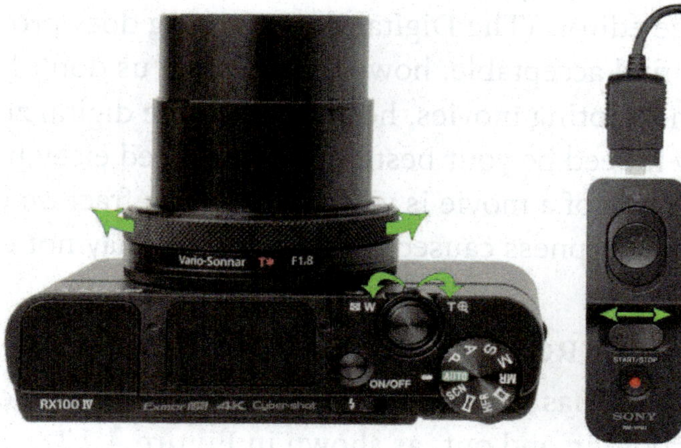

Figure 4.13

Three possible zoom controls.

Of course, you can always shoot *without* the electronic zoom features and crop to the effective magnification you want in your image editor. Clear Image Zoom and Digital Zoom are not available when using Sweep Panorama, Lock-on AF, Auto Object Framing, or Face Detection/Smile Shutter, or when Image Quality is set to RAW or RAW & JPEG. Electronic zooming works fine in Intelligent Auto and Superior Auto modes, but neither mode will try to examine the frame and switch to an appropriate scene mode. When working with those ersatz zooms, the metering mode is locked at Multi, and Focus Area setting is disabled (instead, the focus area frame in the zoomed image is shown by a dotted line).

Sony has made use of digital zoom more confusing than it needs to be, because the RX100 V offers two digital zoom options, Clear Image Zoom and Digital Zoom, *plus* a third type -- Smart Zoom -- that doesn't appear on any menu, but which nevertheless is activated when Image Size is set to Medium or Small. **Figure 4.14** shows the zoom bar that appears when using optical and digital zooming and the zoom lever; when using the control ring to zoom, an arc appears at the upper center of the screen with similar indicators. The four types of zooming are as follows:

- **Optical Zoom Only.** Use the control ring (if defined as a zoom control), zoom lever, or RM-VPR1 remote to zoom in and out between 24mm and 70mm settings. Optical zoom is available at any Quality Setting, including RAW and RAW & JPEG. However, if you switch from Large to Medium, Small or VGA Image Size settings (VGA is available only with the 4:3 Aspect Ratio, as described in Chapter 3), Smart Zoom kicks in, giving you the magnifications shown in **Table 4.1**. As a result, *Optical Zoom Only* actually means *Optical Zoom Mostly*.
- **Clear Image Zoom.** When using this option, some quality is lost, as this kind of zooming doesn't produce any actual additional information; it just *interpolates* the pixels captured optically to simulate a zoomed-in perspective in the range 1.1X to 2X when Image Size is set to Large. Pixels are created to fill the frame with the zoomed image. The magnifications possible with Medium, Small, and VGA Image Sizes are listed in the table.
- **Digital Zoom.** This option gives you even higher magnifications than Clear Image Zoom, with an additional decrease in image quality. This mode uses optical zoom up to 24mm, then switches to Clear Image Zoom for 1.1 to 2.0X magnifications, and kicks in as Digital Zoom from 2.1 to 4.0X magnifications. The additional magnifications available in Medium, Small, and VGA Image Sizes are listed in the table.
- **Smart Zoom.** Smart Zoom isn't selectable from a menu. It automatically becomes available when you have set the camera to M (medium), S (small), or VGA Image Size, and is used in Optical Zoom Only, Clear Image Zoom, and Digital Zoom modes. It provides a limited amount of zooming, but, technically, requires no quality-reducing interpolation. The camera simply produces each "zoomed" image by cropping the

photo to the resolution of the Medium, Small, or VGA Image Size.

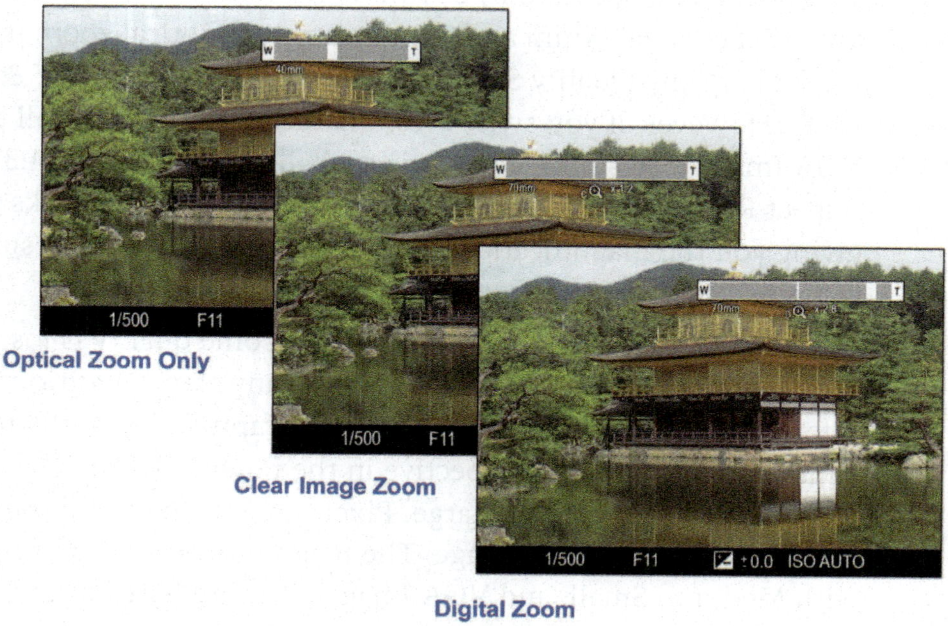

Figure 4.14

The zoom scale shows the amount of magnification and type of zoom in use.

Table 4.1 Zoom Settings

Zoom Setting	Large	Medium	Small	VGA (w/ 4:3 Aspect Ratio)
Optical Zoom Only	24-70mm zoom	24-70mm zoom 1.1X-1.4X Smart Zoom	24-70mm zoom 1.1X-2.0X Smart Zoom	24-70mm zoom 1.1X-7.6X Smart Zoom
Clear Image Zoom	24-70mm zoom 1.1X-2X Clear Image Zoom	24-70mm zoom 1.1X-1.4X Smart Zoom 1.5X-2.8X Clear Image Zoom	24-70mm zoom 1.1X-2.0X Smart Zoom 2.1X-4.0X Clear Image Zoom	24-70mm zoom 1.1X-15X Smart Zoom 2.1X-4.0X Clear Image Zoom
Digital Zoom	24-70mm zoom 1.1X-2.0X Clear Image Zoom 2.1X-4.0X Digital Zoom	24-70mm zoom 1.1X-1.4X Smart Zoom 1.5X-2.8X Clear Image Zoom 2.9X-5.6X Digital Zoom	24-70mm zoom 1.1X-2.0X Smart Zoom 2.1X-4.0X Clear Image Zoom 4.1X-8.0X Digital Zoom	24-70mm zoom 1.1X-7.5X Smart Zoom 7.6X-15X Clear Image Zoom

FINDER/MONITOR

- **Options:** Auto, Viewfinder, Monitor
- **Default**: Auto
- **My preference**: N/A

This option uses the infrared eye sensor located to the right of the viewfinder window, and controls whether the camera turns off the LCD and switches the view to the viewfinder when your eye comes near the EVF. With the default setting of Auto, the screen goes blank and the viewfinder activates when your eye (or any other object) approaches the viewfinder.

Switch to the Viewfinder or Monitor options and the eye sensors no longer initiate a switch from one display to the other. The display is then *always* sent to the viewing device you selected, and the other one is turned off. You might want to use the Monitor option if you are doing work involving critical focusing using the LCD, and as you examine the screen closely, your face will frequently be close to the back of the camera where the Eye-Start sensor might detect it. Or, perhaps, you are shooting at a concert or other venue where the bright LCD can be distracting to others. Choose Viewfinder, and the shooting preview, menus, photos displayed for review during playback, and so forth will be shown only in the EVF.

Of course, if you disable automatic switching between the two, you still might want to have the option of activating the viewfinder or monitor displays manually. To do that, after a fashion, you'll need to assign the FINDER/MONITOR switching function to a key. I'll show you how to do that later in this chapter, when I describe the Custom Key option in the Custom Settings 5 menu. The correct behavior has the unfortunate name Deactivate Monitor, when it actually toggles between the EVF and the LCD monitor. (It also leaves the monitor's backlight illuminated, changes to Setting Effect OFF, and switches the screen display to No. Disp. Info.).

Release w/o Card

- **Options:** Disable, Enable
- **Default:** Disable
- **My preference:** Disable

The ability to trip the shutter without having a memory card installed is not especially useful, unless you want to hand your camera to someone for demonstration purposes and do not want to give them the capability of actually taking a picture. This happens frequently at trade shows, where vendors want you to try out their equipment, but would prefer you not leave the premises with any evidence/image samples, especially if the memory card in question belongs to the vendor rather than you.

On the contrary, it's more likely that you'd prefer to have your own camera inoperable if you've forgotten to insert a memory card. It's easy to miss the orange No Card warning that flashes when the non-picture is taken. Disabling release when a card is absent can help you avoid losing a card (you removed it to load some pictures onto someone else's computer) or having to sheepishly ask the bride and groom if they would be willing to re-stage their wedding.

AEL w/Shutter (Still Image)

- **Options:** On, Off
- **Default:** On
- **My preference:** N/A

This item is On by default so the RX100 V can lock the exposure (as well as the focus in AF-S mode) when you apply light pressure to the shutter release button. Point the camera at your primary subject, and maintain contact with the button while re-framing for a better composition. This technique will ensure that both focus and exposure are optimized for the primary subject.

Set this item to Off and light pressure on the shutter release button will lock only focus, and not the exposure. After choosing Off, you'll need to depress a defined AEL button (I'll show you how to assign that behavior later in this Custom Settings section) when you want to lock the exposure. (Light pressure on the shutter release button will still lock focus.) The only method for locking the exposure will be to press the AEL button you have set up.

You might want to choose the Off option because this will allow you to lock focus on one subject in the scene while locking the exposure for an entirely different part of the scene. To use this technique, focus on the most important subject and keep the focus locked by keeping your finger on the shutter release button while you recompose. You can then point the lens at an entirely different area of the scene to read the exposure, and lock in the exposure with pressure on the AEL button you've defined using the Custom Key Settings option in the Custom Settings 5 menu. Finally, reframe for the most pleasing composition and take the photo.

In your image, the primary subject will be in sharpest focus while the exposure will be optimized for the area that you metered. This technique makes the most sense when your primary subject is very light in tone like a snowman or very dark in tone like a black Lab dog. Subjects of that type can lead to exposure errors, so you might want to expose for an area that's a middle tone, such as grass. I'll discuss exposure in detail in Chapter 7; then, the value of this menu option will be more apparent.

Shutter Type (Still Image)

- **Options:** Auto, Electronic Shutter, Mechanical Shutter
- **Default:** Auto
- **My preference:** It depends on the scene.

Your RX100 V has two shutters and this entry allows you to choose between them. Tucked inside your camera is a high-precision leaf shutter located inside the lens itself (with speeds from 30 seconds to 1/2000th second, plus Bulb, which is available in Manual exposure mode) and a virtual shutter that performs a similar function electronically (and which provides shutter speeds from 30 seconds to 1/32000th second.

The mechanical shutter is capable of opening very quickly and remaining open for the entire exposure, which means the RX100 V's pop-up electronic flash can synchronize at any shutter speed up to and including 1/2000th second. If you've used cameras that have a *focal plane* shutter, you know that flash exposures can only take place when both curtains of the shutter are completely open, which generally limits flash sync to 1/250th second or slower. Faster sync speeds reduce the amount of ambient (non-flash) light reaching the sensor, thereby minimizing the "ghost" effects that can take place when both flash and ambient exposures of a moving subject are recorded. (The flash exposure takes place in an instant, but the ambient light is captured for the full duration of the exposure, even when the subject is moving.)

The electronic shutter has, as you'd expect, no moving parts. Instead of covering the sensor for a moment while the live view image is "dumped" (which must be done with the mechanical shutter), the electronic shutter erases the old image and then is immediately able to begin recording the exposure. At the end of the exposure time, the electronic shutter simply stops capturing photons, stores the image on your memory card, and returns the RX100 V to its live view preview.

You can choose one type or the other here, or select the Auto setting, and allow the camera to decide which type of shutter to use. Here are some additional differences between the two:

- **Mechanical shutter.** The physical shutter is inherently louder, but not by much. Indeed, the sound emitted by the mechanical shutter alone is so soft that, by default, Sony *adds* an electronic shutter sound to provide a healthy click and feedback as you take a picture. If you venture to the Audio Signals entry in the Setup 1 menu (described in Chapter 6), you can switch from the default On to Shutter (only, thus silencing other beeps and chortles), or Off, which deactivates all sounds. When set to Off, only the meekest click can be heard.
- **Electronic shutter.** The virtual shutter produces no sound at all, which can be spooky, but can be remedied by turning on

the shutter sound in the Audio Signals entry. Because the electronic shutter captures an image one row at a time, flash sync is limited to 1/100th second. Because it has speeds up to 1/32000th second, the electronic shutter is excellent in bright environments, such as beach and snow scenes, or when you want the fastest possible frame rates in Continuous shooting and Speed Priority Continuous modes. (Indeed, it is the electronic shutter than makes the camera's faster frame rates for slow motion, and HFR mode for super slow motion possible.)

The electronic shutter has the potential of distorting the image when panning, and Sony recommends switching to the mechanical shutter in such cases. The symptoms you're likely to notice include vertical lines that seem to "lean" and round objects that become elliptical. Flickering lights, including fluorescents and the lighting in many gymnasiums, can produce unsightly banding.

Note that if you are using the electronic shutter and are using Face Registration to record new faces, or trying to capture an image to use for a custom white balance, the RX100 V will switch to the mechanical shutter. The electronic shutter is not available when using Long Exposure noise reduction, and may be deactivated by some PlayMemories apps (discussed in Chapter 5).

Self-Portrait Timer

- **Options:** On, Off
- **Default:** On
- **My preference:** N/A

This is the first entry in the Custom Settings 5 menu. (See **Figure 4.15**.) With its flip-up, reversible LCD monitor, the RX100 V is ideal for shooting selfies in both still and movie modes. The camera reverses the image so the preview looks like what you see in a mirror, rather than what will actually be recorded. (It can be lousy to see ourselves as others see us.)*

** You may need to brush up on your Robert Burns to appreciate this.*

However, the camera also activates a three-second self-timer for still photos, which can be useful most of the time, but not when you're trying to catch the famous movie star you're standing next to off-guard. Turn the timer off, and your selfie will be captured as soon as you press the shutter release.

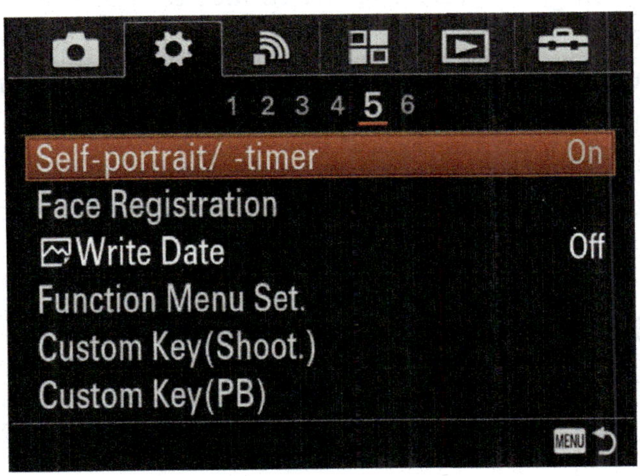

Figure 4.15
Custom Settings 5 menu.

Face Registration

- **Options:** New Registration, Order Exchanging, Delete, Delete All
- **Default:** None
- **My preference:** N/A

This menu entry is used to log into your camera's Face Detection memory the visages of those you photograph often. New Registration allows you to log up to eight different faces. Line up your victim (subject) against a brightly lit background to allow easier detection of the face. A white box appears that you can use to frame the face. Press the shutter button. A confirmation message appears (or a Shoot Again warning suggests you try another time). When Register Face? appears, choose Enter or Cancel, and press the MENU button to confirm.

The Order Exchanging option allows you to review and change the priority in which the faces appear, from 1 to 8. The RX100 V will use your priority setting to determine which face to focus on if several registered faces are detected in a scene. You can also select a specific face and delete it from the registry (say, you broke up with your significant other!) or delete *all* faces from the registry (your SO got custody of the camera). Face data remains in the camera when you delete individual faces, but is totally erased when you select Delete All.

Write Date (Still Image)

- **Options:** On, Off
- **Default:** Off
- **My preference:** Off

This entry tells the camera to superimpose a small date overlay in orange in the lower-right corner of the image. The camera is smart enough to know the orientation of the camera when the picture was taken (horizontal, vertical, upside down) and select the actual lower-right corner. Some like to include this marker as a reminder of when the picture was taken. Here are a couple things to keep in mind:

- Once an image has been taken with the date overlay, it cannot be removed, except through retouching, or cropping it out, which may or may not be practical, depending on the image.
- Only the date, and not the time the image was taken will be overlaid, and if you have the date set incorrectly in your camera, the wrong information will be overlaid on your image.
- If all you want is to keep track of when the picture was taken, that information is embedded in the image file, and can be retrieved by most image editors, catalog programs, and utilities that interpret EXIF data. This is assuming, once again, you have the correct time set in your camera.
- When you print your images using the Date Imprint option in the Specify Printing entry in the Playback 2 menu (described in Chapter 6), your printed photo will have the date printed twice.
- The Write Date feature cannot be used to overlay the date on a RAW image, nor on the JPEG version if you're shooting RAW & JPEG. It's also disabled when shooting in continuous drive modes.

Function Menu Settings

- **Options:** 34 different Function menu settings
- **Default**: Top row: Drive Mode, Flash Mode, Focus Mode, Focus Area, Exposure Compensation, ISO setting. Bottom row: ND Filter, Metering Mode, White Balance, DRO/Auto HDR, Creative Style, Shoot Mode
- **My preference**: N/A

When you press the Fn button, a screen like the one shown in **Figure 4.16**, left pops up, with six settings each in two rows arrayed along the bottom. The default options are illustrated. This entry allows you to change the function of any of the 12 positions in the Function menu, so you can display only those you use most, and arrange them in the order that best suits you. There are 34 different functions available. Browse through the list below, and decide which 12 you want to display on the Function menu.

- Drive Mode
- Self-Timer During Bracket
- Flash Mode
- Flash Comp.
- Focus Mode
- Focus Area
- Exposure Comp.
- ISO
- ISO Auto Minimum Shutter Speed
- ND Filter
- Metering Mode
- White Balance
- DRO/Auto HDR
- Creative Style
- Shoot Mode
- Picture Effect
- Picture Profile
- HFR Frame Rate
- Center Lock-on AF
- Smile/Face Detect
- Auto Dual Record
- Soft Skin Effect
- Auto Obj. Framing
- Image Size
- Aspect Ratio
- Quality
- SteadyShot (Still Image)
- SteadyShot (Movie)
- Zebra
- Grid Line
- Marker Display
- Peaking Level
- Peaking Color
- Gamma Display Assist
- Not Set

When you highlight Function Menu Set. and press OK, the first of two screens appears, as shown in **Figure 4.16**, right. The screen has an entry for each of the positions in the top row, along with the current function (the second screen shows the positions in the bottom row). Highlight the position you want to modify and press OK. You can then select from among these options, all explained in detail elsewhere in this book:

Note that you can select Not Set to leave a position blank if you want to unclutter your screen, or even duplicate an entry in multiple positions, accidentally or on purpose.

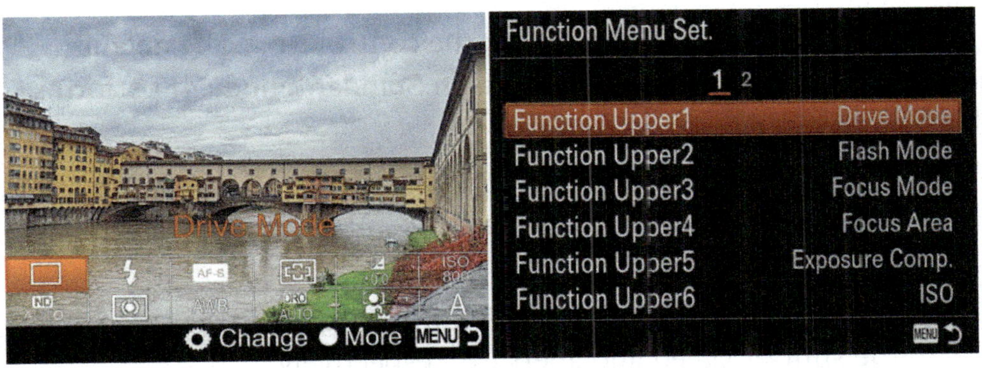

Figure 4.16

Function menu default settings (left.) Function menu settings (right.)

Custom Key Settings (Shoot)

- **Options:** Up to 50 different definitions for Control Ring, C Button, Center Button, Left Button, Right Button
- **Default:** Various
- **My preference:** N/A

This entry allows further customization of as many as five controls on the camera. The number of behaviors for each control varies depending on which you want to re-define. Your custom key definitions override any default definitions for those buttons when in Shooting mode; they retain their original functions in Playback mode.

Because button definition is such a personal choice, I steer away from recommending particular definitions for each of the buttons.

When assigning definitions to keys, keep in mind that certain behaviors can be used *only* you have made them available using a custom key definition. For example, if you want to use the Bright Monitoring feature, which temporarily turns the Live View Setting Effect to Off to increase the brightness level of the screen in dark locations, you must assign it to a key. Eye-AF and Deactivate Monitor are other functions not available unless assigned to a button.

Control Ring Functions

These functions are available for the control ring. The default setting is Standard. When the ring is in Standard mode, it performs the following functions in these modes:

- **Program Auto mode.** Rotating the ring changes shutter speed and aperture to produce different combinations of equivalent exposure, as described in Chapter 7.
- **Shutter Priority/Aperture Priority.** Rotating the ring adjusts the shutter speed and aperture, respectively.
- **Manual exposure.** Rotating the ring adjusts the aperture; the control *wheel* adjusts the shutter speed.
- **Scene mode.** Rotating the ring selects any of the scene modes, essentially duplicating the function of the control wheel.
- **Intelligent Auto/Superior Auto.** Rotating the ring zooms the lens in and out, duplicating the function of the zoom lever.
- **Sweep Panorama.** The ring changes the direction of the panorama, among left/right/up/down.
- **HFR/Movie modes.** After you've selected P, A, S, or M exposure modes for either, the control ring functions as described for Program Auto, Aperture Priority, Shutter Priority, or Manual exposure modes.

- **Manual Focus/Direct Manual Focus modes.** Instead of the behaviors described above, the control ring adjusts or fine-tunes focus.

In addition to Standard and Not Set, you can also assign any of the additional eight functions listed below to the control ring. Note that if you assign shutter speed to the ring, it will duplicate the function of the control wheel in Manual exposure mode. I sometimes use Zoom to allow smoother zooming during movie shooting.

- Standard
- Exposure Comp.
- ISO
- White Balance
- Creative Style
- Picture Effect
- Zoom
- Shutter Speed
- Aperture
- Not Set

C Button, Center Button, Left/Right Button Functions

These functions are available for the other definable buttons on the RX100 V. Note that not all functions are available for all controls. The list below includes behaviors that are all available for use with the C Button, Center Button, Left Button, and Right Button.

- Drive Mode
- Self-timer during Bracket
- Flash Mode
- Flash Comp.
- Focus Mode
- Focus Area
- Exposure Comp.
- ISO
- ISO Auto Minimum Shutter Speed
- ND Filter
- Metering Mode
- White Balance
- DRO/Auto HDR
- Creative Style
- Picture Effect
- Picture Profile
- HFR Frame Rate
- Smile/Face Detect
- Auto Dual Record
- Soft Skin Effect
- Auto Obj. Framing
- SteadyShot (Still Image)
- Steady Shot (Movie)
- Image Size
- Aspect Ratio
- Quality
- Memory
- AEL Toggle
- Center AEL Toggle
- AF/MF Control Toggle
- Center Lock-On AF
- Bright Monitoring
- Focus Magnifier
- Deactivate Monitor
- MOVIE
- Zebra
- Grid Line
- Marker Display Selection
- Peaking Level
- Peaking Color
- Send to Smartphone
- Download Application
- Application List
- Monitor Brightness
- TC/UB Display
- Not Set

There are additional behaviors for the C and Center buttons. **Table 4.2** shows the defaults and extra behaviors for the buttons.

Table 4.2
Control Options

Control	Default	Additional Behaviors
C Button	In-Camera Guide	In Camera Guide, Center AEL Hold, AF/MF Control Hold, and Eye AF.
Center Button	Standard	AEL Hold, Center AEL Hold, AF/MF Control Hold, and Eye AF.
Left Button	Drive Mode	None
Right Button	Flash Mode	None

Custom Key Settings (Playback)

- **Options:** 11 different definitions for the Fn/Send to Smartphone button during Playback
- **Default**: Send to Smartphone
- **My preference**: Enlarge Image

You can also redefine the behavior of the Fn/Send to Smartphone button *during image playback only*. The button retains its Function menu function when in shooting mode. I like having an Enlarge Image button available, because my other Sony cameras, such as my a7R II, have one. You can choose from:

- Finder/Monitor Select
- Send to Smartphone
- Download Application
- Application List
- Delete
- Image Index
- Rotate
- Enlarge Image
- Beauty Effect
- Photo Capture
- TC/UB Display Switch

Zoom Function on Ring

- **Options:** Standard, Quick, Step
- **Default**: Standard
- **My preference**: Standard

If you elect to assign the zoom feature to the control ring using the Custom Keys options just described, you can specify how you want the ring to operate. There are three choices:

- **Standard.** At this default setting, rotating the ring zooms the lens in and out smoothly. I think this is the best choice for shooting movies, because a constant zoom speed (assuming you rotate the ring at a constant speed) is less disconcerting than either of the two behaviors described next. I do feel that zooming while capturing video should be kept to a minimum.
- **Quick.** In this mode, the faster you rotate the ring, the zoom changes more quickly and zooms farther in a given period of time. I find this useful for sports photography, where you might have only a split second to zoom in (or out) to keep the action framed properly.
- **Step.** With this option, the lens will zoom in discrete steps and skip the focal lengths in between. The steps are 24mm, 28mm, 35mm, 50mm, and 70mm. This mode is useful if you want repeatable increments that you can "click" into (although no actual clicking is involved) quickly. If you select this setting, you can still access conventional smooth zooming with the zoom lever, effectively giving you two different zoom modes to choose from.

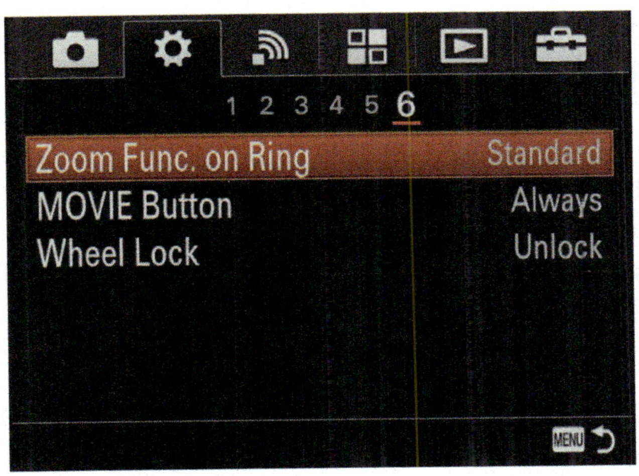

Figure 4.17

Custom Settings 6 menu.

MOVIE Button

- **Options:** Always, Movie Mode Only
- **Default:** Always
- **My preference:** Movie Mode Only

Movie recording can be started in any operating mode by pressing the Movie record button. This feature is on by default, but if you find that you occasionally press the button inadvertently (as I frequently do), you might want to choose the Movie Mode Only. After you do so, pressing the button will have no effect; when you want to record a movie, you'll need to rotate the mode dial to the Movie position. I prefer Movie Mode Only much of the time with this particular camera, because it's small size (compared to some of my other Sony cameras) makes it easy to accidentally start video capture. However, if I am intending to shoot a lot of video, or want to be prepared for impromptu video moments, I switch this button back to Always.

Wheel Lock

- **Options:** Lock, Unlock
- **Default:** Unlock
- **My preference:** Unlock

If you want to avoid accidentally changing settings by inadvertently rotating the control wheel, you can implement this locking option. Choose Lock and the dial is frozen. You can reactivate it by holding the Fn button down for about three seconds.

Chapter 5

Wi-Fi and Application Menus

Your RX100 V is equipped with a built-in Wi-Fi system that can be used for transferring files to a networked computer, a networked HDTV, or a smartphone/tablet computer. As we'll see later, there's also an option (with an app) to use the smartphone or tablet as a remote controller for the camera. The RX100 V includes both traditional Wi-Fi capabilities and, with Android devices, a newer protocol called Near Field Communications (NFC), which allows linking devices directly without an intervening network.

While basic Wi-Fi has become available with an increasing number of digital cameras, your RX100 V goes a giant step further. Once connected to a network or hotspot, you can download from a suite of sensational apps (some free; others for $4.99 or $9.99) from a Sony website for increased versatility. These apps can expand existing features with extra options or add entirely new functions. For example, one app enables you to retouch JPEGs to improve them while two others allow for direct uploading (via Wi-Fi) from the RX100 V to certain social media sites on the Internet. Most impressive of all is the Sky HDR utility that can balance a bright sky with the foregound in a variety of ways.

This chapter first provides an introduction to NFC and making Wi-Fi connections. You'll learn how to transfer photos to a computer or to a smart device. Later, I'll discuss downloading and installing apps, the available apps, and other benefits provided by the wireless connectivity available with Wi-Fi from your home network or from a Wi-Fi hotspot. These days, you can find numerous hotspots where Wi-Fi is provided (often free of charge), at restaurants, supermarkets, stores and theme parks, for example.

As the Application menu hints, the RX100 V is Wi-Fi compatible and can run apps downloaded from the Sony Entertainment app store. In fact, quite a few menu items (such as those shown in **Figure**

5.1) are relevant to the Wi-Fi feature; they're available only after you have connected the RX100 V camera to a Wi-Fi network.

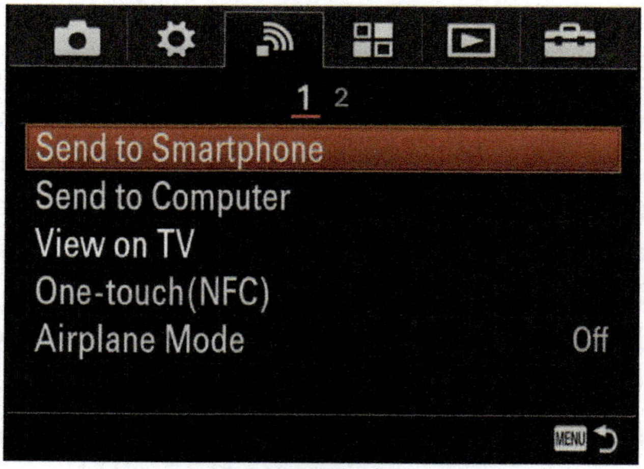

Figure 5.1

Functions in the Wireless 1 menu can be accessed once you're connected.

Although this chapter will cover the Wireless and Application menus in detail, I'm not going to explain each entry in the exact order in which it appears in the camera. Some later entries, such as Access Point Set in the Wireless 2 menu, must be accessed *first* to set up the Wi-Fi connectivity required to use *other* entries, such as "Send to Smartphone." So this chapter will take a more practical approach and describe the entries in the order that will approximate more closely your actual workflow.

Making a Wi-Fi Connection

The first step, of course, is to establish Wi-Fi connectivity. Setting up a link to a network/hotspot can be done in two different ways: manually or using a simplified alternative called WPS (Wi-Fi Protected Setup) Push. Your best bet is to start with WPS, if it's available with your router, before taking the more traditional route, described later in this chapter.

Using WPS Push

Wi-Fi Protected Setup works only when you're in range of a network provided by a wireless router that is equipped with a WPS button. Not all are. Examine your router and look for a button labeled WPS, or with a symbol. Or, find the owner's manual for your router or use a Google search (try "*routername* manual PDF") in order to locate the WPS button, if one is available. Some routers that support WPS provide it with software instead of a physical button; in that case, you'll need to access the router's control panel using a computer and click the button on the WPS page. The WPS Push tactic is great, but it would not work at a Wi-Fi hotspot in a supermarket, for instance, since the network owner is unlikely to use the WPS feature for hundreds of customers.

WHAT'S WPS?

The abbreviation WPS indicates Wi-Fi Protected Setup. This is a security standard that makes it easier and quicker to connect a device, including your RX100 V, to a wireless home network. It eliminates the need to key in the password. Because it's possible for an aggressive hacker to recover the WPS PIN number, some experts suggest turning the router's WPS feature off when you're not actually using it; this may not be possible with all router models but check the owner's manual for the one you own.

Just follow these steps:

1. **Access Wireless 2 menu.** If your router provides WPS, scroll to the WPS Push item in the camera's Wireless 2 menu and press the center button. (See **Figure 5.2**.)
2. **Press router's WPS button.** A screen will appear advising you to press the router's WPS button within 2 minutes. When you press the button (or use the software) to do so, the camera should be able to establish connectivity.
3. **Confirm registration.** Once the connection is established, a screen reporting "Registered. SSID *network name*" appears. Press the center button to confirm.

Registering Manually

You can also select an access point manually when within range of a wireless network; you'll need to know the network password, if one is in place, in order to do so. Just follow these steps:

1. **Access the Wireless 2 menu and scroll to Access Point Set.** (See **Figure 5.2.**) Press the center button. A Wi-Fi Standby screen will appear confirming that the camera is searching for available access points.
2. **Wait for the camera to find your network.** The RX100 V will find the nearby access points (networks) in less than a minute. (See **Figure 5.3**, left.) If there is more than one network or available access point, all of those found will be shown. If your smartphone has a hotspot feature and it's turned on, that "network" may appear as well.

   When several networks are displayed, some may belong to nearby businesses or your neighbors, and you can ignore them (their signal strength is probably weaker than your own network in any case, even if your neighbor's network is not protected by a password). In my case, my wireless router resides in my office; in other, more distant rooms is a wired access point, and, on the second floor, a wireless repeater. Scroll to the one you intend to use and press the center button to confirm.
3. **Input the password (if necessary).** The next screen that appears may have a field for entering your network password, if your router/access point is set up to require one. If not, proceed to Step 4. Otherwise, press the center button and a virtual keyboard will appear. Using this keyboard, enter the password for your network. The keyboard works a bit like the physical multi-tap keyboard found on some (older) cell phones. Use the directional buttons to highlight a letter group, such as abc, def, ghi, and press the center button once to enter the first character in the group, twice for the second character, three times for the third character, and four times for the

fourth. Some of the virtual keys allow you to backspace, delete characters, and toggle between uppercase and lowercase. When finished, highlight OK and press the center button.

4. **IP Address Setting.** The next screen will appear, showing the IP Address Setting as Auto and Priority Connection as Off. (See **Figure 5.3**, right.) These defaults should work perfectly. Select OK and press the center button. A screen will appear showing the camera trying to connect to the network.

   If the Auto IP Address Setting option does not work, and you have some networking expertise, change from Auto to Manual, and a screen appears that allows you to enter the IP address, Subnet Mark, and Default Gateway. You can safely leave the Priority Connection parameter set to Off. Fortunately, you probably won't have to resort to these additional steps.

5. **Confirm connectivity.** After the Wi-Fi connectivity has been made, a screen will appear confirming that your network has been registered. The screen will look like the one shown earlier in **Figure 5.3**, but an orange dot will appear next to the connected network. If you get a screen with a note stating *cannot authenticate,* or that the *input value is invalid,* you'll need to start again at step 1; make sure you have the correct password for the network and be extra careful when keying it in. Remember that when a capital letter is required, you must use the shift feature (an arrow pointing upward) on the virtual keyboard.

6. **Try it again later.** After you have established Wi-Fi connectivity, you can revert to using the RX100 V as usual; a touch of the shutter release button returns it to shooting mode. The camera will retain the connection to the network until you turn it off or it goes into power-saving sleep mode; Wi-Fi is then temporarily disconnected. When you're ready to use Wi-Fi again, activate the RX100 V while in range of the same network, scroll to Access Point Settings in the Wireless

menu, and press the center button. The camera will quickly find your network to re-establish Wi-Fi connectivity.

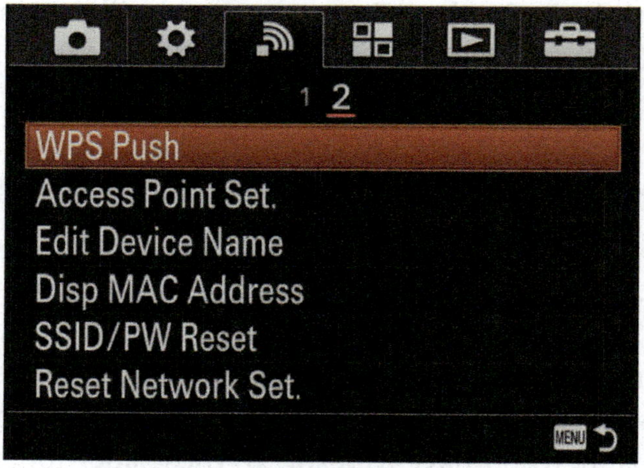

Figure 5.2

WPS Push, located at the top of the Wireless 2 menu, is the fastest way to connect to a network.

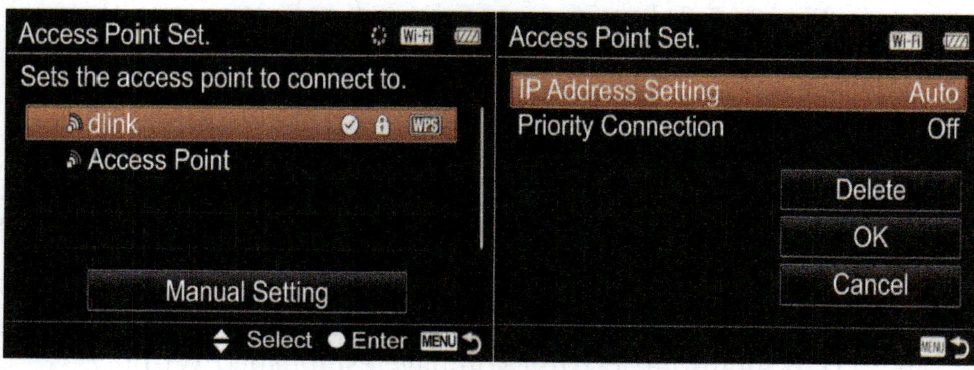

Figure 5.3

Access Point Settings can be used to select an access point/hotspot (left.) IP Address Setting set to Auto and Priority Connection disabled (right.)

If you're connecting to a public Wi-Fi hotspot, the steps should be the same, but you'll most likely find a screen that requires you to agree to the hotspot's terms and conditions. Some hotspots may not require you to enter a password.

Selecting an Access Point Manually

If the desired access point (network) is not displayed on the screen as described in Step 2 above, you may need to enter it yourself. Just follow these steps:

1. **Choose Manual Setting.** Scroll down to Manual Setting (visible at the bottom of **Figure 5.3**, left) and press the center button. The screen shown in **Figure 5.4**, left, appears.
2. **Select Manual Registration.** Press the center button to begin the manual registration process. The screen shown in **Figure 5.4**, right, appears.
3. **Enter SSID.** On the Manual Registration screen, there's a field for entering the SSID name of the access point (network) you plan to use. Press the center button when this field is visible and the virtual keyboard appears. Enter the data. When you're finished press the center button.
4. **Change Security (if necessary).** Again, if you have some networking expertise, you'll know if the security setting on your router is WPA (Wi-Fi Protected Access, the default), WEP (Wired Equivalent Privacy, an older, easily "hacked" protection scheme), or None (effectively, no security). If you want to change the Security setting, highlight that field and press the center button. The screen shown in **Figure 5.5**, left, appears. Select your choice and press the MENU button to return.
5. **Enter password.** The next screen will ask for your password, which you can enter using the virtual keyboard.
6. **Enter WPS PIN (if necessary).** If your WPS connection requires a PIN, you can enter it using the screen shown in b, right.

Take care not to lose the network connection by inadvertently using the Initialize or the Reset Network Settings item of the Wireless menu. If you do so, the camera will eliminate all of your network settings and you'll need to repeat the steps in this section.

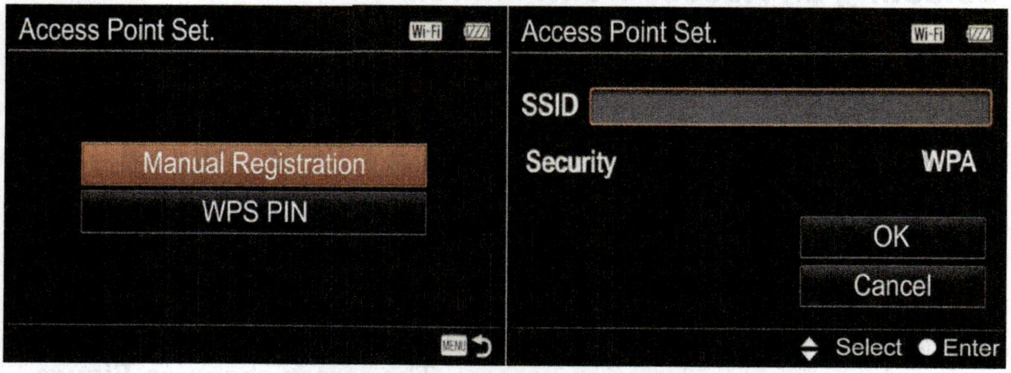

Figure 5.4

Manual registration requires you to complete extra steps. Enter the SSID

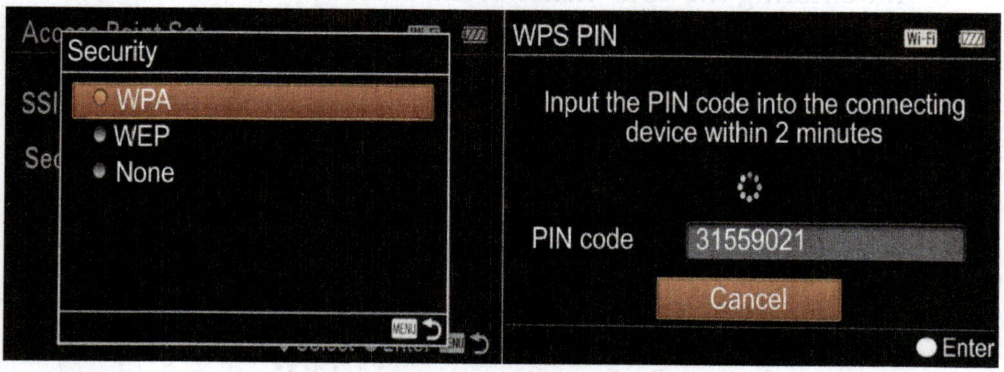

(network/access point name).

Figure 5.5

You can change the security protocol used (left.) If your router requires a WPS PIN, enter it here (right.)

Wi-Fi Settings

The Wireless 2 menu, shown earlier in **Figure 5.2**, has additional entries beyond those we've used so far. Their functions should be fairly obvious:

- **Edit Device Name.** By default, your camera is assigned the device name DSC-RX100M4. Select this entry and you can change it to something else.
- **Disp MAC Address.** Each device on a network has a unique Media Access Control number. You generally have no need to know this, unless you want to block a particular device from your network and use the MAC address to identify the unwanted device.
- **SSID/PW Reset.** Deletes the current SSID and password. You might want to do this for security reasons (say, you load/give/sell your RX100 V to someone else), or need to start over in registering your camera with a network.
- **Reset Network Set.** Removes all network settings from the camera.

Wi-Fi Functions

Once Wi-Fi connectivity has been established, you can consider using other features that I mentioned earlier. Begin by transferring some photos from the RX100 V to your computer that's also connected to the same wireless network. Do note that you must first download and install Sony's PlayMemories Home for Windows, or Sony's Wireless Auto Import for Mac to your computer.

The functions you can access are shown in the Wireless 1 menu, as seen earlier in **Figure 5.1**:

- **Send to Smartphone.** Transfer files to a smart device.
- **Send to Computer.** Send files to a computer.
- **View on TV.** View images with a wireless connection to a compatible HDTV.

- **One-touch (NFC).** Near Field Communications with a compatible Android phone.
- **Airplane Mode.** Disable all wireless functions.

Sending Photos to a Smart Device

To transfer photos from your camera to a smartphone or tablet, the device must be running the free PlayMemories Mobile app for Android or iOS; you can get it from your usual app store. After you have downloaded the PlayMemories Mobile app (for iOS or Android) and are running it in your smart device, you can send one or more images to the smart device. (The app, and hence the camera's Wi-Fi features like this one, are not available in a few countries where many aspects of Internet use are restricted.) This feature does not work for video clips. Here are the steps you'll follow:

1. ***On your smart device:*** Run the PlayMemories Mobile app. Start the app on your smartphone or tablet, so it will be ready to link to your RX100 V after you've completed the network connection.
2. ***On your camera:*** Access the Send to Smartphone item. Access this Wireless 1 menu item in the camera. (The term smartphone actually means smart *device* since it works with a tablet computer, too, in the same manner.) You'll see two options: Select on This Device (which is the camera), or Select on Smartphone.
3. ***On your camera:*** Choose Device. Next, you'll choose the device used to select the images to transfer:
4. **Select on This Device.** The RX100 V will display a screen with three options: This Image, All Images on This Date, and All Images in the Device. Choose one and press the center button.
5. **Select on Smartphone.** Press the center button to specify choosing images on the smartphone.

6. ***On your camera:*** View SSID and password. After you've chosen which device to use for image selection, the camera will display both its unique ID (SSID) and a password.
7. ***On your smart device:*** Join camera's network. Go to your smart device's Wi-Fi screen, where the SSID displayed by the camera should be listed as a Wi-Fi network. Select the camera's network and using the smart device's virtual keyboard, enter the SSID and password that your RX100 V is displaying. Remember, it's all case sensitive so use capital letters when necessary. If you get an *incorrect password* message from the smart device, start again using greater care to be accurate. Click on Join or whatever command your device requires in order to proceed. The camera will display a "Connecting…" message as it links to your smart device. Note: Once you've linked your camera and smart device, the device should retain the password for future use.
8. ***On your smart device:*** Return to the PlayMemories app on your smart device. It should immediately try to connect to the camera's network. If not, tap the Connect to Camera icon. If you selected images on your camera, the transfer will begin immediately. If you decided to select images on your smart device, thumbnails will be shown of the images on the camera. You can select them individually. When finished selecting, tap the Copy icon at the bottom of the screen and the transfer will commence.
9. ***On your smart device:*** View the Images. After the smart device has completed importing files from the RX100 V, you can view the thumbnails on its screen. Naturally, you can enlarge any photo so it fills the device's screen.
10. ***On your smart device:*** Use the smart device to send photos, etc. You can now use any of the smart device's capabilities: modify any of the images, send images to friends via e-mail, upload images to any website, and so on.

Wi-Fi Transfer to a Computer

You can transfer photos from the RX100 V to a computer that's also connected to the same wireless network. Use this Wireless menu item when you're ready to transfer images from the RX100 V via Wi-Fi to a computer that is connected to the network. (Review the items under the Networks heading for advice on establishing Wi-Fi connectivity between your camera and a network.)

Before you can transfer photos to a computer with Wi-Fi, be sure to install the PlayMemories Home software on a Windows computer or Wireless Auto Import to a Mac; you can download the latter from http://support.d-imaging.sony.co.jp/imsoft/Mac/wai/us.html. Then, you'll need to register the RX100 V in the software; this will also instruct the camera as to where photos should be sent in future, using Wi-Fi. The process is automatic after you connect the camera to the computer with the USB cable; the software will recognize it after a few seconds and proceed to register it. Afterward, image transfer will be possible without cable connection.

Use the following steps. These are based on the ones I used with PlayMemories Home in a Windows PC; they may be slightly different if you own a Mac computer and are using the Wireless Auto Import software, as described below.

Begin to authenticate your RX100 V. Before using Wi-Fi, you must sync the two devices. Launch the Sony PlayMemories software, connect the camera to the computer with the USB cable, and turn the camera on to start the process. (If any auto run wizard opens, offering to transfer images, close it.) The Sony Software in the computer will recognize the RX100 V and confirm it; you'll also see a screen on your computer monitor indicating that a compatible device has been found. If the computer software displays a screen indicating that the USB mode must be changed (to Mass Storage), click on Yes. (Surprisingly, this was necessary for me although the USB mode in the camera was at Auto which should have worked without any problem.)

NOTE: When you open the Wireless Auto Import software on a Mac, you will be presented with a screen that says if you want to set this computer as the device that imports files from your camera wirelessly, click Set on the screen. Do so. Then it will ask for your computer's password. Provide it and connect the camera to the computer via a USB cable, and the software will let you set up an account and download any needed software from Sony, as shown on the camera screen.

Proceed with the software-recommended step. When you see the screen on your computer monitor asking how you want to set up Wi-Fi import, the Recommended item will be checked. Click on Next. A Settings Completed screen will appear. Click on Finish.

Disconnect the camera. Since you'll be sending photos from the RX100 V to the computer using Wi-Fi, there's no need for any cable connection from this point on.

Access the Send to Computer menu item. Turn the RX100 V on, access the Wireless menu, and scroll to this item; then, press the center button. The camera will find the network and connect to it; it will then find your computer and make that connection, using Wi-Fi. This can take a minute or two. The camera's LCD will display a confirmation that files are being shared with the computer via Wi-Fi. PlayMemories Home in your computer will display a bar on your monitor confirming the wireless connection to the RX100 V and that it's importing (bringing in) the files on the memory card.

Wait for the file transfer to finish. There is no method for importing only certain files to a computer. The transfer process can be very time consuming if the memory card contains numerous images, especially RAW photos and long movie clips. The camera should shut down automatically after saving the files to your computer; if not, turn it off yourself.

Confirm that the files have arrived. Use any software to access the drive/folder that was the destination for the photos and video clips. You should find them in the expected location, in individual folders. Delete any files that you do not want to keep.

BYPASS SECURITY SOFTWARE

If during Step 4 you get a note on the RX100 V's display screen indicating that the camera could not connect to your computer, the problem is being caused by a computer firewall and you'll need to make a change to allow incoming data to be received. For example, my Norton 360's firewall was set by default to Block incoming data. I changed that to Allow and then all went exactly as discussed in the steps. After the data transfer has been completed, it's essential that you re-activate the blocking features of the firewall so it will again provide full security.

Viewing Images on a TV

As with most other current digital cameras, it's possible to view JPEG photos and video clips on an HDTV when you connect the RX100 V to the TV using an HDMI cable. This is an extra-cost accessory. Buy the Type D cable with a micro HDMI connector at one end (for plugging into the camera) and a conventional HDMI plug to connect to the TV's HDMI port. An inexpensive cable is fine; there's no need to pay more for one of the premium brands unless you need a cable that's longer than about 6 feet. Make the cable connection and you can now display photos and movies on the oversized screen.

After the Wi-Fi connection has been made with a Digital Living Network Alliance/DLNA-compatible (network-enabled or Wi-Fi Direct-enabled) HDTV, you can use this menu item, on the second screen of Wireless options. Use it to display photos on the HDTV without cable connection after Wi-Fi connectivity has been confirmed. The benefit of Wi-Fi Direct is that you do not need to register your access point on the camera before doing so; in other words, the TV need not be connected to the network if you are using Wi-Fi Direct. Movie clips cannot be transferred to a TV for display over Wi-Fi; to show those, connect the camera to the HDTV using an optional Type D HDMI cable.

Use the menu options to instruct the camera as to which device (TV) it should send to, which photos to display (all or only those in a specific folder), and whether the display time should be long or short if using the slide show feature. Press the center button if you do want to use the slide show feature. At any time, you can move to another image for the display by scrolling to the left or right.

It's also possible to transfer JPEG photos, but not videos, to an HDTV without cable connection. If you have a networked TV (or a network-friendly game machine such as PlayStation or Xbox), you can view the images in your camera on that display without using the HDMI cable.

Of course, the HDTV must be DLNA (Digital Living Network Alliance) compliant and it must first be connected to your home network via Wi-Fi as per the instructions that came with the device. The RX100 V must also be communicating with your network via Wi-Fi, of course. (Use the steps provided earlier.)

> There is an exception to the DLNA rule. Some HDTVs are Wi-Fi Direct enabled; if yours is, then it doesn't need to be connected to your network. Mine is not, so I have not been able to try this feature.

There are simply too many types of Wi-Fi enabled HDTV's to provide full specifics on exactly how you'll transfer JPEGs to the device. Sony's published documents specifically recommend their Bravia HDTV, as you might expect, but you can use any DLNA (or Wi-Fi Direct) -enabled TV. A Bravia HDTV does provide a few extra display features that are possible only when using a Sony camera.

In any event, start by accessing the View on TV item in the camera's Wireless menu and press the center button. The camera will confirm the Wi-Fi connection to your network and it will search for a compatible TV. Be sure to consult your TV's instructions for setting the media display component to receive information from the camera. When connectivity with the TV has been confirmed, you can begin the sharing process using connection controls similar to those described earlier in this chapter.

The Application Menu

Unlike most other cameras with Wi-Fi, the RX100 V can download apps from the Sony Entertainment PlayMemories Camera Apps website while Wi-Fi connectivity is active. (Sony does not plan to offer its Camera apps via the other app stores.) This enables you to add extra functions to existing features or to arm the camera with some entirely new functions to expand its versatility. When you connect to the Internet, you can use your camera's simple built-in browser to access the Sony PlayMemories Camera Apps page and download any that are of interest to you.

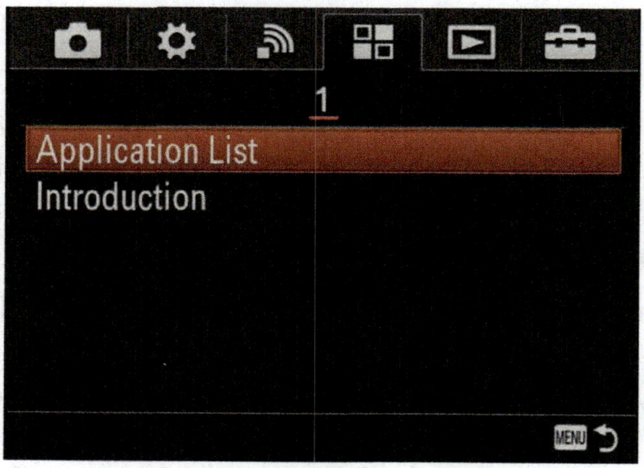

Figure 5.6
The Application menu.

Set up an account with the Sony Entertainment Network website using your computer or tablet. In North America, you can find that website at http://www.sony.net/pmx. There you fill out an online form and set a password, and download/install a browser add-on. Once you've created an account, you can connect your RX100 V to your computer with the included USB cable and download apps directly from your computer through the browser plug-in.

Or, you can establish Wi-Fi communication between your camera and your home network using the Wireless menu, as described earlier in this chapter, and download apps over your network to the camera without the need for a direct connection to your computer. After the Wi-Fi connection has been made, scroll to the Application menu (see **Figure 5.6**) where you'll see two choices: Application List and Introduction.

Application List

- **Options**: N/A
- **Default**: N/A
- **My preference**: N/A

Select Application List and a screen similar to **Figure 5.7** appears. It displays any apps you have installed, plus two management entries: PlayMemories Camera Apps and Application Management.

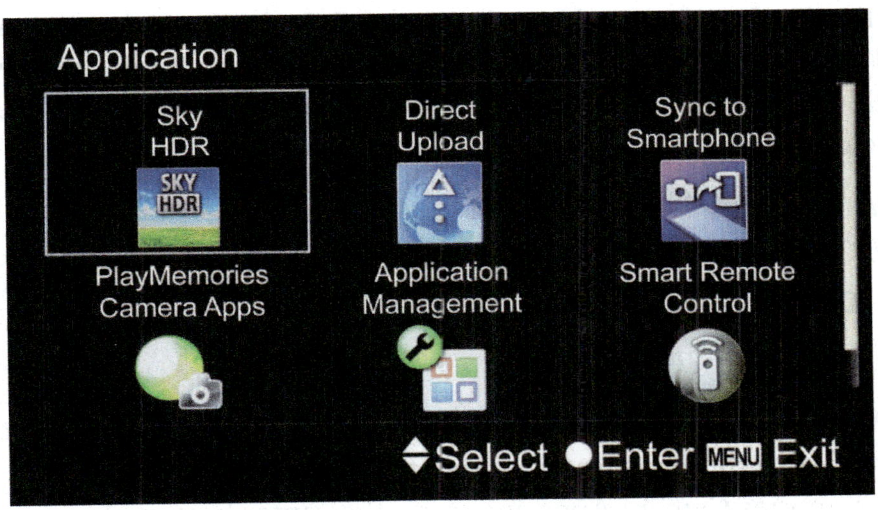

Figure 5.7

The Application List.

Introduction

- **Options:** Service Introduction, Service Availability
- **Default:** N/A
- **My preference:** N/A

Introduction provides two sections. Service Introduction shows you where to find the Sony Entertainment website and mentions that it's not available in a few countries; my camera shows www.sony.net/pmca as the shortcut to it. Service Availability provides details as to countries where Sony can supply apps.

Working with Applications

In general, you'll browse, purchase, and run apps from the Application List screen shown in **Figure 5.7**. You have the options to load applications shown in the list, browse available applications with PlayMemories Camera Apps, or use Application Management. In all three cases, just highlight an icon and press the center button.

PlayMemories Camera Apps

- **Options:** N/A
- **Default:** N/A
- **My preference:** N/A

After you have established Wi-Fi communication and opened an account with the Sony Entertainment Network website, scroll to PlayMemories Camera Apps and press the center button. A screen will appear indicating the camera is searching for an access point (your wireless network). When that's found, the camera will display a screen like the one shown in **Figure 5.8**. You can press the left/right buttons to move between the applications list at right, and the menu icons at left:

- **New.** Displays the most recent (new) apps.
- **All.** Shows all available apps, including free apps.
- **My App.** Shows only the apps installed on your camera.

- **Settings.** Allows you to sign into the Sony network or select your Country/Region.

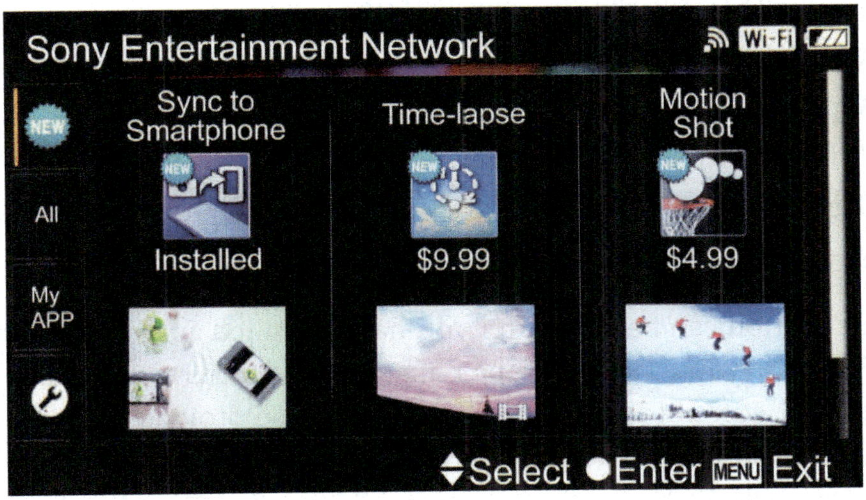

Figure 5.8
PlayMemories

Select an app that's already installed and press the center button to activate it. Or, scroll to an app you want to install, such as Picture Effect+ (which is free of charge) and press the center button. On the next screen, scroll to Install and press the center button; this takes you to a screen where you enter your e-mail address to start the sign-in process (for the Sony app site). Scroll to the bottom of the page and enter your password in the field that appears, again using the on-screen keyboard that appears after you press the center button. (This is the password you had created with the Sony online app store.) Basically you follow the on-screen process which is quite intuitive, although it is tedious to use the on-screen keyboard without a touch-screen LCD.

Scroll to Done and press the center button again. On the following screens, agree to everything (if you do want to proceed) and the camera will begin downloading the app. Afterward, you'll see a screen indicating that the installation was successful. Scroll down to Use the Installed App, and it will appear. Picture Effect+ (for example) is similar to what you'd see if you had accessed the camera's conventional Picture Effect item, but there are some entirely new options for applying special effects to your pictures that you can choose. Scroll among the options and a Help Guide will provide a brief summary of the one you scrolled to.

Camera Apps.

- **Options:** Sort, Manage and Remove, Display Account Information
- **Default:** N/A
- **My preference:** N/A

This section can be used after you have installed apps (see **Figure 5.9**); it allows you to sort the apps, manage and remove apps, and to display your account information. The latter also provides instructions on how to delete your account; the Initialize > Factory Reset item will do so, in addition to re-setting all camera functions to the factory defaults.

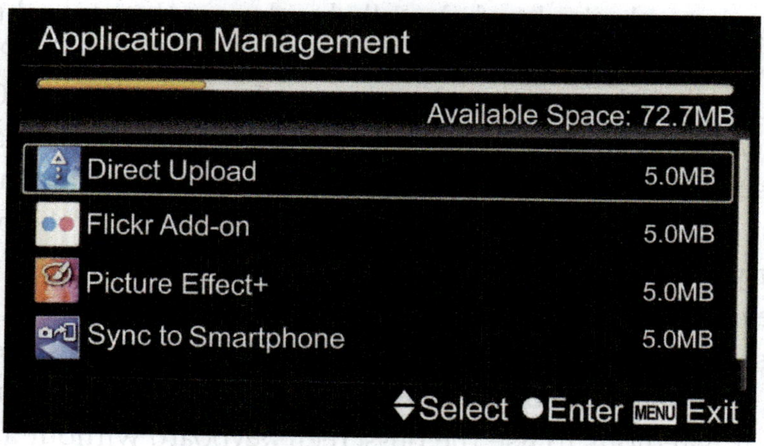

Figure 5.9
Application Management.

Downloading Apps

Here's how you can download apps, step by step:

1. **Sign up for a service account at http://www.sony.net/pmx using a computer.** This is an essential first step and will include specifying a credit card that will be charged for any

apps that are not free. You can also check out the available apps (on your large computer monitor) in order to appreciate the features they will provide if you later install them in your RX100 V.

2. **Log into the app store from the RX100 V.** While the camera is connected to a network via Wi-Fi, scroll to the PlayMemories Camera Apps item in the Application menu. Press the center button and wait a few seconds until you're connected to the Sony Entertainment Network app store.
3. **Find the available apps with the RX100 V.** You'll now be viewing a screen on the camera with tabs along the left side. You can scroll to: New (list only the new camera apps), All (list all available camera apps), and My App (list any apps already downloaded to the camera). Start by scrolling to All; press the center button and you'll be able to view a display of all available apps. Not all of the many icons are visible at any one time so scroll down to view the others. The price for each is shown. If an app is available free of charge, the word Install appears below it instead of the price. If you have previously installed an app, the word Installed appears under it.
4. **Download and install an app.** Scroll to an app you might want to try. Go for a free one initially, such as Direct Upload, and press the camera's center button. A screen will appear with information about that app and how it works. If you do want this app, scroll to the Install bar and press the camera's center button.
5. **Complete the Sign In process.** You'll need to sign in using the password you had created while connected to the Sony website with your computer in step 1. When you scroll to a field and press the center button, the virtual keyboard appears so you can enter the data. When you have finished entering your data in a field, scroll down to END and press the center button.
6. **Wait for the app to upload to your RX100 V.** This can take up to a minute for some apps; a note on the camera's screen

will keep you advised as to the status. Do not turn the camera off during the process. When the app has been installed, you'll get a screen confirming it was successful.

7. **Try the new app.** If you're ready to do so, scroll down to "Use the installed application" bar and press the camera's center button. The other option, "View other applications," is useful in case you want to download other apps right away.
8. **Access your apps.** Access the camera's Application menu to find the list of apps that you have already installed. If there are several, you may need to scroll down to reveal any that are not immediately visible in the display. Scroll to one you want to try and press the center button. This will take you to a screen that will provide guidance on how to proceed with the app.

A TRADITIONAL ALTERNATIVE TO DOWNLOADING APPS

If you prefer not to use Wi-Fi for uploading apps to your RX100 V, it's also possible to do so with the camera connected to a computer with the USB cable. After making that connection, access the www.sony.net/pmx app store and open an account as discussed in Step 5. Connect the RX100 V to your computer with the USB cable. Scroll to an app displayed on your computer monitor (by the Sony Entertainment website), and click on Install. (If there's a fee, you'll need to agree to pay that.) The transfer to the RX100 V will then start; it's automatic and simple. When it's finished, you'll see a note on your computer monitor (from the Sony app store) confirming that the installation has been completed. Disconnect the RX100 V (using the Windows safe eject feature or by dragging the camera icon to the Trash if you're using a Mac). The new app will appear in the list of apps in the camera's Application menu.

Current Sony Apps

At the time of this writing, Sony offered a series of conventional apps, some free and others priced at $4.99 or $9.99 in the US; prices in other countries may be entirely different. Additional apps (all free) include Snapshot Me, Time Lapse LE, Catch Light, Stop Motion, and ID Photo were available in the US. Of course, it's also possible that some other, entirely new conventional apps will be available then.

Sony provides sample video clips, and occasionally still photos, that illustrate how most of the following apps work, how to install them, and the effects you can expect. Check them out at www.sony.net/Products/playmemories/pm/pmca.html.

Several of the conventional apps are various free keyboards such as International, Chinese, Japanese, and Korean; these are self-explanatory so I won't provide a summary. In any event, here's a brief overview of the most popular conventional apps available in the US and Canada at the time I wrote this chapter.

- **Sky HDR ($9.99).** This app was an instant hit when it was introduced in late 2015. It solves the problem of trying to balance a bright sky with a darker foreground, giving you an additional in-camera HDR feature that's been optimized for landscape photography. It comes with three canned "themes," Blue Sky, Sunset, and Graduated ND (see **Figure 5.10**) and includes two custom presets you can define yourself using a multifunction, multi-tabbed menu system. It's easy to adjust the boundary between foreground and sky, and then balance the exposure and white balance between them. (See **Figure 5.10.**) If you do a lot of landscape photography, this is a must-have app.

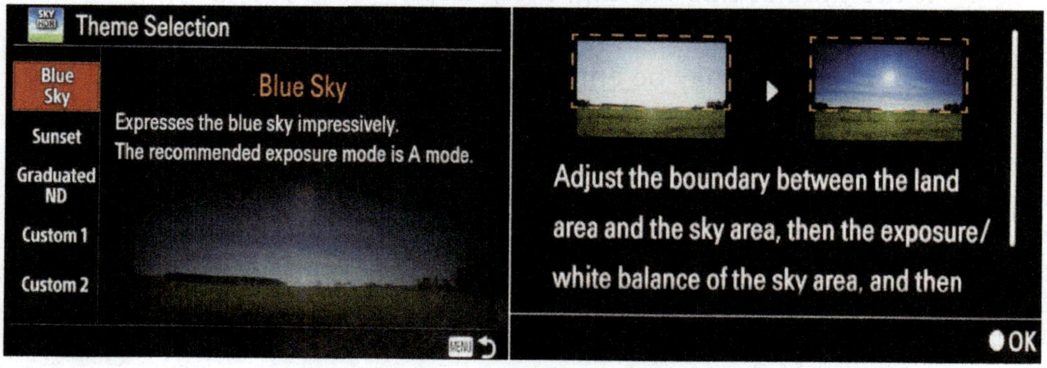

Figure 5.10

Choose a theme with Sky HDR, or create your own preset (left.) Adjust the boundary between sky and foreground (right.)

- **Direct Upload (free).** Use this app to upload photos directly from the RX100 V to Facebook or to the Sony PlayMemories site via Wi-Fi. (Perhaps other sites will be added in future.) Of course, the camera must be connected to a network to do so. Because the 20-megapixel images are huge, they're automatically downsized to 2 megapixels. Select the photos you want to upload and you can specify the destination album. If you're uploading to Facebook, you can also add a comment to each photo, if desired. (You will need to key in your ID and password and that can be tedious; you might consider checking the box that instructs the app to remember this data to eliminate the need to sign in every time.)
- **Flickr Add-On (free).** This is a companion app to Direct Upload and available only after you have installed that one. This app merely adds the ability to upload images directly to Flickr. It becomes part of Direct Upload in the camera's Application menu.
- **Picture Effect+ (free).** The camera already provides many special effects options, but this app adds others and modifies some existing effects for greater versatility. The Partial Color

effect, for example, allows you to fine-tune intensity and make other tweaks.

- **Multi Frame Noise Reduction ($4.99).** As the name implies, this app is similar in concept to the two SCN modes that provide high ISO photos by taking a burst of multiple JPEG frames and compositing them into one after discarding much of the digital noise data. (See Chapter 4 for a discussion of the Anti Motion Blur and Hand-held Twilight modes.) The app is available for use when the camera is set to P, A, S, or M mode so you get a lot more versatility in terms of camera settings than you do with the fully automatic SCN modes. You can set a desired ISO level, exposure compensation, and a Creative Style plus its overrides, for example.
- **Photo Retouch (free).** This app enables you to modify the technical aspects of JPEG photos you've already taken. A variety of tools are available for adjusting aspects such as brightness, saturation, and contrast while you view the photo. The app also offers resizing (downsizing an image), horizon correction, skin softening, and applying the auto portrait framing feature.
- **Smart Remote (free).** Get this app to take advantage of an important feature provided by Wi-Fi: control of the RX100 V from a smart device that's running the PlayMemories Mobile app. (The RX100 V becomes the access point.) Set up the camera pointing toward a bird's nest for example, and you can get a live preview of the scene on the device's LCD screen. You can control the exposure if the camera is set for A or P mode, activate a self-timer, use exposure compensation, and trip the shutter from the smart device to take photos. (You cannot control camera features such as zooming, ISO level, mode, etc.) (See **Figure 5.11.**)
- **Bracket Pro ($4.99).** The RX100 V already provides a feature for autoexposure bracketing, but this app provides a lot more bracketing options. It expands the exposure range to +/-5 EV and provides a simplified interface. More importantly, the app

provides additional features: focus bracket (three shots at various focused distances), shutter speed bracket (three shots, each at a different shutter speed), aperture bracket (three shots at various f/stops), and flash bracketing (two shots, one with and one without flash).

- **Cinematic Photo ($4.99)**. This app is unusual in that it creates cinemagraphs, still photos of which a portion is animated. In other words, it provides a video in which most of the frame is a still photo but with a single animated element.

  For example, your subject might be a friend pouring milk from a clear bottle. The camera will fire 18 JPEGs and then it will provide a preview image with a brush tool that you can use to specify the area that will be animated: depicted as moving in the cinemagraph. In this example, you would brush only the area of the flowing milk so it would be the area depicted as moving; your friend would be static. The painting process is slow since you'll be using the control wheel. After you finish your artistic work, you can view the finished video; if it's not quite right, you can start again with the painting process. A cinemagraph video is about 20 seconds long and 640 x 360 pixels in resolution.

- **Time Lapse ($9.99)**. Activate this really cool app to automatically shoot a series of photos at various intervals with settings made automatically by the camera; use it to record the opening of a blossom during the period from 8 am to 10 am, for example. Because the exposure is locked after the first shot, this feature works best when the brightness of the light will not change (as on a cloudy day) while the series of photos are being made. You can set the interval between shots, the number of photos to be taken, and whether the self-timer will be used. After the series is finished, it's combined into one HD video clip.

  If you don't want a video, you can choose to have the camera merely save the still images as a series. You get seven presets, each providing a different look: Cloudy Sky, Night Sky, Night

Scene, Sunset, Sunrise, Miniature, and Standard. There's also a Custom option with more user control.

- **Multiple Exposure ($4.99).** Some other cameras offer a feature that lets the user take several photos that are composited into one, a straightforward function. Add this app and the RX100 V can also do so, but you get far more versatility. You can select a theme and the app will automatically composite your series of photos into one, after optimizing the exposure. Seven themes are available: Easy Silhouette, Sky, Texture, Rotate, Mirror, Soft Filter, and Manual. If you choose Manual, you can preview the results you'd get with any of the five options and then select the one that will provide the results you prefer.
- **Motion Shot ($4.99).** Also a type of multiple exposure app, this is intended for photos of moving subjects, such as race cars, cyclists, or runners. After you take a sequence of shots with continuous drive, they're composited into one. You can choose the first and last images of the sequence, adjust spacing between the images to be composited, and customize other settings. All of the photos, including the composite, are saved to the memory card. (Check out the sample that Sony provides at https://www.playmemoriescameraapps.com/portal/.)
- **Portrait Lighting ($4.99).** This app can accentuate people's faces by adjusting the contrast and brightness. It can also lighten or darken the background. You can select any of five lighting levels or use a custom setting; the latter lets you choose from six levels of emphasis on either the person or the background. When experimenting, start by making a portrait photo of a friend and use this app to brighten the face and darken the surroundings for a dramatic effect.
- **Light Shaft ($4.99).** Perhaps a bit gimmicky, this app can add a *splash of light* to your photos in one of four different light shapes: Ray, Star, Flare, and Beam. You get some control since you can specify where you want the light shape to fall as well as adjust its intensity, length, width, and number of light rays.

As mentioned earlier, any apps you download will be available for access in the camera's Application menu. If many have been installed, you may need to scroll down to find the icon for the app you want to use. The RX100 V includes an Application Management item as well. This feature offers options that allow you to sort your apps, delete any of them, and display your Sony account information. When you scroll to one of these options, on-screen guidance is provided, such as the steps required to remove an app. (If you remove an app, you can later re-install it if you decide that you do want it -- at no extra charge.) All of this is quite intuitive so experiment with the available options. Pressing the up directional button at any time will return you to the previous screen.

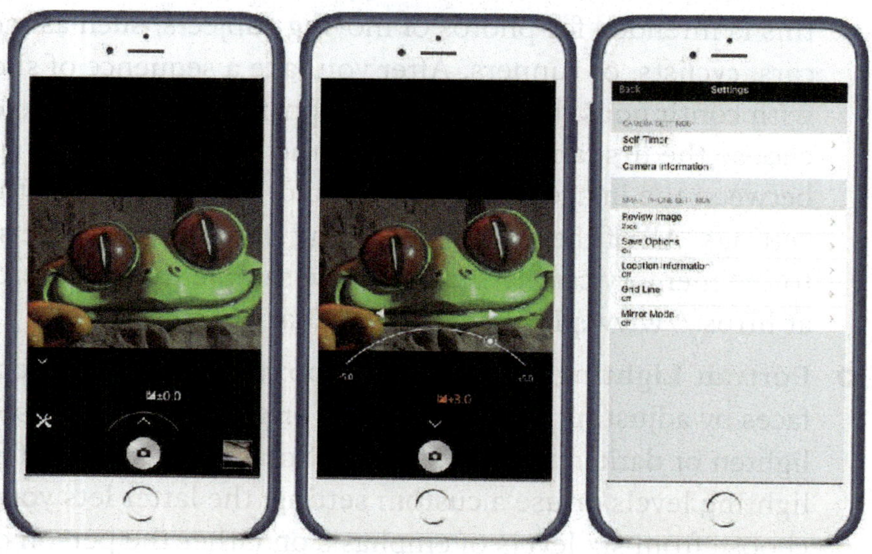

Figure 5.11

Link your camera to your smartphone using the PlayMemories Home app, and you can use the phone as a remote to take pictures (left), adjust exposure compensation (center), and specify other parameters (right).

Near Field Communications (NFC)

If you know Bluetooth, then you already understand much of what you need to know about One-Touch (Near Field Communications). Like Bluetooth, NFC is a radio communications protocol that allows smart devices to establish a link with each other simply by touching them together or moving them close to each other (a few inches is sufficient). Currently, NFC is supported only by Android devices and cameras using a compatible operating system, including the RX100 V.

Pairing your smart device and your camera couldn't be easier:

1. Download PlayMemories Mobile to your Android device.
2. Activate the NFC function of the smart device. An N-like icon should be displayed on your device's screen when NFC is available.
3. Locate the NFC marking on the left side of the RX100 V (when you're holding the camera in shooting position).
4. Touch the marking to the corresponding mark on the smart device for about 1 to 2 seconds.
5. When the devices are paired, the PlayMemories Mobile app launches on the smart device.
6. You may now select One Touch (NFC) in the Wireless 1 menu. The option cannot be used if the camera is in Airplane Mode.
7. You can access applications using NFC, or transfer images on the camera to the smart device.

Chapter 6

Playback and Setup Menus

Even more options are available from the Sony RX100 V's Playback and Setup menus, which allow you to further tailor the camera's behavior; view, print, and protect images; and adjust important camera settings, such as monitor brightness or audio volume.

Playback Menu

This menu controls functions for deleting, protecting, displaying, and printing images. You can bring it up on your screen more quickly by pressing the Playback button first, then the MENU button, which causes the Playback icon to be highlighted on the main menu screen.

The first set of items that are visible on the screen when you activate the Playback menu are shown in **Figure 6.1** below.

- Delete
- View Mode
- Image Index
- Display Rotation
- Slide Show
- Rotate
- Enlarge Image
- Enlarge Initial Magnification
- Enlarge Initial Position
- Protect
- Motion Interval Adjustment
- Specify Printing
- Beauty Effect

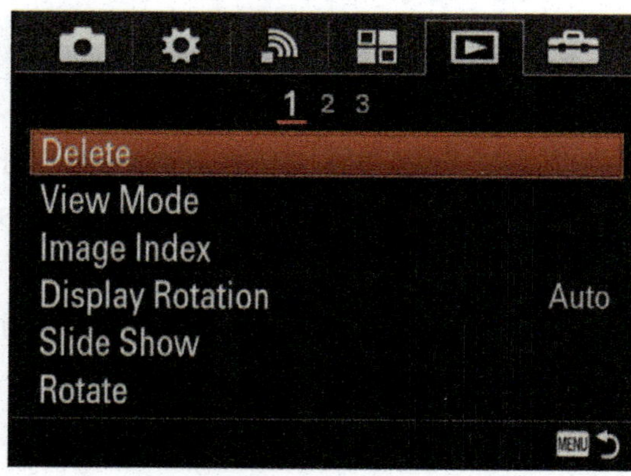

Figure 6.1
Playback menu.

Delete

- **Options:** Multiple Img., All With This Date, All In This Folder
- **Default**: Multiple Img.
- **My preference**: N/A

Sometimes we take pictures or video clips that we know should never see the light of day. Maybe you were looking into the lens and accidentally tripped the shutter. Perhaps you really goofed up your settings. You want to erase that photo *now,* before it does permanent damage to your reputation as a good photographer. Unless you have turned Auto Review off through the Setup menu, you can delete a photo immediately after you take it by pressing the C key (Delete button). Also, you can use that method to delete any individual image that's being displayed on the screen in Playback mode.

However, sometimes you need to wait for an idle moment to erase all pictures that are obviously not "keepers." This menu item makes it easy to remove selected photos or video clips (Multiple Images), or to erase all taken on a certain date or contained in a certain folder, sorted by your currently active view mode (such as folder or date). (Change the type of view using the View Mode option, described next.) Note that there is no delete method (other than Format) that will remove images tagged as Protected (as described below in the section on "Protect").

To remove one or more images (or movie files), select the Delete menu item, and use the up/down direction buttons or the control wheel to choose the Multiple Images option. Press the center button, and the most recent image *using your currently active view* -- Date View, Folder View (Still), Folder View (MP4), or AVCHD View -- will be displayed on the LCD.

Scroll through your images with the left/right directional buttons or control wheel and press the center button when you reach the image you want to tag for deletion; a check mark then appears beside it and an orange check mark appears in the bottom-left corner of the thumbnail.

The number of images marked for deletion is incremented in the indicator at the lower-left corner of the LCD, next to a trash can icon. When you're satisfied (or have expressed your dissatisfaction with the really bad images), press the MENU button, and you will be asked if you're sure you want to proceed. To confirm your decision, press the center button. The images (or video clips) you had tagged will now be deleted. If you choose All in Folder or All With This Date instead of Multiple Images, a screen will ask you to confirm you want to remove all the images in the current folder or shot on that particular date. If you change your mind, press the Playback button to cancel.

Tip: If you want to delete everything on the memory card, it's quicker to do so by using the Format item in the Setup menu, as discussed later in this chapter.

View Mode

- **Options:** Date View, Folder View (Still), Folder View (MP4), AVCHD View, XAVC S HD View, XAVC S 4K View
- **Default**: Folder View (Still)
- **My preference**: Folder View (Still)

Adjusts the way the camera displays image/movie files, which is useful for reviewing only certain types of files, or for deleting only particular types, as described above. You can elect to display files by Date View, Folder View (still photos only), Folder View (MP4 clips only), AVCHD View (just AVCHD movies), or XAVCS clips in both HD (high definition) and 4K modes.

Image Index

- **Options**: 9, 25
- **Default**: 9
- **My preference**: 25

You can view an index screen of your images on the camera's LCD by pressing the down direction button (Index button) while in Playback mode. By default, that screen shows up to 9 thumbnails of photos or movies; you can change that value to 25 using this menu item. Remember to use the View Mode menu item first, to identify the folder (stills, MP4, or AVCHD) that the index display should access; by default, it will show thumbnails of still photos, but you might want to view thumbnails of your movie clips instead.

Display Rotation

- **Options:** Auto, Manual, Off
- **Default**: Auto
- **My preference**: Auto

You can use this function to determine whether a vertical image is rotated automatically during picture review. If you want to rotate the image more, use the Rotate entry, described later in this section.

- **Auto.** The image will be shown in the orientation indicated by information in the image, no matter how the camera itself is rotated during picture review. For example, a vertical image will be shown in the correct orientation, as shown at left in **Figure 6.2**, when the camera is held horizontally. It will be shown smaller in size in order to fit the long dimension of the image into the short dimension of the screen. Rotate the camera 90 degrees, and the RX100 V will automatically rotate the photo so it's *still* shown in the correct orientation, but it will now fill the LCD screen, as you can see in **Figure 6.2** right.
- **Manual.** With this setting, the image is always displayed on the LCD in the same orientation it was taken. That is, a

vertically oriented photo will be displayed in a smaller size, just as it is when using Auto, as shown at left in Figure 6.3. However, when you rotate the camera during picture review, the RX100 V does *not* automatically rotate the image at the same time, so it will be shown with an incorrect orientation (see **Figure 6.3** right).

- **Off.** With this setting, both vertical and horizontal images are displayed to fill the screen as much as possible with the image. Vertical shots are larger, as shown at right in **Figure 6.4**, but the camera must be rotated.

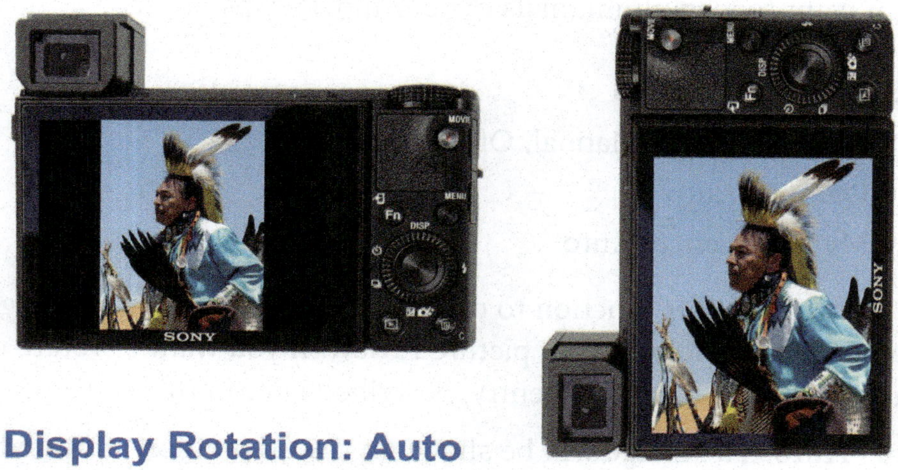

Figure 6.2
Display Rotation: Auto.

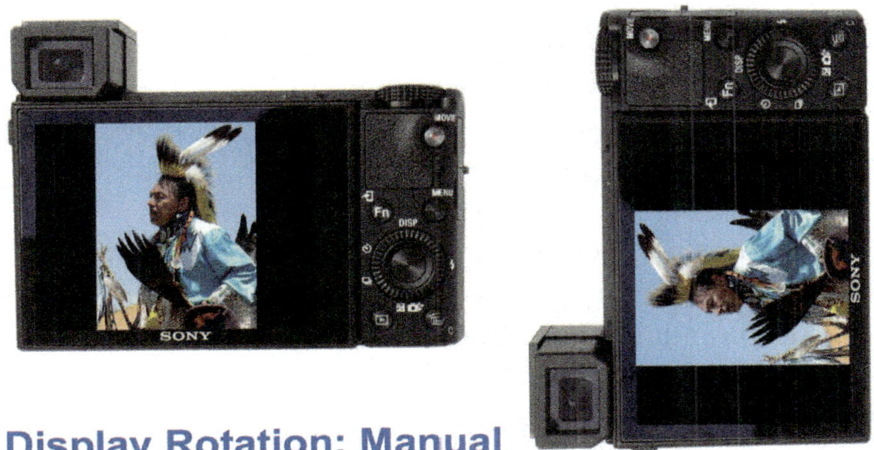

Figure 6.3

Display Rotation: Manual.

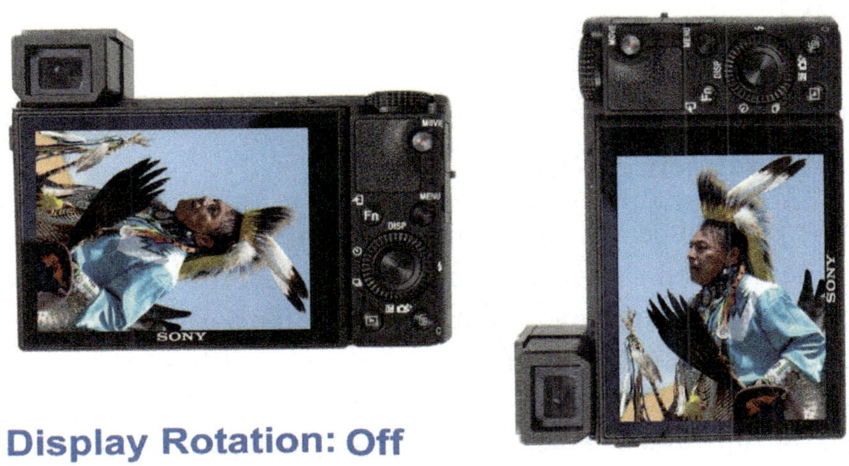

Figure 6.4

Display Rotation: Off.

Slide Show

- **Menu Options:** Repeat (On/Off), Interval: 1 second, 3 seconds, 5 seconds, 10 seconds, 30 seconds
- **Default:** 3 seconds
- **My preference:** N/A

Use this menu option when you want to display all the still images on your memory card (you cannot select which photos are used) in a continuous show. You can display still images in a continuous series, with each one displayed for the amount of time that you set. Choose the Repeat option to make the show repeat in a continuous loop. After making your settings, press the center button and the slide show will begin. You can scroll left or right to go back to a previous image or go forward to the next image immediately, but that will stop the slide show. The show cannot be paused, but you can exit by pressing the MENU button.

Rotate

- **Options:** None
- **Default:** N/A
- **My preference:** N/A

When you select this menu item, you are immediately presented with a new screen showing the current or most recently reviewed image along with an indication that the center button can be used to rotate the image. (This feature does not work with movies.) Scroll left/right to reach the image you want to rotate. Successive presses of the center button will now rotate the image 90 degrees at a time. The camera will remember whatever rotation setting you apply here. You can use this function to rotate an image that was taken with the camera held vertically, when you have set Display Rotation to Manual. Press the MENU button to exit.

Enlarge Image

- **Options:** None
- **Default:** N/A
- **My preference:** N/A

This is the first entry on the second page of the Playback menu (see **Figure 6.5**, left). Whenever you are playing back still images (not movies), you can use this menu entry to magnify the image. Use the control wheel to zoom in and out, and you can scroll around inside the enlarged image using the four direction buttons.

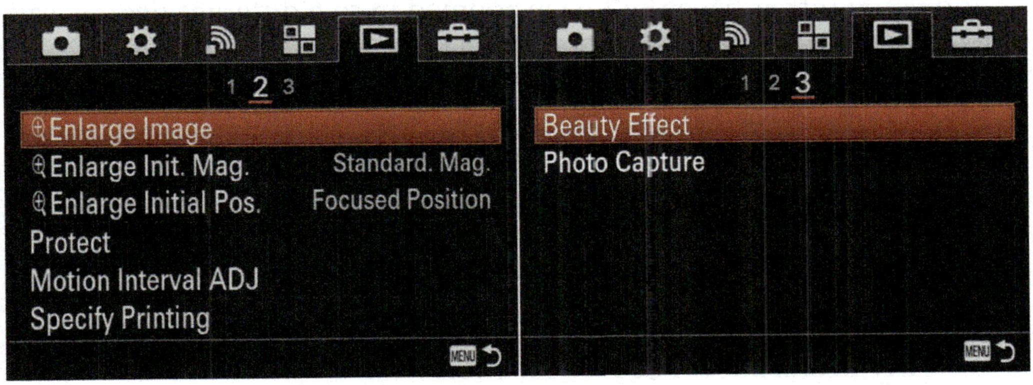

Figure 6.5

The second page of the Playback menu.

Enlarge Initial Magnification

- **Options:** Standard Magnification, Previous Magnification
- **Default:** Standard Magnification
- **My preference:** Standard Magnification

This entry lets you control how much magnification is applied to an image you are reviewing during playback. with the default value, the image is displayed with the standard amount of magnification. That's your best bet for everyday use, and the image is played back with a small, but consistent amount of enlarging. However, if you find you'd rather have the image zoomed in to a different degree, say, because you are examining fine details of your subject, you can choose Previous Magnification. Then, every time you zoom in that same zoom level will be applied without the need to zoom in or out.

Enlarge Initial Position

- **Options:** Focused Position, Center
- **Default:** Focused Position
- **My preference:** Focused Position

This is another helpful tool, telling the camera *how* to position the magnified image. It's usually most useful to zoom in on the point where focus was achieved, so you can check sharpness.. If you'd rather the enlarged image is centered in the middle of the frame, choose Center instead.

Protect

- **Options:** Multiple Images, All in this Folder, All with this Date, Cancel All in this Folder
- **Default:** None
- **My preference:** N/A

You might want to protect certain images or movie clips on your memory card from accidental erasure, either by you or by others who may use your camera from time to time. This menu item enables you to tag one or more images or movies for protection so a delete command will not delete it. (Formatting a memory card deletes everything, including protected content.) This menu item also enables you to cancel the protection from all tagged photos or movies.

To use this feature, make sure to specify whether you want to do so for stills or movies; use the View Mode item in the Playback menu to designate the desired view mode, as described earlier. Then, access the Protect menu item, choose Multiple Images, and press the center button. An image (or thumbnail of a movie) will appear; scroll among the photos or videos using the control wheel to reach the photo you want to tag for protection; press the center button to tag it with an orange check mark at the bottom-left corner of the image. (If it's already tagged, pressing the button will remove the tag, eliminating the protection you had previously provided.)

After you have marked all the items you want to protect, press the MENU button to confirm your choice. A screen will appear asking you to confirm that you want to protect the marked images and give you two options, OK or Cancel. Press the center button to do either. Later, if you want, you can go back and select the Cancel All option for the current view mode to unprotect all of the tagged photos or movies.

Motion Interval Adjustment

- **Options:** Intervals 1-7
- **Default:** 4
- **My preference:** N/A

The RX100 V's Motion Shot Video feature is a playback mode that produces a stroboscopic skip-frame effect when playing back AVCHD or MP4 video. It can look sort of cool, but Sony provides no way to save this video effect. It can only be viewed during playback in the camera. (You might want to check out the Motion Shot app from Sony Entertainment, too.)

To activate Motion Shot, press the down button while viewing a clip, and then the right button to navigate to the Motion Shot Icon (a movie frame overlaid with a series of disks of decreasing size) and press the center button. It's the third icon from the left. You can use this menu entry to change the interval between skip-frames. The same function is available during playback; select the fourth icon from the left.

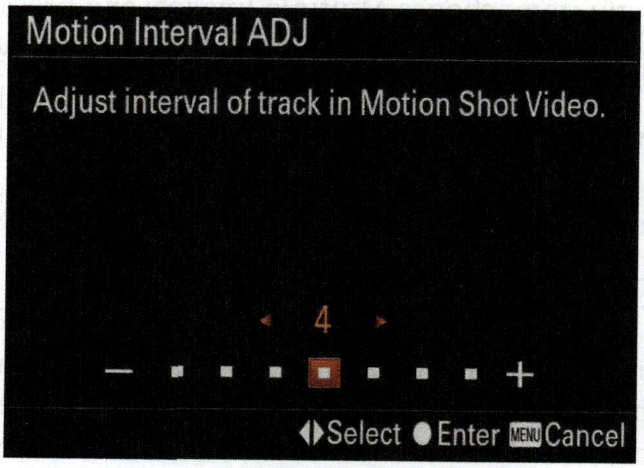

Figure 6.6
Motion interval adjustment.

Specify Printing

- **Options:** Multiple Images, Cancel All, Print Setting
- **Default:** N/A
- **My preference:** N/A

Most digital cameras are compatible with the DPOF (Digital Print Order Format) protocol, which enables you to tag JPEG images on the memory card (but not RAW files or movies) for printing with a DPOF compliant printer; you can also specify whether you want the date imprinted as well. Afterward, you can transport your memory card to a retailer's digital photo lab or do-it-yourself kiosk, or use your own DPOF-compatible printer to print out the tagged images in the quantities you've specified.

Choose multiple images using the View Mode filters described earlier to select to view either by Date or by Folder. Press the center button to mark an image for printing with an orange check mark, and the MENU button to confirm when you're finished. The Print Setting entry lets you choose to superimpose the date onto the print. The date will be added during printing by the output device, which controls its location on the final print.

Beauty Effect

- **Options:** Skin Toning, Skin Smoothing, Shine Removal, Eye Widening, Teeth Whitening
- **Default:** N/A
- **My preference:** N/A

This is the first entry on the sparse third page of the Playback menu (see **Figure 6.5**, right). Now you don't need an image editor to retouch those quickie pictures of family and friends (or yourself) before posting them on social media or sharing via e-mail. This built-in feature gives you five tools to fine-tune faces in a snap, saving a new and improved version while leaving your original image as-is.

View an image you want to adjust and then activate this feature. The camera searches for a face within the shot. Select the face you want to retouch and then press the center button. You can select Skin Toning (adjust the face color); Skin Smoothing (to remove wrinkles and spots); Shine Removal (to reduce unwanted skin sheen); Eye Widening; or Teeth Whitening. Select the effect you want and use the up/down buttons to specify the degree of retouching from 1 to 5. Press the center button to apply each effect. You can then use the left/right buttons to move on to a different effect, or press the center button again to confirm.

When finished with the first face, you can select the same image and apply the Beauty Effect to a different face in the same photo. This feature cannot be used with panoramas or movies, and may not work with faces that are very small or difficult to detect (say, the subject is wearing a large hat or glasses).

Photo Capture

- **Options:** Capture frames
- **Default:** N/A
- **My preference:** N/A

This entry allows you to capture still frames during image review, and save them as JPEG files. Individual movie frames have a respectable amount of resolution (about 2 megapixels in a Full HD video), so you might want to make some frame grabs. Just select Photo Capture, review the movie, and press the down button, highlight Pause with the left/right buttons, and press the center button. Then use the slow-forward or slow-rewind buttons to inch through the video frame by frame, stopping at the frame you want to capture. Then highlight the Photo Capture icon (just to the left of the Volume icon) and press the center button to save the frame as a still image.

Setup Menu

Use the lengthy Setup menu to adjust infrequently changed settings, such as language, date/time, and power-saving options. The six five items in the Setup menu are shown in **Figure 6.7**.

1	2	3
• Monitor Brightness • Viewfinder Brightness • Finder Color Temperature • Gamma Display Assistance • Volume Settings • Audio Signals	• Upload Settings • Tile Menu • Mode Dial Guide • Delete Confirm. • Display Quality • Power Save Start Time	• Function for Viewfinder Close • NTSC/PAL Selector • Demo Mode • TC/UB Settings • HDMI Settings • 4K Output Selection
4	**5**	**6**
• USB Connection • USB LUN Setting • USB Power Supply • Language • Date/Time Setup • Area Setting	• Copyright Info • Format • File Number • Select REC Folder • New Folder • Folder Name	• Recover Image Database • Display Media Information • Version • Certification Logo (non-US/Canada models only) • Setting Reset

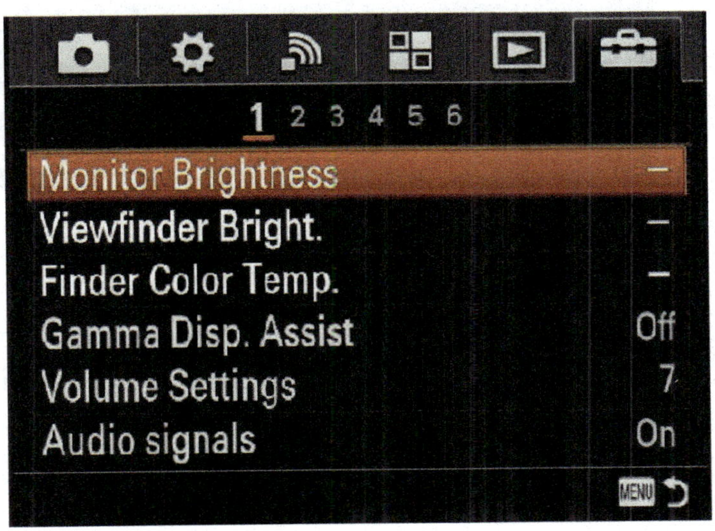

Figure 6.7
The Setup menu.

Monitor Brightness

- **Options:** Manual, Sunny Weather
- **Default:** Manual
- **My preference:** Manual

When you access this menu item, two controls appear. The first is a Brightness bar (shown just above the grayscale/color patches in **Figure 6.8**). It's set to Manual adjustment by default, but press the center button and you can change it to Sunny Weather for a brighter display. You might resort to this setting if you're shooting outdoors in bright sun and find it hard to view the LCD even when shading it with your hand.

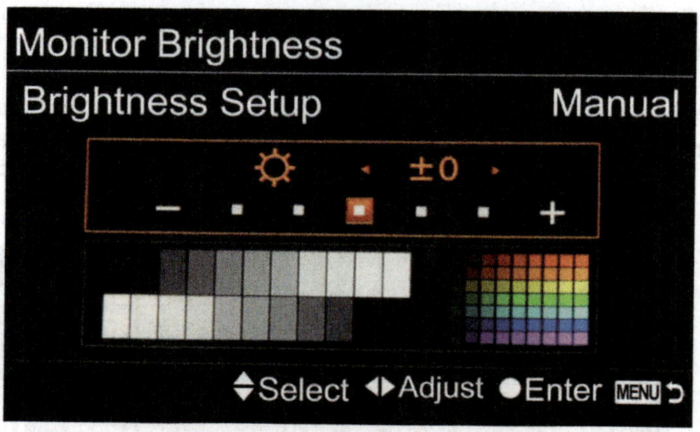

Figure 6.8
Adjust monitor brightness.

If you set Sunny Weather, the LCD brightness will automatically increase, making the display easier to view in very bright light. This makes the display unusually bright so use it only when it's really necessary. Remember too that it will consume a lot more battery power, so have a spare battery available.

The grayscale steps and color patches can be used as you manually adjust the screen brightness using the left/right direction buttons. Scroll to the right to make the LCD display brighter or scroll to the left to make the LCD display darker, in a range of plus and minus 2 (arbitrary) increments. As you change the brightness, keep an eye on the grayscale and color chart in order to visualize the effect your setting will have on various tones and hues. The zero setting is the default and it provides the most accurate display in terms of exposure, but you might want to dim it when the bright display is distracting while shooting in a dark theater, perhaps. A minus setting also reduces battery consumption but makes your photos appear to be underexposed (too dark).

I prefer to choose Manual but then leave the display at the zero setting. This ensures the most accurate view of scene brightness on the LCD for the best evaluation of exposure while previewing the scene before taking a photo.

Viewfinder Brightness

- **Options:** Auto, Manual
- **Default:** Auto
- **My preference:** Manual

This entry operates exactly the same as the Monitor Brightness option just described, except that there is no need for a Sunny Weather entry for the electronic viewfinder. A notice will appear on the LCD monitor advising you to look through the viewfinder and make your adjustments.

Finder Color Temperature

- **Options:** +2 to -2
- **Default:** 0
- **My preference:** N/A

While looking through the viewfinder, press the left/right buttons to adjust the color balance of the finder to make it appear warmer (using the left button) or colder/bluer (using the right button), according to your preference.

Gamma Display Assist

- **Options:** Assist Off, Assist Auto, Assist S-Log
- **Default:** Assist Off
- **My preference:** Assist Off

As you'll learn in Chapter 10, video captured using the S-Log gamma curve have a very low degree of contrast, allowing post processing that results in a very wide dynamic range in the finished footage. Check out Chapter 10 if S-Log (or, indeed, most of this description) is, like the letter *gamma,* Greek to you. While the low contrast is good news when you're processing the vide, it's not much fun to review when you're checking out a clip in the camera.

This setting tells the RX100 V to adjust the contrast back to normal *during playback only* so you can review your video more easily. The default value is Off. If you select Auto, instead, any movies which have been captured with a Picture Profile of S-Log2 will be played back using a correction factor with the tongue-tying name "S-Log2>709(800%)." No correction is applied when you're reviewing movies captured using a gamma value other than S-Log2.

The third setting *always* displays video using the S-Log2>709(800%). effect. You'd use this if you are shooting movies with S-Log2 gamma exclusively.

Volume Settings

- **Options:** 0-15
- **Default:** 2
- **My preference:** N/A

This menu item affects only the audio volume of movies that are being played back in the camera. It does not affect recording volume. It's grayed out unless you have selected movies, as opposed to stills, with the Still/Movie Select menu item. When you select Volume Settings, the camera displays a scale of loudness from 0 to 15; scroll up/down to the value you want to set and it will remain in effect until changed.

You might want to use this menu item to pre-set a volume level that you generally prefer. However, you can also adjust the volume whenever you're displaying a movie clip, to set it to just the right level. To do so, press the down direction button and use the left/right direction buttons to raise or lower the volume.

Audio Signals

- **Options:** On, Shutter, Off
- **Default**: On
- **My preference**: N/A

Use this item to turn off the sounds the camera makes as feedback, including the electronic shutter sound that is emitted when using both the electronic and mechanical shutters. You can turn sounds on or off, or specify that only the shutter sound is heard. Remember that an electronic shutter sound is produced when using *both* the mechanical and electronic shutters. If you turn audio signals off, the mechanical shutter is very, very quiet, and the electronic shutter is totally silent. I like to leave sounds on for feedback, but turn them off for stealth shooting and in quiet venues.

Upload Settings

- **Options**: On, Off
- **Default**: On
- **My preference**: Off

The Upload Settings for Eye-Fi cards does not appear in the menu unless you have inserted an Eye-Fi card into the camera's memory card slot. An Eye-Fi card is a special type of SD card that connects to an available wireless (Wi-Fi) network and uploads the images from your memory card to a computer on that network. The Upload Settings option on the Setup menu lets you either enable or disable the use of the Eye-Fi card's transmitting capability. So, if you want to use an Eye-Fi card just as an ordinary SD card, simply set this item to Off, which saves a bit of power drawn by the card's Wi-Fi circuitry.

Tile Menu

- **Options:** On, Off
- **Default:** Off
- **My preference:** Off

This is the first entry on the second page of the Setup menu. (See **Figure 6.9**.) The Tile menu is a holdover from the NEX era, and features icons representing the six main menu tabs. While it might be marginally useful when you first begin working with your RX100 V, it's really an unnecessary intermediate step. Turn it Off and when you press the MENU button, you'll be whisked to the conventional menu system, where you can quickly navigate to the tab you want.

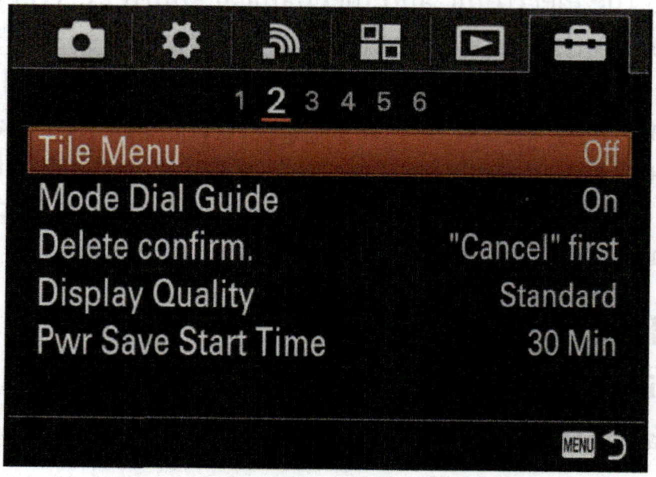

Figure 6.9

The Setup 2 menu.

Mode Dial Guide

- **Options:** On, Off
- **Default:** On
- **My preference:** Off

The On setting activates an on-screen description of the current Shooting mode as you rotate the mode dial. You might want to enable this extra help when you first begin using your camera, and turn it off after you're comfortable with the various mode dial settings.

Delete Confirm

- **Options:** Delete First, Cancel First
- **Default:** Cancel First
- **My preference:** Delete First

Determines which choice is highlighted when you press the trash button to delete an image. The default Cancel First is the safer option, as you must deliberately select Delete and then press the center button to actually remove an image. Delete First is faster; press the trash button, then the center button, and the unwanted image is gone. You'd have to scroll down to Cancel if you happened to have changed your mind or pressed the trash button by mistake.

Display Quality

- **Options:** Standard, High
- **Default:** Standard
- **My preference:** Standard

You can specify the image quality of the display, switching from the default Standard to High (which uses more battery power). While you might discern a small difference when viewing on an external monitor, most of the time the camera display isn't reliable for judging images anyway, so sticking to Standard quality is usually your best bet.

Power Save Start Time

- **Options:** 30 minutes, 5 minutes, 2 minutes, 1 minute, 10 seconds
- **Default:** 1 minute
- **My preference:** 5 minutes

This item is more critical than you might think, given the RX100 V predilection for gobbling power from the tiny battery. It lets you specify the exact amount of time that should pass before the camera goes to "sleep" when not being used. The default of 1 minute is a short time, useful to minimize battery consumption. You can select a much longer time before the camera will power down, or a much shorter time. I use 5 minutes most of the time to avoid having to "waken" the camera frequently. If I'm wandering around with long periods of time between shots, I may set it to 2 minutes. In street photography or sports mode, I use 30 minutes to make sure my camera will always be ready for action. But, of course, I tend to carry at least two spare batteries with me at all times.

Function for Viewfinder Close

- **Options:** Power Off, Not Power Off
- **Default:** Power Off
- **My preference:** Power Off

This is the first item on the third page of the Setup menu. (See **Figure 6.10.**) You can specify what happens when you retract the EVF and pop it back down into the camera body. I like to use the Power Off setting, as I use the EVF most of the time. When I tuck it away that usually means I am done shooting, and it's convenient to power down the RX100 V at the same time. If you frequently alternate between shooting with the viewfinder and framing using *only* the LCD monitor, you might want to choose Not Power Off, so you can hide the viewfinder and continue shooting without it in snapshot mode. With the EVF retracted, the camera is even more compact and easy to tuck away in a pocket for fast retrieval. (This camera makes an excellent point-and-shoot.)

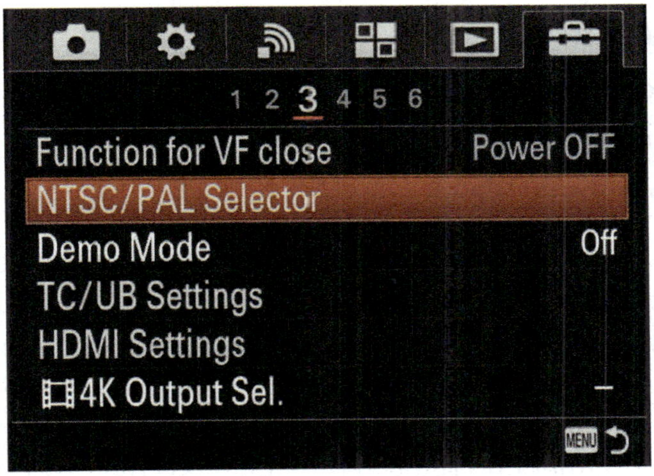

Figure 6.10

The Setup 3 menu.

NTSC/PAL Selector

- **Options**: NTSC, PAL
- **Default**: Depends on the country where the camera is sold
- **My preference**: N/A

It allows you to switch the camera between the two major television video systems, NTSC (used in the North and South America, Korea, Japan, and some other Pacific countries), and PAL, which is used in Europe, the Middle East, and elsewhere. To switch from one video system to another, you must be using a memory card that was formatted while the camera was using that video system. Otherwise, you'll be prompted to reformat the card or use a different card. Your camera will be set up at the factory to default to the video system used in your country. If you switch to the alternate system, the start-up screen will display a message "Running on NTSC" or "Running on PAL" to make sure you're aware of the change. Note that a few countries in South America (Brazil, Argentina, Paraguay, and Uruguay) use a modified PAL system, while others, including

Bulgaria, France, Greece, Guiana, Iran, Iraq, Monaco, Russia, and Ukraine use a third system, called SECAM.

Demo Mode

- **Options:** On, Off
- **Default:** Off
- **My preference:** N/A

This is a semi-cool feature that allows your camera to be used as a demonstration tool, say, when giving lectures or showing off at a trade show. When activated, if the camera is idle for about one minute it will begin showing a protected AVCHD movie, which is not impressive on the camera's built-in LCD, but can have a lot more impact if the camera is connected to a large-screen HDTV through the HDMI port. You may not have seen this feature discussed much in other guides; that's because it can only be deployed if you use the included AC adapter/USB cable. Most of us have no need for it, but if you *do* want to do demos, or if you shoot time-lapse images over long periods of time, you'll want to buy one. If you're properly equipped, just follow these steps:

1. Use the File Format entry in the Camera Settings 2 menu and select AVCHD as the movie format, as explained in Chapter 3. Demo Mode works only with AVCHD files.
2. Shoot the clip that you want to use as your demonstration, in AVCHD format.
3. In the Playback 1 menu, access the View Mode and select AVCHD View so that only AVCHD videos will appear.
4. In the Playback 2 menu, choose Protect and select the demo clip, which should be the movie file with the oldest recorded date and time.
5. Connect the camera to the AC adapter. Because Demo Mode uses a lot of juice, it operates only when the external power source is connected.

6. Demo Mode will no longer by grayed out in the Setup 2 menu. Select it and choose On.
7. After about one minute of idling, the demo clip will begin playing. Note that, because the AC adapter is connected, your automatic power-saving setting is ignored, and Demo Mode will not operate if no movie file is stored on your memory card.

TC/UB Settings

- **Options:** TC/UB Display Settings, TC Preset, UB Preset, UB Time Rec, TC Format, TC Run, TC Make
- **Default:** TC/UB Display Settings: Counter
- **My preference:** N/A

The Time Code (TC) and User Bit (UB) settings are information that can be embedded and used to sync clips and sound when editing movies. I'll describe this advanced feature in a little more detail in Chapter 10, but pro movie-making techniques are largely beyond the scope of this book.

HDMI Settings

- **Options:** Listed below
- **Default:** Listed below
- **My preference:** N/A

You can view the display output of your camera on a high-definition television (HDTV) when you connect it to the RX100 V if you make the investment in an HDMI cable (which Sony does not supply); get the Type D with a micro-HDMI connector on the camera end. (Still photos can also be displayed using Wi-Fi, without cable connection, as discussed earlier.) When connecting HDMI-to-HDMI, the camera automatically makes the correct settings. If you're lucky enough to own a TV that supports the Sony Bravia synchronization protocol, you can operate the camera using that TV's remote control when this item is On. Just press the Link Menu button on the remote, and then use the device's controls to delete images, display an image index of photos in the camera, display a slide show, protect/unprotect images in the camera, specify printing options, and play back single images on the TV screen. The settings available are as follows:

- **HDMI Resolution (Auto, 2160/1080p, 1080p, 1080i).** The camera can adjust its output for display on a high-definition television when at the Auto setting. This usually works well with any HDTV. If you have trouble getting the image to display correctly, you can set the resolution manually here to 2160/1080p (for 4K and Full HD), 1080p, or 1080i.
- **24p/60p Output.** You can select either 60p or 24p output to the HDMI port when connected to a 1080 60i compatible television and Record Setting (described in Chapter 4) has been set to 24p 24M (FX), 24p 17M (FH), or 24p 50M. If a different setting was used, this setting is ignored, and the output conforms to the HDMI Resolution setting above instead.
- **HDMI Info. Display.** Choose On or Off. Choose On if you want the shooting information to display when the camera is connected to an HDTV television/monitor using an HDMI cable. Select Off if you don't want to show the shooting information on the display. You might want to suppress the shooting information when you're showing your images as a slide show.
- **TC Output.** Choose on or off to enable/disable including time code in the HDMI output signal. Use On if you are outputting to professional video equipment and want to include the time code information. Note that the time code is *data* and will not actually appear on the screen. If this setting is on and you are sending the signal to a television or some other device, the image may not appear properly. Change this setting to off when outputting to devices not equipped to handle TC information.
- **REC Control.** This setting is available only when TC Output is set to on. Choose on or off. The setting allows you to start and stop REC Control-compatible external video recorders

connected to the camera. A REC or STBY icon will be displayed on the camera's screen as appropriate.

- **CTRL for HDMI.** This option can be useful when you have connected the camera to a non-Sony HDTV and find that the TV's remote control produces unintended results with the camera. If that happens, try turning this option Off, and see if the problem is resolved. If you later connect the camera to a Sony Bravia sync-compliant HDTV, set this menu item back to On.
- **HDMI Audio Out.** Enable/disable audio output through the HDMI port.

4K Output Selection

- **Options:** Memory Card+HDMI, HDMI Only (30p), HDMI Only (24p), HDMI Only (25p)
- **Default:** N/A
- **My preference:** N/A

When your RX100 V is connected to an external video recorder or playback device and set to Movie mode, you can use this setting to specify how 4K movies are recorded and output. Note that when using one of these choices, the camera's movie counter does not appear on the screen. If Dual Video REC is on, Smile/Face Detection, Lock-on Autofocus, Center Lock-on Autofocus, and Eye AF are disabled. Your choices are as follows:

- **Memory Card+HDMI.** A 4K movie in 30p is saved on the camera's internal memory card *and* output to the external device. Use this if you want two copies of your video, including one on the memory card. **Reminder:** It is mandatory to use an SDXC 64GB memory card.
- **HDMI Only (30p).** A 4K movie in 30p is output only to the external device, and not recorded on your memory card. HDMI Info. Display is disabled.
- **HDMI Only (24p).** A 4K movie in 24p is output only to the external device. HDMI Info. Display is disabled.

- **HDMI Only (25p).** If the NTSC/PAL Selector described earlier is set to PAL, you can use this option to shoot a 4K movie in 25p, and output only to the external device. HDMI Info. Display is disabled.

USB Connection

- **Options:** Auto, Mass Storage, MTP, PC Remote
- **Default:** Auto
- **My preference:** N/A

This setting, the first in the Setup 4 menu (see **Figure 6.11**), allows you to select the type of USB connection protocol between your camera and computer.

- **Auto.** Connects your camera to your computer or other device automatically, choosing either Mass Storage or MTP connection as appropriate.
- **Mass Storage.** In this mode, your camera appears to the computer as just another storage device, like a disk drive. You can drag and drop files between them.
- **MTP.** This mode, short for Media Transfer Protocol, is a newer version of the PTP (Picture Transfer Protocol) that was standard in earlier cameras. It allows better two-way communication between the camera and the computer and is useful for both image transfer and printing with PictBridge-compatible printers.

- **PC Remote.** This setting is used with Sony's Remote Camera Control software to adjust shooting functions and take pictures from a linked computer.

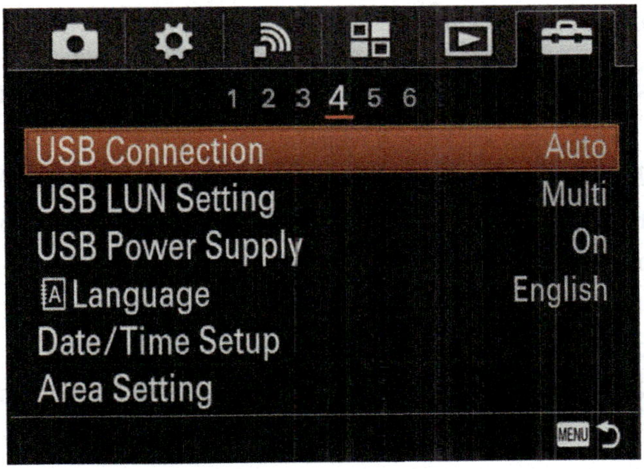

Figure 6.11
The Setup 4 menu.

USB LUN Setting

- **Options:** Multi, Single
- **Default**: Multi
- **My preference**: N/A

This entry specifies how the camera selects a Logical Unit Number when connecting to a computer through the USB port. Normally, you'd use Multi, which allows the camera to adjust the LUN as necessary, and is compatible with the PlayMemories Home software. Use Single to lock in a LUN if you have trouble making a connection between your camera and a particular computer. PlayMemories Home software will usually not work when this setting is active. But don't worry; Single is rarely necessary.

USB Power Supply

- **Options**: On, Off
- **Default**: On
- **My preference**: On

When set to on, the camera receives charging power from a connected computer or other device through the micro USB cable link. Use this setting if you want to charge the RX100 V's battery when connected to a computer or other device. Set to off, and power is not supplied. You'd want to use this to avoid draining power from the computer host. Although I most frequently connect my camera to a desktop computer, if I am using a laptop, I set this to off, as I have plenty of NP-BX1 batteries and recharging the laptop is sometimes inconvenient.

Language

- **Options:** English, French, Italian, Spanish, Chinese languages
- **Default**: Language of country where camera is sold
- **My preference**: N/A

If you accidentally set a language you cannot read and find yourself with incomprehensible menus, don't panic. Just find the Setup menu, the one with the red tool box for its icon, and scroll down to the line that has a symbol that looks like an alphabet block "A" to the left of the item's heading. No matter which language has been selected, you can recognize this menu item by the "A." Scroll to it, press the center button to select this item, and scroll up/down among the options until you see a language you can read.

Date/Time Setup

- **Options:** Daylight Savings, Date/Time, and Date Format
- **Default:** None
- **My preference:** N/A

Use this option to specify the date and time that will be embedded in the image file along with exposure information and other data. Having the date set accurately also is important for selecting movies for viewing by date. Use the left/right direction buttons to navigate through the choices of Daylight Savings Time On/Off; year; month; day; hour; minute; and date format. You can't directly change the AM/PM setting; you need to scroll the hours past midnight or noon to change that setting. Use the up/down direction buttons or rotate the control wheel to change each value as needed.

Area Setting

- **Options:** World time zones
- **Default:** None
- **My preference:** N/A

When you select this option, you are presented with a world map on the LCD. Use the left/right direction buttons to scroll until you have highlighted the time zone that you are in. Once the camera is set up with the correct date and time in your home time zone, you can use this setting to change your time zone during a trip, so you will record the local time with your images without disrupting your original date and time settings. Just scroll back to your normal time zone once you return home.

Copyright Info

- **Options:** Write Copyright Info, Set Photographer, Set Copyright, Display Copyright Info
- **Default:** Off
- **My preference:** Add all information

This is the first item on the Setup 5 menu. (See **Figure 6.12**.) Your choices include:

- **Write Copyright Info.** Turn On to embed copyright information in your image file; Off to disable this feature. If you choose On, a copyright symbol will appear on the shooting screen to indicate that copyright data is being written to the image file.
- **Set Photographer.** Enter the name of the photographer. Highlight this and press the center button to move to the next screen, where a blank line appears. Highlight that and press the center button, and the text entry screen appears. It functions much like the multi-tap cell phone keypads in the pre-smartphone era: highlight a button and press the center button multiple times to enter a particular character. For example, if you highlight the "abc" button, pressing once inserts an "a," twice a "b," and three times a "c." When finished, highlight OK and press the center button to return to the initial screen, where you can highlight OK again and press the center button a last time to confirm.
- **Set Copyright.** Define your copyright terms, such as *Cpr. 2016 David D. Busch*. Strictly speaking, "Cpr." should be used rather than a lowercase c between two parentheses. Text is entered as described above.
- **Disp. Copyright Info.** Displays whatever copyright information you've specified.

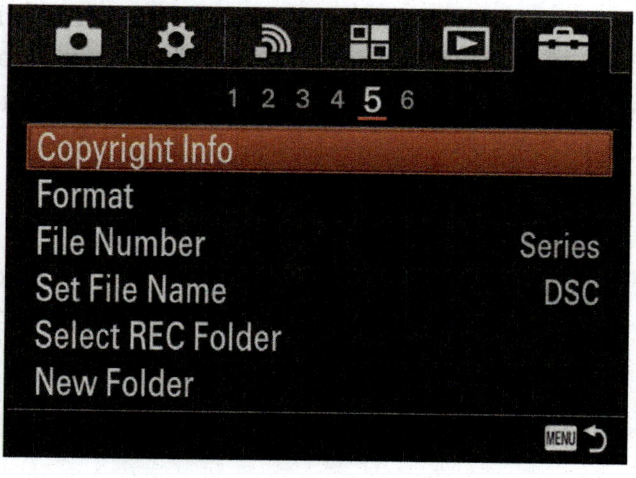

Figure 6.12
The Setup 5 menu.

Format

- **Options:** OK, Cancel
- **Default:** None
- **My preference:** N/A

As you'd guess, you'll use Format to re-format your memory card while it's in your RX100 V. To proceed with this process, choose the Format menu item and select OK and press the center button to confirm, or Cancel to chicken out.

Use the Format command to erase everything on your memory card and to set up a fresh file system ready for use. This procedure removes all data that was on the memory card, and reinitializes the card's file system by defining anew the areas of the card available for image storage, locking out defective areas, and creating a new folder in which to deposit your images. It's usually a good idea to reformat your memory card in the camera (not in your camera's card reader using your computer's operating system) before each use. Formatting is generally much quicker than deleting images one by one. Before formatting the card however, make sure that you have saved all your images and videos to another device; formatting will delete everything, including images that were protected.

File Number

- **Options:** Series, Reset
- **Default:** Series
- **My preference:** N/A

The default for the File Number item is Series, indicating that the RX100 V will automatically apply a file number to each picture and video clip that you make, using consecutive numbering; this will continue over a long period of time, spanning many different memory cards, and even if you reformat a card. Numbers are applied from 0001 to 9999; when you reach the limit, the camera starts back at 0001. The camera keeps track of the last number used in its internal memory. So, you could take pictures numbered as high as 100-0240 on one card, remove the card and insert another, and the next picture will be numbered 100-0241 on the new card. Reformat either card, take a picture, and the next image will be numbered 100-0242. Use the option when you want all the photos you take to have consecutive numbers (at least, until your camera exceeds 9999 shots taken).

If you want to restart numbering back at 0001 frequently, use the Reset option. In that case, the file number will be reset to 0001 *each* time you format a memory card or delete all the images in a folder, insert a different memory card, or change the folder name format (as described in the next menu entry). I do not recommend this since you will soon have several images with exactly the same file number.

Select REC Folder

- Options: Folder
- Default: None
- My preference: N/A

This entry allows you to choose a storage folder. Although your camera will create new folders automatically as needed, you can create a new folder at any time (using the New Folder entry, described next), and switch among available folders already created on your memory card. (Of course, a memory card must be installed in the camera.) This is an easy way to segregate photos by folder. For example, if you're on vacation, you can change the Folder Name convention to Date Form (described next). Then, each day, create a new folder (with that date as its name), and then deposit that day's photos and video clips into it. A highlighted bar appears; press the up/down buttons to select the folder you want to use, and press the center button.

New Folder

- **Options**: N/A
- **Default**: None
- **My preference**: N/A

This item will enable you to create a brand new folder each time you open this entry and switch the selected folder to the new one. Press the center button, and a message like "10100905 folder created" or "102MSDCF folder created" appears on the LCD. The alphanumeric format will be determined by the Folder Name option you've selected (and described next), either Standard Form or Date Form.

Folder Name

- **Options:** Standard Form, Date Form
- **Default**: Standard Form
- **My preference**: N/A

This is the first entry in the Setup 6 menu. (See **Figure 6.13**.) If you have viewed one of your memory card's contents on a computer, you noticed that the top-level folder on the card is always named DCIM. Inside it, there's another folder created by your camera. Different cameras use different folder names, and they can co-exist on the same card. For example, if your memory card is removed from your Sony camera and used in, say, a camera from another vendor that also accepts Secure Digital or Memory Stick cards, the other camera will create a new folder using a different folder name within the DCIM directory.

By default, the camera creates its folders using a three-number prefix (starting with 100), followed by MSDCF. As each folder fills up with 999 images, a new folder with a prefix that's one higher (say, 101) is used. So, with the "Standard Form," the folders on your memory card will be named 100MSDCF, 101MSDCF, and so forth.

You can select Date Form instead, and the camera will use a *xxxymmdd* format, such as 10060904, where the 100 is the folder number, 6 is the last digit of the year (2016), 09 is the month, and 04 is the day of that month. If you want the folder names to be date-oriented, rather than generic, use the Date Form option instead of Standard Form. This entry allows you to switch back and forth between them, both for folder creation (using the New Folder entry described above) and REC folder preference (also described above).

Whoa! Sony has thrown you a curveball in this folder switching business. Note that if you are using Date Form naming, you can *create* folders using the date convention, but you can't switch among them when Date Form is active. If you *do* want to switch among folders named using the date convention, you can do it. But you have to switch from Date Form back to Standard Form. *Then* you can change to any of the available folders (of either naming format). So, if you're on that vacation, you can select Date Form, and then choose New Folder each day of your trip, if you like. But if, for some reason, you want to put some additional pictures in a different folder (say, you're revisiting a city and want the new shots to go in the same folder as those taken a few days earlier), you'll need to change to Standard Form, switch folders, and then resume shooting. Sony probably did this to preserve the "integrity" of the date/folder system, but it can be annoying.

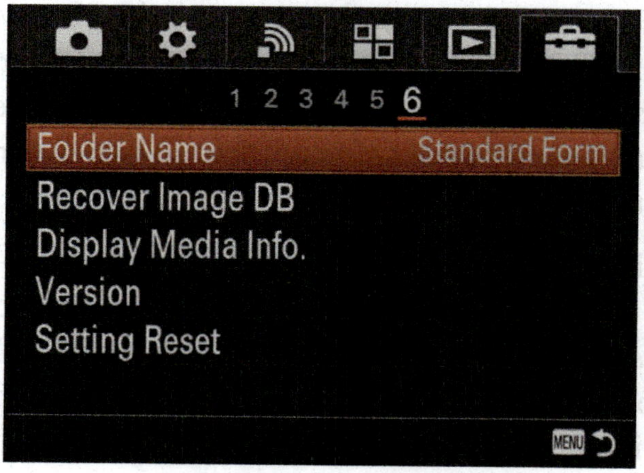

Figure 6.13
The Setup 6 menu.

Recover Image Database

- **Options:** OK, Cancel
- **Default:** None
- **My preference:** N/A

The Recover Image DB function is provided in case errors crop up in the camera's database that records information about your movies. According to Sony, this situation may develop if you have processed or edited movies on a computer and then re-saved them to the memory card that's in your camera. I have never had this problem, so I'm not sure exactly what it would look like. But, if you find that your movies are not playing correctly in the camera, try this operation. Highlight this menu option and press the center button, and the camera will prompt you, "Check Image Database File?" Press the center button to confirm, or the MENU button to cancel.

Display Media Information

- **Options:** None
- **Default:** None
- **My preference:** N/A

This entry gives you a report of how many still images and how many movies can be recorded on the memory card that's in the camera, given the current shooting settings. This can be useful, but that information is already displayed on the screen when the camera is being used to shoot still photos (unless you have cycled to a display with less information), and the information about minutes remaining for movie recording is displayed on the screen as soon as you press the Record button. But, if you want confirmation of this information, this menu option is available.

Version

- **Options**: None
- **Default**: N/A
- **My preference**: N/A

Select this menu option to display the version number of the firmware (internal operating software) installed in your camera. From time to time, Sony updates the original firmware with a newer version that adds or enhances features or corrects operational bugs. When a new version is released, it will be accompanied by instructions, which generally involve downloading the update to your computer and then connecting your camera to the computer with the USB cable to apply the update. It's a good idea to check occasionally at the Sony website, www.esupport.sony.com, to see if a new version of the camera's firmware is available for download. (You can also go to that site to download updates to the software that came with the camera, and to get general support information.)

Certification Logo (Non-US/Canada Models Only)

- **Options**: None
- **Default**: N/A
- **My preference**: N/A

This information-only entry displays various certification logos indicating the camera has met specifications mandated by other countries. It's included in cameras intended for non-US/Canada sales so that the logos can be tailored for specific areas through firmware updates, rather than printed notices on the bottom of the cameras themselves.

Setting Reset

- **Options:** Camera Settings Reset, Initialize.
- **Default:** N/A
- **My preference:** N/A

If you've made a lot of changes to your camera's settings, you may want to return the features to their defaults so you can start over without manually going back through the menus and restoring everything. This menu item lets you do that. Your choices are as follows:

- **Camera Settings Reset.** Resets the main shooting settings to their default values.
- **Initialize.** Resets *all* camera settings to their default settings, including the time/date and downloaded applications.

Chapter 7

Shooting Modes and Exposure Control

In the most basic sense, exposure is all about light. Exposure can make or break your photo. Correct exposure brings out the detail in the areas you want to picture, providing the range of tones and colors you need to create the desired image. Poor exposure can cloak important details in shadow, or wash them out in glare-filled featureless expanses of white.

Getting a Handle on Exposure

You're probably well aware of the traditional "exposure triangle" of aperture (quantity of light and light passed by the lens), shutter speed (the amount of time the shutter is open), and the ISO sensitivity of the sensor -- all working *proportionately* and *reciprocally* to produce an exposure. The trio is itself affected by the amount of illumination that is available to work with. So, if you double the amount of light, increase the aperture by one stop, make the shutter speed twice as long, or boost the ISO setting 2X, with any one of those changes you'll get exactly twice as much exposure. Similarly, you can *increase* any of these factors while *decreasing* one of the others by a similar amount to keep the same exposure.

Working with any of the three controls involves trade-offs. Larger f/stops provide less depth-of-field, while smaller f/stops increase depth-of-field (and potentially at the same time can *decrease* sharpness through a phenomenon called *diffraction*). Shorter shutter speeds do a better job of reducing the effects of any camera/subject motion, while longer shutter speeds make that motion blur more likely. Higher ISO settings increase the amount of visual noise and artifacts in your image, while lower ISO settings reduce the effects of noise. (See **Figure 7.1**.)

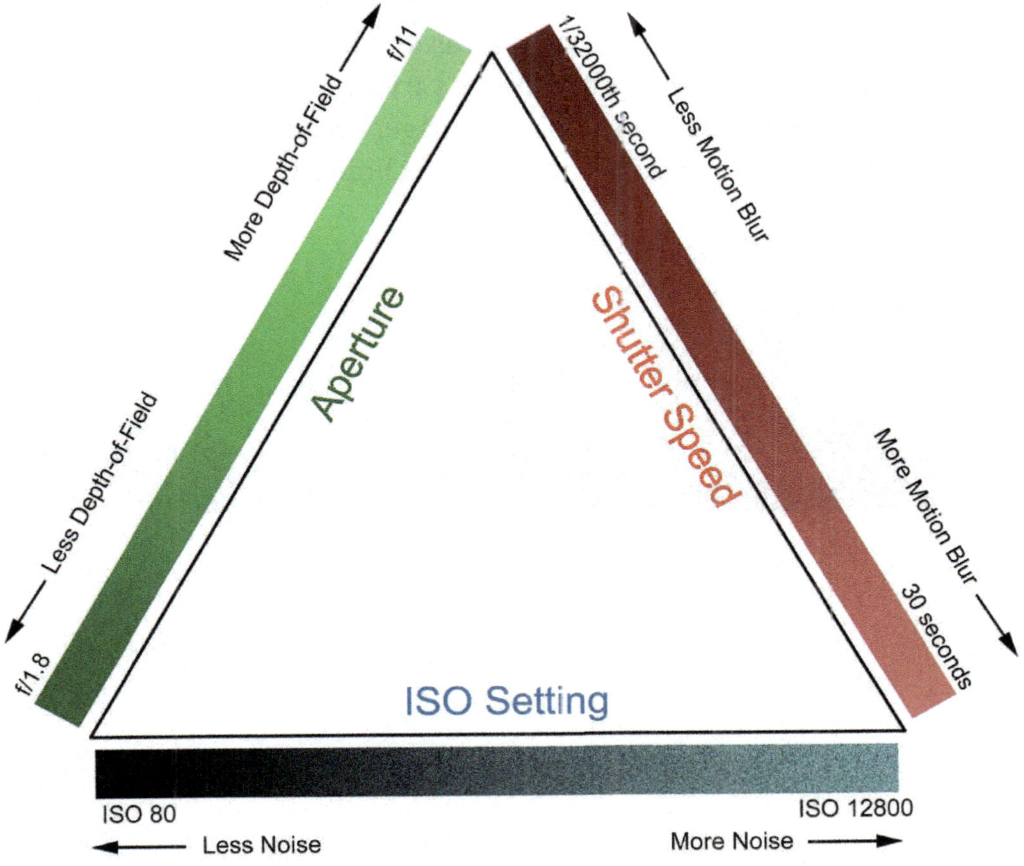

Figure 7.1

The traditional exposure triangle includes aperture, shutter speed, and ISO sensitivity.

You'll often need to make choices about which details are important, and which are not, so that you can grab the tones that truly matter in your image. That's part of the creativity you bring to bear in realizing your photographic vision.

For example, look at two bracketed exposures presented in **Figure 7.2**. For the image at top left, the highlights (chiefly the clouds at upper left and the top-left edge of the skyscraper) are well exposed, but everything else in the shot is seriously underexposed. The version at the top right, taken an instant later with the tripod-mounted camera, shows detail in the shadow areas of the buildings, but the highlights are completely washed out. The camera's sensor simply can't capture detail in both dark areas and bright areas in a single shot. With digital camera sensors, it's tricky to capture detail in both highlights and shadows in a single image, because the number of tones, the *dynamic range* of the sensor, is limited.

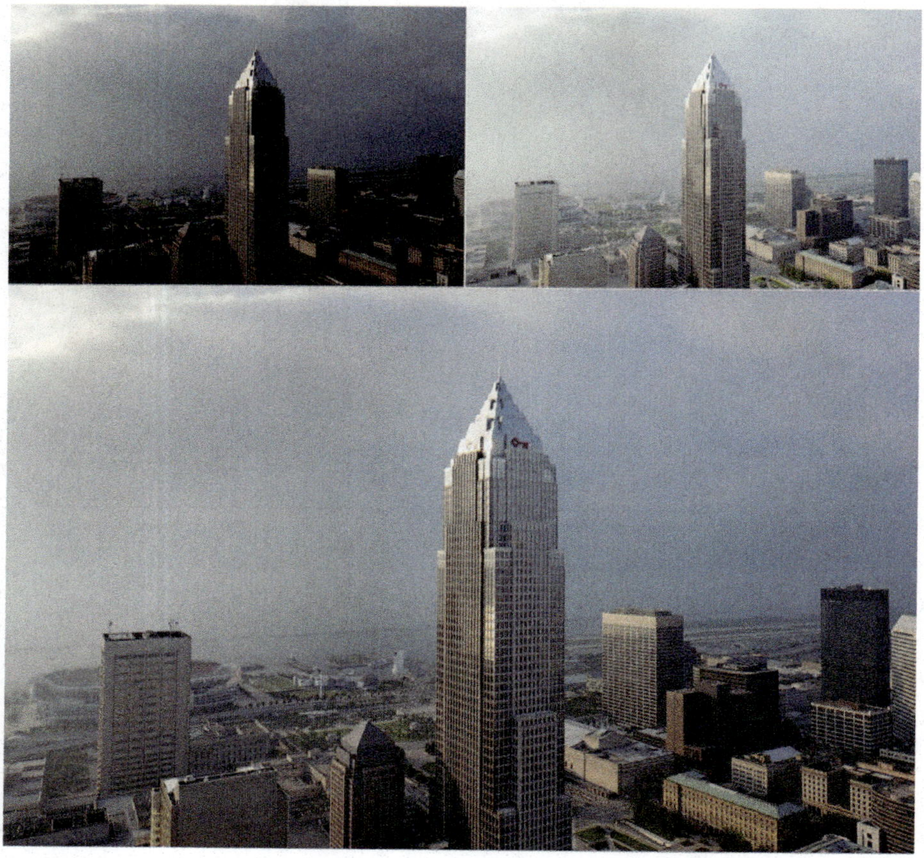

Figure 7.2

At top left, exposure for the highlights loses shadow detail. At top right, exposure for the highlights washes out the background. Bottom, combining the two exposures produces the best compromise.

The solution is to resort to a technique called High Dynamic Range (HDR) photography. It's included as a built-in feature of the camera (through the DRO/HDR Photography entry the Camera Settings 5 menu). However, I elected to produce the image shown at the bottom of the figure by merging the two original shots using a Photoshop/Photoshop Elements feature called Merge to HDR. There are also specialized software tools like Photomatix (about $100 from www.hdrsoft.com), Google's HDR Efex Pro 2 as part of the free Nik Collection or, for Macs only, Aurora HDR ($39.95 from www.aurorahdr.com).

I'll explain more about HDR photography, and how to explore it with your RX100 V later in this chapter. For now, though, I'm going to concentrate on showing you how to get the best exposures possible without resorting to such tools, using only the features of your camera.

Quantity of light, light passed by the lens, the amount of time the shutter is open, and the sensitivity of the sensor all work proportionately and reciprocally to produce an exposure. That is, if you double the amount of light, increase the aperture size by one stop, make the shutter speed twice as long, or double the ISO, you'll get twice as much exposure. Similarly, you can reduce any of these and reduce the exposure when that is preferable.

As we'll see however, changing any of those aspects in P, A, or S mode does not change the actual exposure; that's because the camera also makes changes when you do so, in order to maintain the same exposure. That's why Sony provides other methods for modifying the exposure in those modes.

F/STOPS AND SHUTTER SPEEDS

Especially if you're new to advanced cameras, it's worth quickly reviewing some essential concepts. For example, the lens aperture, or f/stop, is a ratio, much like a fraction, which is why a "standard" full-stop aperture of f/2 (just 1/3-stop smaller than your camera's f1.8 maximum aperture) is larger than f/4, just as 1/2 is larger than 1/4. However, f/2 is actually *four times* as large as f/4. (Think back to high school geometry where we learned that to double the area of a circle, you multiply its diameter by the square root of two: 1.4.)

The full f/stops available with the RX100 V's f/1.8 lens are f/2, f/2.8, f/4, f/5.6, f/8, and f/11 (the smallest f/stop available with this camera.) Each higher number indicates an aperture that's half the size of the previous number. Hence, it admits half as much light as the one before. Figure 7.3 shows a simplified representation. (I've brightened the iris to make it more visible.)

Of course, you can also set intermediate apertures with the RX100 V, such as f/6.3 and f/7.1, which are the 1/3-stop increments between the full stops f/5.6 and f/8.

Shutter speeds are actual fractions (of a second), so that 1/60, 1/125, 1/250, 1/500, 1/1000, and so forth represent 1/60th, 1/125th, 1/250th, 1/500th, and 1/1000th second. Each higher number indicates a shutter speed that's half as long as the one before. (And yes, intermediate shutter speeds can also be used, such as 1/640 or 1/800th second.) To avoid confusion, Sony uses quotation marks to signify long exposures: 0.8", 2", 2.5", 4", and so forth; these examples represent 0.8-second, 2-second, 2.5-second, and 4-second exposures, respectively.

Figure 7.3

Top row (left to right): f/2, f/2.8, f/4; bottom row: f/5.6, f/8, f/11.

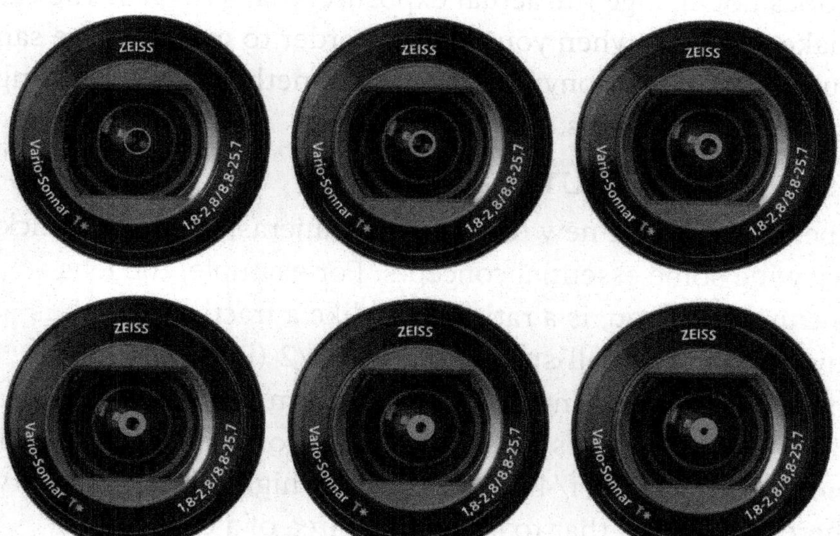

Equivalent Exposure

One of the most important aspects in this discussion is the concept of "equivalent exposure." This term means that exactly the same amount of light will reach the sensor at various combinations of aperture and shutter speed. Whether we use a small aperture (large f/number) with a long shutter speed or a wide aperture (small f/number) with a fast shutter speed, the amount of light reaching the sensor can be exactly the same. **Table 7.1** shows equivalent exposure settings using various shutter speeds and f/stops; in other words, any of the combination of settings listed will produce exactly the same exposure.

Table 7.1

Equivalent Exposures

Shutter Speed	f/stop
1/125th second	f/11
1/250th second	f/8
1/500th second	f/5.6
1/1,000th second	f/4
1/2,000th second	f/2.8
1/4,000th second	f/2

When you set the camera to P mode, it sets both the aperture and the shutter speed that should provide a correct exposure, based on guidance from the light metering system. In P mode, you cannot change the aperture or the shutter speed individually, but you can shift among various aperture/shutter speed combinations by rotating the control wheel, providing what is called *program shift*. (If you use program shift, an asterisk will appear next to the P on your display screens to let you know you've made an adjustment.) Just rotate the control wheel counterclockwise to change to a slower shutter speed/smaller aperture, or clockwise to switch to a higher shutter speed/larger aperture. (See **Figure 7.4.**)

Moreover, if you change the ISO, the camera will set a different combination automatically. As the concept of equivalent exposure indicates, the image brightness will be exactly the same in every photo you shoot with the various combinations because they all provide the same exposure.

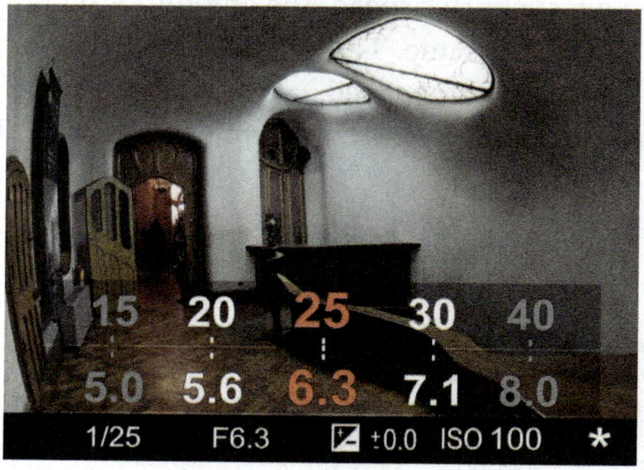

Figure 7.4

In Program mode, rotate the control wheel to change to an equivalent exposure.

In Aperture Priority and Shutter Priority (S) modes, you can change the aperture or the shutter speed, respectively, by rotating the control wheel (unless you've defined another control to perform that function using the Custom Keys entry in the Custom Settings 5 menu). The camera will then change the other factor to maintain the same exposure. I'll cover all of the operating modes and the important aspects of exposure with each mode in this chapter.

How the RX100 V Calculates Exposure

Your camera calculates exposure by measuring the light that passes through the lens and reaches the sensor, based on the assumption that each area being measured reflects about the same amount of light as a neutral gray card that reflects a "middle" gray of about 12- to 18-percent reflectance.

Tip: The photographic "gray cards" you buy at a camera store have an 18-percent gray tone; your camera is calibrated to interpret a somewhat darker 12-percent gray. Yes, I know you've been told that your camera is set to an 18-percent gray standard in other books or in classes you've attended. That's an unfortunate myth that's been lingering for ages. You'll understand why that's so after I've explained how a gray tone is used to measure exposure.

That "average" middle gray assumption is necessary, because different subjects reflect different amounts of light, and your RX100 V doesn't measure the amount of light *falling* on your subject -- it measures the amount of light *reflected* by that subject. In a photo containing, say, a white cat and a dark gray cat, the white cat might reflect five times as much light as the gray cat. An exposure based on the amount of light reflected from the white cat will cause the gray cat to appear to be black, while an exposure based only on the gray cat will make the white cat appear washed out.

Correctly Exposed

The image shown in **Figure 7.5**, left represents how a photograph might appear if the exposure were calculated by measuring the light reflecting from the middle gray patch, which, for the sake of illustration, we'll assume reflects approximately 12 to 18 percent of the light that strikes it. The exposure meter in the RX100 V sees an object that it thinks is a middle gray, calculates an exposure based on that, and the patch in the center of the strip is rendered at its proper tonal value. Best of all, because the resulting exposure is correct, the black patch at left and white patch at right are rendered properly as well.

When you're shooting pictures with your RX100 V, and the meter happens to base its exposure on a subject that averages that "ideal" middle gray, then you'll end up with similar (accurate) results. The camera's exposure algorithms are concocted to ensure this kind of result as often as possible, barring any unusual subjects (that is, those that are backlit, or have uneven illumination). The camera has three different metering modes (described next), each of which is equipped to handle certain types of unusual subjects, as I'll outline.

Overexposed

Figure 7.5, center, shows what would happen if the exposure were calculated based on metering the leftmost, black patch. The light meter sees less light reflecting from the black square than it would see from a gray middle-tone subject, and so figures, "Aha! I need to add exposure to brighten this subject up to a middle gray!" That lightens the "black" patch, so it now appears to be gray.

But now the patch in the middle that was *originally* middle gray is overexposed and becomes light gray. And the white square at right is now seriously overexposed and loses detail in the highlights, which have become a featureless white. Our human subject is similarly overexposed.

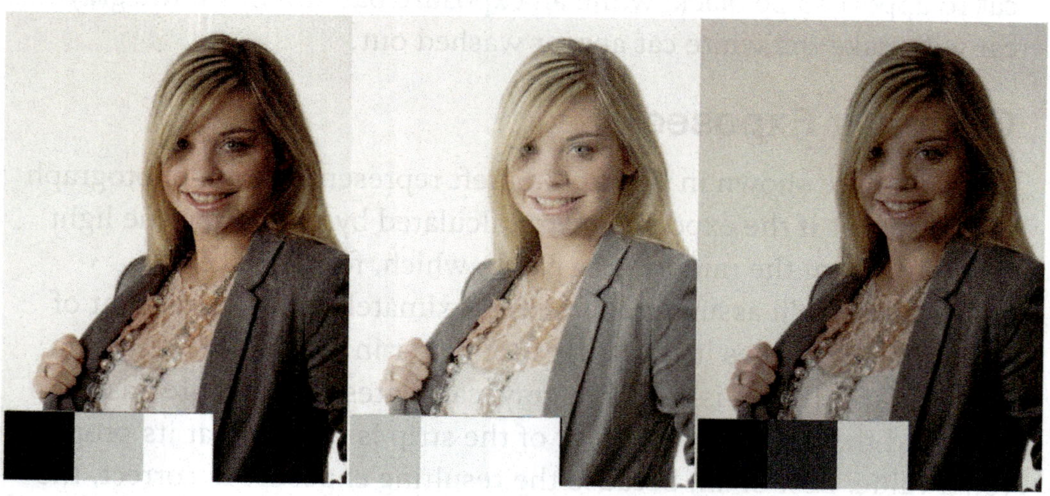

Figure 7.5

Calculating exposure by metering the center, left, and right patches.

Underexposed

The third possibility in this simplified scenario is that the light meter might measure the illumination bouncing off the white patch, and try to render that tone as a middle gray. A lot of light is reflected by the white square, so the exposure is *reduced*, bringing that patch closer to a middle gray tone. The patches that were originally gray and black are now rendered too dark. Clearly, measuring the gray card -- or a substitute that reflects about the same amount of light -- is the only way to ensure that the exposure is precisely correct. (See **Figure 7.5**, right.)

As you can see, the ideal way to measure exposure is to meter from a subject that reflects 12 to 18 percent of the light that reaches it. If you want the most precise exposure calculations, the solution is to use a stand-in, such as the evenly illuminated gray card I mentioned earlier. The standard Kodak gray card reflects 18 percent of the light that reaches it, what is considered to be a middle gray. But, as I said earlier, your RX100 V is calibrated for a somewhat darker tone than that middle gray, roughly 13 percent gray, so you would need to *add* about one-half stop *more* exposure than the value metered from the card.

Another substitute for a gray card is the palm of a human hand (the backside of the hand is too variable). But a human palm, regardless of ethnic group, is even brighter than a standard gray card, so instead of one-half stop more exposure, you need to add one additional stop. That is, if your meter reading is 1/500th of a second at f/11, use 1/500th second at f/8 or 1/250th second at f/11 instead. (Both exposures are equivalent.)

If you actually wanted to use a gray card, place it in your frame near your main subject, facing the camera, and with the exact same even illumination falling on it that is falling on your subject. Then, use the Spot metering function (described in the next section) to calculate exposure. Of course, in most situations, it's not necessary to do this. Your camera's light meter will do a good job of calculating the right exposure, especially if you use the exposure tips in the next section. But, I felt that explaining exactly what is going on during exposure calculation would help you understand how your RX100 V's metering system works.

Tracking Down the Gray Card Confusion

Why are so many photographers under the impression that camera light meters are calibrated to the 18-percent "standard," rather than the true value, which may be 12 to 14 percent, depending on the vendor? You'll find this misinformation in an alarming number of places. I've seen the 18-percent "myth" taught in camera classes; I've found it in books, and even been given this wrong information from the technical staff of camera vendors. (They should know better -- the same vendors' engineers who design and calibrate the cameras have the right figure.)

The most common explanation is that during a revision of Kodak's instructions for its gray cards in the 1970s, the advice to open up an extra half stop was omitted, and a whole generation of shooters grew up thinking that a measurement off a gray card could be used as-is. The proviso returned to the instructions by 1987, it's said, but by then it was too late. Next to me is a 2006 version of the instructions for KODAK Gray Cards, Publication R-27Q (still available from a variety of sources under license, despite the demise of Kodak). The directions read (with a bit of paraphrasing from me in italics):

- For subjects of normal reflectance increase the indicated exposure by 1/2 stop.
- For light subjects use the indicated exposure; for very light subjects, decrease the exposure by 1/2 stop. *(That is, you're measuring a subject that's lighter than middle gray.)*
- If the subject is dark to very dark, increase the indicated exposure by 1 to 1-1/2 stops. *(You're shooting a black subject.)*

Exploding the gray card myth still begs a couple of questions. Where did the 18-percent figure come from, and how can 18-percent gray be a "middle" gray? Shouldn't 50 percent be considered middle gray? For the answers, we need to resurrect a pioneering exposure method (originally for black-and-white photography) perfected by Ansel Adams called the *Zone System*. Adams divided the entire range of tonal values into a single chart with zones numbered from 0 to X (using Roman numbers, although the Romans didn't have a zero as such). Zone 0 is the darkest possible black, and Zone X is the lightest possible white. Each Zone indicates one stop more or less exposure than the following or preceding Zone.

As you might guess, Zone V, in the middle, represents a "middle gray" under the Zone System, and it happens to correspond to a gray value that reflects 18 percent of the light falling on it. That's because our eyes respond to light *logarithmically*, so that 18-percent gray appears to be a middle tone visually. However, photographic exposure, in contrast, changes *arithmetically*, in terms of stops. What we're really talking about is two different scales, the visual, in which 18-percent gray represents a middle tone to our eyes, and other processes, such as the printing process, in which black is black (0%), white is white (100%), and the middle tone is halfway between (at 50%). It's really only important to know the difference if you work in, say, the printing industry, or want to befuddle your photographer friends with an explanation. The 18-percent gray figure is useful because we want our middle gray to correspond to what we see.

So, why aren't cameras calibrated to 18-percent gray? The truth is that photographic camera manufacturers don't really care about the Zone System or scientific explanations. Their main concern is to make your pictures look good, and calibrate their cameras' exposure systems to help ensure that they do. Sony uses a specification called the *Recommended Exposure Index*, last updated in 2006, which allows the manufacturer to specify a camera model's exposure method arbitrarily, based on the vendor's opinion of what values produce pleasing, well-exposed images within its range of ISO settings. REI lends itself especially to the most common metering systems, such as the evaluative metering found in the RX100 V, and other Sony cameras. Sony, like other camera vendors, has selected a calibration point that, they feel, produces the best overall exposures.

EXTERNAL METERS CAN BE CALIBRATED

The light meters built into your RX100 V are calibrated at the factory and can only be changed using the Fine Tune Optimal Exposure option (Custom Setting b7 on the D4s; b6 on the D4). But if you use a hand-held incident or reflective light meter, you *can* calibrate it, using the instructions supplied with your meter. Because a hand-held meter can be calibrated to the 18-percent gray standard (or any other value you choose), my rant about the myth of the 18-percent gray card doesn't apply.

The Importance of ISO

Another essential concept when discussing exposure, ISO control allows you to change the sensitivity of the camera's imaging sensor. Sometimes photographers forget about this option, because the common practice is to set the ISO once for a particular shooting session (say, at ISO 100 or 200 for bright sunlight outdoors, or ISO 800 or 1600 when shooting indoors) and then forget about ISO. Or some shooters simply leave the camera set to ISO Auto. That enables the camera to change the ISO it deems necessary, setting a low ISO in bright conditions or a higher ISO in a darker location. That's fine, especially since you can specify the highest and lowest ISO sensitivities you want to deploy, and select the slowest shutter speed you want to use before Auto ISO kicks in, using the ISO and Auto ISO Minimum Shutter Speed entries in the Camera Settings 4 menu. (Explained in Chapter 3.)

However, often you'll want to set a specific ISO yourself. You can choose sensitivity settings from ISO 80 to 12800 directly. When shooting movies, only ISO 125 to ISO 12800 can be chosen directly. You cannot specify an ISO setting when you are shooting in Intelligent Auto, Superior Auto, any scene mode, or Sweep Panorama mode. The camera always uses ISO Auto (which is labeled Auto in the ISO menu and is second from the top in the selection column). Don't be confused by the top entry, Multi Frame Noise Reduction (MFNR), which can be set to specific ISO values or to its own Auto mode. In the latter case, its label will read "ISO Auto." (See **Figure 7.6.**)

When using Multi Frame Noise Reduction, you can specify Auto (the camera selects an appropriate ISO) or select from ISO 200 to ISO 25600. In MFNR mode, the RX100 V will take multiple photos and merge them together to provide an image with reduced noise.

Tip: When shooting in the Program (P), Aperture Priority , and Shutter Priority (S) modes, all discussed soon, changing the ISO does not change the exposure. If you switch from using ISO 100 to ISO 1600 in A mode for example, the camera will simply set a different shutter speed. If you change the ISO in S mode, the camera will set a different aperture, and in P mode, it will set a different aperture and/or shutter speed. In all of these examples, the camera will maintain the same exposure. If you want to make a brighter or a darker photo in P, A, or S mode, you would need to set + or - exposure compensation, as discussed later. However, when you use the Manual (M) mode, changing the ISO also changes the exposure, as discussed shortly.

In ISO Auto mode, you can specify a minimum ISO of 125 to ISO 3200, and a maximum ISO of 125 to ISO 12800, as explained in more detail in Chapter 3. When enabled, the camera will select an ISO that should be suitable for the conditions: a low ISO on a sunny day and a high ISO in a dark location. In Intelligent Auto, Superior Auto, Scene Selection, or Sweep Panorama modes, ISO Auto is the only available option.

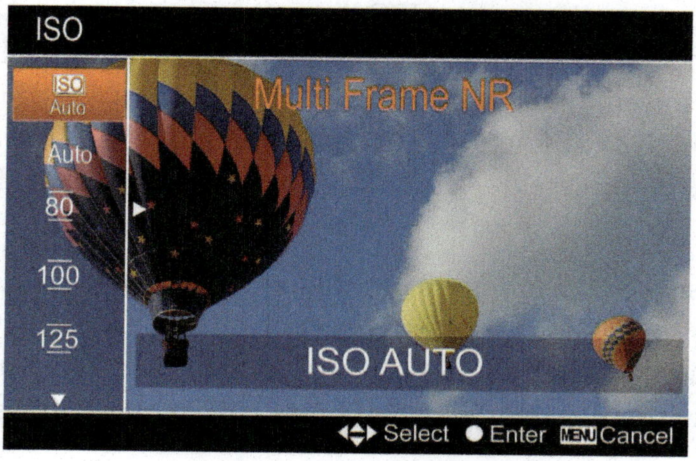

Figure 7.6

Left column, from top: Multi Frame Noise Reduction, ISO Auto, and ISO 80, 100, and 125 settings. You can scroll down to additional ISO values up to 12800.

Choosing a Metering Method

The Sony RX100 V has three different schemes for evaluating the light received by its exposure sensors. The quickest way to choose among them is to assign Metering Mode to a key using the Custom Key settings in the Custom Settings 6 menu, as described in Chapter 4. Then, you can press the defined key to produce the Metering Mode screen; then scroll up/down among the options. Without a custom key, the default method for choosing a metering mode is to use the Camera Settings 5 menu entry (see **Figure 7.7**), the Function menu, or Quick Navi menu.

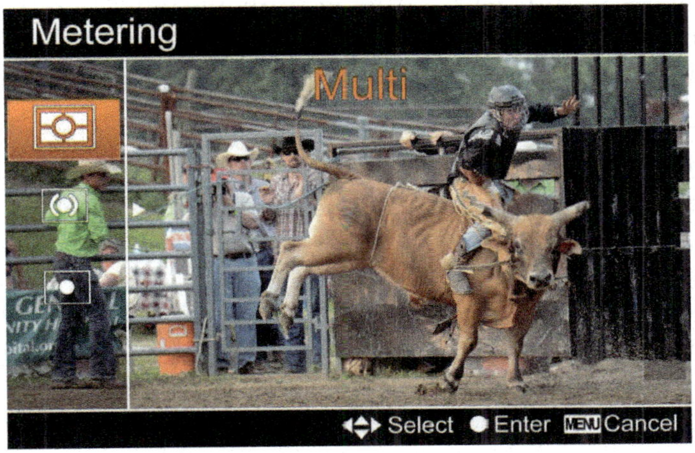

Figure 7.7.

The RX100 V provides three options for metering mode: Multi (the default), Center, and Spot (left, top to bottom).

- **Multi.** In this "intelligent" (multi-segment) metering mode, the camera meters the entire sensor frame, and then evaluates the measurements to make an educated guess about what kind of picture you're taking, based on examination of exposure data derived from thousands of different real-world photos. For example, if the top section of a picture is much lighter than the bottom portions, the algorithm can assume that the scene is a landscape photo with lots of sky. This mode is the best all-purpose metering method for most pictures.

The Multi system can recognize a very bright scene and it can automatically increase the exposure to reduce the risk of a dark photo. This will be useful when your subject is a snow-covered landscape or a close-up of a bride in white. Granted, you may occasionally need to use a bit of exposure compensation, but often, the exposure will be close to accurate even without it. (In my experience, the Multi system is most successful with light-toned scenes on bright days. When shooting in dark, overcast conditions, it's more likely to underexpose a scene of that type.)

- **Center.** This (center-weighted) metering was the only available option with cameras some decades ago. In this mode you get conventional metering without any "intelligent" scene evaluation. The light meter considers brightness in the entire frame but places the greatest emphasis on a large area in the center of the frame, as shown in **Figure 7.8**, left, on the theory that, for most pictures, the main subject will not be located far off-center.

  Of course, Center metering is most effective when the subject in the central area is a mid-tone. Even then, if your main subject is surrounded by large, extremely bright or very dark areas, the exposure might not be exactly right. (You might need to use exposure compensation, a feature discussed shortly.) However, this scheme works well in many situations if you don't want to use one of the other modes.

- **Spot.** This mode confines the reading to a very small area in the center of the image, as shown in **Figure 7.8**, right. (When you use the Flexible Spot autofocus options, however, the spot metering will be at the area where the camera sets focus.) The Spot meter does not apply any "intelligent" scene evaluation. Because the camera considers only a small target area, and completely ignores its surroundings, Spot metering is most useful when the subject is a small mid-tone area. For example, the "target" might be a tanned face, a medium red blossom, or a gray rock in a wide-angle photo; each of these is a mid-tone.

And that is important as you will recall from our example involving the cats.

The Spot metering technique is simple if you want to Spot meter a small area that's dead center in the frame. If the "target" is off-center, you would need to point the lens at it and use the AE Lock technique discussed later in this chapter. For **Figure 7.8**, Spot metering was used at right to base the exposure on an area in the center of the frame.

If you Spot meter a light-toned area or a dark-toned area, you will get underexposure or overexposure respectively; you would need to use an override for more accurate results. On the other hand, you can Spot meter a small mid-tone subject surrounded by a sky with big white clouds or by an indigo blue wall and get a good exposure. (The light meter ignores the subject's surroundings so they do not affect the exposure.) That would not be possible with Center-weighted metering, which considers brightness in a much larger area.

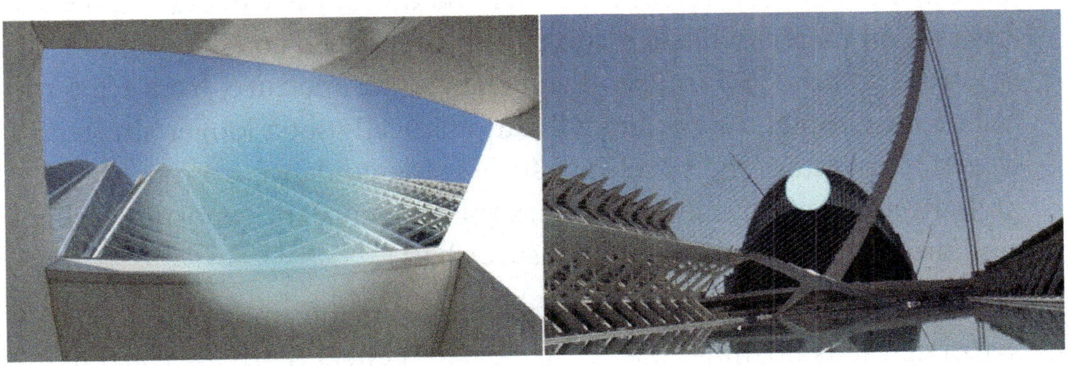

Figure 7.8

Center metering emphasizes the center area (left). Meter from precise areas in an image using Spot metering.

Choosing an Exposure Mode

After you set a desired metering mode, you have several methods for choosing the appropriate shutter speed and aperture, semi-automatically or manually. Spin the mode dial to the exposure mode that you want to use. If the Mode Dial Guide is activated in the Setup 2 menu (as described in Chapter 6), you'll see a display that briefly explains what the selected mode does. Your choice of which is best for a given shooting situation will depend on aspects like your need for extensive or shallow depth-of-field (the range of acceptably sharp focus in a photo) or the desire to freeze action or to allow motion blur. The semi-automatic Aperture Priority and Shutter Priority modes discussed in the next section emphasize one aspect of image capture or another, but the following sections introduce you to all four of the modes that photographers often call "creative."

Aperture Priority Mode

When using the A mode, you specify the lens opening (aperture or f/stop) with the control wheel. After you do so, the camera (guided by its light meter) will set a suitable shutter speed considering the aperture and the ISO in use. If you change the aperture, from f/5.6 to f/11 for example, the camera will automatically set a longer shutter speed to maintain the same exposure, using guidance from the built-in light meter. (I discussed the concept of equivalent exposure earlier and provided the equivalent exposure chart).

Aperture Priority is especially useful when you want to use a particular lens opening to achieve a desired effect. Perhaps you'd like to use the smallest aperture (such as f/11) to maximize depth-of-field (DOF), to keep the entire subject sharp in a close-up picture. Or, you might want to use a large aperture (small f/number like f/4) to throw everything except your main subject out of focus, as in **Figure 7.9**. Maybe you'd just like to "lock in" a particular f/stop, such as f/8, because it allows your lens to provide the best optical quality. Or, you might prefer to use f/2.8 even though your RX100 V's lens has a maximum aperture of f/1.8, because you want the best compromise between shutter speed and optical quality.

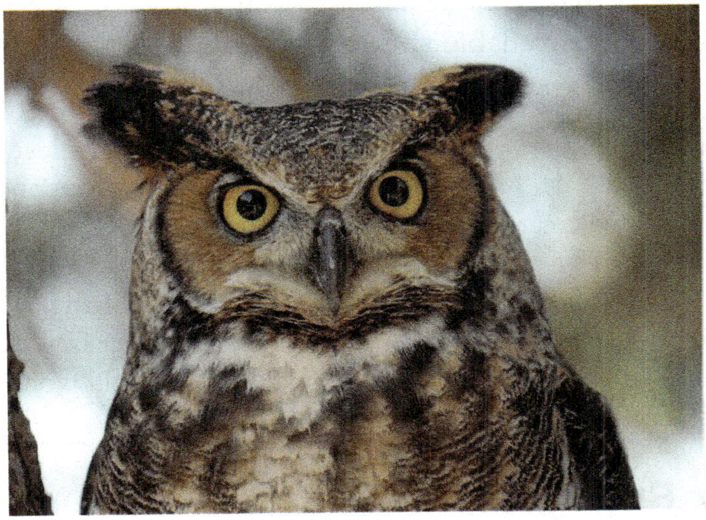

Figure 7.9

Use Aperture Priority mode to "lock in" a wide aperture (denoted by a large f/number) when you want to blur the background.

Aperture Priority can even be used to specify a *range* of shutter speeds you want to use under varying lighting conditions, which seems almost contradictory. But think about it. You're shooting a soccer game outdoors with a telephoto and want a relatively fast shutter speed, but you don't care if the speed changes a little should the sun duck behind a cloud. Set your camera's shooting mode to A, and adjust the aperture using the control wheel until a shutter speed of, say, 1/1,000th second is selected at the ISO level that you're using. (In bright sunlight at ISO 400, that aperture is likely to be around f/11.) Then, go ahead and shoot, knowing that your RX100 V will maintain that f/11 aperture (for sufficient DOF as the soccer players move about the field), but will drop down to 1/800th or 1/500th second if necessary should a light cloud cover part of the sun.

When the camera cannot provide a good exposure at the aperture you have set, the +/- symbol and the shutter speed numeral will blink in the LCD display. The blinking warns that the camera is unable to find an appropriate shutter speed at the aperture you have set, considering the ISO level in use and over- or underexposure will occur. That's the major pitfall of using Aperture Priority: you might select an f/stop that is too small or too large to allow an optimal exposure with the available shutter speeds.

Tip: Remember that your RX100 V has a built-in physical 3-stop neutral-density filter you can activate any time the smallest available aperture of f/11 isn't sufficient to allow the slow shutter speed you want to use for creative effect. You can enable the ND filter in the Camera Settings 5 menu, the Function menu, or the Quick Navi screen. You can even define a button to activate it, using the Custom Keys options discussed in Chapter 4. When the filter is active, instead of using, say 1/30th second at f/11, you could work with 1/4 second at f/11 instead at the same ISO setting.

Shutter Priority (S) Mode

Shutter Priority is the inverse of Aperture Priority. You set the shutter speed you'd like, using the control wheel, and the camera sets an appropriate f/stop considering the ISO that's in use. When you change the shutter speed, the camera will change the aperture to maintain the same (equivalent) exposure using guidance from the built-in light meter. Shutter Priority mode gives you some control over how much action-freezing capability your digital camera brings to bear in a particular situation. In other cases, you might want to use a slow shutter speed to add some blur to a sports photo that would be mundane if the action were completely frozen (see **Figure 7.10**).

Take care when using a slow shutter speed such as 1/8th second, because you'll potentially get blurring from camera shake unless you're using a tripod or other firm support. Of course, this applies to any mode, but in most modes the camera displays a camera shake warning icon when the shutter speed is long. In Chapter 3, I explain how to switch among the RX100 V's three SteadyShot modes (plus Off), Intelligent Active, Active, and Standard.

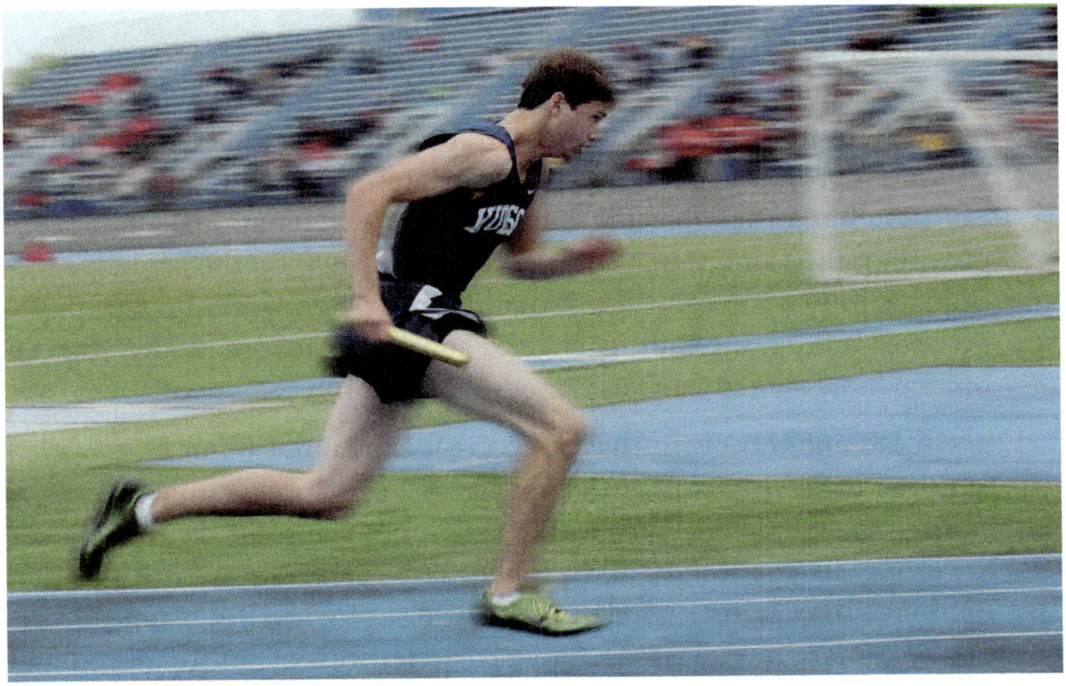

Figure 7.10

Set a slow shutter speed when you want to introduce blur into an action shot, as with this panned image of a relay runner.

As in Aperture Priority, you can encounter a problem in Shutter Priority mode; this happens when you select a shutter speed that's too long or too short for correct exposure under certain conditions. I've shot outdoor soccer games on sunny fall evenings and used Shutter Priority mode to lock in a 1/1,000th second shutter speed, only to find that my camera refused to produce the correct exposure when the sun dipped behind some trees and there was no longer enough light to shoot at that speed, even with the lens wide open.

Program Auto (P) Mode

The Program mode uses the camera's built-in smarts to set an aperture/shutter speed combination, based on information provided by the light meter. If you're using Multi metering, the combination will often provide a good exposure. Rotate the control wheel and you can switch to other aperture/shutter speed combinations, all providing the same (equivalent) exposure. The P on the screen changes to P*. You can't use Program Shift when working with flash. To reverse Program Shift, change to another exposure mode (you can immediately switch back to P mode) or turn the camera off.

In the unlikely event that the correct exposure cannot be achieved with the wide range of shutter speeds and apertures available, the shutter speed and aperture will both blink. (The solution is to set a lower ISO in bright light and a higher ISO in dark locations until the blinking stops.) The P mode is the one to use when you want to rely on the camera to make reasonable basic settings of shutter speed and aperture, but you want to retain the ability to adjust many of the camera's settings yourself. All overrides and important functions are available, including ISO, white balance, metering mode, exposure compensation, and others.

Making Exposure Value Changes

Sometimes you'll want a brighter or darker photo (more or less exposure) than you got when relying on the camera's metering system. Perhaps you want to underexpose to create a silhouette effect, or overexpose to produce a high-key (very light) effect. It's easy to do so by using the RX100 V's exposure compensation features, available only in P, S, A, M, Panorama, and Movie modes. In Manual exposure mode, exposure compensation can be dialed in only when ISO Auto is activated, as the camera will leave your shutter speed and aperture settings undisturbed and add or subtract exposure by changing ISO sensitivity instead. There are several ways to set exposure compensation:

- **Down button.** Unless you've redefined it, just press the down directional button and rotate the control wheel to specify plus or minus three stops of exposure compensation, in one-third stop increments. This is the fastest method.
- **Exposure Compensation menu.** You can also venture to the Camera Settings 4 menu, where the Exposure Comp. entry will let you set plus or minus three stops of exposure using the control wheel.
- **Function menu.** Unless you've redefined your Function menu to remove it, exposure compensation can also be applied by pressing the Fn button and using the Function menu. Its default position is fifth from the left in the top row of functions. The Function menu entry also lets you choose up to three stops of compensation.
- **Quick Navi menu.** When the Quick Navi screen is visible, press the Fn button and navigate to the exposure scale in the middle to add or subtract up to three stops of exposure compensation. Note that the flash exposure compensation scale shares this space; toggle between the two with the up/down button.

In my experience, adding exposure compensation is the option that's most often necessary. I'll often set +2/3 when using Multi metering if the camera underexposed my first photo of a light-toned scene. With Center-weighted or Spot metering, +1.3 or an even higher level of plus compensation is almost always necessary with a light-toned subject. Since the camera provides a live preview of the scene (when Setting Effect is turned on), it's easy to predict when the photo you'll take is likely to be obviously over- or underexposed. When the histogram display is on, you can make a more accurate prediction about the exposure; I'll discuss this feature shortly. Of course, you can also use plus compensation when you want to intentionally overexpose a scene for a creative effect.

You won't often need to use minus compensation. This feature is most likely to be useful when metering a dark-toned subject, such as close-ups of black animals or dark blue buildings, for example. Since these dark-toned subjects lead the camera to overexpose, set -2/3 or -1 compensation (when using Multi metering) for a more accurate exposure. (The amount of minus compensation that you need to set may be quite different when using the other two metering modes.) Minus compensation can also be useful for intentionally underexposing a scene for a creative effect, such as a silhouette of a sailboat or a group of friends on a beach.

Any exposure compensation you set will remain active for all photos you take afterward. The camera provides a reminder as to what value is currently set in some display modes. Turning the RX100 V off and then back on does not set compensation back to zero; when you no longer need to use it, be sure to do so yourself. If you inadvertently leave it set for +1 or -1 for example, your photos taken under other circumstances will be overexposed or underexposed.

Manual Exposure (M) Mode

Part of being an experienced photographer comes from knowing when to rely on your RX100 V 's automation (including Intelligent Auto, Superior Auto, P mode, and SCN mode settings), when to go semi-automatic (with Shutter Priority or Aperture Priority), and when to set exposure manually (using M). Some photographers actually prefer to set their exposure manually. This is quite convenient since the camera is happy to provide an indication of when your settings will produce over- or underexposure, based on its metering system's judgment. It can even indicate how far off the "correct" (recommended) exposure your photo will be at the settings you have made.

I often hear comments from novices first learning serious photography claiming that they must use Manual mode in order to take over control from the camera. While a back-to-basics approach does force you to learn photographic principles, it's not always necessary. For example, you can control all important aspects when using semi-automatic A or S mode as discussed in the previous sections. This allows you to adjust depth-of-field (the range of acceptable sharpness) or the rendition of motion (as blurred or as frozen). You can set a desired ISO level; that will not change the exposure. You would use exposure compensation when you want a brighter or a darker photo.

Manual mode provides an alternative that allows you to control the aperture and the shutter speed and the exposure simultaneously. For example, if you want to seriously underexpose a backlit subject to create a silhouette effect, you probably won't get exactly the desired effect with A or S mode while experimenting with various levels of exposure compensation. Instead, switch to M mode, set an appropriate ISO, and then set an aperture/shutter speed that might provide the intended exposure. After taking a test shot, change the aperture slightly until you get an image with the interpretation of the scene that you want.

The Basic M Mode Technique

Depending on your proclivities, you might not need to use M mode very often, but it's still worth understanding how it works. Here are your considerations:

- Rotate the mode dial to M.
- Use the control ring to adjust aperture and the control wheel to adjust shutter speed (unless you've swapped their functions, as described in Chapter 6). The setting that is currently active will be highlighted in orange.
- As you adjust the settings, an enlarged label showing the current shutter speed will be displayed on the screen, along with the usual shutter speed display at the bottom. If you have Exposure Set Guide in the Custom Settings 2 menu set to On, additional enlarged labels showing the changing shutter speed will scroll along the bottom of the screen, unless you choose the Graphic display mode with the DISP button. In that case, scales will show the current shutter speed and aperture at the same time.
- Any change you make to either factor affects the exposure, of course, so if you have Live View Display in the Custom

Settings 2 menu set to Setting Effect ON, you'll see the display getting darker or brighter as you change settings.

- If the display you're viewing includes the histogram graph, that will provide an even better indication of the exposure you'll get as you set different apertures or shutter speeds. I'll explain histograms later in this chapter.

A guide at the bottom of the monitor or viewfinder indicates whether your current settings yield a correct exposure as metered.

- **LCD monitor**. A label reading MM appears at the bottom of the screen. To use the exposure suggested by the camera, adjust the shutter speed or f/stop until the MM guide reads -+ 0.0. Over and underexposure is indicated by + and - readouts.
- **Viewfinder.** An analog scale from -3 to +3 appears. To use the camera's suggested exposure, adjust shutter speed or aperture until the indicator is centered at the 0 point.

Long Exposures

You can specify exposures as long as 30 seconds when using P, A, or S modes. In Manual exposure mode, you can select B (for bulb exposure), located *after* the 30-second option. Bulb cannot be selected when using Auto HDR, Continuous Shooting, or Multi Frame Noise Reduction.

In Bulb mode, you can press and hold the shutter release button, and the shutter will remain open as long as the button is depressed. Standing there with your finger on the trigger, so to speak, can produce vibration, so I prefer to use a wired release with a locking button, such as the Sony RM-VPR1 ($65), which plugs into the multi terminal connector on the camera.

Adjusting Exposure with ISO Control in M Mode

As mentioned in the previous section, changing the ISO level is another method of changing the exposure in M mode, whether you adjust it yourself manually, or activate Auto ISO and let the camera do it for you when you add or subtract exposure compensation.

Most photographers control the aperture and/or shutter speed exclusively to adjust exposure, sometimes forgetting about the option to adjust ISO. The common practice is to set the ISO once for a particular shooting session (say, at ISO 100 outdoors on a bright days or ISO 1600 when shooting indoors). There is also a tendency to use the lowest ISO level possible because of a concern that high ISO levels produce images with obvious digital noise (such as a grainy effect). However, changing the ISO is a valid way of adjusting exposure in M mode.

Indeed, I find myself using ISO adjustment as a convenient alternate way of adding or subtracting EV (exposure values) when shooting in Manual mode, and as a quick way of choosing equivalent exposures when in automatic or semi-automatic modes. For example, I've selected a manual exposure with both f/stop and shutter speed suitable for my image using, say, ISO 400. I can change the exposure in full-stop increments by adjusting the ISO sensitivity. The difference in image quality/noise is not much different at ISO 200 or ISO 800 than at ISO 400, and this exposure control method allows me to shoot at my preferred f/stop and shutter speed while retaining control of the exposure.

Or, perhaps, I am using Shutter Priority mode and the metered exposure at ISO 400 is 1/500th second at f/11. If I decide on the spur of the moment I'd rather use 1/500th second at f/8, I can press the quickly switch to ISO 200. Of course, it's a good idea to monitor your ISO changes, so you don't end up at ISO 6400 or above accidentally; a setting like that will result in more digital noise (graininess) in your image than you would like. In M mode, you can use Auto ISO, as discussed in the section that follows. Higher ISO levels are necessary only when shooting in a very dark location where a fast shutter speed is important; this might happen during a sports event in a dark arena, for example.

Using ISO Auto

ISO Auto is a powerful feature, available in PSAM and Movie modes. In your camera's Fn and Camera Settings 5 ISO menus, it's designated as Auto; the setting labeled ISO Auto is actually Multi Frame Noise Reduction, and it's easy to get the two confused. ISO Auto provides two major benefits. First, if the shutter speed and aperture settings in use won't provide a proper exposure, ISO Auto can adjust the ISO setting to compensate. Second, you can use ISO Auto to "lock in" a particular shutter speed or aperture (or both, in Manual mode), and use ISO sensitivity to compensate for changing or low-light conditions.

In the first case, suppose you were shooting a moving subject in Aperture Priority mode and your selected f/stop would result in a shutter speed of 1/8th second at ISO 400. All the image stabilization in the world can't protect you from blur caused by *subject* movement. If you were using ISO Auto with the RX100 V and had specified a minimum shutter speed of 1/30th second in the Camera Settings 5 menu (as described in Chapter 3), the camera's exposure system would automatically increase ISO from 400 to 1600. Most of us would prefer a slight increase in noise from the ISO boost than a blurry photograph.

With the RX100 V, the minimum (slowest) shutter speed allowed before ISO Auto kicks in can be specified in the Camera Settings 5 menu. The setting has no effect when you're using Shutter Priority, as the shutter speed you choose is locked in. But in Program and Aperture Priority modes, you can choose that minimum. If you were shooting action and wanted to ensure that P and A modes would try to use a shutter speed of 1/250th second or faster, you could select that speed as the minimum speed before ISO Auto would increase sensitivity. If you were shooting subjects with little movement, you might select 1/8th second and count on the camera and/or lens's image stabilization to give you sharp results. For most general applications, a minimum of 1/30th second should work well.

We're not done yet. ISO Auto also allows you to choose a *minimum* and *maximum* ISO speed to be used. If you want to avoid noise, you could set the Minimum ISO to 100 and the Maximum to 800, and still gain the benefits of using ISO Auto. If you wouldn't mind seeing a little noise, you could set the Maximum somewhat higher. Coupled with Minimum Shutter speed (with the RX100 V), ISO Auto gives you quite a bit of flexibility in controlling the range of shutter speeds and apertures used.

Don't forget that in Manual exposure mode, you can use ISO Auto in a special way. As you might expect, the shutter speed and aperture are selected by you and fixed at those settings until you change them. However, if ISO Auto is active, you can add or subtract exposure compensation, as described earlier, by rotating the exposure compensation dial on top of the camera, or by using the menu, Function menu, or a physical ISO control.

Exposure Bracketing

While exposure compensation lets you adjust exposure, sometimes you'll want to quickly shoot a series of photos at various exposures in a single burst. Doing so increases the odds of getting one photo that will be exactly right for your needs, and is particularly useful when assembling high dynamic range (HDR) composite images manually. This technique is called bracketing.

Years ago, before high-tech cameras became the norm, it was common to bracket exposures when shooting color slide film especially, by taking three (or more) photos at different exposures in Manual mode. Eventually, exposure compensation became a common feature as cameras gained semi-automatic modes; it was then possible to bracket exposures by setting a different compensation level for each shot in a series, such as 0, -1, and +1 or 0, -1/3 and +2/3.

Today, cameras like the RX100 V give you a lot of options for automatically bracketing exposures. When Bracket is active, you can take a series of consecutive photos: one at the metered ("correct") exposure, and others with more or less exposure. **Figure 7.11** shows an image with the metered exposure (center), flanked by exposures of 2/3 stop more (left), and 2/3 stop less (right).

Bracketing cannot be performed when using Auto mode, any SCN mode, Sweep Panorama mode, or when using the Smile Shutter or Auto HDR features. If flash is used, you must take the photos one at a time, manually, rather than in a continuous burst. Exposure bracketing can be used with both RAW and JPG capture. When it's set, the camera will fire the shots in a sequence if you keep the shutter release button depressed; you can also decide to shoot the photos one at a time.

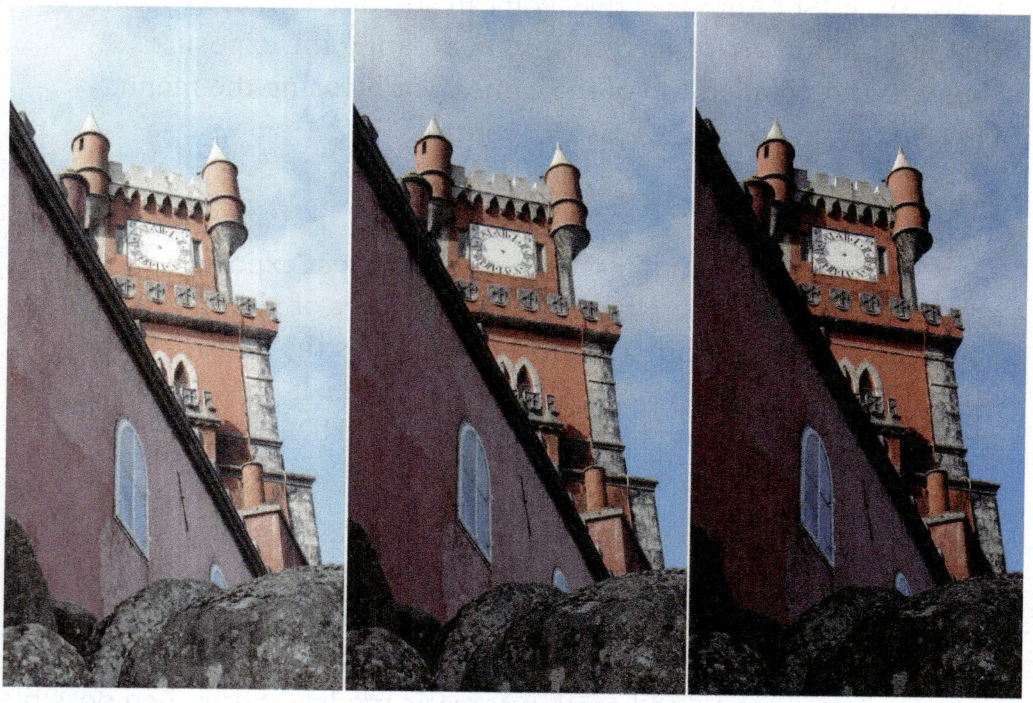

Figure 7.11

Metered exposure (center) accompanied by bracketed exposures of 2/3 stop more (left) and 2/3 stop less (right).

Bracketing is activated using the Drive settings, which can be found in the Camera Settings 3 menu, Function menu, and summoned by pressing the left directional button or some other button you've defined as the Drive button. Four different bracketing modes can be selected: continuous bracket, single bracket, white balance bracket, and DRO (dynamic range optimizer) bracket, plus an additional Self-Timer During Bracketing option for exposure bracketing (this option must be activated using the Bracket Settings entry of the Camera Settings 3 menu).

Continuous Bracketing

This mode captures three, five, or nine images in one burst when the shutter release is held down, bracketing them 0.3, 0.7, 1.0, 2.0, or 3.0 stops apart. When you highlight Cont. Bracket in the Drive menu, the left/right buttons are used to select the increment between shots and the number of shots. In Manual exposure (when ISO Auto is disabled), or in Aperture Priority, the shutter speed will change. If ISO Auto is set in Manual exposure, the bracketed set will be created by changing the ISO setting. In Shutter Priority, the aperture will change. Use continuous mode when you want all the images in the set to be framed as similarly as possible, say, when you will be using them for manually assembled high dynamic range (HDR) photos.

You can use flash when continuous bracketing is active, and the RX100 V will adjust the *flash output* for each exposure, using the bracketing increment you specify. The shutter speed and aperture will not change. Because of the time required for the flash to recycle, you'll need to press the shutter button each time to take subsequent images (effectively switching the camera into Single Bracket mode, described next). Continuous Bracketing (and Single Bracketing) is disabled when using Superior Auto, SCN modes, or Sweep Panorama.

Only the last shot in the set is displayed when using Auto Review. With all types of bracketing, the exposure/bracket scale at the bottom of the EVF or LCD monitor (in Display All Info mode) will display indicators showing the number of images shot and the relative amount of underexposure or overexposure.

Don't forget that you can dial in exposure compensation, and *that* will affect the amount of over/underexposure applied while bracketing, too. You can bracket your exposures based on something other than the base (metered) exposure value. Set any desired exposure compensation, either a plus or a minus value. Then set the Bracketing level you want to use. The camera will bracket exposures as over, under, and equal to the *compensated* value.

Single Bracketing

This mode captures one bracketed image in a set of three or five shots each time you press the shutter release, bracketing them 0.3, 0.7, 1.0, 2.0, or 3.0 stops apart. The left/right buttons are used to select the increment and number of shots. In this mode, you can separate each image by an interval of your choice. You might want to use this variation when you want the individual images to be captured at slightly different times, say, to produce a set of images that will be combined in some artistic way. As with Continuous Bracketing, you can elevate and use the built-in flash, and the camera will adjust the flash output rather than the shutter speed or aperture.

Tip: The 1.0 to 3.0 EV options are the ones you might try first when bracketing if you plan to perform High Dynamic Range magic later on in Photoshop (with Merge to HDR), Elements (with Photomerge), or with another image editor that provides an HDR feature. That will allow you to combine images with different exposures into one photo with an amazing amount of detail in both highlights and shadows. To get the best results, mount your camera on a tripod, shoot in RAW format, and use BRK C3.0EV to get three shots with 3 EV of difference in exposure. Of course, with this camera, you also have the option of using the Auto HDR feature as well; this can provide very good results in the camera without the need to use any special HDR software.

White Balance Bracketing

In this mode, the camera shoots three images, each with a different adjustment to the color temperature. While you can't specify which direction the color bias is tilted, you can select Lo (the default) for small changes, or Hi, for larger changes using the left/right buttons. Only the last shot taken is displayed during Auto Review.

DRO Bracketing

This mode takes three images, with Lo (the default) or Hi adjustments to the dynamic range optimization. Use the left/right buttons to specify the degree of adjustment. Again, only the last shot taken is displayed during Auto Review. You'll find more about Dynamic Range Optimizing and HDR in an upcoming section.

Dealing with Digital Noise

Digital noise is that random grainy look with colorful speckles that some like to use as a visual effect, but most consider to be objectionable. That's because it robs your image of detail even as it adds that "interesting" texture. Noise is caused by two different phenomena: high ISO levels and long exposures. The RX100 V offers a menu item to minimize high ISO noise. In Chapter 3, I discussed the Camera Settings 6 menu item that you can use to modify the noise reduction processing; you might want to review the sections about High ISO NR and Long Exposure NR as a refresher.

High ISO Noise

Digital noise commonly appears when you set an ISO above ISO 1600 with the RX100 V. High ISO noise appears as a result of the amplification by the digital image process to increase the effective sensitivity of the sensor. While higher ISOs do pull details out of dark areas, they also amplify non-signal information randomly, creating noise.

High ISO Noise Reduction is very useful, although at default, it also tends to make images slightly softer as blurring the noise pattern also blurs some intricate details. The higher the ISO, the more aggressive the processing will be, depending on whether you've specified Normal or Low. The Low level for NR provides images that are more grainy but with better resolution of fine detail. Even if you've chosen Off, the camera still applies some noise reduction.

High ISO NR is grayed out when the camera is set to shoot only RAW format photos. The camera does not use this feature on RAW format photos since noise reduction -- at the optimum level for any photo -- can be applied in the software you'll use to modify and convert the RAW file to JPEG or TIFF. (If you shoot in RAW & JPEG, the JPEG images, but not the RAW files, will be affected by this camera feature.) I'll discuss Noise Reduction with software in more detail in the next section.

Long Exposure Noise

A similar digital noise phenomenon occurs during long time exposures, which allow more photons to reach the sensor, increasing your ability to capture a picture under low-light conditions. However, the longer exposures also increase the likelihood that some pixels will register as random, "phantom," photons, often because the longer an imager collects photos during an exposure, the hotter it becomes, and that heat can be mistaken by the sensor as actual photons. The camera tries to minimize this type of noise automatically; there is no separate control you can adjust to add more or less noise reduction for long exposures.

Long exposure noise reduction is used with JPEG exposures longer than one full second. (This feature is not used on RAW photos and in continuous shooting, bracketing, Panorama mode, Sports Action, and Hand-held Twilight scene modes.) When it's active, long exposure noise reduction processing removes random pixels from your photo, but some of the image-making pixels are unavoidably vanquished at the same time.

It's possible that you prefer the version made without NR, and you can achieve that simply by shooting RAW. Indeed, noise reduction can be applied with most image-editing programs. You might get even better results with an industrial-strength product like Nik Dfine, part of

Google's Nik collection, or Topaz DNoise or Enhance (www.topazlabs.com). You can apply noise reduction to RAW photos with Sony's Image Data Converter or any other versatile converter software. Some products are optimized for NR with unusually sophisticated processing, such as Photo Ninja (www.picturecode.com) and DXO Optics Pro's version 9 or higher (www.dxo.com).

SPECIAL MODES FOR BEST HIGH ISO QUALITY

As I'll discuss in the section on scene modes, the RX100 V offers two modes for use in low light at high ISO for superior image quality. When you use Hand-held Twilight and Anti Motion Blur, the camera shoots a series of photos and composites them into one after discarding most of the digital noise. These are automatic modes so they're not ideal for all types of serious photography but they certainly provide the "cleanest" images possible at high ISO with your camera.

Using Dynamic Range Optimizer

Dynamic Range Optimizer (DRO) and Auto HDR (discussed next) are features you can select from the Camera Settings 5 menu or the Function menu, as explained in Chapter 3. When enabled, the camera will examine your images as they are exposed, and, if the shadows appear to have detail even though they are too dark, will attempt to process the image so the shadows are lighter, with additional detail, without overexposing detailed highlights. The processed image is always saved as a JPEG, so if you are shooting RAW you won't notice a difference.

Here is how the DRO and Auto HDR features work:

- **DRO Off.** No optimization. You're on your own; the camera will not apply extra processing even to your JPEG photos. Of course, if you are shooting RAW (or RAW & JPEG) photos, you can apply DRO effects to your photo when converting it with the downloadable Image Data Converter SR software. (Other programs have different tools for lightening shadow areas and/or darkening highlight areas.) Use Off when shooting subjects of normal contrast, or when you want to capture an image just as you see it, without modification by the camera.

- **DRO.** Press the left/right buttons after scrolling to DRO Auto and you can then set a specific intensity level for the Dynamic Range Optimizer, from Level 1 through Level 5.

  If you do not want to set a specific level, simply scroll to DRO Auto and allow the camera to decide on the amount of increased dynamic range. With the Auto setting, the camera dives into your image, looking at various small areas to examine the contrast of highlights and shadows, making modifications to each section to produce the best combination of brightness and tones with detail. In my experience, Auto provides a mid level of DRO that's worth leaving on at all times.

- **HDR Auto.** In this mode, the RX100 V creates a high dynamic range photo. It starts by taking three JPEG photos, each at a different exposure; the three are then composited into one by the processor using the best-exposed areas from each photo. The final image will have a high dynamic range effect, with great detail in shadow areas and increased detail in bright areas. You can specify how dramatic the effect should be.

  After scrolling to DRO/Auto HDR, press the center button and then use the left/right buttons and set an HDR Level, from 1.0 EV to 6.0 EV. (One EV equals one stop of exposure). The higher the level you set, the greater the exposure difference will be among the three photos the camera will shoot to produce one with High Dynamic Range. There's no "best" setting; it depends on your personal preference. At a very high EV level, the effect will be dramatic, but the photo may not appear to be "natural" looking. See the section that follows for more on HDR photography.

The primary method for DRO processing is lightening the dark tones and mid tones of an image. The higher the level of DRO you set, the more significantly the processor will lighten those areas; that causes digital noise to be more and more noticeable, especially in photos made at ISO 800 and at higher ISO levels. This is one reason why you would not always want to set Level 4 or 5 for DRO, particularly when using a high ISO setting. The other reason is that very high DRO produces a somewhat unnatural looking effect with all shadow areas lighter than "normal." Auto and Levels 1 to 3 retain the most natural-looking effect.

When you activate DRO, you have your choice of specifying the aggressiveness of the processing (from Level 1 through Level 5), in which case it will *always* be applied at the level you specify. Or, you can set the feature to Auto and let the camera decide the ideal amount of optimization (or even when to apply it at all). Auto is usually your best choice, because the camera is pretty smart about choosing which images to process, and which to leave alone. Indeed, the camera's programming usually does a better job than a similar feature available in the Image Data Converter SR software you may have installed on your computer.

Figure 7.12 shows an image with DRO turned off, and using Level 1, Level 3, and Level 5 optimization. (The differences between, say Level 1 and 2, or 2 and 3 are subtle and wouldn't show up well on the printed page, so I skipped the even-numbered levels.) The printed page also doesn't show that DRO tends to increase the amount of noise in an image as it works more aggressively; it's usually a good idea to avoid using the feature at high ISO levels where noise tends to be a real problem under any conditions.

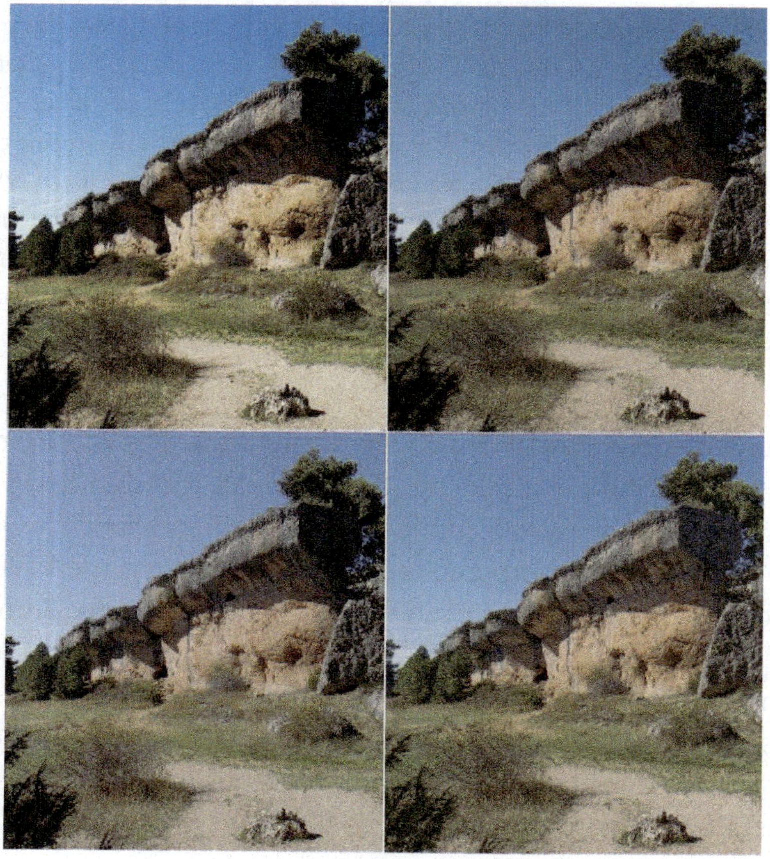

Figure 7.12

DRO Off (upper left); Level 1 (upper right); Level 3 (lower left); and Level 5 (lower right).

Working with HDR

High dynamic range (HDR) photography is quite the rage these days, and entire books have been written on the subject. Suppose you wanted to photograph a dimly lit room that had a bright window showing an outdoors scene. Proper exposure for the room might be on the order of 1/60th second at f/2.8 at ISO 200, while the outdoors scene probably would require f/11 at 1/400th second. That's almost a 7 EV step difference (approximately 7 f/stops) and well beyond the dynamic range of any digital camera, including the Sony RX100 V. (An additional problem, of course, is the mixed illumination: daylight outdoors and probably tungsten or fluorescent lamps indoors. Pro photographers sometimes gel the windows with corrective film so that inside/outside illumination matches.)

Until camera sensors gain much higher dynamic ranges (which may not be as far into the distant future as we think), special tricks like DRO and HDR photography will remain basic tools. With the Sony RX100 V, you can create in-camera HDR exposures, or shoot HDR the old-fashioned way -- with separate bracketed exposures that are later combined in a tool like Photomatix or Adobe's Merge to HDR image-editing feature. I'm going to show you how to use both.

Auto HDR

The camera's in-camera Auto HDR feature is simple and surprisingly effective in creating high dynamic range images. It's also remarkably easy to use. It can be dialed in using the DRO/Auto HDR entries found in the menu, Function menu, and any key you might define with that function.

Although Auto HDR combines only three images to create a single HDR photograph, in some ways it's as good as the manual HDR method I'll describe in the section after this one. For example, it allows you to specify an exposure differential of six stops/EV between the three shots, whereas the camera shooting bracketed exposures is limited to no more than three EV between shots.

Figure 7.13, left illustrates how the three shots that the camera's Auto HDR feature merges might look. There is a one-stop differential between each of the images, from the underexposed image at top, the intermediate exposure in the middle, and the overexposed image at the bottom. The in-camera HDR processing is able to combine the three to derive an image similar to the one shown in **Figure 7.13**, right, which has a much fuller range of tones.

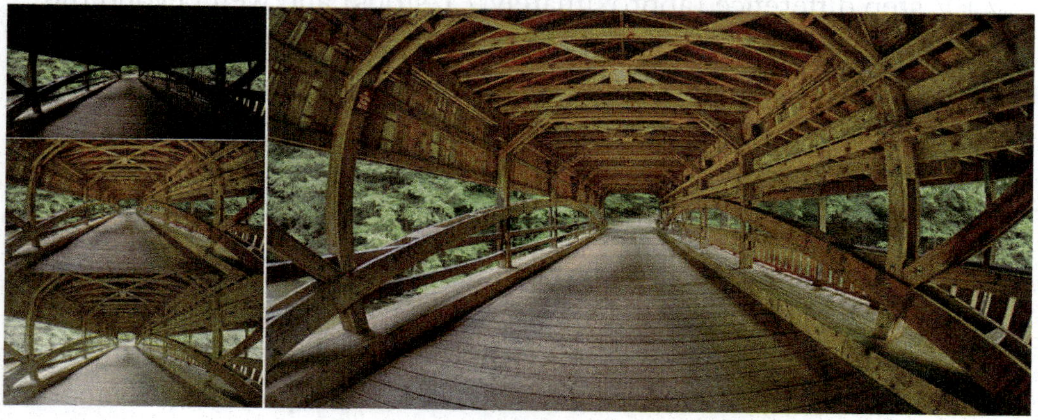

Figure 7.13

The three images can be automatically combined...(left) to produce this merged high dynamic range (HDR) image.

To use the camera's HDR feature, select it in the Camera Settings 5 menu's DRO/Auto HDR entry, or from the Fn menu. You can manually specify an increment from 1 EV to 6 EV, or choose Auto and allow the camera to select the appropriate differential. When you press the shutter release, the camera will take all three shots consecutively, align the images (because, if the camera is hand-held, there is likely to be a small amount of movement between shots), and then save one JPEG image to your memory card. The feature does not work if you have selected RAW or RAW+JPEG formats.

Bracketing and Merge to HDR

If your credo is "If you want something done right, do it yourself," you can also shoot HDR manually, without resorting to the camera's HDR mode. Instead, you can shoot individual images either by manually bracketing or using the camera's auto bracketing modes, described earlier in this chapter.

When you're using Merge to HDR Pro, you'd take several pictures, some exposed for the shadows, some for the middle tones, and some for the highlights. The exact number of images to combine is up to you. Four to seven is a good number. Then, you'd use the Merge to HDR Pro command to combine all of the images into one HDR image that integrates the well-exposed sections of each version.

Here's how.

The images should be as identical as possible, except for exposure. So, it's a good idea to mount the camera on a tripod, use a remote release, and take all the exposures in one burst. Just follow these steps:

1. **Set up the camera.** Mount the camera on a tripod.
2. Set the camera to shoot a bracketed burst of five to nine images with an increment of at least 2 EV.

   The description of how to do this will be found earlier in this chapter. As I noted there, you can set the camera to shoot up to nine exposures, each one increment apart, and use any or all of them for your HDR merger. For my example,, in **Figure 7.14**, left, I selected the best four out of nine images captured.
3. **Choose an f/stop.** Set the camera for Aperture Priority and select an aperture that will provide a correct exposure at your initial settings for the series of manually bracketed shots. *And then leave this adjustment alone!* You don't want the aperture to change for your series, as that would change the depth-of-field and, potentially, the image size of some elements. You want the camera to adjust exposure *only* using the shutter speed.

4. **Choose manual focus.** You don't want the focus to change between shots, so set the camera to manual focus, and carefully focus your shot.
5. **Choose RAW exposures.** Set the camera to take RAW files, which will give you the widest range of tones in your images. (This is an advantage of manually creating HDR files; the camera's Auto HDR feature can't be used when RAW or RAW+JPEG is active.)
6. **Take your bracketed set.** Press the button on the remote (or carefully press the shutter release or use the self-timer) and take the set of bracketed exposures.
7. **Continue with the Merge to HDR Pro steps listed next.** You can also use a different program, such as Photomatix or Nik software, if you know how to use it.

The next steps show you how to combine the separate exposures into one merged high dynamic range image. **Figure 7.14**, right shows the results you can get from a four-shot bracketed sequence.

1. **Copy your images to your computer.** If you use an application to transfer the files to your computer, make sure it does not make any adjustments to brightness, contrast, or exposure. You want the real raw information for Merge to HDR Pro to work with.
2. **Activate Merge to HDR Pro.** Choose File > Automate > Merge to HDR Pro.
3. **Select the photos to be merged.** Use the Browse feature to locate and select your photos to be merged. You'll note a check box that can be used to automatically align the images if they were not taken with the camera mounted on a rock-steady support. This will adjust for any slight movement of the camera that might have occurred when you changed exposure settings.
4. **Choose parameters (optional).** The first time you use Merge to HDR Pro, you can let the program work with its default parameters. Once you've played with the feature a few times,

you can read the Adobe Help files and learn more about the options than I can present in this non-software-oriented camera guide.

5. **Click OK.** The merger begins.
6. **Save.** Once HDR merge has done its thing, save the file to your computer.

If you do everything correctly, you'll end up with a photo like the one shown at right in **Figure 7.14**.

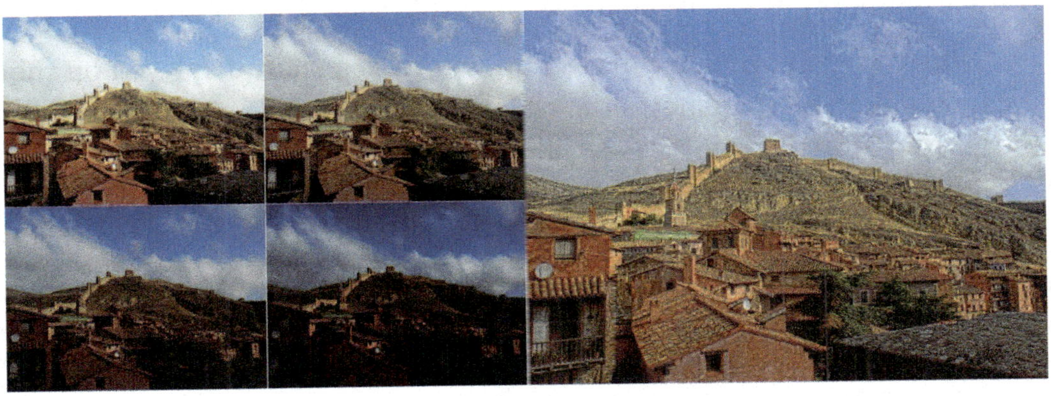

Figure 7.14

Fourbracketed photos (left) and the finished image (right.)

What if you don't have the opportunity, inclination, or skills to create several images at different exposures, as described? If you shoot in RAW format, you can still use Merge to HDR, working with a *single* original image file. What you do is import the image into Photoshop several times, using Adobe Camera Raw to create multiple copies of the file at different exposure levels.

For example, you'd create one copy that's too dark, so the shadows lose detail, but the highlights are preserved. Create another copy with the shadows intact and allow the highlights to wash out. Then, you can use Merge to HDR to combine the two and end up with a finished image that has the extended dynamic range you're looking for. (This concludes the image-editing portion of the chapter. We now return you to our alternate sponsor: photography.)

Exposure Evaluation with Histograms

While you may be able to improve poorly exposed photos in your image-editing software or with DRO or HDR techniques, it's definitely preferable to get the exposure close to correct in the camera. This will minimize the modifications you'll need to make in post-processing, which can be very time-consuming and will degrade image quality, especially with JPEGs. A RAW photo can tolerate more significant changes with less adverse effects, but for optimum quality, it's still important to have an exposure that's close to correct.

Instead, you can use a histogram, which is a chart displayed on the camera's screen that shows the number of tones that have been captured at each brightness level. Two types of histograms are available, a "live" histogram that appears at the lower-right corner of the screen in Shooting mode, and a larger, more detailed version that appears in Histogram mode during playback. The live version can help you make exposure decisions as you shoot, whereas the playback version is useful in determining corrections to be made before you take your next shot. I'll explain both versions, but first it's useful to understand exactly what you're seeing when you view a histogram.

The Live Histogram

The camera's live histogram offers the most reliable method for judging the exposure as you shoot (although the Zebra feature described in Chapter 4 can be used to isolate specific problems involving blown highlights). A pair of live histograms are also available for display for both the viewfinder and monitor; activate both with the DISP Button (Monitor/Finder) item in the Custom Settings 4 menu, as discussed in Chapter 4. After activating, press the DISP button a few times to reach the display that includes the histogram, which will be shown at lower right in the viewfinder and LCD monitor screens.

In Shooting mode, you'll get a luminance (brightness) histogram that shows the distribution of tones and brightness levels across the image given the current camera settings, including exposure compensation, Dynamic Range Optimizer (DRO) level in use, or the aperture, shutter speed, and ISO that you have set if using Manual mode. This live histogram (displayed before taking a photo) is useful for judging whether the exposure is likely to be satisfactory or whether you should use a camera feature to modify the exposure. When the histogram looks better, take the photo. I'll show you how to evaluate histograms later in this chapter.

The Playback Histograms

You can view histograms in Playback mode, too; press the DISP button until the display shown in **Figure 7.15** appears. The top graph, called the luminance or brightness histogram, is conventional, showing the distribution of tones across the image. Each of the other three histograms is in a specific color: red, green, and blue. That indicates the color channel you're viewing in that histogram: red, green, or blue. These additional graphs allow you to see the distribution of tones in the three individual channels. It takes a lot of expertise to interpret those extra histograms and, frankly, the conventional luminance histogram is the only one that many photographers use.

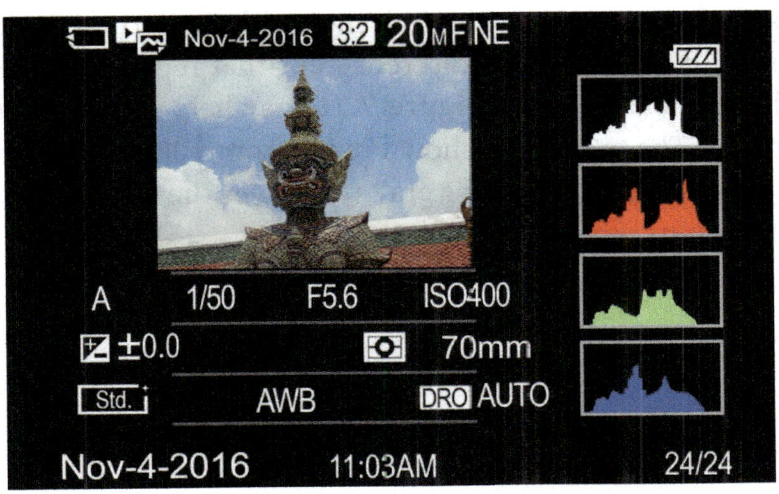

Figure 7.15

The Playback histograms show you the tonal distribution of a photo you've already taken.

As a bonus in Playback mode, another feature is available when the histograms are visible: any areas of the displayed image that are excessively bright, or excessively dark, will blink. This feature, often called "blinkies," warns that you may need to change your settings to avoid loss of detail in highlight areas (such as a white wedding gown) or in shadow areas (such as a black animal's fur). The camera also includes the Zebra feature to indicate overexposure, as discussed in Chapter 4. You can use the histogram information along with the flashing blinkie and Zebra alerts to guide you in modifying the exposure, and/or setting the DRO feature (discussed earlier), before taking the photo again.

Tonal Range

Histograms help you adjust the tonal range of an image, the span of dark to light tones, from a complete absence of brightness (black) to the brightest possible tone (white), and all the middle tones in between. Because all values for tones fall into a continuous spectrum between black and white, it's easiest to think of a photo's tonality in terms of a black-and-white or grayscale image, even though you're capturing tones in three separate color layers of red, green, and blue.

Because your images are digital, the tonal "spectrum" isn't really continuous: it's divided into discrete steps that represent the different tones that can be captured. **Figure 7.16** may help you understand this concept. The gray steps shown range from 100-percent gray (black) at the left, to 0-percent gray (white) at the right, with 20 gray steps in all (plus white).

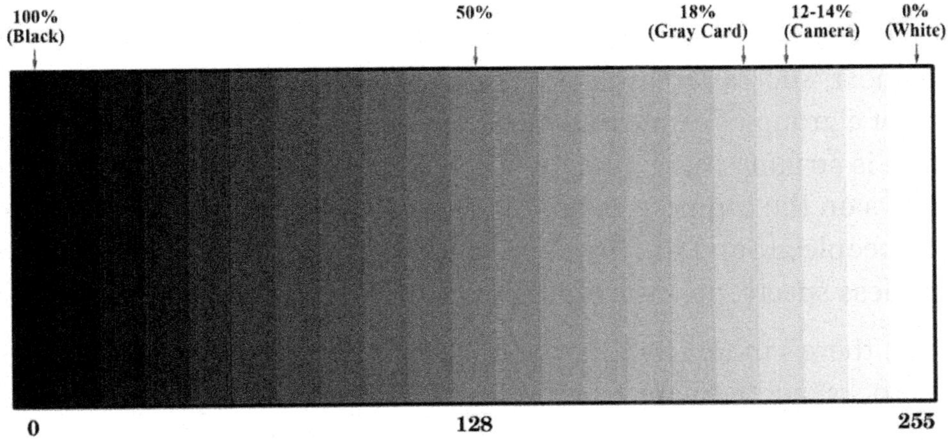

Figure 7.16

A tonal range from black (left) to white (right) and all the gray values in between.

Along the bottom of the chart are the digital values from 0 to 255 recorded by your sensor for an image with 8 bits per channel. (8 bits of red, 8 bits of green, and 8 bits of blue equal a 24-bit, full-color image.) Any black captured would be represented by a value of 0, the brightest white by 255, and the midtones would be clustered around the 128 marker.

Grayscale images (which we call black-and-white photos) are easy to understand. Or, at least, that's what we think. When we look at a black-and-white image, we think we're seeing a continuous range of tones from black to white, and all the grays in between. But, that's not exactly true. The blackest black in any photo isn't a true black, because some light is always reflected from the surface of the print, and if viewed on a screen, the deepest black is only as dark as the least-reflective area a computer monitor can produce. The whitest white isn't a true white, either, because even the lightest areas of a print absorb some light (only a mirror reflects close to all the light that strikes it), and, when viewing on a computer monitor, the whites are limited by the brightness of the display's LCD or LEDs picture elements. Lacking darker blacks and brighter, whiter whites, that continuous set of tones doesn't cover the full grayscale tonal range.

The full scale of tones becomes useful when you have an image that has large expanses of shades that change gradually from one level to the next, such as areas of sky, water, or walls. Think of a picture taken of a group of campers around a campfire. Since the light from the fire is striking them directly in the face, there aren't many shadows on the campers' faces. All the tones that make up the *features* of the people around the fire are compressed into one end of the brightness spectrum -- the lighter end.

Yet, there's more to this scene than faces. Behind the campers are trees, rocks, and perhaps a few animals that have emerged from the shadows to see what is going on. These are illuminated by the softer light that bounces off the surrounding surfaces. If your eyes become accustomed to the reduced illumination, you'll find that there is a wealth of detail in these shadow images.

This campfire scene would be a nightmare to reproduce faithfully under any circumstances. If you are an experienced photographer, you are probably already wincing at what is called a *high-contrast* lighting situation. Some photos may be high in contrast when there are fewer tones and they are all bunched up at limited points in the scale. In a low-contrast image, there are more tones, but they are spread out so widely that the image looks flat. Your digital camera can show you the relationship between these tones using a histogram.

Histogram Basics

Your camera's histograms are a simplified display of the numbers of pixels at each of 256 brightness levels, producing an interesting mountain range effect. Although separate charts may be provided for brightness and the red, green, and blue channels, when you first start using histograms, you'll want to concentrate on the brightness histogram.

Each vertical line in the graph represents the relative number of pixels in the image for each brightness value, from 0 (black) on the left to 255 (white) on the right. The vertical axis measures that relative number of pixels at each level. Ideally, all the tones in an image will fall within one of those two values. If not, there may be a spike at the left edge of the histogram, meaning that some black tones were clipped off, or, there may be a spike at the right edge, where some of the highlight details were clipped.

Contrast, Too

Although histograms are most often used to fine-tune exposure, you can glean other information from them, such as the relative contrast of the image. **Figure 7.17** shows a set of three generic histograms captured from an image-editing program, accompanied, at left, by images having normal (top), high (center), and low (bottom) contrast.

In the normal image, most of the pixels are spread across the image, with a healthy distribution of tones throughout the midtone section of the graph. That large peak at the right side of the graph represents all those light tones in the sky. A normal-contrast image you shoot may have less sky area, and less of a peak at the right side, but notice that very few pixels hug the right edge of the histogram, indicating that the lightest tones are not being clipped because they are off the chart.

Increasing the contrast of an image produces a histogram like the one shown at center in **Figure 7.17**. In this case, the tonal range is now spread over the entire width of the chart, but, except for the bright sky, there is not much variation in the middle tones; the mountain "peaks" are not very high. When you stretch the grayscale in both directions like this, the darkest tones become darker (that may not be possible) and the lightest tones become lighter (ditto). In fact, shades that might have been gray before can change to black or white as they are moved toward either end of the scale.

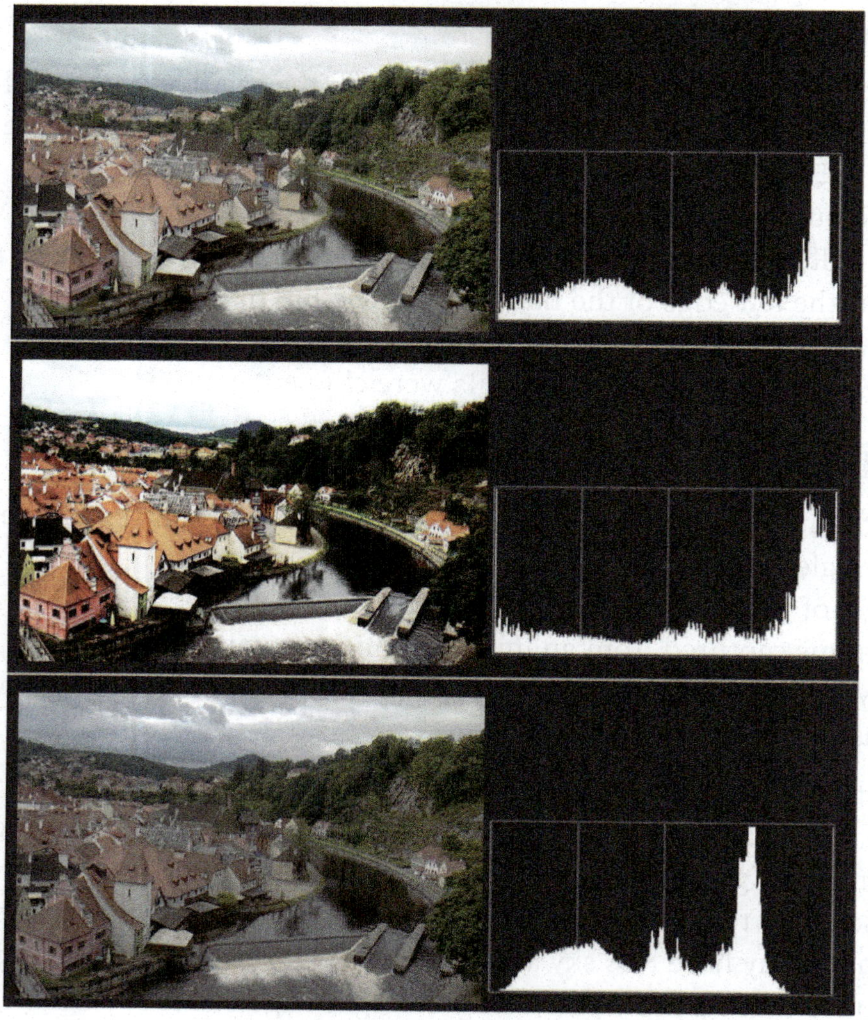

Figure 7.17

Normal contrast (top); high contrast (center); low contrast (bottom.)

The effect of increasing contrast may be to move some tones off either end of the scale altogether, while spreading the remaining grays over a smaller number of locations on the spectrum. That's exactly the case in the example shown. The number of possible tones is smaller and the image appears harsher.

With a lower-contrast image, like the one shown at bottom in the figure, the basic shape of the previous histogram will remain recognizable, but gradually will be compressed together to cover a smaller area of the gray spectrum. The squished shape of the histogram is caused by all the grays in the original image being represented by a limited number of gray tones in a smaller range of the scale.

Instead of the darkest tones of the image reaching into the black end of the spectrum and the whitest tones extending to the lightest end, the blackest areas of the scene are now represented by a light gray, and the whites by a somewhat lighter gray. The overall contrast of the image is reduced. Because all the darker tones are actually a middle gray or lighter, the scene in this version of the photo appears lighter as well.

Understanding Histograms

Although the histograms I just showed you display how these charts change depending on the contrast of an image, an important thing to remember when working with the histogram display in your camera is that changing the exposure does *not* change the contrast of an image. The curves illustrated in the previous three examples retain exactly the same basic shape when you increase or decrease exposure. I repeat: The proportional distribution of grays shown in the histogram doesn't change when exposure changes; it is neither stretched nor compressed. However, the tones as *a whole* are moved toward one end of the scale or the other, depending on whether you're increasing or decreasing exposure. You'll be able to see that in some illustrations that follow.

So, as you reduce exposure, tones gradually move to the black end (and off the scale), while the reverse is true when you increase exposure. The contrast within the image is changed only to the extent that some of the tones can no longer be represented when they are moved off the scale.

To change the *contrast* of an image, you must do one of four things:

- **Change the camera's contrast setting** using one of the Creative Styles, which each has a contrast adjustment. I explain Creative Styles in Chapter 9, which covers some advanced options.
- **Use your camera's shadow-tone "boosters."** As previously discussed, both DRO and Auto HDR processing can adjust the contrast of your final image.
- **Alter the contrast of the scene itself,** for example by using a fill light or reflectors (if available) to add illumination to shadows that are too dark.
- **Attempt to adjust contrast in post-processing** using your image editor or RAW file converter. You may use features such as Levels or Curves (in Photoshop, Photoshop Elements, and many other image editors), or work with HDR software to cherry-pick the best values in shadows and highlights from multiple images.

Of the four of these, the third -- changing the contrast of the scene -- is the most desirable, because attempting to fix contrast by fiddling with the tonal values is unlikely to be a perfect remedy. However, adding a little contrast can be successful because you can discard some tones to make the image more contrasty. However, the opposite is much more difficult. An overly contrasty image rarely can be fixed, because you can't add information that isn't there in the first place.

What you *can* do is adjust the exposure so that the tones *that are already present in the scene* are captured correctly, even if the contrast itself remains the same. **Figure 7.18**, top, shows the histogram for an image that is badly underexposed. You can guess from the shape of the histogram that many of the dark tones to the left of the graph have been clipped off. There's plenty of room on the right side for additional pixels to reside without having them become overexposed.

So, you can increase the exposure (either by changing the f/stop or shutter speed, or by adding an EV value) to produce the corrected histogram shown in **Figure 7.18**, center.

Conversely, if your histogram looks like the one shown in **Figure 7.18**, bottom, , with bright tones pushed off the right edge of the chart, you have an overexposed image, and you can correct it by reducing exposure. In addition to the histogram, the camera has its Highlights and Zebra options, which, when activated, shows areas that are overexposed with flashing tones ("blinkies") in the picture review screen, or, with Zebra, by stripes in the overexposed areas in your live view image. Depending on the importance of this "clipped" detail, you can adjust exposure or leave it alone. For example, if all the dark-coded areas in the review are in a background that you care little about, you can forget about them and not change the exposure, but if such areas appear in facial details of your subject, you may want to make some adjustments.

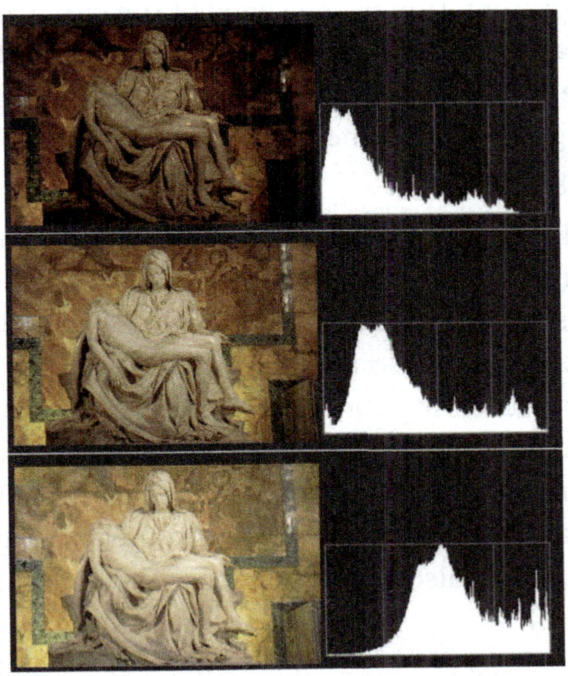

Figure 7.18

Underexposed (top); properly exposed (center); overexposed (bottom.)

In working with histograms, your goal should be to have all the tones in an image spread out between the edges, with none clipped off at the left and right sides. Underexposing (to preserve highlights) should be done only as a last resort, because retrieving the underexposed shadows in your image editor will frequently increase the noise, even if you're working with RAW files. A better course of action is to expose for the highlights ("exposing to the right"), but, when the subject matter makes it practical, fill in the shadows with additional light, using reflectors, fill flash, or other techniques rather than allowing them to be seriously underexposed.

A histogram graph includes a *representation* of up to 256 vertical lines on a horizontal axis (but not 256 actual lines; only the general shape of the resulting curve is shown). The graph shows the number of pixels in the image at each brightness level, from 0 (black) on the left side to 255 (white) on the right. The 3-inch LCD doesn't have enough pixels to show each and every one of the 256 lines; instead, it provides a representation of the shape of the curve, often resembling a mountain range. The more pixels at a given level, the higher the "peak" will be at that position. If no bar appears at a particular position along the scale in the graph, there are no pixels at that particular brightness level.

A typical histogram produces a mountain-like shape, with most of the pixels bunched in the middle tones, with fewer pixels at the dark and light ends of the scale. Ideally, though, there will be at least some pixels at either extreme, so that your image has both a true black and a true white representing some details. Learn to spot histograms that represent over- and underexposure, and add or subtract exposure using exposure compensation, as described earlier. (The D-Range Optimizer is also a useful feature when you want to get more detail in shadow areas; it can also slightly increase the amount of detail in highlight areas.)

The key is to make settings that will produce a histogram with a more even distribution of tones. A corrected histogram exhibits a mountain-like shape with a tall wide peak in the center of the scale (denoting the many mid-tone areas), and a good distribution of tones overall. This histogram indicates that the image exhibits detail in both the dark and the light tones since there's no spike at either end of the graph. Typically, this is the type of histogram you want for an accurate exposure. Of course, you'll sometimes want to create a special effect like a silhouette or a high-key look (mostly light tones); then your histogram will look entirely different.

As noted earlier, the histogram can also warn you of very high or very low contrast in an image. If all the tones are bunched up in one area of the graph (usually around the center), the photo will be low in contrast. You can increase the contrast level with the Creative Style item as discussed at the end of this chapter, or do so later with software.

Automatic and Specialized Shooting Modes

After the long discussion of exposure control and other issues, let's get back to the remaining shooting modes. When you set the Intelligent Auto or the Superior Auto mode, the camera will use its programmed intelligence to try to identify the type of scene and set itself accordingly. These "autopilot" modes are useful when you suddenly encounter a picture-taking opportunity and don't have time to decide exactly what settings you might want to make in a semi-automatic or manual mode. Instead, you can spin the mode dial to one of the Auto modes, or, if you have a little more time, to the most appropriate scene mode, and fire away, knowing that you have a fighting chance of getting a usable or very good photo.

The RX100 V also offers more specialized modes, for use in particular situations: Sweep Panorama and two special scene modes that provide surprisingly fine quality at high ISO levels -- Hand-held Twilight and Anti Motion Blur.

Auto and Scene Modes

The two Auto modes and the scene modes are especially helpful when you're just learning to use your RX100 V, because they let you get used to composing and shooting, and obtaining excellent results, without having to struggle with unfamiliar controls to adjust things like shutter speed, aperture, ISO, and white balance. Once you've learned how to make those settings, you'll probably prefer to use P, A, S, and M modes since they provide more control over shooting options.

The fully automatic modes may give you few options for overrides, or none at all. For example, the AF mode, AF area, ISO, white balance, Dynamic Range Optimizer, and metering mode are all set for you. In most modes, you can select the drive setting and the flash mode, though not all settings for those options are available. You cannot adjust exposure compensation or Creative Styles in any of these modes. Here are some essential points to note about the Intelligent Auto, Superior Auto, and SCN modes.

- **Intelligent Auto.** This is the setting to use when you hand your camera to a total stranger and ask him or her to take your picture posing in front of the Eiffel Tower. All the photographer has to do is press the shutter release button. Every other crucial decision is made by the camera's electronics, and many settings, such as ISO, white balance, metering mode, exposure compensation, and focus settings are not available to you for adjustment. However, you still are able to set the drive mode to Continuous shooting, add self-timer (but not to Bracketing), and you can set the flash mode for the pop-up flash to Auto Flash, Fill Flash or Flash Off. If the camera detects a subject suitable for a scene mode, it will switch to that mode and display its choice in the upper-left corner of the screen.
- **Superior Auto.** This mode is exactly like Intelligent Auto, but provides an extra benefit. In scenes that include extremely bright areas as well as shadow areas, the camera can activate its Auto HDR (high dynamic range) feature to provide more shadow detail. And in dark locations, when an extremely high ISO will be used, the camera can activate a special mode that fires several shots and composites them into one after discarding the digital noise data. The same flash modes as those for Intelligent Auto are available.

- **Portrait.** The first of the scene modes that you'll encounter, this mode tends to use wide apertures (large f/numbers) and faster shutter speeds. This is intended to provide shallow depth-of-field to blur the background while minimizing the risk of blurry photos caused by camera shake or subject movement. It's also optimized to provide "soft" skin tones. The drive mode cannot be set to Continuous shooting, but you can do the following: set the self-timer for 2, 5, or 10 second delays; select AF-S, MF, or DMF focus in the Function submenu; and set the flash mode to Auto Flash, Fill Flash, or forced off; and adjust Face Detection parameters.
- **Sports action.** In this mode, the Camera favors fast shutter speeds to freeze action and it switches to Continuous drive mode to let you take a quick sequence of pictures with one press of the shutter release button. (You can select Speed Priority Continuous if you want a higher frame rate.) Continuous Autofocus is activated to continually refocus as a subject approaches the camera or moves away from your shooting position, but you can change to MF or DMF in the Function menu. Flash is disabled by default, but you can activate Fill Flash if you like in the Function menu. Smile/Face Detection is also available.
- **Macro.** This mode is similar to the Portrait setting, favoring wider apertures to isolate your close-up subjects, and fast shutter speeds to eliminate the camera shake that's accentuated at close focusing distances. However, if your camera is mounted on a tripod, you might want to use Aperture Priority mode instead. That will allow you to specify a smaller aperture (larger f/number) for additional depth-of-field to keep an entire three-dimensional subject within the range of acceptably sharp focus.
- **Landscape.** The camera tries to use smaller apertures for more depth-of-field to try to render the entire scene sharply; it also boosts saturation slightly for richer colors. You can set Fill Flash and can use the self-timer; most other settings are not available in this mode.

- **Sunset.** Increases saturation to emphasize the red tones of a sunrise or sunset. You can use the Fill Flash or Flash Off settings, but most other adjustments are unavailable to you.
- **Night Scene.** This is another mode for low-light photography. Similar to Night Portrait, but the flash is forced off. Use a tripod if at all possible or set the camera on a solid object, because the shutter speed will be long in low light. Most settings are not available, other than the Self-timer.
- **Hand-held Twilight.** This is one of the two special modes designed for use in low light when hand-holding the RX100 V camera. The camera will set a high ISO (sensitivity) level to enable it to use a fast shutter speed to minimize the risk of blurring caused by camera shake. (In extremely dark conditions however, the shutter speed may still be quite long.) When you press the shutter release button, the camera takes six shots in a quick series. The processor then composites them into one after discarding most of the digital noise data for a "cleaner" image than you'd get in a conventional high ISO photo. You'll get one image that's of surprisingly fine quality. Flash is never fired in this mode and you have access to virtually no camera options.
- **Night Portrait.** This mode is intended for taking people pictures in dark locations with flash using a long shutter speed. The Flash mode is set to Slow Sync. A nearby subject will be illuminated by flash while a distant background (such as a city skyline) will be exposed by the available light during the long exposure. Because the shutter speed will be long, it's necessary to use a tripod or set the camera on something solid like the roof of a car. If using an OSS-designated lens with a SteadyShot stabilizer, make sure it's on, unless the camera is mounted on a tripod; in that case, turn the stabilizer off using the SteadyShot item in the Setup menu. You can use the Self-timer or the Remote Commander in Night Portrait mode.
- **Anti Motion Blur.** Similar to Hand-held Twilight, this mode is also designed for use in dark locations, but it's more

effective at reducing blurring that might be caused by a subject's motion or by a shaky camera. That's because the camera will set an even faster shutter speed; that may require it to set a higher ISO level. (Of course, in an extremely dark location, the shutter speed may still be a bit long.) Again, the camera fires a series of six shots and composites them into one with minimal digital noise.

- **Pet.** Optimized for capturing the antics of your furry (or scaled/feathered) friends, with bright colors and contrast.
- **Gourmet.** Produces bright colors that make food appear even more appetizing.
- **Fireworks.** Mount your camera on a tripod or other sturdy support, and this setting will give you the long exposures needed to capture a spectacular burst.
- **High sensitivity.** Suitable for still images and dark movie scenes under low illumination, using higher ISO settings to allow capture without flash (for stills) or auxiliary lighting (for both stills and movies).

Sweep Panorama Mode

I showed you some panorama techniques in Chapter 3, but here's a recap. A conventional panorama mode has been available for several years with many other cameras, especially those with a built-in lens. That allows you to shoot a series of photos, with framing guided by an on-screen display; make sure they overlap correctly and you can then "stitch" them together in special software to make a single, very wide, panoramic image. Some cameras can even do this for you with in-camera processing but most (though not all) require you to use a tripod. Your Sony camera offers the most convenient type of panorama mode; it's automatic (but allows you to use some overrides) and it can produce very good results without a tripod. Of course, it's easier to keep the camera perfectly level while shooting the series when using a tripod, but that's not always practical. Here are a few tips to consider:

- **Choose a direction.** You can select one of four directions for your panorama: right, left, up, or down. Select any of these options in the Camera Settings 1 menu, using the Panorama Direction item. It's only available when the camera is set to Sweep Panorama mode. The default setting, right, is probably the most natural for many people; it requires you to pan the camera from the left to the right across a wide vista. Occasionally, you might want to use one of the other options. The up or down motion is the one you'll need to make a panoramic photo of very tall subjects, such as skyscrapers and nearby mountains.
- **Change settings while in Panorama mode.** When you select this Shooting mode, the camera presents you with a large arrow and urgent-sounding instructions to press the shutter button and move the camera in the direction of the arrow. Don't let the camera intimidate you with this demand; what it is neglecting to tell you is that you can take all the time you want, and that you are free to change certain settings before you shoot.

  Press the MENU button and you can set the focus mode, white balance, and metering mode. Other useful functions include exposure compensation; Image Size in the Image Size menu, which lets you set either the Standard or the Wide panorama option; and the Creative Style modes in the Brightness/Color menu. Once you have those settings fine-tuned to your satisfaction, *then* go ahead and press the shutter release button.
- **Smooth and steady does it.** While keeping the shutter release button depressed, immediately start moving the camera smoothly and steadily in an arc; pivot your feet or the camera on a tripod head and keep going until the shutter stops clicking. The on-screen guide that appears during the exposure will help you keep the speed and direction of movement right. If you moved the camera at a speed that was too fast or too slow, you'll get an error message and the camera will prompt you to start over.

- **Beware of moving objects.** The Sweep Panorama mode is intended for stationary subjects, such as mountain ranges, city skylines, or expansive gardens. There's nothing to stop you from shooting a scene that contains moving cars, people, or other objects, but be aware of problems that can arise in that situation. Because you're taking multiple overlapping shots that are then stitched into a single image, the camera may capture the same car or person two or more times in slightly different positions; this can result in a truncated or otherwise distorted picture of that particular subject. Press the Playback button to view your just completed panorama; press the center button to view a moving playback of the image.

Chapter 8

Mastering the Mysteries of Autofocus

Designing a fast, efficient autofocus system was one of the challenges facing the designers of Sony's super-compact RX100 series of cameras, including the RX100 V. The mirrors found in traditional SLRs (and Sony's own A-mount SLT cameras) provide a distinct advantage: they make it possible to direct some of the incoming illumination to a separate electronic autofocus system that's fast and accurate. At the moment of exposure, focus is locked, and the mirror flipped up out of the way, allowing the light to pass through the camera body to the film or digital sensor.

Fixed-lens cameras like the RX100 V have no mirror, so there's no way to insert an outboard AF system into the light path. Instead, with previous models of the RX100 series, autofocus was achieved by interpreting the contrast of the image on the sensor. This contrast detect auto focus (CDAF) system requires focusing and refocusing the lens until the sharpest image has been obtained. A certain degree of "hunting" is required as the focus is adjusted back and forth. That's generally slower than the autofocus technology used by cameras with optical/mirror viewfinders and separate autofocus systems, although the AF system found in previous RX100 IV was considered excellent for its type.

The reason for that was its special sensor. Most sensors have their photo diodes (which capture the photons) and image-processing circuitry in a single layer, moving the information to the edges before processing can begin. The RX100 V uses a back side illuminated (BSI) sensor, which places the photosites on the surface of the sensor facing the back of the lens, where the light emerges, and, in the Exmore RS, with the circuitry on layers glued underneath. This new "stacked" configuration allows a larger photosensitive surface for capturing photos, and makes it possible to include the image-processing circuitry directly under the photosites, so the information can be processed much more quickly. The data readout of the chip was more than five times faster than that of sensors used in RX100 models before the Mark IV.

But that was then, and this is now. For the RX100 V, has retained the advanced BSI sensor, but upgraded it for even faster AF performance. In doing so, Sony has combined the original *contrast detection* method of autofocus, which was slower, but inherently very accurate, with a much speedier *phase detection* system to produce a single *hybrid* AF scheme that combines speed with accuracy. The RX100 V's autofocus is much faster.

However, to achieve the best focus possible for a given shot, there is one additional logistical problem to overcome: the camera doesn't really know, for certain, *what* subject *you* want to be in sharp focus. It may select an object and lock in focus with lightning speed -- even though it's not the center of interest in your photograph. Or, the camera may lock focus too soon, or too late. This chapter will help you understand the options available with your Sony RX100 V in order to help the camera understand what you want to focus on, when, and maybe even why.

Getting into Focus

Learning to use the RX100 V's autofocus system is easy, but you do need to fully understand how the system works to get the most benefit from it. Once you're comfortable with autofocus, you'll know when it's appropriate to use the manual focus option, too. The important thing to remember is that focus isn't absolute. For example, some things that appear to be in sharp focus at a given viewing size and distance might not be in focus at a larger size and/or closer distance. That family portrait hanging over the mantle may look fine when you're seated on the sofa, but it appears less sharp when examined from two feet away.

In addition, the goal of optimum focus isn't always to make things look sharp. For some types of subjects, not all of an image needs be sharp. Controlling exactly what is sharp and what is not is part of your creative palette. Use of depth-of-field characteristics to throw part of an image out of focus while other parts are sharply focused is one of the most valuable tools available to a photographer. But selective focus works only when the desired areas of an image are in focus properly. For the digital camera photographer, correct focus can be one of the trickiest parts of the technical and creative process.

As I said in the introduction to this chapter, there are two major focusing methods used by modern digital cameras: phase detection, used by all digital cameras with mirrors, including the fixed-mirror Sony models like the a77 II; and contrast detection, which was the primary focusing method employed by all cameras using LCD and electronic viewfinders until very recently.

Contrast Detection

Contrast detection relies on examining the image formed on the sensor, and how it works is illustrated, if over-simplified, in **Figure 8.1**. At top in the figure, the transitions between the edges of the vertical wood grain grooves are soft and blurred because of the low contrast between them. The traditional contrast detection autofocus system looks only for contrast between edges, and those edges can run in any direction. At the bottom of the figure, the image has been brought into sharp focus, and the edges have much more contrast; the transitions are sharp and clear. Although this example is a bit exaggerated so you can see the results on the printed page, it's easy to understand that when maximum contrast in a subject is achieved using contrast detection, it can be deemed to be in sharp focus.

Contrast detection works best with static subjects, because, lacking the RX100 V's speedy sensor, it is inherently slower and not well-suited for tracking moving objects. Contrast detection works less well in dim light, because its accuracy depends on its ability to detect variations in brightness and contrast. You'll find that contrast detection works better with faster lenses, too, because larger lens openings admit more light that can be used by the sensor to measure contrast. Here are some of the advantages and disadvantages of CDAF.

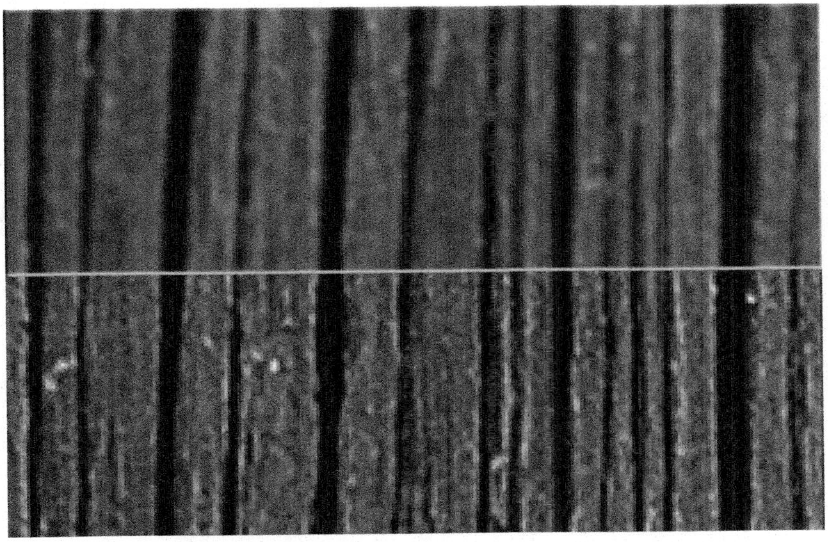

Figure 8.1

Using the contrast detection method of autofocus, a camera can evaluate the increase in contrast in the edges of subjects, starting with a blurry image (top) and producing a sharp, contrasty image (bottom).

Phase Detection

With phase detection, each autofocus sampling area (either a separate sensor with dSLRs and SLT models or pixels embedded in the sensor in the case of cameras like the RX100 V are divided into two halves. The two halves are compared, much like (actually, exactly like) a two-window rangefinder used in surveying, weaponry, and non-SLR cameras such as the venerable Leica M film models. The contrast between the two images changes as focus is moved in or out, until sharp focus is achieved when the images are "in phase," or lined up. **Figure 8.2** can help you visualize how this works.

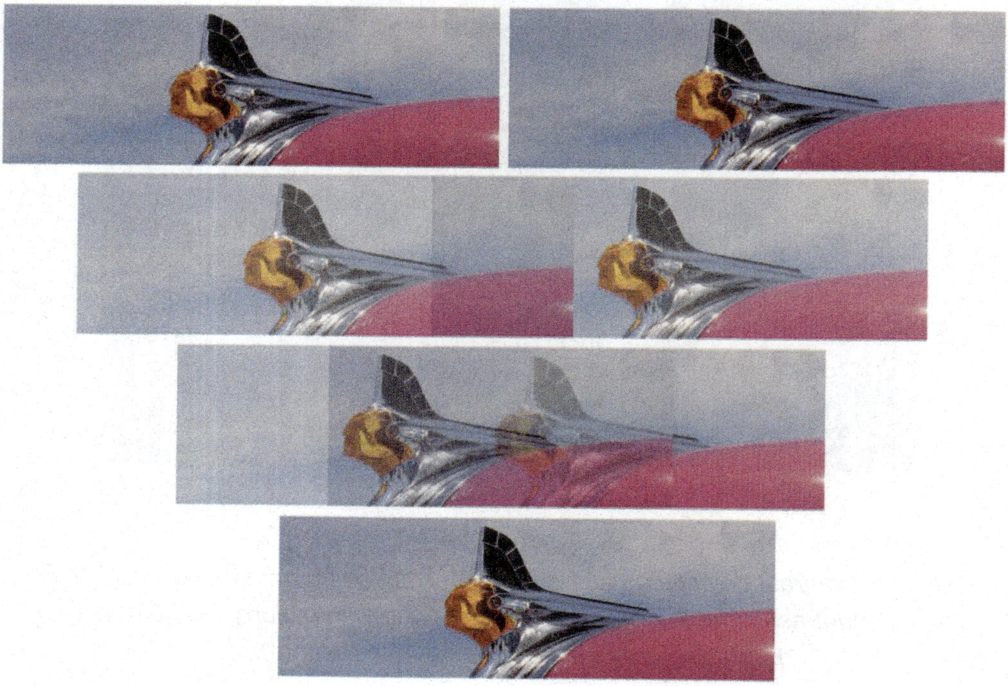

Figure 8.2

Phase detection "lines up" portions of your image using rangefinder-like comparison to achieve focus.

The rangefinder approach of phase detection tells the camera exactly how much out of focus the image is, and in which direction (focus is too near, or too far), thanks to the amount and direction of the displacement of the split image.

The camera can snap the image into sharp focus and line up the vertical lines in much the same way that rangefinder cameras align two parts of an image to achieve sharp focus. Even better, because it knows the amount of focus travel needed, the camera is able to adjust the speed of the lens's AF motor to move the lens elements slowly or quickly, depending on how much focus adjustment is needed.

Because of the speed advantages of phase detection, makers of mirrorless cameras have been adding on-chip phase detect points to their sensors. Sony, because it designs and makes its own sensors, has been able to do a stellar job with this. The RX100 V has a whopping 315 phase detect pixels embedded in its sensor, shown in **Figure 8.3**.

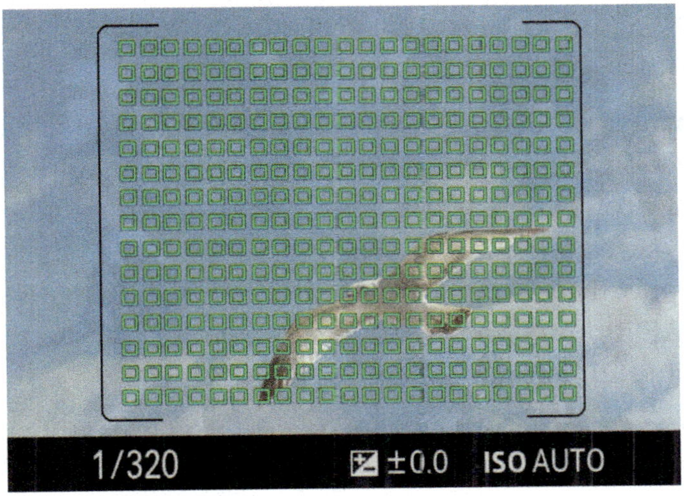

Figure 8.3

The RX100 V's phase detection points cover the majority of the frame.

Comparing the Two Types

Your RX100 V actually uses *both* types of autofocus in many situations. It first applies the speedy phase detection to move the focusing elements of the lens in the correct direction by an appropriate amount. No hunting back and forth is required. Then, the camera uses the highly-accurate contrast detection, if needed, to fine-tune the focus precisely. You can see why Sony elected to do this if you review the advantages of each type of AF:

- **Contrast detection works with many image types.** Contrast detection, unlike phase detection, doesn't require subject matter to have lines that are vertical or horizontal. Any subject that has edges running in any direction can be used to achieve sharp focus, as long as the subject is brightly lit. The RX100 V's AF illuminator can often compensate at close ranges for lack of illumination.
- **Contrast detection can focus on large areas of the scene.** Focus is achieved with the actual sensor image, so focus point selection is simply a matter of choosing which part of the sensor image to use. (This point is highlighted by the fact, discussed below, that in Flexible Spot mode, you can move the Autofocus Area to many parts of the sensor.)
- **Contrast detection can focus on larger areas of the scene.** Whereas phase detection focus can be achieved *only* at the points that fall on one of the 315 special autofocus sensor pixels, with contrast detection much larger portions of the image can be used as focus zones. Focus is achieved with the actual sensor image, so focus point selection is simply a matter of choosing which part of the sensor image to use. (This point is highlighted by the fact, discussed below, that in Flexible Spot mode, you can move the Autofocus Area to many parts of the sensor, whereas with a phase detection system, you can move the Autofocus Area only to a specific locations where the special autofocus sensors used for phase detection are located.)

- **Phase detection 'knows" which direction to focus.** The split image seen by phase detection sensors reveal instantly whether focus is too close or too far. As I mentioned earlier, there is no need to "hunt" for the focus point, as the AF system can immediately adjust in the proper direction. That boosts focus speed considerably.
- **Phase detection "knows" how far out of focus a subject is.** The separation between the two halves of the image let the AF system know whether the subject is grossly out of focus, or whether only a slight adjustment is needed. That means faster autofocus, too.
- **Phase detection isn't as dependent on scene brightness.** As long as the split images are illuminated well enough for the AF system to make an evaluation, greater or lesser amounts of light don't have as much of an effect on speed and accuracy. Remember, the reason phase detect systems operate less well at smaller f/stops is because the baseline diameter of the aperture is smaller.

Focus Modes and Options

Now that you understand the fundamental principles of how the RX100 V achieves focus, let's discuss the practical application of these principles to your everyday picture-taking activities, by setting the various modes and options available for the autofocus system. We'll also discuss the use of manual focus, and when that method might be preferable to autofocus.

As you've come to appreciate by now, the RX100 V offers many options for your photography. Focus is no exception. Of course, as with other aspects of this camera, you can set the shooting mode to either Auto option or a scene mode such as Sports Action, and the camera will do just fine in most situations, using its default settings for autofocus. But, if you want more creative control, the choices are there for you to make.

FOCUS MODES/FOCUS AREA MODES

Your camera has a lot of modes! To keep the various focus options straight, remember that *focus modes* determine *when* the camera focuses: either once or continuously using autofocus, or manually. *Focus area modes* determine *where* in the frame the RX100 V collects the information used to achieve autofocus.

So, no matter what shooting mode you're using, your first choice is whether to use autofocus or manual focus. Yes, there's also a Direct Manual Focus (DMF) option, discussed in Chapter 3, but that *still* provides autofocus, with the option of *fine-tuning* focus manually before taking the shot. Manual focus presents you with great flexibility along with the challenge of keeping the image in focus under what may be difficult conditions, such as rapid motion of the subject, darkness of the scene, and the like. Later in this chapter, I'll cover manual focus as well as DMF. For now, I'll assume you're going to rely on the camera's conventional AF mode.

The Sony RX100 V has two basic AF modes: AF-S (Single-shot autofocus) and AF-C (Continuous autofocus). Once you have decided on which of these to use, you also need to tell the camera how to select the area used to measure AF. In other words, after you tell the camera *how* to autofocus, you also have to tell it *where* to direct its focusing attention. I'll explain both *AF modes* and *AF area modes* in more detail later in this section.

MANUAL FOCUS

When you select manual focus (MF) in the Focus Mode entry in the Camera Settings 4 menu, using the Function menu, or by switching using a defined button, the RX100 V lets you set the focus yourself by turning the control ring around the lens. There are some advantages and disadvantages to this approach. While your batteries will last slightly longer in manual focus mode, it will take you longer to focus the camera for each photo. And unlike older 35mm film SLRs, digital cameras' electronic viewfinders and LCDs are not designed for optimum manual focus. Pick up any advanced film camera and you'll see a big, bright viewfinder with a focusing screen that's a joy to focus on manually. So, although manual focus is still an option for you to consider in certain circumstances, it's not as easy to use as it once was. I recommend trying the various AF options first, and switching to manual focus only if AF is not working for you. And then be sure to take advantage of the focus peaking feature and the automatic frame enlargement (MF Assist) which can make it easier to determine when the focus is precisely on the most important subject element. And remember, if you use the DMF mode, you can fine-tune the focus after the AF system has finished its work.

Focus Pocus

Back in the pre-AF days, manual focusing was problematic because our eyes and brains have poor memory for correct focus, which is why your eye doctor must shift back and forth between sets of lenses and ask "Does that look sharper or was it sharper before?" in determining your correct prescription. Similarly, manual focusing involves jogging the focus ring back and forth as you go from almost in focus, to sharp focus, to almost focused again. The little clockwise and counterclockwise arcs decrease in size until you've zeroed in on the point of correct focus. What you're looking for is the image with the most contrast between the edges of elements in the image.

The Sony RX100 V can assess sharpness quickly, and it's also able to remember the progression perfectly, making the entire process fast and precise. Unfortunately, even this high-tech system doesn't really know with any certainty *which* object should be in sharpest focus. Is it the closest object? The subject in the center of the frame? Something lurking *behind* the closest subject? A person standing over at the side of the picture? Many of the techniques for using autofocus effectively involve telling the camera exactly what it should be focusing on.

Adding Circles of Confusion

But there are other factors in play, as well. You know that increased depth-of-field brings more of your subject into focus. But more depth-of-field also makes autofocusing (or manual focusing) more difficult because the contrast is lower between objects at different distances. So, autofocus with a 70mm zoom setting may be easier than at a 24mm zoom setting because the longer lens has less apparent depth-of-field.

To make things even more complicated, many subjects aren't polite enough to remain still. They move around in the frame, so that even if the camera's lens is sharply focused on your main subject, the subject may change position and require refocusing. An intervening subject may pop into the frame and pass between you and the subject you meant to photograph. You (or the camera) have to decide whether to focus on this new subject, or to remain focused on the original subject. Finally, there are some kinds of subjects that are difficult to bring into sharp focus because they lack enough contrast to allow the camera's AF system (or our eyes) to lock in. Blank walls, a clear blue sky, or other low-contrast subject matter may make focusing difficult.

If you find all these focus factors confusing, you're on the right track. Focus is, in fact, measured using something called a *circle of confusion*. An ideal image consists of zillions of tiny little points, which, like all points, theoretically have no height or width. There is perfect contrast between the point and its surroundings. You can think of each point as a pinpoint of light in a darkened room. When a given point is out of focus, its edges decrease in contrast and it changes from a perfect point to a tiny disc with blurry edges (remember, blur is the lack of contrast between boundaries in an image). (See **Figure 8.2.**)

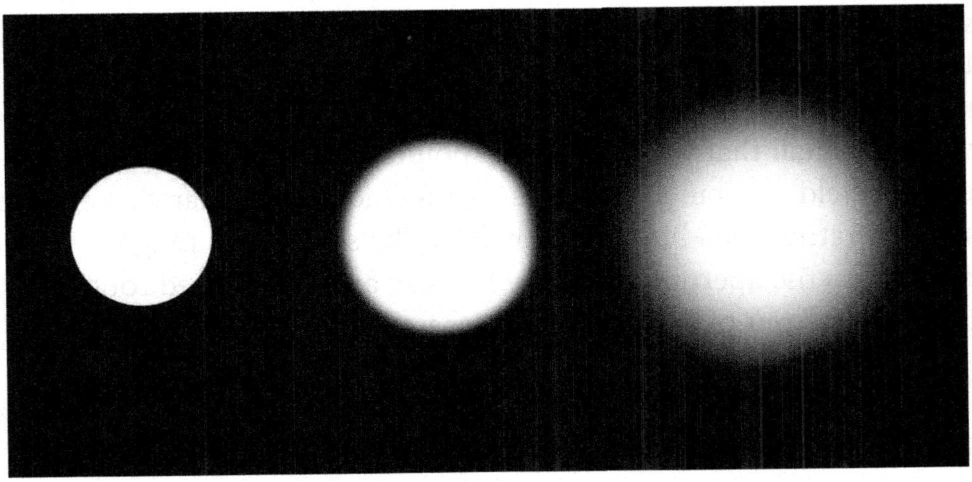

Figure 8.4

When a pinpoint of light (left) goes out of focus, its blurry edges form a circle of confusion (center and right).

If this blurry disc -- the circle of confusion -- is small enough, our eye still perceives it as a point. It's only when the disc grows large enough that we can see it as a blur rather than as a sharp point that a given point is viewed as being out of focus. You can see, then, that enlarging an image, either by displaying it larger on your computer monitor or by making a large print, also magnifies the size of each circle of confusion. Moving closer to the image does the same thing. So, parts of an image that may look perfectly sharp in a 5 x 7-inch print viewed at arm's length, might appear blurry when blown up to 11 x 14 inches and examined at the same distance. Take a few steps back, however, and the image may look sharp again.

To a lesser extent, the viewer also affects the apparent size of these circles of confusion. Some people see details better at a given distance and may perceive smaller circles of confusion than someone standing next to them. For the most part, however, such differences are small. Truly blurry images will look blurry to just about everyone under the same conditions.

Technically, there is just one plane within your picture area, parallel to the back of the camera (actually the sensor) that is in sharp focus. That's the plane in which the points of the image are rendered as precise points. At every other plane in front of or behind the focus plane, the points show up as discs that range from slightly blurry to extremely blurry. In practice, the discs in many of these planes will still be so small that we see them as points, and that's where we get depth-of-field: the range of planes that includes discs that we perceive as points rather than blurred splotches. The size of this range increases as the aperture is reduced in size and is allocated roughly one-third in front of the plane of sharpest focus, and two-thirds behind it. (See **Figure 8.5**.)

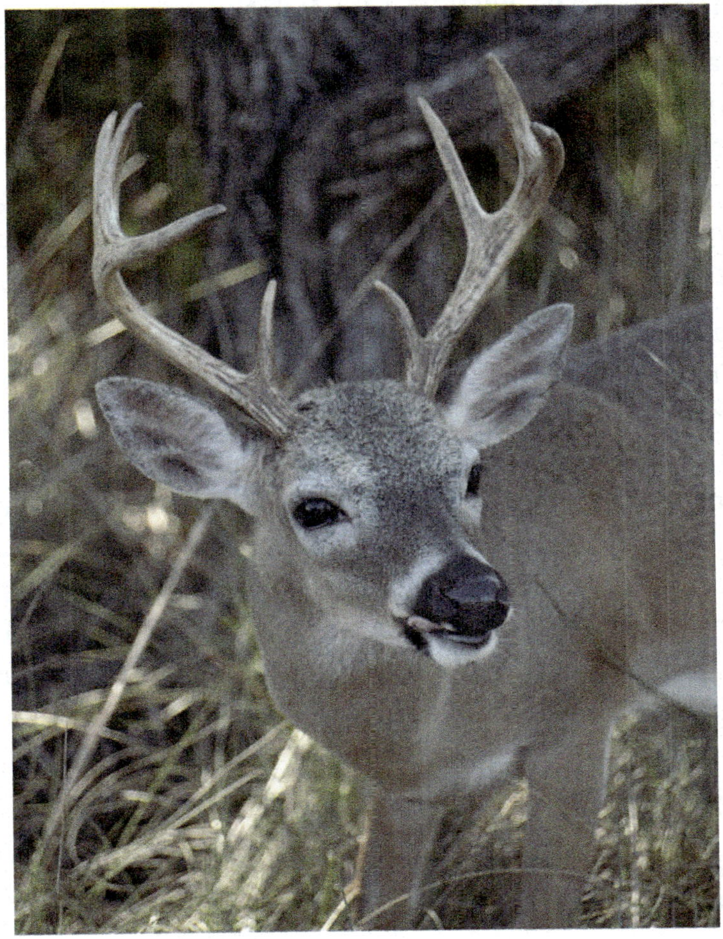

Figure 8.5

The focused plane (the deer's head) is sharp, but the area behind it (the background) are blurred because the depth-of-field (the range of acceptably sharp focus) is shallow in this image.

Your Autofocus Mode Options

Manual focus can come in handy, as I'll explain later in this chapter, but autofocus is likely to be your choice in the great majority of shooting situations. Choosing the right AF mode and the way in which focus points are selected is your key to success. Using the wrong mode for a particular type of photography can lead to a series of pictures that are all sharply focused -- on the wrong subject.

But autofocus isn't some mindless beast out there snapping your pictures in and out of focus with no feedback from you. There are several settings you can modify to regain a fair amount of control. Your first decision should be which of the autofocus modes to select: Single-shot (AF-S) or Continuous AF (AF-C). DMF first uses autofocus, and then allows you to fine-tune focus manually. Press the MENU button, go to the Camera Settings 4 menu, and navigate to the line for Focus Mode. Press the center button, then highlight your autofocus mode choice from the submenu, and press the center button again. You can also set autofocus mode by pressing the Fn button and using the Function menu.

FOCUS INDICATOR

At the lower-left corner of your screen, you'll find a green focus confirmation indicator that's active while focusing is underway. It consists of a round green disk. If the *disk glows steadily*, the image is in focus; if it's flashing, focus has failed. Only the disk appears when using AF-S; in AF-C mode, the disk is surrounded by the brackets and indicates that the focus plane may change if the subject moves. If the *brackets are flashing and no disk appears*, focusing is in progress; if the *disk is flashing*, focusing has failed. (See **Figure 8.6**.)

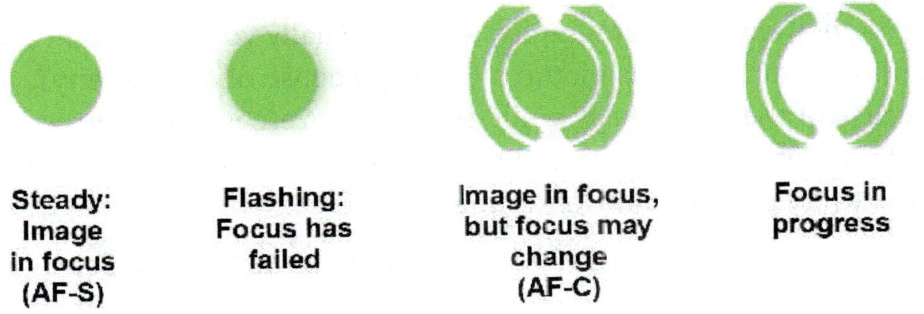

Figure 8.6

The focus indicator icon shows focus status.

Single-Shot AF (AF-S) Mode

With Single-Shot AF (AF-S), the camera will lock in focus when you press the shutter release (or defined AF start button) and will not adjust focus if your subject moves or you change the distance between you and your subject, as long as you hold down the button.

In AF-S mode, focus is locked. By keeping the button depressed halfway, you'll find you can reframe the image by moving the camera to aim at another angle; the focus (and exposure) will not change. Maintain pressure on the shutter release button and focus remains locked even if you recompose, or if the subject begins running toward the camera, for example.

In this chapter, I'm assuming that you're using P, A, S, or M mode where you have full control over the camera features. This is important because the camera will use *only* AF-S in either Intelligent Auto or Superior Auto modes, in any scene mode *except* Sports Action, in Sweep Panorama, and whenever the Smile Shutter feature is active. And it will set Continuous AF (AF-C) only in Movie mode, regardless of what focus mode you've selected for still images.

When sharp focus is achieved in AF-S mode, the solid green focus indicator appears in the lower-left corner of the screen and you'll hear a little beep. One or more green focus confirmation frames will also appear to indicate the area(s) of the scene that will be in sharpest focus.

For non-action photography, AF-S is usually your best choice, as it minimizes out-of-focus pictures (at the expense of spontaneity). Because of the small delay while the camera zeroes in on correct focus, you might experience slightly more shutter lag. This mode uses less battery power than Continuous AF.

If you have set the RX100 V for Pre-AF in the Custom Settings 3 menu, you may notice something that seems strange: the camera's autofocus mechanism will begin seeking focus even before you touch the shutter release button. In this mode, no matter which AF method is selected, the camera will continually alter its focus as it is aimed at various subjects, *until* you press the shutter release button halfway. At that point, the camera locks focus in Single-shot AF mode.

Continuous AF (AF-C) Mode

When Continuous AF is active, focus is constantly readjusted as your subject (or you) move. The difference between Single-shot AF and Continuous AF comes at the point the shutter release button (or defined focus start button) is pressed halfway. (See the discussion of *back button focus* later in this chapter.)

Switch to this mode when photographing sports, young kids at play, and other fast-moving subjects. In this mode, the camera can lock focus on a subject and retain that focus if the subject is not moving toward the camera or away from your shooting position. You'll see a green circle surrounded by brackets. (There will be no beep.) But if the camera-to-subject distance begins changing, the camera instantly begins to adjust focus to keep it in sharp focus, making this the more suitable AF mode with moving subjects.

Setting the AF Area

So far, you have allowed the camera to choose which part of the scene will be in the sharpest focus using its focus detection points called *AF areas* by Sony. However, you can also specify a single focus detection point that will be active. Use the Function menu, or press the MENU button, navigate to the Focus Area item in the Camera Settings 4 menu, press the center button, and select one of the options. Press the center button again to confirm. Here is how the AF Area options work:

- **Wide.** The camera chooses the appropriate focus area(s) in order to set focus on a certain subject in the scene. There are no focus brackets visible on the screen until you press the shutter release button halfway to lock focus. At that point, the camera displays one or more pairs of green focus indicators to show what area(s) of the image it has used to set focus on. If Face Detection is active, the AF system will prioritize faces when making its decision as to where it should set focus. You'll see several pairs of brackets when several parts of the scene are at the same distance from the camera. Even if you set one of the other options, Wide is automatically selected in certain shooting modes, including both Auto and all SCN modes. Use this mode to give the camera (rather than you) complete control over where to focus. (See **Figure 8.7**, left.)
- **Center.** Activate this AF area and the camera will use only a single focus detection point in the center of the frame to set focus. Initially a pair of black focus brackets appears on the screen. Touch the shutter release button and the camera sets and locks focus on the subject in the center of the image area; the brackets then turn green to confirm the area that will be in the sharpest focus in your image. (See **Figure 8.7**, right.) Choose this option if you want the camera to always focus on the subject in the center of the frame. Center the primary subject (like a subject in a wide-angle landscape composition), allow the camera to focus on it, maintain slight pressure on the shutter release button to keep focus locked, and re-frame the scene for a more effective, off-center, composition. Take the photo at any time and your subject (which is now off-center) will be in the sharpest focus.

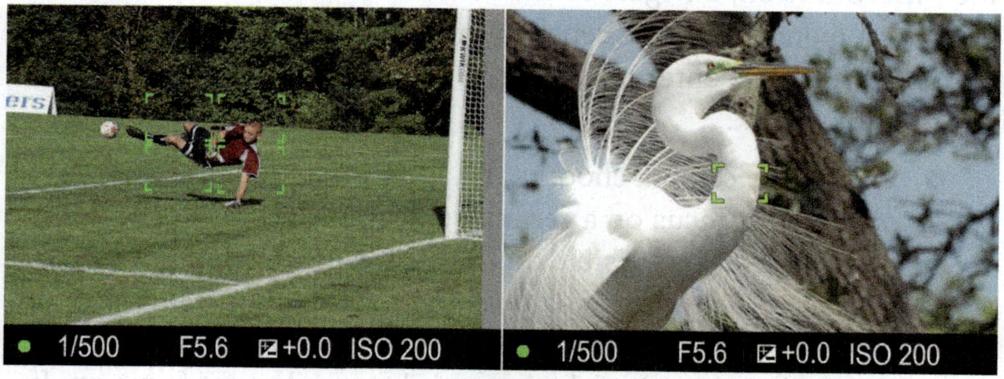

Figure 8.7

With Wide AF Area, the camera displays one or more brackets to indicate the specific area(s) of the scene that will be in sharpest focus. (Left) In the Center AF Area mode, the camera displays the focus brackets in the center of the screen; the brackets turn green after focus has been set. (Right.)

- **Flexible Spot.** This mode enables you to move the camera's focus detection point (focus area) around the scene to any one of multiple locations, using the directional buttons. When opting for Flexible Spot, you can use the left/right buttons to choose Small, Medium, or Large spots, as shown in **Figure 8.8**, left. The relative size of these focus zones is shown in **Figure 8.8**, right.

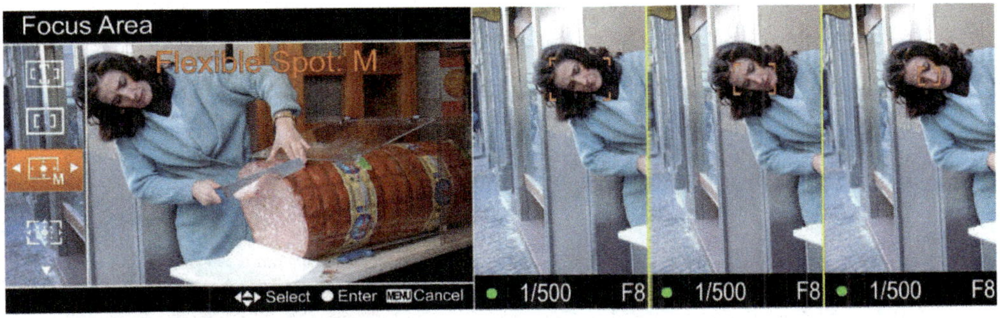

Figure 8.8

When selecting Flexible Spot, you can use the left/right buttons to specify Small, Medium, or Large spots.

Press the center button to activate Flexible Spot focusing; a small pair of focus brackets appears in the center of the screen along with four triangles pointing toward the four sides of the screen. (See **Figure 8.9**.) The triangles merely indicate that the AF area can be moved in any direction. Use the directional controls to move the orange brackets around the screen through an overlapping array of 19 x 17 (Small), 17 x 17 (Medium), or 17 x 15 (Large) focus zones. You can switch sizes as you compose your image by rotating the control wheel.

This allows great versatility in the placement of the active focus detection point. Move the orange brackets until they cover the most important subject area and touch the shutter release button. The brackets will turn green and the camera will beep to confirm that focus has been set on the intended area.

This mode can be especially useful when the camera is mounted on a tripod and you'll be taking photos of the same scene for a long time, while the light is changing, for example. Move the focus area to cover the most important subject, and it will always focus on that point when you later take a photo.

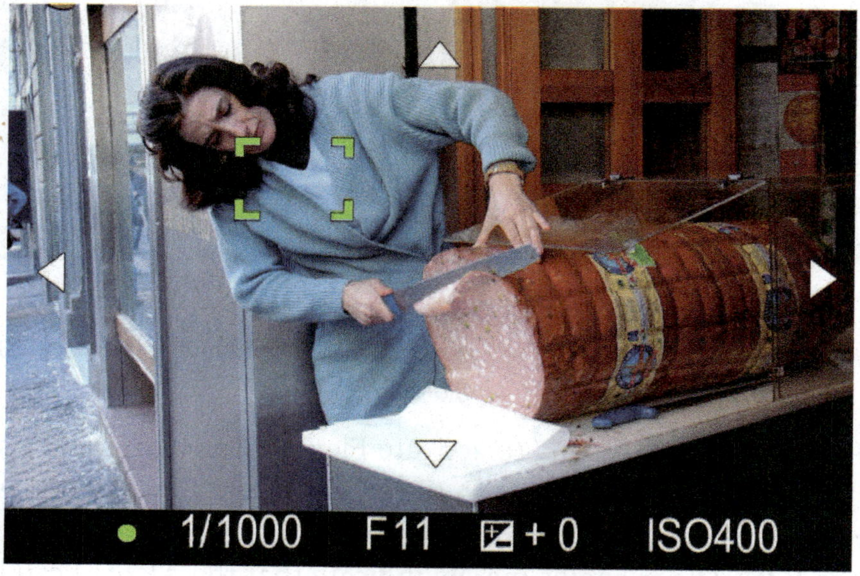

Figure 8.9

When the Flexible Spot AF Area mode is initially selected, the active focus detection point is delineated with orange brackets that turn green when focus is confirmed and locked; the arrows at each side of the screen indicate that you can move the brackets in any of the four directions.

- **Expand Flexible Spot.** If the camera is unable to lock in focus using the selected focus point, it will also use the eight adjacent points to try to achieve focus.
- **Lock-On AF.** In this mode, the camera locks focus onto the subject area that is under the selected focus spot when the shutter button is depressed halfway. Then, if the subject moves (or you change the framing in the camera), the camera will continue to refocus *on that subject*. You can select this mode only when the focus mode is set to Continuous AF (AF-C).

  This option is especially powerful, because you can activate it for any of the five focus area options described above. That is, once you've highlighted Lock-On AF on the selection screen, you can then press the left-right directional button and choose

Wide, Center, Flexible Spot (Small, Medium, or Large), or Expand Flexible Spot.

When the shutter release is pressed down halfway, the camera will lock on a subject, using the "rules" of your selected area mode. That is, in Lock-On AF: Wide, the camera selects the focus area; with Lock-On AF: Center, the center of the frame is used to lock onto a subject; in Flexible Spot mode, you can move the focus zone around before pressing the shutter release halfway to lock on (and rotate the control wheel to select the size of the Flexible Spot). (See **Figure 8.10**.) The next section will explain how Lock-On AF differs from its cousin, Center Lock-On AF.

Just as you're limited in the use of the AF mode in certain operating modes, there's a limitation with AF Area as well. For example, Flexible Spot is not available for selection in automatic modes: in either Auto mode or any SCN mode, the camera will always use Multi as the AF Area mode.

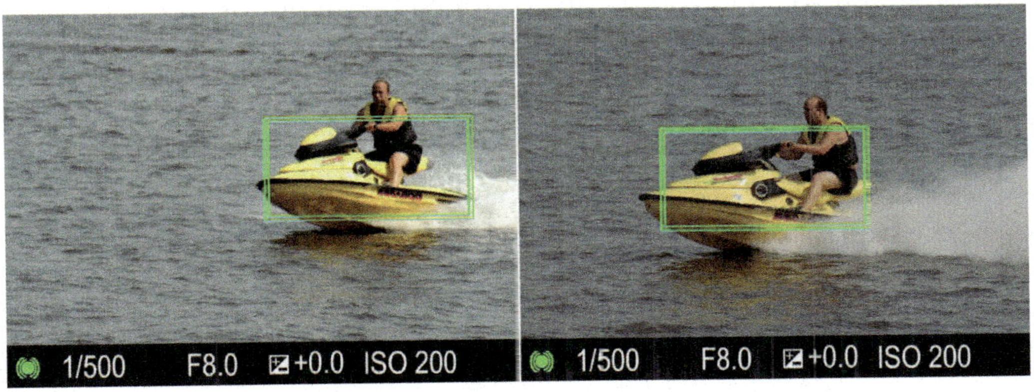

Figure 8.10

Lock-On AF can follow your subject as it moves within the frame.

Face Detection and Eye AF

As hinted already, the RX100 V has a couple more tricks up its sleeve for setting the AF area. By default, Smile/Face Detection in the Camera Settings menu is on, enabling the camera to attempt to identify any human faces in the scene. If it finds one or more faces, the camera will surround each one (up to eight in all) with a gray frame on the screen. (Later, I'll discuss a feature that allows you to specify favorite faces that the camera should prioritize.) If it judges that autofocus is possible, it will turn the frame white to indicate the face given priority. (See **Figure 8.11**.) When you press the shutter button halfway down to lock autofocus, the frame will turn green, confirming autofocus. The camera will also attempt to adjust exposure (including flash, if activated) as appropriate for the scene.

Personally, I often prefer to exercise my own control as to exactly where the camera should focus, but when shooting quick snaps during a party, Face Detection can be a useful feature. It's also an ideal choice if you need to hand the camera to someone to photograph you and your family or friends at an outing in the park. However, it really comes in useful when you couple it with Eye AF when Continuous AF is selected in the Camera Settings 4 menu.

THE EYES HAVE IT

I like to use Face Detection in tandem with Eye AF. By default, the control wheel's center button activates Eye AF while you hold the button down. When active, simply point the camera at a face and press the defined key. The camera will magically identify the face and focus on the eye that's closest to the camera. If no eye is detected, the RX100 V reverts to face detection. If it cannot find a face, Eye AF will fail to lock in. But if you'd like to be amazed, set your camera as follows:

- Continuous AF
- Lock-On AF: Flexible Spot
- Eye AF

The camera will almost unerringly locate faces and focus on the eye of your subject. It's great for candid portraits, weddings, or child photography. As I noted in Chapter 4, to use Eye AF, you must assign that function to a custom key.

Figure 8.11

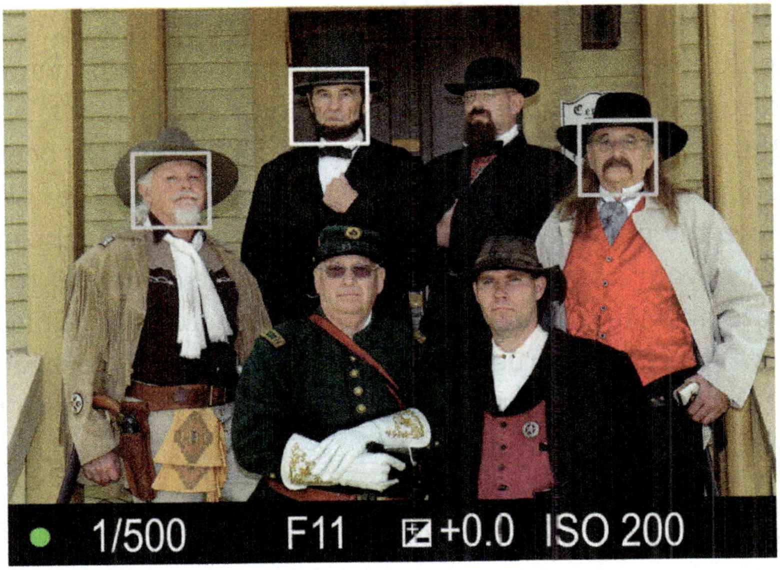

Face Detection will find faces, giving priority to registered faces.

Center Lock-On AF

The next trick the camera can perform is called Center Lock-On AF, which is a separate feature from the Lock-On AF that you can activate with a half-press of the shutter release. Center Lock-On AF must be activated with its Camera Settings 6 menu entry. It's designed to maintain focus on a specific subject as it moves around the scene that you're shooting, using the colors of your subject to identify and track it. Don't confuse this feature with Continuous AF (AF-C), the mode you would use in action photography with a subject running toward you, for example. AF-C's *predictive focus* feature is often called "AF tracking" by other cameras and by many photographers. The RX100 V offers that feature too, with AF-C mode autofocus, but it's not the same as Center Lock-On or Lock-On AF.

The Center Lock-On AF function *can* change focus as a person approaches the camera, but it's not intended for that purpose with a fast-action subject. And this feature is far more versatile than

Continuous AF mode alone. Once the camera knows what your preferred subject is, it can maintain focus as it moves around the image area, as a person might do while mingling with a large group of friends at a party. (See **Figure 8.12.**)

Turn on Center Lock-On AF in the Camera Settings 6 menu. (You cannot do so when the camera is set for Hand-held Twilight, Anti-Motion Blur, Sweep Panorama or manual focus.) When it's been activated, a small white square initially appears in the center of the screen. Move the position of the square with the directional controls until it covers your intended subject and press the center button. The small square now changes to a larger double square that's called the *target frame*. You have instructed the camera as to your preferred subject. If the camera is set to AF-C mode, the camera tracks a focus subject when the shutter button is pressed halfway. To use Center Lock-On AF, just follow these steps:

1. **Deactivate Lock-On AF.** You won't be able to activate Center Lock-On AF if its Lock-On AF cousin is enabled. Visit the Function menu and choose Wide, Center, Flexible Spot, or Expand Flexible Spot.
2. **Activate Center Lock-On AF.** Next, stop by the Camera Settings 6 menu and enable Center Lock-On AF.
3. **Activate.** Press the center button to activate.
4. **Choose subject.** Align the camera so the subject you want to track is within the selection box. Press the center button again to select that subject.
5. **Start tracking.** Once the camera figures out which areas of the image under the selection box include your subject, it will outline the subject with a double white border, using the Wide focus area. The camera will now use the live view image to track the subject and keep that subject in focus.

   Move the camera around to change your composition or wait until your targeted subject begins moving around. Note that the target frame will remain on your subject, confirming that it will be in the sharpest focus when you take a photo. Changes in lighting, lack of contrast or color contrast with the background, extra small or extra large subjects, and anything moving very rapidly can confuse Center Lock-On AF, but it's generally quite effective. Note that once you take a picture, you must go through the menu/custom key rigmarole again; this mode is not "sticky."

6. **Don't panic.** If your subject moves out of the frame, the RX100 V will remember what it was tracking for several seconds, and relock on it if it appears in the frame again within that time. If tracking is totally lost, the camera resumes its normal AF behavior until you select another subject to track.
7. **Stop tracking.** You can press the center button again to stop tracking your subject.

There are a few other benefits with Center Lock-On AF when using the camera when Face Detection is also active. Let's say you have designated the intended target as your friend Jack's face. If Jack leaves the room while being tracked and then returns to the scene, Center Lock-On AF will remember it and focus on Jack again. Whenever a face is your target, the camera can continue tracking that person even if the face is not visible; it will then make the body the target for tracking. If you also activate the camera's Smile Shutter feature (in the Camera Settings menu) in addition to Face Detection, the camera will not only track the targeted face, but it will take a photo if your subject smiles.

Center Lock-On AF allows you to choose the subject to track, rather than rely on the camera to track whatever object focus is originally locked on, as with Lock-On AF, described next. In addition, it can also be used in Movie mode, which can be very handy when you want to track a moving subject as you capture video. It cannot be used when Lock-On AF is active.

There are some special considerations when using this feature if the target subject is a human face. The camera "remembers" the face selected, so if the subject disappears from the frame and then returns, the camera locks in on that face again. If you're using the Smile Shutter function, then the RX100 V will not only track the individual's face, but release the shutter and take a picture if your subject smiles!

Center Lock-On may not work if the subject is moving too quickly, is too small or too large to be isolated effectively, has only reduced contrast against its background, or if the ambient light is too dark or changes dramatically while you're tracking.

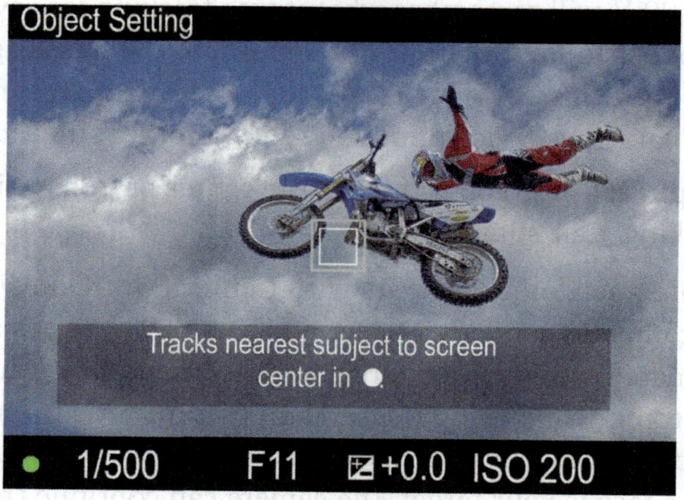

Figure 8.12

Press the center button to start Center Lock-On AF, and press the button again when your subject is within the selection frame.

Lock-On AF

Lock-On AF is the other tool for tracking a moving subject. Lock-On AF is easier than Center Lock-On AF, because you can turn it on and forget it. It does, however, only work in still photography mode; you can't use it when shooting movies. To use Lock-On AF, just follow these steps:

1. **Choose AF-C.** This feature works only when you are using continuous autofocus because, well, it refocuses continually.
2. **Deactivate Center Lock-On.** You can't use Lock-On and Center Lock-On at the same time.
3. **Activate Lock-On AF.** Use the Function menu and choose Focus Area. Scroll down past the Expand Flexible Spot entry and highlight Lock-On AF.
4. **Choose Focus Area.** Surprise! Using Lock-On AF does *not* mean you lose access to the four AF area modes. With Lock-On AF highlighted, use the left/right controls to select Wide, Center, Flexible Spot, or Expand Flexible Spot. That will give you both Lock-On AF *and* the area mode you prefer. If you switch from AF-C to AF-S, you lose the lock-on capabilities, and the camera just reverts to whatever focus area mode you select here.
5. **Start tracking.** When you activate focus by pressing the shutter release halfway, the camera will use your selected focus area option to lock in focus, as always. However, now, once focus has been locked, the camera will *track* your subject as it roams around the screen. You'll see the green focus area rectangles moving as your subject moves (or you reframe the image with the camera). If a face is detected, a tracking rectangle around the face will be shown. (You'll learn more about face detection in an upcoming section.)

Continual Focus Differences

The RX100 V includes four ways of continuing to focus as a subject moves around a frame. Here are their differences:

- **AF-C**. When the shutter release is pressed halfway, the camera focuses on a subject and continues to refocus as the subject moves. AF-C is activated in the Focus Mode entry of the Function menu, Quick Navi menu, or Camera Settings 4 menu. Works in both still and movie modes.
- **Pre-AF.** The camera tries to focus, even if the shutter release has not been pressed halfway down. The RX100 V operates continuously in AF-C mode (and will single-focus in AF-S mode), and uses a lot of battery power. Pre-AF works in both still and movie modes.
- **Center Lock-on AF.** The RX100 V racks an object that was in the center of the frame when you press the center button. Center Lock-on AF is activated from menu and cannot be used when Lock-on AF is active. Center Lock-on AF operates in both still and movie modes.
- **Lock-On AF.** Tracks an object in an area you select. You may choose Wide, Center, Flexible Spot, and Expanded Flexible Spot focus areas. Lock-on AF is activated in the Focus Area settings (including Fn and Quick Navi menus) and cannot be used when Center Lock-on AF is active. Lock-on AF operates only in still photography mode.

Using Manual Focus

As I noted earlier, manual focus is not as straightforward as with an older manual focus 35mm SLR equipped with a focusing screen optimized for this purpose and a readily visible focusing aid. But Sony's designers have done a good job of letting you exercise your initiative in the focusing realm, with features that make it easy to determine whether you have achieved precise focus. It's worth becoming familiar with the techniques for those occasions when it makes sense to take control in this area.

Here are the basic steps for quick and convenient setting of focus:

- **Select Manual Focus.** After you do so (in the Focus Mode entry in the Camera Settings 4 menu), the letters MF will appear in the LCD display when you're viewing the default display that includes a lot of data. (You can change display modes by pressing the DISP button.)
- **Aim at your subject and turn the control ring.** As soon as you start turning the control ring, the image on the LCD is enlarged (magnified) to help you assess whether the center of interest of your composition is in focus. (That is, unless you turned off this feature, called MF Assist, through the Custom Settings 1 menu.) Use the up/down/left/right direction controls to move around the magnified image area until you're viewing the most important subject element, such as a person's eyes. Turn the control ring until that appears to be in the sharpest possible focus.

  The enlargement lasts two seconds before the display returns to normal; you can increase that with the MF Assist Time menu item. In situations where you want to use manual focus without enlargement of the preview image, you can turn this feature off in the Custom Settings menu, using the MF Assist item.
- **If you have difficulty focusing, zoom in if possible and focus at the longest available focal length.** If you're using a zoom lens, you may find it easier to see the exact effect of slight changes in focus while zoomed in. Even if you plan to take a wide-angle photo, zoom to telephoto and rotate the ring to set precise focus on the most important subject element. When you zoom back out to take the picture, the center of interest will still be in sharp focus.
- **Use Peaking of a suitable color.** On by default in Shooting mode, focus peaking provides a colored overlay around edges that are sharply focused; this makes it easier to determine when your subject is precisely focused. The overlay is white, but you can change that to another color when necessary. The

alternate hue may be needed to provide a strong contrast between the peaking highlights and the color of your subject. Access the Peaking Color item of the Custom Settings 2 menu to adjust the color. To make the overlay even more visible, select High in the Peaking Level item; you can also turn peaking Off with this item, if desired.

- **Consider using the DMF option.** Your third option is DMF, or Direct Manual Focus. Activate it and the camera will autofocus with Single-shot AF and lock focus when you press the shutter release button halfway. As soon as focus is confirmed, you can turn the control ring to make fine-tuning adjustments, as long as you maintain slight pressure on the shutter release button. The MF Assist magnification will be activated immediately.

  This method gives you the benefit of autofocus but gives you the chance to change the exact point of focus, to a person's eyes instead of the tip of the nose, for example. This option is useful in particularly critical focusing situations, when the precise focus is essential, as in extremely close focusing on a three-dimensional subject. Because depth-of-field is very shallow in such work, you'll definitely want to focus on the most important subject element, such as the pistil or stamen inside a large blossom. This will ensure that it will be the sharpest part of the image.

- **Specify magnification parameters.** As you'll remember from Chapter 4, You can enable/disable Manual Focus Assist, specify the length of time the image is magnified, and even tell the RX100 V and even choose the initial focus magnification (x1.0 or x5.3) in the Custom Settings 4 menu.

Useful Menu Items for AF

I discussed how to set all the autofocus options, which are scattered among the Camera Settings and Custom Settings menus, plus how to define Custom Keys to activate certain features in Chapters 3 and 4. If you need a recap, here is a list of the RX100 V autofocus and manual focus features that you should keep in mind.

- **Pre-AF.** This stills-only option activates autofocus all the time, so you don't have to press down the shutter release. It takes AF-C to the next level, but uses a lot of power.
- **AF Illuminator.** This Setup menu item is set at Auto by default, indicating that the illuminator on the front of the camera will provide a burst of light in a dark location when using in AF-S mode. That provides a bright target for the autofocus system, and is effective out to about 10 feet. Turn this feature off when you feel the red burst might be intrusive.
- **Face Registration.** Mentioned briefly earlier in this chapter, this Custom Settings 5 menu item is quite versatile, and was described in Chapter 3. You can register up to eight faces that should get priority in terms of autofocus and then specify the order of priority from the most important faces to the least important.

  To register a face, point the camera at the person's face, make sure it's within the large square on the screen, and press the shutter release button. Do so for several faces. When you're taking a photo of a scene that contains more than one registered face, the camera will prioritize faces based on which were the first to be registered in the process you used.

  Take advantage of the Order Exchanging option of this menu item so the faces you consider the most important are prioritized. When you access it, the camera displays the registered faces with a number on each; the lower the number the higher the priority. You can now change the priority in which the faces will be recognized, from 1 (say your youngest child) to 8 (perhaps your cousin twice removed). You can also use the Delete or the Delete All options to delete one or more faces from the registry, such as your ex and former in-laws.

- **Smile Shutter.** If you activate this feature in the Smile/Face Detection entry in the Camera Settings 7 menu, the face detection system will try to find smiling faces. In fact, it will not take a photo until it finds at least one. Within the Smile/Face Detection menu, if you scroll down to Smile Shutter, you can press the left/right buttons to select Normal Smile, Big Smile, or Small Smile. Set the one you want and the camera will watch for a smile of that magnitude; it will cover the relevant face(s) with an orange frame which will turn green after focus is set. And as mentioned earlier, when the camera will be tracking a face using the Lock-On AF feature while Smile Shutter is on, it will prioritize this face while doing so.

Autofocus Summary

Here's a summary of autofocus considerations that were discussed elsewhere in this book, primarily here and in Chapters 3 and 4 under the explanations of the various autofocus settings. I'll recap the most important aspects here, as a quick guide to help you locate the longer discussions. **Table 8.1** provides some guidelines for particular types of subjects. Remember that some of these are also available in the Function menu.

- **Focus Mode (Camera Settings 3).** Choose focus modes from AF-S, AF-C, DMF, and MF.
- **Focus Area (Camera Settings 4).** Select the number and location of autofocus points used, from Wide, Center, Flexible Spot, and Expanded Flexible Spot.
- **AF Illuminator (Stills) (Camera Settings 4).** Enables/disables use of the AF illuminator as an autofocus aid.
- **Focus Magnifier** (Camera Settings 6). Enlarges image during manual focus.

- **Center Lock-On AF (Camera Settings 6).** When activated, automatically tracks focused subject when shooting stills and movies. Mutually exclusive with Lock-On AF.
- **Smile/Face Detection (Camera Settings 7).** Sets focus, exposure, and white balance for detected faces, both registered and unregistered.
- **MF Assist (Custom Settings 1).** Turns manual focus magnifier on or off.
- **Focus Magnifier Time (Custom Settings 1).** Length of time focus magnifier remains active.
- **Peaking Level/Color (Custom Settings 2).** These two settings specify the color outline of manually focused sharp areas.
- **Pre-AF (Stills) (Custom Settings 3).** Enables/disables AF start when camera is brought up to the eye.
- **Face Registration (Custom Settings 5).** Allows you to register up to eight faces.

Table 8.1
Focus Guidelines

Subject	Focus Mode	Focus Area	Lock-On AF	Smile/Face Detection	Eye AF
Portraits	AF-S	Flexible Spot	Off	On	Yes
Street photography	AF-C	Wide	On	On	As needed
General sports action	AF-C	Expanded Flexible Spot	On	Off	No
Birds in Flight	AF-C	Expanded Flexible Spot	On	Off	No
Football, soccer, basketball	AF-C	Expanded Flexible Spot	On	Off	Off
Kids, Pets	AF-C	Wide	On	On	Yes
Track events, auto racing	AF-C	Wide	On	Off	No
Landscapes	AF-S	Wide	Off	Off	No
Concerts, performance	AF-S	Flexible Spot	Off	On	Yes

Chapter 9

Advanced Techniques

Of the primary foundations of great photography, only one of them -- the ability to capture a compelling image with a pleasing composition -- takes a lifetime (or longer) to master. The art of *making* a photograph, rather than just *taking* a photograph, requires an aesthetic eye that sees the right angle for the shot, as well as a sense of what should be included or excluded in the frame; a knowledge of what has been done in the medium before (and where photography can be taken in the future); and a willingness to explore new areas. The more you pursue photography, the more you will learn about visualization and composition. When all is said and done, this is what photography is all about.

The other basics of photography -- equally essential -- involve more technical aspects: the ability to use your camera's features to produce an image with good tonal and color values; to achieve sharpness (where required) or unsharpness (when you're using selective focus); and to master appropriate white/color balance. It's practical to learn these technical skills in a time frame that's much less than a lifetime, although most of us find there is always room for improvement. You'll find the basic information you need to become proficient in each of these technical areas in this book.

Now it's time to begin exploring advanced techniques that enable you to get stunning shots that will have your family, friends, and colleagues asking you, "How did you *do* that?" These more advanced techniques deserve an entire book of their own, but there is plenty of room in this chapter to introduce you to some clever things you can do with your RX100 V.

Exploring Ultra-Fast Exposures

Fast shutter speeds (such as 1/1,000th second) can stop action because they capture only a tiny slice of time: a high-jumper frozen in mid-air, perhaps. The Sony RX100 V has a top shutter speed of 1/32,000th second for ambient light exposures. Electronic flash can also freeze motion by virtue of its extremely short duration -- as brief as 1/50,000th second or less. When you're using flash, the short duration of the actual burst of light can freeze a moving subject; that can also give you an ultra-quick glimpse of a moving subject when the scene is illuminated only by flash.

The RX100 V is fully capable of immobilizing all but the very fastest movement if you use a shutter speed no higher than about 1/2,000th second. That's the top speed of your camera when using its mechanical shutter. Switch to the all-electronic shutter instead, and the RX100 V can use a full range of shutter speeds from 30 seconds to 1/32000th second. Of course, the top speeds from 1/4000th second to 1/32,000th second are generally overkill when it comes to stopping action; I can rarely find a situation where even 1/4,000th second is required to freeze high-speed motion. Indeed, virtually all sports action can be frozen at such speeds, and for many sports a slower shutter speed is actually preferable -- for example, to allow the wheels of a racing automobile or motorcycle, or the propeller on a classic aircraft, to blur realistically, as I'll show you shortly.

There may be a few situations where faster shutter speeds are required. If you wanted to use an aperture of f/1.8 at ISO 80 outdoors in bright sunlight, say to throw a background out of focus with the shallow depth-of-field available at f/1.8, a shutter speed of 1/4,000th second would more than do the job. You'd need a faster shutter speed only if you were shooting a snowy scene or you were on a beach or, perhaps you had set an ISO higher than ISO 80 (and you probably wouldn't do that if your goal were to use the widest aperture possible). Under *less* than full sunlight, I doubt you'd even need to use a shutter speed of 1/4,000th second in any situations you're likely to encounter. After all, your RX100 V has a 3-stop neutral-density filter which reduces the amount of light passing through the lens to the sensor.

But while ultra-high shutter speeds may not be required for day-to-day photography, your camera's capabilities do open the door to exploring some unseen perspectives that can only be captured by using tiny slices of time. You can have a lot of fun exploring the kinds of pictures you can take using very brief exposure times, if you decide to take advantage of the action-stopping shutter speeds (between 1/1,000th and 1/32,000th second) Here are a few ideas to get you started:

Sports Action

I was a sports photographer for a daily newspaper for many years, and my personal preference has always been to use a shutter speed slow enough to introduce enough blur to convey a feeling of motion in my shots. But there's a lot to be said for freezing a peak moment with a fast shutter speed, in order to show the tension of the moment, say, a pole vaulter's flex to clear the bar, a long jumper's mid-air stretch to gain a few more inches, or a sprinter straining to sail over an imposing array of hurdles (see **Figure 9.1**).

To reliably capture a moment without blur, you'll need to use a shutter speed of 1/2000th second or faster. Visit the Custom Settings 4 menu's Shutter Type entry and choose Electronic Shutter. While the Auto setting does allow using the full range of shutter speeds, explicitly selecting Electronic Shutter will enable you to take advantage of the e-shutter's quick response at all shutter speeds.

In addition to providing extremely fast shutter speeds, the electronic shutter increases the speed of continuous shooting and speed priority continuous shooting. That's because, with the mechanical shutter, the shutter curtains must close before the previous image is "dumped" to allow a new exposure, but the e-shutter performs this step electronically, and at a much higher speed.

Note that the RX100 V will force use of the mechanical shutter, regardless of your setting, if you're using a custom white balance or face registration, and long exposure noise reduction and the Bulb setting are disabled (30 seconds is the longest exposure available with the electronic shutter). If you're shooting indoors, say, basketball games under some types of fluorescent and "arena" lighting, the innate cycling of such lights (which is invisible to the eye) may cause banding and light/dark areas when using the electronic shutter.

Electronic flash can be used with the electronic shutter at speeds no faster than 1/100th second. While the e-shutter is inherently silent, the RX100 V produces a comforting "click" sound when you take pictures. To enable a totally soundless mode, visit the Audio Signals entry in the Setup 1 menu and choose Off.

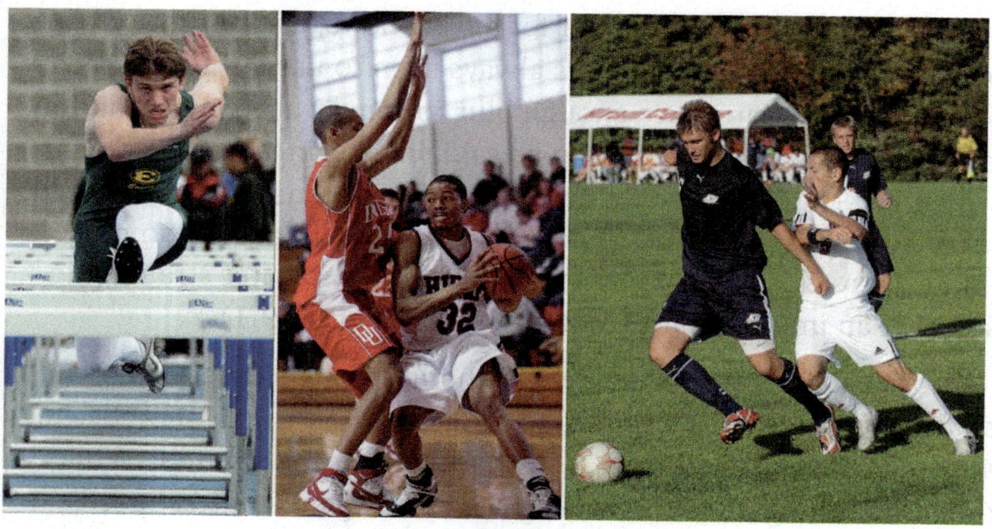

Figure 9.1
Fast shutter speeds can freeze action at its peak.

Capture Unseen Perspectives

Some things are *never* seen in real life, except when viewed in a stop-action photograph. M.I.T. professor Dr. Harold Edgerton's famous balloon burst photographs were only a starting point for the inventor of the electronic flash unit. Freeze a hummingbird in flight for a view of wings that never seem to stop. Or, capture the splashes as liquid falls into a bowl, as shown in **Figure 9.2**, left. No electronic flash was required for this image (and wouldn't have illuminated the water in the bowl as evenly). Instead, a clutch of high-intensity lamps and an ISO setting of 3200 allowed the camera to capture this image at 1/4,000th second.

Electronic flash works well for freezing the motion of a nearby subject when flash is the only source of light, but your RX100 V's built-in flash provides illumination only from the front (unless you point it upward with your finger for bounce flash). Ambient light shooting gives you a great deal more flexibility in placement of lights, and the opportunity to preview the effects of those lights. In most cases, you'll need to boost the ISO sensitivity to ISO 3200 to ISO 6400 (unless you have uncommonly bright artificial illumination) if you want to use very high shutter speeds to freeze falling objects or capture water droplets as they spray upward.

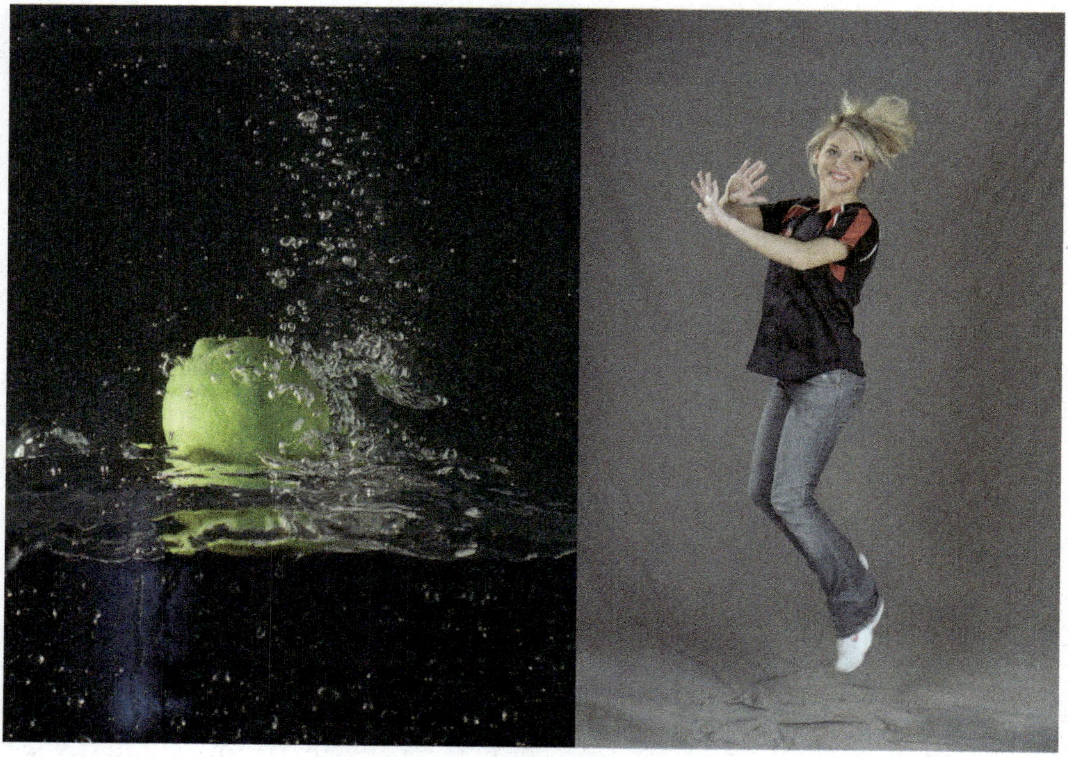

Figure 9.2

Using fast shutter speeds to freeze action.

Take Revealing Images

Fast shutter speeds can help you reveal the real subject behind the façade, by freezing constant motion to capture an enlightening moment in time. Legendary fashion/portrait photographer Philippe Halsman used leaping photos of famous people, such as the Duke and Duchess of Windsor, Richard Nixon, and Salvador Dali, to illuminate their real selves. Halsman said, "*When you ask a person to jump, his attention is mostly directed toward the act of jumping and the mask falls so that the real person appears.*" Try some high-speed portraits of people you know in motion to see how they appear when concentrating on something other than the portrait. (See **Figure 9.2**, right.)

Create Unreal Images

High-speed photography can also produce photographs that show your subjects in ways that are quite unreal. A helicopter in mid-air with its rotors frozen or a motocross cyclist leaping over a ramp, but with all motion stopped so that the rider and machine look as if they were frozen in mid-air, makes for an unusual picture. (See the frozen rotors at top in **Figure 9.3**.) When we're accustomed to seeing subjects in motion, seeing them stopped in time can verge on the surreal.

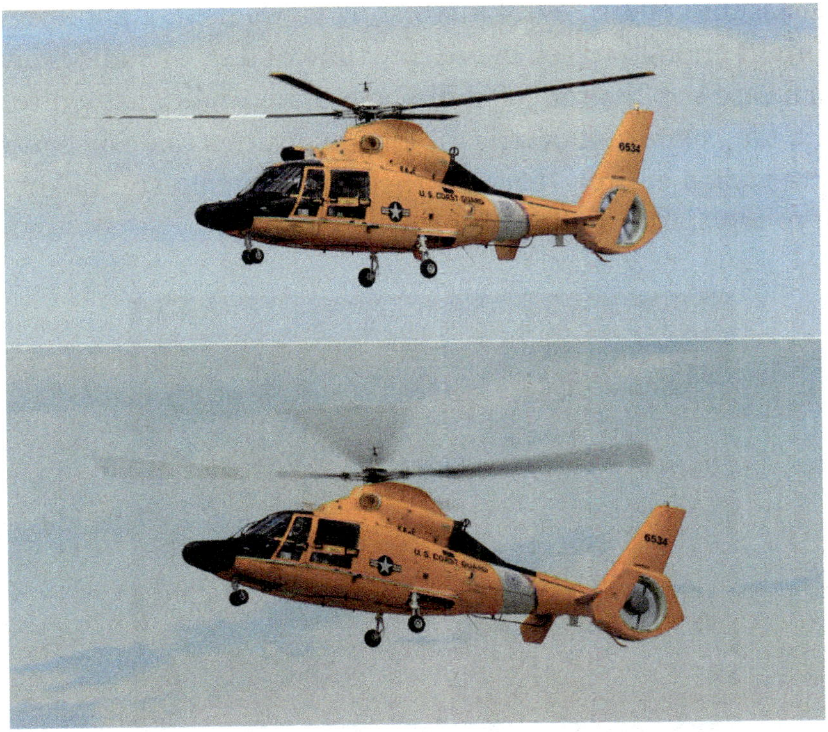

Figure 9.3

Freezing a helicopter's rotors with a fast shutter speed makes for an image that doesn't look natural (top); a little blur helps convey a feeling of motion (bottom).

Long Exposures

Longer exposures are a doorway into another world, showing us how even familiar scenes can look much different when photographed over periods measured in seconds. At night, long exposures produce streaks of light from moving, illuminated subjects like automobiles or amusement park rides, or objects that are light sources themselves, like the fireworks shown in **Figure 9.4**. Or, you can move the camera or zoom the lens to get interesting streaks from non-moving light sources, such as the holiday lights. Extra-long exposures of seemingly pitch-dark subjects can reveal interesting views using light levels barely bright enough to see by. At any time of day, including daytime (in which case you'll often need the help of neutral-density filters to make the long exposure practical), long exposures can cause moving objects to vanish entirely, because they don't remain stationary long enough to register in a photograph.

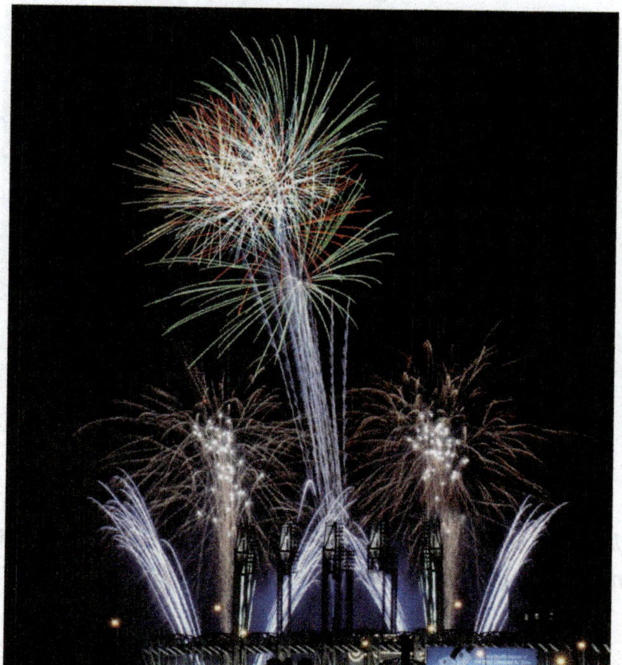

Figure 9.4

Long exposures can produce interesting streaks of light.

Because the RX100 V produces such good images at longer timed exposures, up to 30 seconds (and at even longer bulb exposures), and there are so many creative things you can do with long-exposure techniques, you'll want to do some experimenting. Get yourself a tripod or another firm support and take some test shots with long exposure noise reduction both enabled and disabled in the Setup menu (to see whether you prefer low noise or high detail) and get started.

As I noted in Chapter 7, you can make exposures as long as 30 seconds when using P, A, or S modes. In Manual exposure mode, bulb exposures can be even longer (but not available if you're using any mode that produces multiple exposures within the same frame, such as Auto HDR, Continuous/Speed Priority Continuous, or Multi Frame Noise Reduction). In bulb mode, hold down the shutter release for the duration of the exposure, or use a wired release with a locking button, such as the Sony RM-VPR1 ($65), which plugs into the Multi/USB terminal.

If you want to experiment with long exposures, here are some things to try:

- **Make people invisible.** One very cool thing about long exposures is that objects that move rapidly enough won't register at all in a photograph, whereas the subjects that remain stationary are portrayed in the normal way. That makes it easy to produce people-free landscape photos and architectural photos at night, or even in full daylight if you use the camera's built-in neutral density filter. They'll have to be walking *very* briskly and across the field of view (rather than directly toward the camera) for this to work. At night, it's much easier to achieve this effect with the 20- to 30-second exposures that are possible in low light without any filter.
- **Create streaks.** If you aren't shooting for total invisibility, long exposures with the camera on a tripod can produce some interesting streaky effects. Your camera's built-in three-stop neutral-density filter will let you shoot at f/22 and 1/6th second in daylight. Indoors, you can achieve interesting streaks

with slow shutter speeds, which is a technique I often use when photographing ballet dancers.

The RX100 V's neutral-density filter, available from the Camera Settings 5 menu, is a gray (non-colored) filter that reduces the amount of light passing through the lens, without adding any color or effect of its own.

- **Produce light trails.** At night, car headlights, taillights, and other moving sources of illumination can generate interesting light trails. Your camera doesn't even need to be mounted on a tripod; hand-holding the camera for longer exposures adds movement and patterns to your trails. If you're shooting fireworks, a longer exposure -- with the camera on a tripod -- may allow you to combine several bursts into one picture.
- **Blur waterfalls, etc.** You'll find that waterfalls and other sources of moving liquid produce a special type of long-exposure blur, because the water merges into a fantasy-like veil that looks different at different exposure times, and with different waterfalls. Cascades with turbulent flow produce a rougher look at a given longer exposure than falls that flow smoothly. Although blurred waterfalls and rapids have become almost a cliché, there are still plenty of variations for a creative photographer to explore, as you can see in **Figure 9.5.**

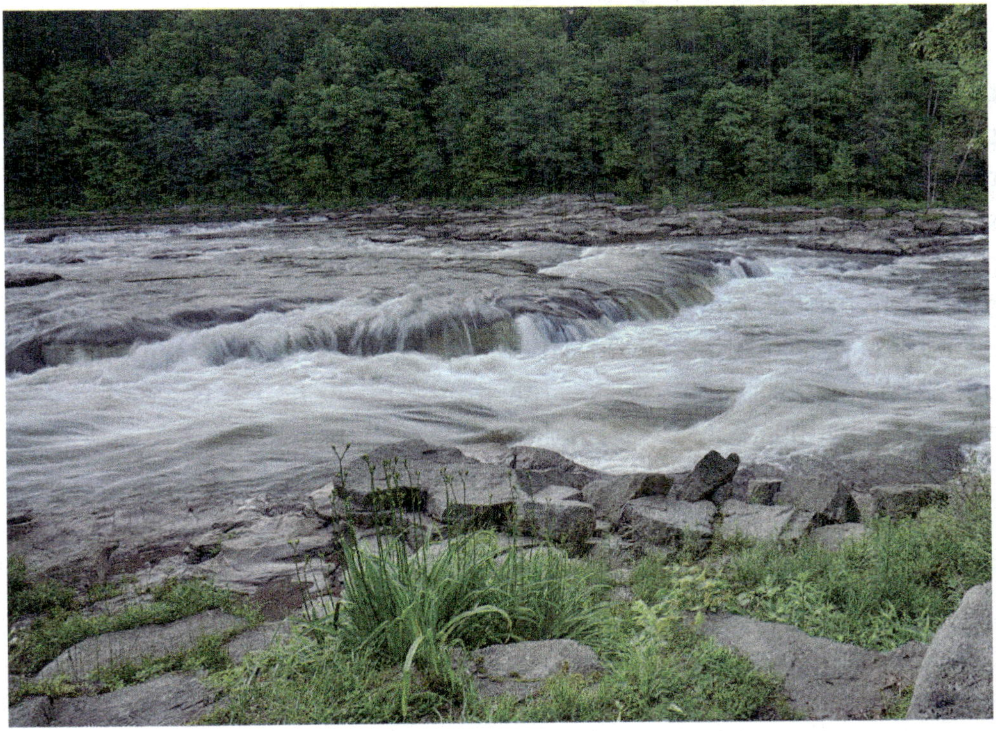

Figure 9.5

A one-second shutter speed blurred the water in these rapids.

Continuous Shooting

The RX100 V's continuous shooting modes are indispensable for the sports photographer. They're also useful for anyone photographing an event in which, even if you have lightning-fast reflexes, a decisive moment may occur a fraction of a second after you've completed an exposure. To improve your chances, you will often use the standard Continuous Shooting setting, which allows capturing images continuously at *up to* (and note that qualification) 24 frames per second, so you can shoot consecutive images non-stop until the camera's buffer fills. This almost never happens, so, effectively, you can keep firing off shots at that rate until your memory card fills up, or the battery is dead, or the camera overheats.

That's a lot of shooting. Given an average burst of about eight frames per sequence at the camera's highest frame (nobody really takes 15 to 20 shots or more of one pass), you can capture hundreds of different sequences before you need to swap cards. Of course, for some types of action (such as football), even longer bursts come in handy, because running and passing plays often last 5 to 10 seconds; there's also a change in character as, say, the action on a basketball court changes from as player maneuvers for position, and then drives to the hoop. (See **Figure 9.6**.)

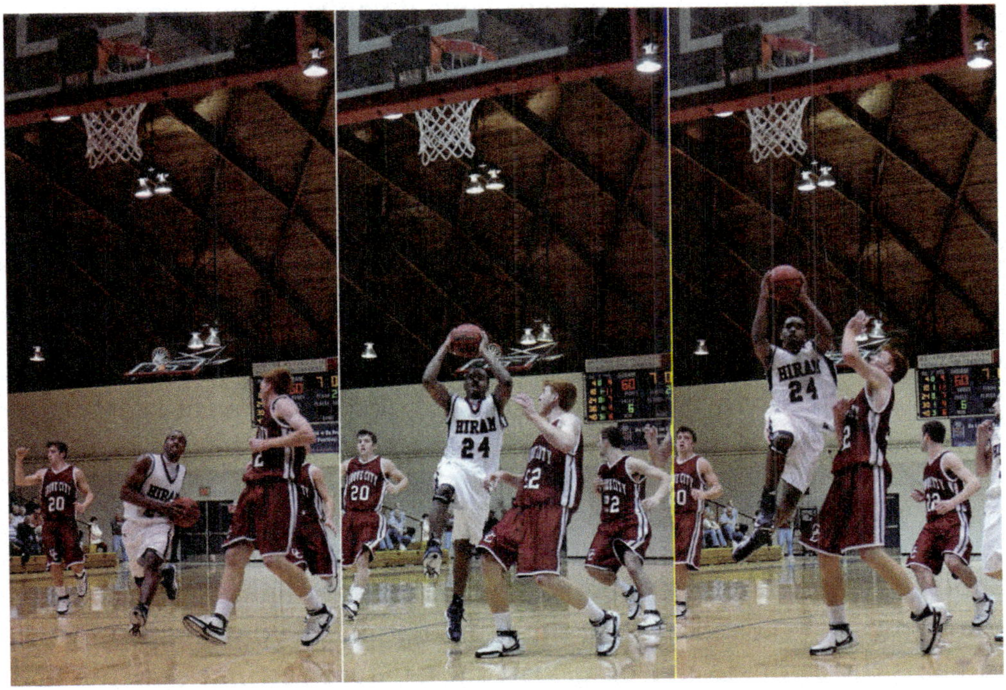

Figure 9.6

Continuous shooting allows you to capture an entire sequence of exciting moments as they unfold.

There are three ways to activate the RX100 V's continuous advance option in the Drive mode menu. You'll find the Drive Mode entry in the Camera Settings 3 menu; you can press the Drive button (left direction button), access the Function menu, where you'll find Drive Mode at the left side of the Fn menu (unless you've deleted or moved it.) Then navigate to the Cont. Shooting option, and press the left/right buttons to select Hi (24 fps), Med (10 fps) or Lo (3.5 fps.) The camera will automatically switch to the electronic shutter, which is what makes the highest speeds possible.

If you set the AF mode (in the Function submenu) to AF-C, Continuous autofocus will be available in all continuous drive modes. This feature is useful when a moving subject is approaching the camera or moving away from it; the RX100 V will continuously adjust to focus on the subject as the distance changes, so the entire set of photos should be sharply focused.

Continuous shooting is not available if you're using Sweep Panorama; if you select a scene mode other than Sports Action; when DRO/Auto HDR is set to Auto HDR; when Smile Shutter is enabled; or Picture Effect is set to Soft Focus, HDR Painting, Rich-tone Mono, Miniature, Watercolor, or Illustration. Continuous shooting is also disabled if ISO is set to Multi Frame Noise Reduction or your battery level is low.

Keep in mind that continuous shooting does not guarantee capturing the "decisive moment" every time. A 90 mph fastball moves 13.2 feet between frames at 10 fps, so if you want to catch the moment the ball hits a player's bat, you'll need some luck and good timing.

Even if the RX100 V is fast enough to change *exposure* between shots, that may not be a good thing if, say, bright lights pass through the frames as you shoot while the illumination on your main subject remains the same. In this case, visit the Custom Settings 3 menu, and set the AEL w/Shutter entry to Off.

Continuous shooting is not available if you're using Sweep Panorama; if you select a scene mode other than Sports Action; when DRO/Auto HDR is set to Auto HDR; when Smile Shutter is enabled; or Picture Effect is set to Soft Focus, HDR Painting, Rich-tone Mono, Miniature, Watercolor, or Illustration. Continuous shooting is also disabled if ISO is set to Multi Frame Noise Reduction or your battery level is low.

The biggest problem with shooting at the top frame rate is that the camera doesn't show you a live view of what you're capturing; the image on the LCD or viewfinder seems to lag a frame or two behind (although it's difficult to tell the difference when shooting at such a high speed), and may black out between frames. Nor can you review any of your images until the camera has finished writing all the images in its buffer to your memory card. This is a significant drawback for sports shooters, or anyone who is accustomed to being able to view their images almost continually through an optical viewfinder like those found on conventional dSLRs.

Customizing White Balance

Back in the film days, both color transparency and color negative ("print") films were standardized, or balanced, for a particular "color" of light. Most were balanced for daylight, but you could also buy "tungsten" balanced color negative and transparency film for shooting under incandescent lamps that produced light of an amber color. This type of film had a bluish color balance, intended to moderate the effect produced by light that was amber. Digital cameras like the Sony RX100 V can be adjusted for specific white balance options suitable for particular types of illumination.

This is important because various light sources produce illumination of different "colors," although sometimes we are not aware of the difference. Indoor illumination tends to be somewhat amber when using light bulbs that are not daylight balanced, while noonday light outdoors is close to white, and the light early and late in the day is somewhat red/yellow.

White balance is measured using a scale called color temperature. Color temperatures were assigned by heating a theoretical "black body radiator" (which doesn't reflect any light; all illumination comes from its radiance alone) and recording the spectrum of light it emitted at a given temperature in degrees Kelvin. So, daylight at noon has a color temperature in the 5,500- to 6,000-degree range. Indoor illumination is around 3,400 degrees. Hotter temperatures produce bluer images (think blue-white hot) while cooler temperatures produce redder images (think of a dull-red glowing ember). Because of human nature, though, bluer images are actually called "cool" (think wintry day) and redder images are called "warm" (think ruddy sunset), even though their color temperatures are reversed.

Take a photo indoors under warm illumination with a digital camera sensor balanced for cooler daylight and the image will appear much too red/yellow. An image exposed outdoors with the white balance set for incandescent (tungsten) illumination will seem much too blue. These color casts may be too strong to remove in an image editor from JPEG files. Of course, if you shoot RAW photos, you can later change the WB setting to the desired value in RAW converter software; this is a completely "non-destructive" process so full image quality will be maintained.

Mismatched white balance settings are easier to achieve accidentally than you might think, even for experienced photographers. I'd just arrived at a Dwight Yoakam concert after shooting some photos indoors with electronic flash and had manually set WB for Flash. Then, as the concert began, I resumed shooting using the incandescent stage lighting -- which looked white to the eye -- and ended up with a few shots like Figure 9.7, left. Eventually, I caught the error during picture review and changed my white balance. Another time, I was shooting outdoors, but had the camera white balance still set for incandescent illumination. The excessively blue image is shown in **Figure 9.7**, right.

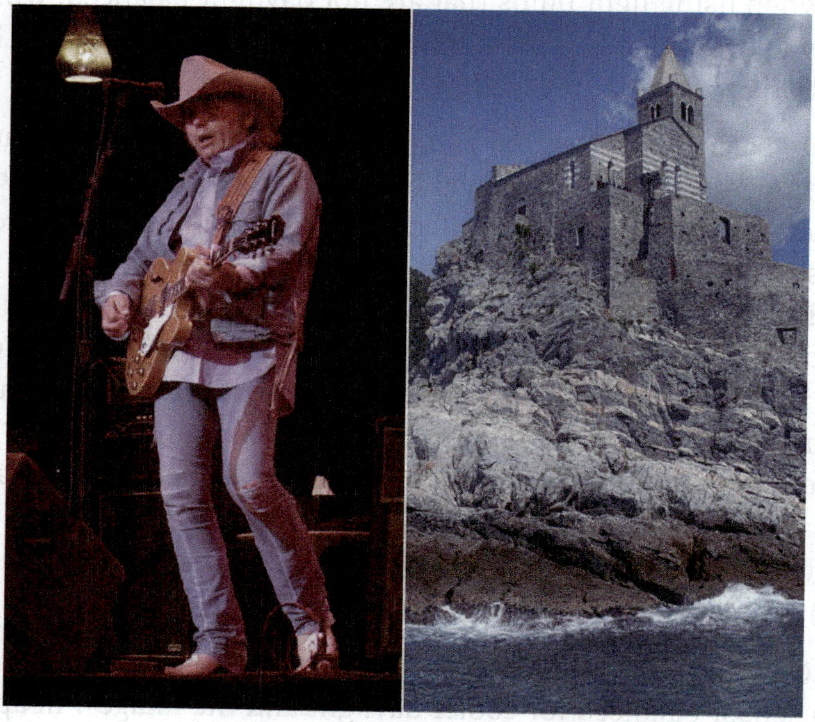

Figure 9.7

An image exposed indoors with the WB set for electronic flash will appear too reddish (left); using the incandescent setting outdoors makes an image too blue (right).

The Auto White Balance (AWB) setting, available from the White Balance entry in the Camera Settings 5 menu, Function menu, or a key defined with that function, examines your scene and chooses an appropriate value based on its perception of the color of the illumination and even the colors in the scene. However, the process is not foolproof (with any camera). Under bright lighting conditions, it may evaluate the colors in the image and still assume the light source is daylight and balance the picture accordingly, even though, in fact, you may be shooting under extremely bright incandescent illumination. In dimmer light, the camera's electronics may assume that the illumination is tungsten, and if there are lots of reddish colors present, set color balance for that type of lighting. With mercury vapor or sodium lamps, correct white balance may be virtually impossible to achieve with any of the so-called presets. In those cases, you should use flash instead, or Custom WB with JPEGs, or shoot in RAW format and make your corrections after importing the file into your image editor with a RAW converter.

The RX100 V provides many WB presets, each intended for use in specific lighting conditions. You can choose from Daylight, Shade, Cloudy, Incandescent (often called Tungsten by photographers), four types of Fluorescent (Warm White, Cool White, Day White, and Daylight), and Flash. However, the RX100 V also offers a method for setting a desired color temperature/filter as well as a custom WB feature.

The Daylight preset provides WB at 5,200K, while the Shade preset uses 7,000K to give you a warming effect that's useful in the bluish light of a deeply shaded area. The chief difference between direct sun and an area in shade, or even incandescent light sources, is nothing more than the proportions of red and blue light. The spectrum of colors used by the RX100 V is continuous, but it is biased toward one end or the other, depending on the white balance setting you make.

However, some types of fluorescent lights produce illumination that has a severe deficit in certain colors, such as only particular shades of red. If you looked at the spectrum or rainbow of colors encompassed by such a light source, it would have black bands in it, representing particular wavelengths of light that are absent. You can't compensate for this deficiency by adding all tones of red. That's why the fluorescent setting of your Sony may provide less than satisfactory results with some kinds of fluorescent bulbs. If you take many photographs under a particular kind of non-compatible fluorescent light, you might want to investigate specialized filters intended for use under various types of fluorescent light, available from camera stores, or develop skills in white balance adjustment using an image editor or RAW converter software program. However, you do get four presets for fluorescent WB with the RX100 V and one of these should provide close to accurate white balance with the common types of lights.

It's when you find that AWB and the various presets simply cannot produce pleasing white balance in certain lighting conditions that you'll need the other options (discussed shortly): use the white balance adjustment feature, set a specific color temperature, or calibrate the WB system to set a custom white balance.

Fine-Tuning Preset White Balance

After you scroll to any of the WB options (AWB, Daylight, Shade, etc.), pressing the right directional button reveals the White Balance Adjustment screen, with a grid, shown in **Figure 9.8**. This feature allows you to fine-tune the white balance by biasing it toward certain colors. Use any of the four directional keys to move the orange dot (cursor) from the center of the grid: upward to bias the WB toward green (G), downward toward magenta (M), right toward amber , or left toward blue . You can move the cursor seven increments (although Sony doesn't reveal exactly what those increments are) in any of the four directions.

Naturally, you can also move the orange dot to any point within the grid: toward amber/magenta for example. While biasing the WB, examine the scene in the LCD or viewfinder preview display; stop making adjustments when the white balance looks fine. Tap the shutter release to escape from the WB settings adjustments. Let's look at the options in more detail:

- **Cooler or warmer.** Pressing the left/right directional buttons changes the white balance to cooler (left) or warmer (right) along the blue/amber scale. There are seven increments, and the value you "dial in" will be shown in the upper-left corner of the screen as an A-B value (yes, the labels are *reversed* from the actual scale at the right side of the screen). The red dot will move along the scale to show the value you've selected. Typically, blue/amber adjustments are what we think of as "color temperature" changes, or, "cooler" and "warmer." These correspond to the way in which daylight illumination changes: warm at sunrise and sunset, very cool in the shade (because most of the illumination comes from reflections of the blue sky), and extremely blue at high noon. Indoor light sources can also be cooler or warmer, depending on the kind of light they emit.
- **Green/magenta bias.** Press the up/down buttons to change the color balance along the green (upward) or magenta (downward) directions. Seven increments are provided here,

too, and shown as vertical movement in the color balance matrix at the right of the screen. Color changes of this type tend to reflect special characteristics of the light source; certain fluorescent lights have a "green" cast, for example.

- **Either or both.** Because the blue/amber and green/magenta adjustments can be made independently, you're free to choose just one of them, or both if your fine-tuning requires it.
- **Never mind.** If you want to cancel all fine-tuning and shift back to neutral, just press the down directional button. The red dot in the color chart will be restored to the center position.

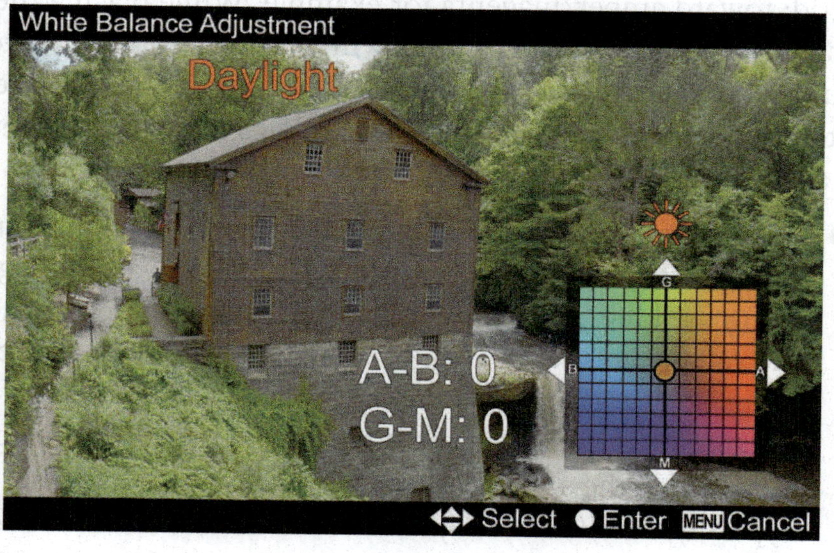

Figure 9.8

Use this feature when you want to fine-tune white balance when using AWB or any of the presets.

Setting White Balance by Color Temperature

If you want to set a specific white balance based on color temperature, choose C. Temp/Filter in the White Balance menu and press the right button. You'll next see a display of color temperatures arrayed along the bottom of the screen. Press the right button a second time to view an adjustment screen similar to the one shown in **Figure 9.8**, but with a scrolling list of color temperatures displayed along the right edge of the screen. Here's how to use this feature.

- **Change color temperature.** Rotate the control wheel on the camera back to select a specific color temperature in 100K increments, from 2,500K (a level that makes your image much bluer, to compensate for amber illumination) to 9,900K (a level that makes images much redder to correct for light that is extremely blue in color). The live preview changes as you scroll to give you an indication as to the white balance you can expect at any K level. If you have a color temperature meter accessory, or reliable tips that guide you in making the optimal setting, this WB feature will be particularly useful. Even if you don't have that accessory or useful information, you may want to experiment with this setting using the live preview, especially if you are trying to achieve creative effects with color casts along the spectrum from blue to red.
- **Fine-tune the color temperature.** In addition to color temperature, you can change the blue/amber or green/magenta bias, exactly as described earlier; move the cursor in any direction with the directional keys. If you change your mind, press the MENU button to cancel the bias adjustments you've made.

This feature corresponds to the use of CC (Color Compensation) filters that were used to compensate for various types of lighting when shooting film. When you use C. Temp/Filter, the color filter value you set takes effect in conjunction with the color temperature you set. In other words, both of these settings work together to give you very precise control over the degree of color correction you are using.

Setting a Custom White Balance

If you often shoot in locations that are illuminated by artificial light of unusual colors, the best bet is to set a custom white balance. This calls for teaching (calibrating) the WB system to render white as white under a specific type of illumination. When white is accurately rendered, other colors will look accurate as well. You can use this feature under more common types of lighting too; it's very useful under tungsten lamps for example, when the Incandescent WB option does not adequately correct for the amber color of the light. Custom WB is the most accurate way of getting the right color balance, short of having a special meter that gives you a precise reading of color temperature. It's easy to do with the RX100 V. Just follow these steps:

1. Navigate to White Balance in the Camera Settings 5 or Function menus.
2. Use the direction buttons or the control wheel to scroll up/down through the list of white balance options until the Set icon at the very bottom is highlighted. Don't select the Custom 1, Custom 2, or Custom 3 entries, located just above it. These are white balance memory register "slots" you can use to store customized white balance settings that you have previously specified.
3. Press the center button. The LCD will display a message telling you to press the shutter button to capture the white balance data. (Custom 1, 2, and 3 are used later to *choose* a custom WB setting you have saved; Custom Set *creates* that setting.)
4. Point the camera at a white object (such as a sheet of white paper) large enough to fill the small circle that's displayed in the center of the frame. Your target must be in the same light as the subject you plan to photograph, not in some entirely different part of the scene where the illumination is different.
5. Press the shutter release button. The target (such as the sheet of white paper) that you had aimed at, as well as the custom

white balance data, appears on the LCD or EVF screen. (The image is not recorded to the memory card.)

6. The white balance of the target you photographed will appear at the bottom of the screen, along with an invitation to choose one of the three registers to store that setting. Rotate the control wheel to specify the register and press the center button to enter it and return to live view.
7. Press the center button to return to the live view on the LCD. Henceforth, you can select that Custom register to load a particular set of white balance parameters.

Using Creative Styles

This option, the next-to-last entry on the Camera Settings 5 menu, gives you six basic Creative Styles with fixed combinations of contrast, saturation, and sharpness. They each have a number prefix on the screen: 1: Standard, 2: Vivid, 3: Neutral, 4: Portrait, 5: Landscape, 6: B&W. Each *also* appears a second time (without the number prefix) and with the addition of Clear, Deep, Light, Night, Autumn, Sepia, and Sunset. You can adjust the contrast, saturation, and sharpness of the non-numbered versions using the left/right buttons to choose an attribute, and the up/down buttons to adjust that attribute. You can apply Creative Styles when you are using any Shooting mode except Superior Auto, Intelligent Auto, or any of the scene modes. When working with Creative Styles, you can *adjust* the parameters within each preset option to fine-tune the rendition. First, look at the "stock" creative styles, each labeled with the number prefix:

- **1: Standard.** This is, as you might expect, your default setting, with a good compromise of sharpness, color saturation, and contrast. Choose this, and your photos will have excellent colors, a broad range of tonal values, and standard sharpness that avoids the "oversharpened" look that some digital pictures acquire.
- **2: Vivid.** If you want more punch in your images, with richer colors, heightened contrast that makes those colors stand out, and standard sharpness, this setting is for you. It's good for

flowers, seaside photos, any picture with expanses of blue sky, and on overcast days where a punchier image can relieve the dullness.

- **3: Neutral.** Reduces saturation and sharpness to produce images with more subdued tones. Use this if you plan on tweaking your photos in an image editor and you want a basic image without any of the enhancements of the other styles.
- **4: Portrait.** You'll get reduced saturation, contrast, and sharpness for a more "gentle" rendition that often works well for people pictures, especially skin tones. This style is a good choice if you're planning on fine-tuning those aspects of your JPEG photos in your computer and don't want the camera to overdo any of them.
- **5: Landscape.** As with the Vivid setting, this option boosts saturation (especially in blues and greens) and contrast to give you rich scenery and purple mountain majesties, even when your subject matter is located far enough from your camera that distant haze might otherwise be a problem. There's extra sharpness, too, to give you added crispness when you're shooting Fall colors, for example.
- **6: B/W.** This is useful if you want to shoot monochrome photos in the camera, so you won't need to modify color photos in software. This style will allow you to change the contrast and sharpness, but not the saturation (because there are no colors to saturate).

As mentioned earlier, those six are repeated without the number prefix, and augmented with seven additional Creative Styles:

- **Clear.** Sony recommends this style for "clear tones" and "limpid colors" in the highlights, especially when you're capturing "radiant light." The description is a bit artsy, but I've found this style useful for foggy mornings and other low-contrast scenes.
- **Deep.** Darker and more somber images result from this style.

- **Light.** Recommended for bright, uncomplicated color expressions. I like it for high-key images with lots of illumination and few shadows.
- **Sunset.** Accentuates the red tones found in sunrise and sunset pictures.
- **Night Scene.** Contrast is adjusted to provide a more realistic night-time effect.
- **Autumn Leaves.** Boosts the saturation of reds and yellows for vivid Fall colors.
- **Sepia.** Provides a warm brownish, old-timey tone to images.

To adjust the level of Contrast, Saturation, and/or Sharpness for any numbered Creative Styles, scroll to a style you want to use (in the Camera Settings 5 menu) and use the left/right keys to display a line at the bottom of the screen showing the available adjustments of the three parameters. Use the left/right direction buttons to scroll among Contrast, Saturation, and Sharpness. With the parameter you want to modify highlighted, press the up/down direction buttons to change the values in a range of -3 to +3. Press the center button to confirm. Here is a summary of how changing the parameters in a Creative Style will affect your images:

- **Sharpness.** Increases or decreases the contrast of the edge outlines in your image, making the photo appear more or less sharp, depending on whether you've selected 0 (no sharpening), +3 (extra sharpening), to -3 (softening). Remember that boosting sharpness also increases the overall contrast of an image, so you'll want to use this parameter in conjunction with the contrast parameter with caution.
- **Contrast.** Compresses the range of tones in an image (increase contrast from 0 to +3) or expands the range of tones (from 0 to -3) to decrease contrast. Higher-contrast images tend to lose detail in both shadows and highlights, whereas lower-contrast images retain the detail but appear more flat and dull, without any snap.

- **Color Saturation.** You can adjust the richness of the color from low saturation (0 to -3) to high saturation (0 to +3). Lower saturation produces a muted look that can be more realistic for certain kinds of subjects, such as humans. Higher saturation produces a more vibrant appearance, but can be garish and unrealistic if carried too far. Boost your saturation if you want a vivid image, or to brighten up pictures taken on overcast days. (Remember, however, Vivid and Landscape provide high saturation even at the zero level.) As I noted earlier, saturation cannot be changed for the Black & White Creative Style.

To modify Creative Styles, just follow these steps:

1. **Access Creative Style menu.** Use the Camera Settings 5 menu entry, or press the Fn button and navigate to the Creative Style entry.
2. **Choose a style to apply.** In the Creative Style screen, the styles are shown in the left-hand column. (You must scroll down to see all of them.) If you want to modify one of the styles shown, press up/down to highlight that style, and press the center button to activate it.
3. **Select a parameter to modify.** You can adjust the contrast, saturation, and sharpness of any of the styles in the left column. Highlight the style you want to adjust/replace, and press the right directional button.
4. **Select an attribute to change.** The icons at the bottom of the image area represent (left to right): Image Style, Contrast, Saturation, and Sharpness. Press left/right to highlight the attribute you'd like to modify.
5. **Enter your adjustments.** To change the style that appears in the box you selected at left, highlight the Image Style icon and press up/down to choose one of the 13 styles.
6. **Make other adjustments.** To modify the currently selected style, press left/right to highlight Contrast, Saturation, or

Sharpness, described earlier, then press up/down to add/subtract from the default zero values.

7. **Confirm and exit.** Press the center button to confirm your changes. If you redefined one of the six slots, that style will appear in the listing in the left column henceforth and can be selected quickly by following Steps 1 and 2 above.

Don't confuse the Picture Effects feature with the Creative Styles. The Picture Effects are intended to provide special effects in-camera, such as Pop Color, Posterization, and Soft Focus. Since I have discussed them in detail in Chapter 3, I won't do so here. And you may remember that the RX100 V can use apps, including some that can modify the look of your photos.

Chapter 10

Introduction to Movie Making

As we've seen during our exploration of its features so far, the RX100 V is superbly equipped for taking still photographs of very high quality in a wide variety of shooting environments. But this camera's superior level of performance is not limited to stills. It's highly capable in the movie-making arena as well. It can shoot Full and Standard HD (high-definition) and UHD (ultra-high-definition) clips. Sony has also provided overrides for controlling all important aspects of your video.

So, even though you may have bought your camera primarily for shooting stationary scenes, you acquired a device that's also great for recording high-quality movies. Whether you're looking to record informal movies of the family on vacation, the latest viral video for YouTube, or a set of scenes that will be painstakingly crafted into a cinematic masterpiece using editing software, the RX100 V will perform admirably. That's a lot to ask of such a tiny camera, but it's up to the task.

It can shoot HD video at 1920 x 1080 resolution using Sony's AVCHD encoding, plus MP4 video, which allows both 1920 x 1080 full HD and 1280 x 720 standard HD. It also can capture HD video in the newer XAVC S format. The RX100 V adds the ability to capture superior 4K video (3840 x 2160-pixel resolution) using XAVC S 4K. The latter is especially useful (even though there is a 5 minute recording limit to avoid overheating) because, unlike the previous model IV, the camera oversamples its clips from 5K video, producing even higher image quality in the finished footage. I'll explain all these movie formats, and how to choose between them, later in this chapter.

The camera also uses something called Picture Profiles, to tailor color, saturation, sharpness, and some video-centric attributes. You can visualize Picture Profiles as Creative Styles for video. This chapter will show you the fundamentals of shooting video; and then later you'll learn about some of your camera's more advanced features, including 4K video.

Some Fundamentals

Recording a video with the RX100 V is extraordinarily easy to accomplish -- just press the button labeled MOVIE with the red dot at the upper-right corner of the camera's back to start. Sony has tucked the button off to the side to reduce the chance that you'll start recording a movie accidentally. That's because video can, if you choose, be captured with the mode dial set to *any* exposure position; there's no need to activate a special Movie mode. Any mode dial position except HFR (high frame rate) works for conventional movie shooting. If you start recording in Sweep Panorama mode, however, the camera will actually use P mode and the video won't be a panorama. After you press the button, the camera will confirm that it's recording with a red REC and numerals showing the elapsed time in the EVF and LCD monitor. Press the button again when you want to stop recording.

Before you start, though, there are some settings to prepare the camera to record the scene the way you want it to. The procedure for setting up the camera for recording video is not immediately obvious, either from the camera's menus or from Sony's manuals. I will unravel that mystery for you, and throw in a few other tips to help improve your movies.

I'll show you how to optimize your settings before you start shooting video, but here are some considerations to be aware of as you get started. Many of these points will be covered in more detail later in this chapter:

- **Use the right card.** Because movie capture, is, basically, full-time "continuous" shooting, you'll need to use a memory card with sufficient capacity and a fast enough write speed to handle the streams of video you'll be shooting.
- **For AVCH or MP4 format.** Sony recommends using an SD, SDHC, or SDXC memory card with Class 4 or UHS Speed

Class U1, or faster. You can also use Sony Memory Sticks of the Pro Duo II, PRO-HG, or Micro II variety. With slow cards, your recording may stop after a minute or two until the card is able to offload the captured video from your camera.

- **For XAVC S format.** Sony *requires* SDXC memory cards 64GB or larger, and Speed Class 10 or UHS Speed Class 1 (U1) or faster write speeds. If you do not have such a card inserted, the camera will display a stern warning message and refuse to record in this format. If you want to record at the fastest bit rates (camera-to-card writing speed, which I'll explain shortly), such as 100 megabits per second, the ante is upped to UHS Speed Class 3 (U3).

  The camera can shoot a continuous movie of just under 30 minutes when shooting HD video (a limitation on cameras not classified as camcorders), or 20 minutes for MP4/MPEG4 at the 1920 x 1080 60p 28M Record Setting. (This is a limitation imposed by the maximum 4GB file size allowed by that format). If you reach either limit, you can stop recording and start shooting the next clip right away; this assumes there's enough space on the memory card and adequate battery power. Of course, you will miss about 30 seconds of the action. (Also see the later item about keeping the camera cool; you may have to stop recording every five minutes when using the highest resolution formats.) Of course, that assumes there's enough space on your memory card and adequate battery power.

- **Avoid extraneous noise.** Try not to make too much noise when changing camera controls. Zooming, as noted next, is a particular problem from a noise standpoint. And don't make comments as you shoot that you do not want to hear on the audio track.

- **Minimize zooming.** While it's great to be able to use the zoom for filling the frame with a distant subject, think twice before zooming. The sound made by the RX100 V's internal zoom motor will be picked up and will be audible when you play back a movie. As well, remember that any more than the occasional minor zoom will be very distracting visually to those who watch your videos. And use of *digital* zoom, as described in Chapter 4, will definitely degrade video quality. Don't use the digital zoom if quality is more important than recording a specific subject, such as a famous movie star at a distance. The one saving grace of digital zoom, compared to optical zoom, is that it is totally silent.

- **Use a fully charged battery.** A fresh battery will allow about one hour of filming at normal (non-Winter) temperatures, but that can be shorter if there are many focus adjustments. Individual clips can be no longer than 29 minutes, however.
- **Keep it cool.** Video quality can suffer terribly when the imaging sensor gets hot so keep the camera in a cool place. When shooting on hot days especially, the sensor can get hot more quickly than usual; when there's a risk of overheating, the camera will stop recording and it will shut down about five seconds later. The current time limit is about five minutes; Sony has been releasing firmware upgrades for some of its cameras that lengthen this, so keep a lookout for updates. When you approach the time limit, give the camera time to cool down before using it again. And remember that when you record a couple of very long clips in a series, the sensor will start to get warm; it's better to wait a few minutes to let it cool before starting to record another clip. You may need to stop every five minutes as a cooling off period. The tiny 1-inch sensor of the RX100 V accumulates heat quickly.

  This limitation generally won't affect serious movie makers, who tend to shoot a series of short scenes that are assembled into a finished movie with an editor. But if you plan to set up your camera and shoot your kid's school pageant non-stop for an hour, you're out of luck.

- **Press the Movie button.** You don't have to hold it down. Press it again when you're done to stop recording. It's recessed so that, with some care, you will not press it inadvertently. (In truth, I find myself accidentally pressing it frequently while shooting stills, so I've gone ahead and selected the Movies Only behavior for the button in the Custom Settings menu.)

Choose Your File Format

Go to the File Format entry in the Camera Settings 2 menu (first discussed in Chapter 3) and select the file format for your movies. You can set it to XAVC S 4K, XAVC S HD, AVCHD, or MP4 (an abbreviation for MPEG-4). (See Figure 10.1.) These formats determine what resolutions, frame rates, and bit transfer rates are available for capturing movies, and what options you have when viewing and editing your clips after they've been captured.

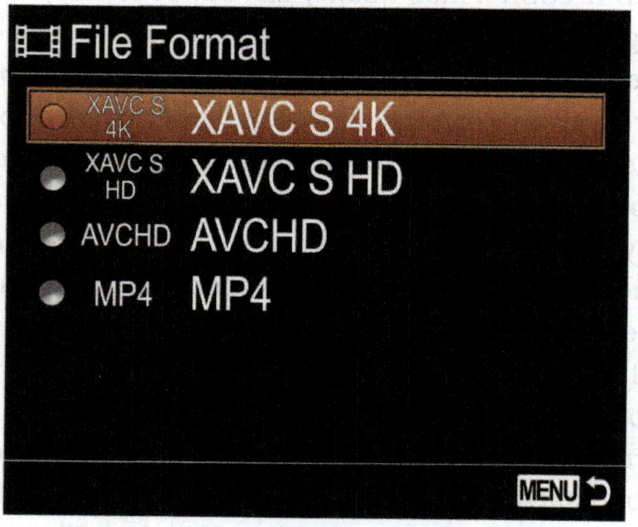

Figure 10.1
Select the File Format for your movies.

- **XAVC S 4K.** This format allows you to capture Ultra High Definition video at 4K (3840 x 2160-pixel resolution). Two frame rates (images captured per second) and bit rates (speed transferred from the camera to your memory card) are available. I'll explain frame and bit rates in the next section.

  This is the highest quality video available with the RX100 V. Even though you must have an HDTV capable of displaying 4K video to view your movies at their full resolution, XAVC S 4K can be *downsampled* using software like Adobe Premiere Pro (for PCs and Macs) or Final Cut Pro X (for Macs only) to produce finished video with HD (1920 x 1080) resolution that is actually of better quality than comparable movies originated in HD format.

As noted above, the heat generated on the RX100 V's tiny 1-inch sensor when recording at this resolution is such that you are limited to about five minutes (or sometimes less) of recording time before you'll need to stop and allow the sensor to cool. The only way around this limitation is to output your camera's internal video to an external video recorder through the HDMI port on the right side of the camera when held in shooting position.

- **XAVC S HD.** This version has the same restrictions in terms of memory card requirements (64GB SDXC) and recording time (including the 5-minute limit when not using an external recorder), but produces movies in Full HD, 1920 x 1080 resolution. Your movies will be better quality than what you might get with the AVCHD format (described next), but will still be viewable on a standard HDTV.

  One option available with XAVC S HD not offered with other formats is the ability to shoot at 120 frames per second. That high frame rate can be converted to video with slow-motion playback, using movie-editing software. Clips captured at 120 fps will appear 4X slower when played back at 30 fps.
- **AVCHD.** This older format, developed by Sony and Panasonic for use with their cameras and camcorders, produces 1920 x 1080 resolution movies (Full HD) that can be displayed on any HDTV, edited using compatible software, and used to produce Blu-Ray and other types of DVDs. You'd want to use this format if you want high-quality movies, your needs are simple, and you don't have image-editing software that can handle XAVC.
- **MP4.** This plain vanilla format is compatible with more types of editing and viewing software, including user-friendly programs like Windows Movie Maker, Apple iMovie, and other

utilities compatible with Apple's QuickTime. It can produce clips in both Full HD and Standard HD (1280 x 720) pixel resolutions. Its highest resolution version (60p/28 megabits/second) is roughly the same quality as AVCHD's comparable setting.

Choose Your Record Setting

Also in the Camera Settings 2 menu, you'll find the Record Setting item, which allows you to choose the frame rate, bit rate, and, with the MP4 format, the resolution, for your movies. These key settings are as follows:

- **Frame rate.** The number of unique "pictures" captured per second, each representing a slice of time that, when viewed continuously, provides the dimension of motion.
- **Bit rate.** The bit rate reflects the amount of compression needed to squeeze a frame's information into the video file, similar to the Extra Fine, Fine, and Standard JPEG compression options for still photographs. The faster the bit transfer rate, the less compression and the higher the quality of the video at a given resolution.
- **Resolution.** XAVC S HD and AVCHD produce video with fixed 1920 x 1080 resolution, so-called Full HD. XAVC S 4K creates movies with a fixed 3840 x 1260-pixel resolution. MP4 offers both 1920 x 1080 (Full HD) and 1280 x 720 (Standard HD) resolutions.

Figure 10.2 shows the Record Setting menu options available when the AVCHD file format has been selected. I'll explain each of the parameters in more detail next:

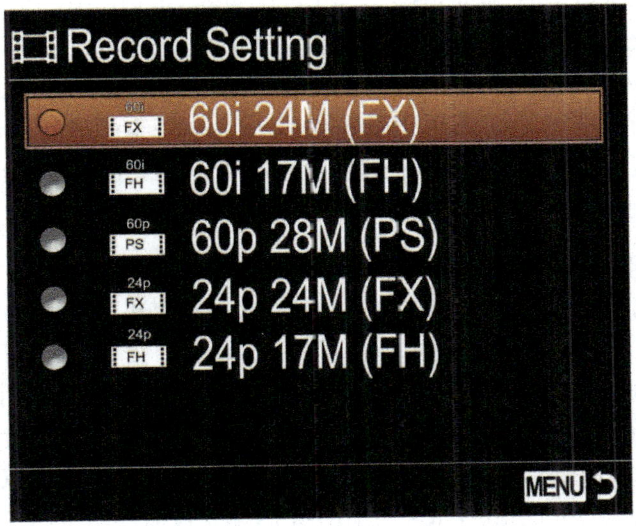

Figure 10.2

Five choices are available in the Record Setting screen when shooting AVCHD.

Frame Rates

Frame rates can be confusing, even for intermediate movie shooters, partially because they come in pairs, such as 30/25 or 60/50 fields per second, followed by cryptic *i* or *p* suffixes. The differences derive from the two "realms" of motion images, film and video, and two "worlds" of display technology (the NTSC standard used in the United States, Japan, and many other countries, and the PAL standard used in much of the rest of the world).

The standard frame rate for motion picture film is 24 fps, while the video rates for NTSC are 30/60/120 fps (with 25/50/100 fps used in PAL countries). Line-by-line scanning during capture and playback can be done in one of two ways:

- **Interlaced scanning.** Odd-numbered lines (lines 1, 3, 5, 7, ... and so forth) are captured with one pass, and then the even-numbered lines (2, 4, 6, 8, ...and so forth) are grabbed. For example, with the 1080/60i format, roughly 60 pairs of odd/even line scans, or 60 *fields* are captured each second. (The actual number is 59.94 fields per second.) Interlaced scanning was developed for and works best with analog display systems such as older television sets. It was originally created as a way to reduce the amount of bandwidth required to transmit television pictures over the air. Modern LCD, LED, and plasma-based HDTV displays must de-interlace a 1080i image to display it. (See **Figure 10.3**.) Interlacing gives us the *i* used to describe frame rates.

- **Progressive scanning.** Also called *sequential scanning,* progressive scanning is used with newer displays. Instead of two interlaced fields, the entire image is scanned as consecutive lines (lines 1, 2, 3, 4, and so forth). This happens at a rate of 30, 60, or 120 frames per second (not fields), or, more precisely, 29.97 frames per second at the 30 fps rate. (As I mentioned, all these numbers apply to the NTSC television system used in the United States, Canada, Japan, and some other countries; other places use systems like PAL, where the nominal scanning figures are 25/50/100 rather than 30/60/120.)

Note that the 24 fps frame rate used to simulate motion picture film is also captured using progressive scanning, because that most closely simulates actual motion picture *film* capture, in which, of course, each frame's information is captured at the same instant. Digital cameras using scanning (a so-called *rolling shutter*) like the RX100 V can't perfectly emulate film's instantaneous capture. A more expensive *global shutter* like that found in higher-end video systems is required.

Lacking a global shutter, there is a possibility of introducing artifacts or distortion under certain conditions, such as when you pan too quickly. (This effect is called *rolling shutter distortion* or the "*Jello effect.*") That is, because of the way the lines of video are displayed in sequence, if the camera moves too quickly in a sideways motion, some of the lines may not show up on the screen quickly enough to catch up to the rest of the picture. As a result, objects in your video can become somewhat distorted or you may experience a jiggling effect and/or loss of detail. So, if at all possible, make your pans smooth and steady, and slow them down to a comfortable pace. But, fortunately, the RX100 V's faster image capture more closely approximates a global shutter's "look," reducing that undesirable Jello effect, even though a rolling shutter is, in fact, being used.

Indeed, Sony claims that with the upgrade to the Mark V, the video look is as close to a global shutter as they've ever been able to achieve in a non-professional video camera.

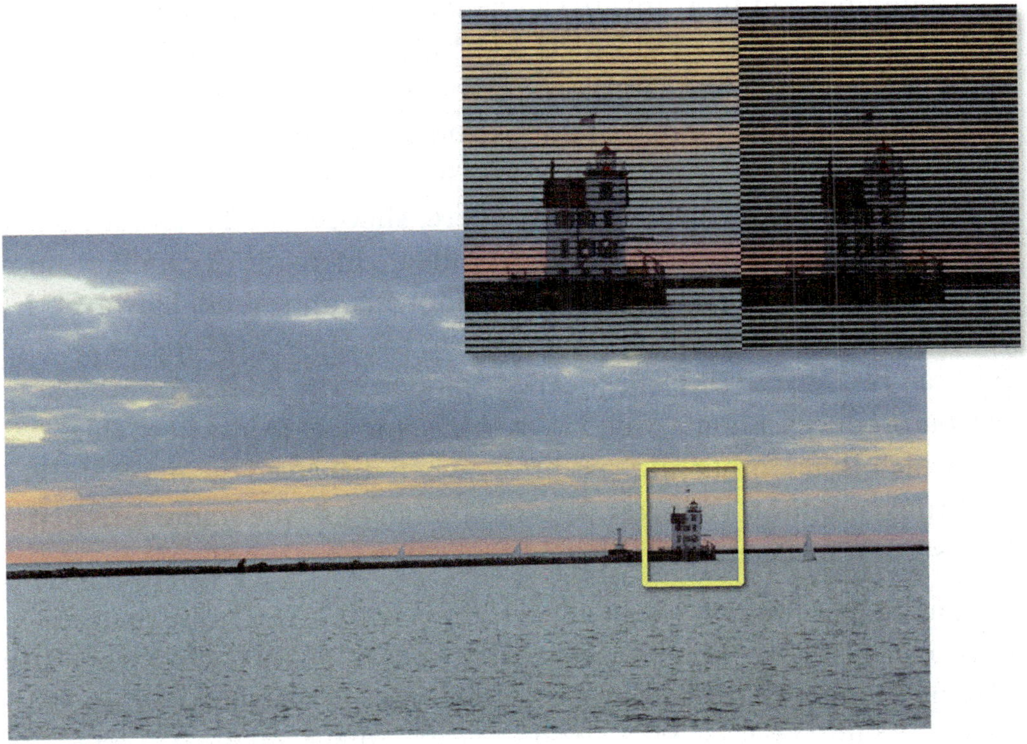

Figure 10.3

The inset shows how lines of the image alternate between odd and even in an interlaced video capture.

One related problem with interlaced scanning appears when capturing video of moving subjects. Half of the image (one set of interlaced lines) will change to keep up with the movement of the subject, while the other interlaced half retains the "old" image as it waits to be refreshed. Flicker or *interline twitter* results. That makes your progressive scan (p) options a better choice for action photography. Interlaced video frame rates are indicated with an (i) designation; for example, within the AVCHD choices, 60i 24M (FX) indicates interlaced video, while 60p 28M (PS) represents progressive scan video. (I'll explain the 24M/28M part in the next section.)

Computer-editing software can handle either type (although AVCHD, XAVC S 4K, and XAVC S HD may not be compatible with the programs you own), and convert between them. The choice between 24 fps and 60 fps (or 25 fps and 50 fps) is determined by what you plan to do with your video. The short explanation is that, for technical reasons I won't go into here, shooting at 24 fps (or 25 fps) gives your movie more of the so-called "cinematic" look that film would produce, which is excellent for showing fine detail. However, if your clip has moving subjects, or you pan the camera, 24 fps (or 25 fps) can produce a jerky effect called "judder." The 60 fps (or 50 fps) option produces a home-video look that some feel is less desirable, but which is smoother and less jittery when displayed on an electronic monitor. I suggest you try both and use the frame rate that best suits your tastes and video-editing software.

The higher frame rates (60 and 120 fps with NTSC) can be used to produce slow-motion movies with no loss in quality, simply by playing them back (or editing them to play back) at 30 fps. This is easy to do in iMovie or Movie Maker for Windows, giving you half-speed or quarter-speed movies with very high quality.

Bit Rates

The final specification in choosing a Record Setting is *bit rate.* Bit rates represent the speed of transfer from your camera to your memory card or external video recorder. The higher the bit rate, the more demands made on your media in storing that data quick enough to keep pace with the video capture. But, as I noted at the beginning of this section, the higher the bit rate, the less compression and, correspondingly, more information that is captured, and so the image quality of your final movie is better.

That's because, just as with JPEG still images, the raw resolution of an image isn't the only factor in calculating how much information is available. All Full HD (1920 x 1080 pixel) movies are not created equal. Just as JPEG images undergo some degree of compression to reduce their file size, the codecs used to store movies on your memory card also must compress the image to fit the available bit transfer rates. So, lower frame rates translate into lower quality, smaller movie files, and less space required on your memory card. Higher frame rates mean better quality, large movie files, and more memory card real estate consumed.

Higher average bit rates range from 6 Mbps (megabits per second) for 1280 x 720 (720p) MP4 movies, to as much as 28 Mbps maximum for AVCHD, 60p full-HD clips. When using XAVC formats, the demands are even higher: 50 Mbps with XAVC S HD and 60 to 100 Mbps with XAVC S 4K.

Tables 10.1 to 10.4 show the frame rates, bit rates, and resolution of the various recording settings for video. Note that frame rates of 30/25, 60/50, and 120/100 represent NTSC/PAL systems, respectively. When choosing your Record Setting from among the available options, you'll need to take into account how much quality you actually need, the "look" you want (video or 24 fps motion picture looks), and the bit rates your memory card can handle. Also keep in mind that higher frame rates require more robust memory cards, and the highest rates (120p/100p, available only with XAVC S HD) are so demanding that certain camera options are not available, including DRO/Auto HDR, both types of digital zoom, face detection, and Monitor/Viewfinder brightness.

Which of the many options should you choose? It depends in part on your needs. When you have very little remaining space on your memory cards, or if your video clip is intended strictly for upload to a website, you might choose MP4, which provides either full HD or standard HD clips. The MP4 format is also more "upload friendly;" in other words, it's the format you'll want to use if you plan to post video clips on a website, including video-sharing sites. If your plan is to primarily shoot videos that you'll show to friends and family on an HDTV set, choose AVCHD. That format gives you better quality, but can be harder to manipulate and edit on a computer than MP4 videos. For more sophisticated productions, you'll want to select XAVC S HD or XAVC S 4K.

My preference: I prefer to use XAVC S at 60p/50M for robust, high-quality video that can be edited using an advanced video-editing program. When I am shooting quick-and-dirty video, perhaps to upload to online sites, MP4 at 1280 x 720/30p/6M does the job. If I know my video will be edited with Windows Movie Maker or iMovie, my choice is MP4 at 1920 x 1080/60p/28m.

Tip: Vacation shooters often find that they want to shoot decent video *and* good still photos on a day's excursion. In that case, I switch from XAVC S 60p/50M to XAVC S 30p/50M and visit the Camera Settings 1 menu and access the Image Size (Dual Rec.) and Quality (Dual Rec) entries to choose L:17M and Extra Fine (respectively). That gives me 5472 x 3080-pixel still shots and Full HD video.

Table 10.1

XAVC S 4K

Record Setting	Resolution	Bit Rate
30p/25p 100M	3840 x 2160	Approx. 100 Mbps
30p/25p 60M	3840 x 2160	Approx. 60 Mbps
24p 100M (NTSC only)	3840 x 2160	Approx. 100 Mbps
24p 60 M (NTSC only)	3840 x 2160	Approx. 60 Mbps

Table 10.2

XAVC S HD

Record Setting	Resolution	Bit Rate
60p/50p 50M	1920 x 1080	Approx. 50 Mbps
30p/25p 50M	1920 x 1080	Approx. 50 Mbps
24p 50M (NTSC only)	1920 x 1080	Approx. 50 Mbps
24p 50 M (NTSC only)	1280 x 720	Approx. 50 Mbps
120p/100p 50M	1280 x 720	Approx. 50 Mbps

Table 10.3

AVCHD

Record Setting	Resolution	Bit Rate
60i/50i 24M (FX)	1920 x 1080	Approx. 24 Mbps
60i/50i 17M (FH)	1920 x 1080	Approx. 17 Mbps
60p/50p 28M (PS)	1920 x 1080	Approx. 28 Mbps
24p/25p 24M (FX)	1920 x 1080	Approx. 24 Mbps
24p/25p 17M (FH)	1920 x 1080	Approx. 17 Mbps

Table 10.4

MP4

Record Setting	Resolution	Bit Rate
1920 x 1080 60p/50p 28M	1920 x 1080	Approx. 28 Mbps
1920 x 1080 30p/25p 16M	1920 x 1080	Approx. 16 Mbps
1280 x 720 30p/25p 6M	1280 x 720	Approx. 6 Mbps

Choosing an Exposure Mode

You can set the mode dial to any mode position other the HFR (high frame rate) when you want to shoot conventional movies. (MR isn't a mode; it's a memory slot storing up to three specific settings.) Pressing the Movie button while using any of these modes automatically shifts the RX100 V into video mode (unless you've set the button to activate video in movie mode only in the Custom Settings 5 menu). Rotating the mode dial to the Movie position does have several advantages: it activates black bars at the top and bottom of the frame so you can preview your image before you start capture. In other modes, the black bars don't appear until you actually begin shooting.

Your camera can be set to one of the compatible shooting mode positions on the mode dial when you begin capturing video. Or, if you've switched to the Movie position on the mode dial, you'll be given the opportunity to select an exposure mode. The first entry on the Camera Settings 8 menu (which is grayed out when the mode dial is not set to the Movie position) can be used to specify one of these four exposure modes.

- **Program (P) mode.** This mode works well, allowing the camera to set the aperture/shutter speed and giving you access to the other fine-tuning features (unlike scene and Automatic modes, which limit your choices). Program shift (to other aperture/shutter speed combinations) can be used before you start recording, but it will not be available during actual recording. The RX100 V is programmed to not use shutter speeds slower than 1/25th-1/125th second (depending on the frame rate selected), unless you have activated the Auto Slow Shutter option, as explained later in this chapter.
- **Aperture Priority mode.** Use this to retain full control over the specific aperture; in that case, you can preset a desired aperture and you can also change it anytime while recording. Be careful however, especially if you have set a specific ISO level. If you switch to a very small aperture while recording in

low light, your movie clip may darken; this is particularly likely if you're using a low ISO sensitivity. And if you switch to a very wide aperture on a sunny day, especially if using a high ISO, your video will become too bright. Of course, you can see the change in brightness in the live view display before recording a movie and while you're recording.

As with P mode, the camera will not select shutter speeds that are inappropriately slow for your frame rate, unless Auto Slow Shutter is activated. You'll find more on specifying shutter speeds for movies later in this chapter. While "fades to black" (and fade ins, by reversing the process) are possible in Aperture Priority mode, you may need to activate the built-in ND filter and use the ISO 125 setting (the lowest allowed for movie shooting) to achieve a true fade, because the smallest aperture available with this camera is f/11. Rotate the control ring or control wheel to fade as you shoot.

- **Shutter Priority (S) mode.** Switch to Shutter Priority mode if you want control over the shutter speed; this is a more advanced technique in Movie mode. You can preset a shutter speed (as fast as 1/12,800th second, which can be used to simulate a "fade to black") and you can change it while recording. Again, be careful as to your settings to avoid a very dark or overly bright video, especially if you have set a specific ISO level. The live view display before and during recording will help to guide you.

  There are some special considerations with shutter speeds when shooting video that I'll address later in this chapter. Specific speeds should be chosen with care. In Shutter Priority mode, the camera *can* select shutter speeds as slow as 1/4 second, which can produce blurry images due to uncorrectable camera shake.

- **Manual (M) mode.** You can choose any aperture, and any shutter speed from 1/4 to 1/12,800th second, except when using XAVC S HD format, where shutter speeds below 1/125th second are locked out. I don't recommend using the

Manual (M) exposure mode initially, but you might want to experiment with it later.

Stop That!

Earlier, I mentioned that shutter speeds must be chosen with care. If you're steeped in still photography shooting, you might think that setting your camera to a faster shutter speed will help give you sharper video frames. But the choice of a shutter speed for movie making is a bit more complicated than that. As you might guess, it's almost always best to leave the shutter speed at 1/30th or 1/60th second, and allow the overall exposure to be adjusted by varying the aperture and/or ISO sensitivity. We don't normally stare at a video frame for longer than 1/30th or 1/24th second, so while the shakiness of the *camera* can be disruptive (and often corrected by your camera's in-lens and in-body image stabilization), if there is a bit of blur in our *subjects* from movement, we tend not to notice. Each frame flashes by in the blink of an eye, so to speak, so a shutter speed of 1/30th or 1/60th second works a lot better in video than it does when shooting stills. Even shots with lots of movement are often sufficiently sharp at 1/60th second.

Higher shutter speeds actually introduce problems of their own. If you shoot a video frame using a shutter speed of 1/250th second, the actual moment in time that's captured represents only about 12 percent of the 1/30th second of elapsed time in that frame. Yet, when played back, that frame occupies the full 1/30th of a second, with 88 percent of that time filled by stretching the original image to fill it. The result is often a choppy/jumpy image, and one that may appear to be *too* sharp.

The reason for that is more social imprinting than scientific: we've all grown up accustomed to seeing the look of Hollywood productions that, by convention, were shot using a shutter speed that's half the reciprocal of the frame rate (that is, 1/48th second for a 24 fps movie). Movie cameras use a rotary shutter (achieving that 1/48th second exposure by using a 180-degree shutter "angle"), but the effect on our visual expectations is the same. For the most "film-like" appearance, use 24 fps and 1/60th second shutter speed.

Faster shutter speeds do have some specialized uses for motion analysis, especially where individual frames are studied. The rest of the time, 1/30th or 1/60th of a second will suffice. If the reason you needed a higher shutter speed was to obtain the correct exposure, use a slower ISO setting, or a neutral-density filter to cut down on the amount of light passing through the lens. A good rule of thumb is to use 1/60th second or slower when shooting at 24 fps; 1/60th second or slower at 30 fps; and 1/125th second or slower at 60 fps.

Note that while you *can* shoot at shutter speeds slower than the frame rate (that is, 1/15th second while shooting at 60p), that's not really what happens. The camera grabs a 1/60th second frame as usual, and then duplicates it four times as consecutive frames. When played back, changes between the frames occur only every 1/15th of a second, but won't have the same "blurriness" they would have had if actually exposed for that longer period of time.

Image Stabilization

Because movie making typically uses relatively slow shutter speeds (as described in the last section), a steady camera or your RX100 V's SteadyShot capabilities help produce the sharpest frames. In the Camera Settings 8 menu, you'll find a SteadyShot entry with the movie frame icon next to it (the last entry in the menu), which allows you to specify the type of image stabilization to be used while you're capturing video. Your choices, which differ dramatically from what you can select when choosing still photos (only On/Off) include:

- **Intelligent Active.** Because your subject matter remains fairly constant from frame to frame, your camera is able to analyze the pixels of each frame and determine which comprise subject matter that is not moving, which pixels represent subjects that are moving within the frame, and which pixels fit neither category: that is, those caused by *camera* movement. It is able to move all the pixels in the frame to cancel out camera movement, performing this magic by slightly cropping at the edges.

This electronic image stabilization has long been a staple tool for video, and works well with still cameras given movie-making capabilities. Unlike conventional in-body image stabilization, which shifts the sensor around, everything is done using the RX100 V's fast image-processing chip. You'd want to use this mode to steady your image if capturing video while walking around in hand-held cinema vérité mode.

- **Active.** This mode is roughly the same as Intelligent Active, but is less aggressive and produces less cropping. Use this mode to reduce the amount of cropping when capturing video with less energetic movement.
- **Standard.** Uses the RX100 V's optical image stabilization only, so no cropping occurs and, as a result, less anti-shake is provided.
- **Off.** All image stabilization is disabled. Use this when the camera is mounted on a tripod and SteadyShot is not required.

Focus Concerns

Unless you're using blur for creative effect, or selective focus to isolate or include subject matter, most of the time you'll be working with your RX100 V's autofocus capabilities. I explained autofocus in some detail in Chapter 8.

You should be aware of one autofocus limitation that applies to movie-making: the only AF mode available is AF-C (continuous autofocus.) If you have selected Single-Shot AF or DMF (direct manual focus) while capturing still images and switch to movie mode, the RX100 V automatically switches to AF-S for the duration.

But there's good news, too. The most important, and most dramatic improvement of the RX100 V over the RS100 IV is the addition of sensor-based phase detection autofocus. There is much less "hunting" for focus, which is typical of cameras that use only phase detection. Of course, Sony had fine-tuned the RX100-series AF capabilities such that even the previous model, without phase detection, performed well for movie-shooting. Here are some special concerns in video shooting.

- **Turn on autofocus.** Make sure autofocus is turned on through the Focus Mode entry of the Camera Settings menu, Function menu, or Quick Navi screen. You also have the option of using manual focus, or even Direct Manual Focus, with focus peaking.

  I find that manual focus is fine for situations such as a stage play where the actors will usually be at roughly the same distance to your position during the entire performance, and for more sophisticated productions where precise focus is a must, or when changing focus during a shot (*focus pulling*) is used creatively (although that technique is somewhat difficult with this tiny camera!). In other cases, however, you'll probably want to rely on the camera's effective full-time continuous autofocus ability while recording a video clip.

- **Try Flexible Spot AF Area**. Although the Wide autofocus area mode is probably your best bet for general-purpose video shooting, You should try Flexible Spot AF Area (discussed in Chapter 8) while recording a video clip, too. This feature is most suitable for a static scene you'll record with the camera on a tripod, where an important small subject is off-center and will remain in the same location. By placing the AF Area exactly on that part of the scene, you'll be sure that the focus will remain on the most important part of the scene during the entire recording. (In truth, you could use manual focus for the same purpose.)

  If you decide to try this, compose the scene as desired before pressing the record button. Set the AF Area to Flexible Spot in the Focus Area options of the Camera Settings, Function, and Quick Navi menus. An orange bracket will appear on the screen, indicating the current location of the active focus detection point. Move the brackets with the direction buttons so they cover the primary subject and press OK (the center button) to confirm. You can now begin recording the video, confident that the focus will always be on your primary subject (assuming it does not move while you're recording).

Manual Focus Concerns

Manual focus is an important tool for serious videographers. I suppose, avid movie shooters may just want to use the tiny RX100 V as a movie shooting tool. It could happen. If you do choose to work with manual focus, be aware the Focus Magnifier tool, commonly used for stills when you rotate the focus ring, is not enabled for video shooting by default. You must assign a function button to that behavior, giving you a defined key that is essentially redundant when you are taking still photographs. Sony, in its wisdom, does not currently allow separate button definitions for stills and video.

Audio

When it comes to making a successful video, audio quality is one of those things that separates the professionals from the amateurs. We're used to watching top-quality productions on television and in the movies, yet the average person has no idea how much effort goes in to producing what seems to be "natural" sound. Much of the sound you hear in such productions is actually recorded on carefully controlled sound stages and "sweetened" with a variety of sound effects and other recordings of "natural" sound.

Your RX100 V has a pair of stereo microphones on its top surface that perform fairly well, considering the size of this camera. Unfortunately, there is no way to plug in an external microphone into the unadorned camera. There are some workarounds, however, which range from not-expensive to expensive. You can always record the sound separately, using an outboard recorder like the Sony PCM-M10 portable linear PCM voice recorder ($399 list price, but often available for much less), which has a pair of electret condenser stereo microphones and 4GB of memory. Sophisticated movie-editing software, including Adobe Premiere Pro, will allow you to sync up your soundtrack with the video.

If you've got about $1,700 to $2,000 burning a hole in your pocket and you seriously want to use the RX100 V for sophisticated video applications, the Atomos Shogun 4K HDMI/12G SDI recorder, with a 7-inch monitor is virtually the standard tool for videographers on a tight budget. Equipped with your choice of magnetic or solid-state drive storage, it can gobble up your camera's so-called "clean" 4K HDMI output at up to 30 fps, and 1080p HD video at up to 120 fps. It has a pair of XLR mic inputs, and the high-resolution touch-screen monitor makes viewing or reviewing your video, and navigating through the device's menus easy.

While it may seem a little far-fetched to envision your RX100 V linked to such gear, in the real world it's more likely that a serious videographer using some other camera or camcorder will have a separate audio or audio/video recorder as I've just described, and may want to use this feature-rich little Sony camera as a backup, as a second camera, or just to fool around and see what can be done.

In any case, whether you're using the camera's built-in microphones or connecting it to more professional recording equipment, here are some tips that will help you get better audio. Since recording high-quality audio is such a challenge, it's a good idea to do everything possible to maximize recording quality:

- **Turn off any sound makers you can.** Little things like fans and air handling units aren't obvious to the human ear, but will be picked up by the microphone. Turn off any machinery or devices that you can plus make sure cell phones are set to silent mode. Also, do what you can to minimize sounds such as wind, radio, television, or people talking in the background.
- **Make sure to record some "natural" sound.** If you're shooting video at an event of some kind, make sure you get some background sound that you can add to your audio as desired in postproduction. You can just allow the camera's built-in mics to record the ambient sound, or capture it with a separate recorder and mix it in later with your movie-editing software.
- **Consider recording audio separately.** Note that you don't really need a recorder like the Sony PCM-M10 to capture audio separately. The secret is to forget about lip-syncing. There's nothing that says you can't record narration *separately* and add it later, even with the simplest movie-editing software. Did you think the narrators of documentaries actually went out on location for every sequence? It's more likely that at least some of the narration was recorded in a studio and inserted into the production during editing. It's actually an easy thing to do if you learn how to use simple software video-editing programs like iMovie (for the Macintosh) or Windows Movie Maker (for Windows PCs). Any time the speaker is off-camera, you can work with separately recorded narration rather than recording the speaker on-camera. This can produce much cleaner sound,

and allow you to record the narration several times to get it exactly right.

- **Wind noise reduction.** The RX100 V does offer a low-cut filter feature that can further reduce wind noise; it's accessed with the Wind Noise Reduction item of the Camera Settings 9 menu, as discussed in Chapter 3. However, this processing feature also affects other sounds, and so should be used with caution.

Lights, Camera, Action!

You're ready to begin shooting. Just press the record button with the red dot in the center. You don't have to hold it down. Press it to start recording and press it again when you're done. Shoot a short test clip and view it to make sure that the settings you made are producing the overall effect you want. If not, change some settings (White Balance or Creative Style or Exposure Compensation, for example) and try again. Just keep these things in mind:

- **Don't forget you have a dual recording option.** If you are shooting an XAVC S (either HD or 4K) at 30p or 24p, or AVCHD movies at 60i or 24p, you can elect to record an MP4 simultaneously, giving you a standard, lower quality MPEG video that can be viewed immediately without needing to process with a video-editing program. Use the Dual Video REC option in the Camera Settings menu to activate this capability. Dual video recording is disabled if you've activated the RX100 V's "electronic" image stabilization feature, Intelligent Active SteadyShot. The image processing required for that mode is too intensive to allow simultaneously recording in two video formats.
- **Exposure compensation works while filming.** I found this feature to be quite remarkable. Although the autoexposure system works very well (especially with Multi metering) to vary the aperture when the ambient lighting changes, you can certainly dial in exposure compensation when you need to do so or want to do so for a certain effect.

If the preview display (when Live View Display is set to Setting Effect On in the Setup menu) suggests that your movie will be dark (underexposed) and if it does not get brighter after you set plus compensation, there's another problem: the camera cannot provide a good exposure for the movie at the ISO that you have set (as discussed earlier). Switch to a higher ISO level until the brightness is as desired or switch to ISO Auto to enable the camera to set a higher ISO level to prevent the "underexposure."

- **Use AE Lock.** Occasionally, you may find that you start having an exposure problem during recording; this might happen when pointing the lens toward a light-tone area that causes the camera to begin underexposing. While plus compensation will allow you to increase brightness, it's preferable to use the defined AE Lock button (you can define the C button to AEL hold or AEL toggle using the Custom Keys entry of the Custom menu, as described in Chapter 4) to maintain a pleasing exposure during the entire video clip.

  Why would you need this feature? Let's say you're filming entertainers against grass and foliage, but you're moving the camera and will soon be filming a second group against a white sky. As soon as you do so, the backlighting will cause the video to get darker. Don't let that happen. Before pointing the lens toward the backlit area, press the defined AEL button and keep it depressed. This will prevent the exposure from changing as you point the lens toward the backlit part of the scene. This is preferable to waiting until an underexposure problem starts and then setting plus exposure compensation that suddenly makes the video brighter.

- **Useful functions.** Remember that you can specify an ISO sensitivity, white balance, Creative Style, Picture Profiles (explained later in this chapter), a Picture Effect (for special effects), any of the three metering modes, and the level of exposure compensation. You can also set an override in the Creative Style for a specific level of sharpness, contrast, and saturation, if desired or use a Picture Profile for other parameters. The DRO and Auto HDR features will not be available, however. You'll recall that these functions are not available in fully automatic modes; if you set them while using another mode and then switch to a fully automatic mode for recording the video, the camera will revert back to the defaults.

- **Playback.** You'll find information about video playback, including the interesting but not very useful Motion Shot feature in Chapter 6. This chapter deals with *shooting* video only.

Advanced Features

Your RX100 V has even more tricks tucked away within its menus, including some advanced features that are likely to be of interest only to serious videographers. All the things your camera can do in the movie-making realm deserve a book of their own, but there is room here to introduce them to you for further study.

Shooting in 4K

While 4K video still seems new and exotic, given the usual pace of technology, it's very likely that your next HDTV will have 4K capabilities (if your current set does not), and cable/satellite/streaming systems as well as Blu-Ray discs will all make the leap sooner than any of us expect. I've already made a switch to 4K video with my "big" camera -- a Sony a7R II -- and have resisted doing the same with my RX100 V only because of the overheating issues. There are times when I *do* need to record more than five minutes of video at a time.

So, it seems wise to at least become familiar with your camera's 4K capabilities, even if you don't plan to use them extensively at the present time. After all, as I've noted, 4K video can easily be converted to more conventional Full HD movies with the right movie editor, and produce *better-quality* Full HD to boot.

The key thing to know is that your RX100 V can record 4K video internally, export 4K video to an external recorder, such as the Atmos

Shogun described earlier under the audio section, or to *both* simultaneously. If you want to record *only* to the memory card, you don't need to do anything special other than select XAVCS 4K under the File Format entry and your desired frame/bit rate under Record Setting (both in the Camera Settings 2 menu).

If you prefer to output your 4K video to the HDMI port, or HDMI port *and* the memory card, you need to visit the 4K Output Selection entry in the Setup 3 menu. Set the mode dial to Movie and attach your RX100 V to the external device using a micro HDMI cable. Then, your choices are as follows:

- **Memory Card+HDMI.** With this setting, your video is written to the internal compatible SDXC memory card, *and* output to an external recorder/playback device.
- **HDMI Only (30p).** The camera does not record on the SDXC card, and sends the "clean" 4K signal only to the external recorder/playback device in 30p format. In fact, with this setting (and the one that follows), both the EVF and LCD monitor are disabled, and you must view the image being captured on the external recorder's LCD instead. Center Lock-On AF and Face Detection are disabled in either HDMI Only mode.
- **HDMI Only (24p/25p).** The camera does not record on the SDXC card, and sends the "clean" 4K signal only to the external recorder/playback device in 24p format (25p with PAL systems).

Frame Guides

Frame guides are a useful way of visualizing the area that will be captured within a larger visible display. In ancient times, interchangeable lens rangefinder film cameras that used an optical viewfinder would have bright frame outlines appear, often automatically when a particular lens was mounted on the camera, and sometimes through the use of an attachment that fit over the built-in viewfinder. In the digital age, frame guides have been popular with digital cameras that use an optical viewfinder, providing a masked off display to preview the actual image area that will be captured in crop or video modes. Cameras with electronic displays, like the RX100 V, don't necessarily need frame guides, because the capture area can be enlarged and masked off electronically to show only the actual image area.

Even so, frame guides are a popular tool for videographers, because they allow viewing the area outside the actual frame that will be captured (the "look-around area") so you can monitor moving subjects before they enter the frame. In professional productions, it's useful to look at the region outside the captured frame to detect when boom microphones, careless crew members, or other objects threaten to intrude on the frame.

The RX100 V offers a variety of frame guides that can be turned on or off in the Custom Settings menu, including grid lines, aspect ratios, frame center markings, and "safety" areas. These markers appear *only* on the EVF or LCD monitor, and not in the captured video itself (see **Figure 10.4** for example placement).

- **Marker Display.** This Custom Settings menu entry works in conjunction with the Marker Settings option (described next), and simply turns settings on or off.
- **Marker Settings.** This menu entry allows you to specify Center, Aspect Ratio, Safety Zone, or Guide Frame. Each can be specified individually, and turned on or off independently, so you can display any, all, or none.
- **Center.** This crosshair can be used to determine whether your subject is placed in the exact center of the screen.
- **Aspect.** Use these guides to frame your image so the important subject matter is contained within a desired aspect ratio, or to frame the image for later cropping to that aspect ratio. You can select from 4:3, 13:9, 14:9, 15:9, 1.66:1, 1.85:1, or 2.35:1. These conform to various movie formats in common use. (Star Wars, for example, was filmed in CinemaScope, with a 2.35:1 aspect ratio.)

- **Safety Zone.** It's common to shoot movies knowing in advance that they will be cropped down eventually for display in a slightly different format. The director simply makes sure that the important parts of the frame are included in the "safety zone" that will never be cropped out. For example, you wouldn't want to put two characters who are talking to each other at opposite ends of the entire frame, but would instead locate them in the safety zone so both would be visible. Your camera's safety zone display can be set for 80 percent or 90 percent of the frame to represent the area that will always be shown when the movie is viewed on a standard HDTV.
- **Guide Frame.** This grid is used to help you determine whether horizontal and vertical lines are skewed, and can also be used as a Rule of Thirds guide for composition.

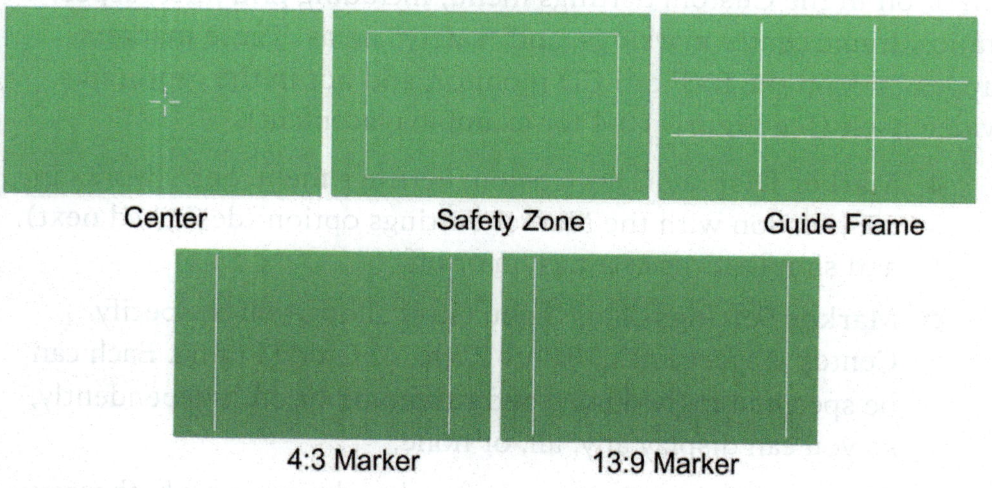

Figure 10.4
Video guide markers.

Time Codes and User Bits

The Time Code (TC) and User Bit (UB) settings are information that can be embedded and used to sync clips and sound when editing movies. Advanced video shooters find SMPTE (Society of Motion Picture and Television Engineers)-compatible time codes embedded in the video files to be an invaluable reference during editing. To oversimplify a bit, the time system provides precise *hour:minute:second:frame* markers that allow identifying and synchronizing frames and audio. The time code system includes a provision for "dropping" frames to ensure that the fractional frame rate of captured video (remember that a 24 fps setting actually yields 23.976 frames per second, while 30 fps capture gives you 29.97 actual "frames" per second) can be matched up with actual time spans.

Using time codes and user bits is a college-level film school class on its own, but I'm going to provide a quick overview to get your started. If you're at the stage where you're using time codes, you don't need this primer, anyway. However, the RX100 V's TC/UB Settings entry in the Setup menu includes the following options:

- **TC Preset.** Sets the time code. If you'll be shooting 60i/50i, you can choose time codes from 00:00:00:00 (hours, minutes, seconds, frame) to 23:59:59:29 or 23:59:59:24, respectively. With 24p, you can set multiples of four from 0 to 23 frames. If you own the RMT-VP1K remote commander, the time code can be reset to zero using a button on the controller.
- **UB Preset.** Sets the user bit, which is a marker you can insert in your video, say to designate a scene or take. There are four digits in each user bit (for example, 01:02:03:04), and the digits are each hexadecimal in nature, so you could create a code like C0 FF EE if you were feeling facetious.
- **TC Format.** Sets the recording method for the time code. You can choose from DF (drop frame) or NDF (non-drop frame) formats. Drop frames are a way of compensating for the discrepancy between the nominal number of frames per second and the actual number (for example, 30 fps yields 29.97 actual

frames per second, and 60 fps gives you 59.95 frames per second). In drop-frame format, the camera will skip some time code numbers at intervals to eliminate the discrepancy. The first two frame numbers are removed every minute except for every tenth minute (think of it as a leap year). You may notice a difference of several seconds per hour when using the non-drop frame option.

- **TC Run.** Sets the count up format for the time code. You can choose Rec Run, in which the time code counts up only when you are actually capturing video; or Free Run (also known as Time of Day), which allows the time code to run up even between shooting clips. The latter is useful when you want to synchronize clips between multiple cameras that are shooting the same event. When using Free Run, even if the cameras record at different times, you'll be able to match the video that was captured at the exact same moment during editing.
- **TC Make.** Sets the recording format for the time code on the recording medium. Choose Preset to record a new time code, or Regenerate to read the previous time code setting and record the new time code consecutively. When Regenerate is selected, the time code advances no matter what TC Run setting has been selected.
- **UB Time Rec.** Sets whether or not to record the time as a user bit.

Picture Profiles

If you've been taking photos for a while, you're probably familiar with all the fixes and tweaks you can do with your still images within image editors like Photoshop. It's relatively easy to adjust color tones, contrast, sharpness, and other parameters prior to displaying or printing your photo. Movies are a little trickier, because any given video typically consists of *thousands* of individual photos, captured at 24 frames per second (or faster), with the possibility that each and every frame within a particular sequence might need fixes or creative adjustments.

Shooting video does not preclude doing post-processing during editing. Indeed, many videographers deliberately shoot relatively low-contrast video in order to capture the largest dynamic range possible, and then fine-tune the rendition later using their editing software. Picture Profiles let you do that -- and also allow you to adjust your camera so that the video you capture is *pre-fine-tuned* in order to reduce or eliminate the amount of post-processing you do later.

The RX100 V is furnished with seven "canned" picture profiles, which you can think of as Creative Styles for movies. The 13 parameters included in these profiles can be further adjusted by you to better suit the "look" you are striving for in your videos. You can connect your camera to a TV or monitor using the HDMI Out connector and an HDMI cable, view the image produced by the camera on the larger screen, and then make adjustments to the picture profile. I described the process in how-to form briefly in Chapter 3.

Needless to say, creating and using Picture Profiles is a highly technical aspect of video making, at least in terms of the amount of knowledge you need to have to correctly judge what changing one of the 13 parameters will do to your video. I hope to get you started with a quick description of what those parameters do, so you'll have a starting point when you start to explore them.

Gamma, Gamma Ding Dong

The seven Picture Profile presets in the Camera Settings menu already have their own default values, each adjusted for a particular type of shooting, using various gamma and color tone settings. Thanks to our evolutionary heritage, humans don't see differences in tones in a linear manner. An absolutely smooth progression of pixels from absolute black to pure white (with 0 representing black and 256 representing white) would not look like a continuous gradient to our eyes. We'd be unable to detect differences in shadows and highlights that have the same change in tonal values as midtones. So, everything from computer monitors to printers use a correction factor (gamma) to cancel out the differences in the way we see tones.

This correction takes the form of a curve, called a *gamma curve*. If you remember your geometry, the x and y axes on a graph are used to define the shape of a curve, and in the case of gamma curves, the values use logarithmic units (ack!) to define the slope. That's where the terms S-log2 and other mind-numbing jargon comes from. The whole shebang is needed to reconcile the ability of sensors to capture, video systems to display, and printers to output a range of tones in a linear way with the actual tones we perceive non-linearly. Gamma correction and gamma compression are used to help make sure that what we get is what we see. While gamma correction between computer platforms (that is, between Macs and PCs) may be different, the actual gamma values defined by video standards like NTSC and PAL are fixed and well-known. Picture Profiles allow you to configure your camera to capture video using a desired amount of gamma and color tone correction.

The seven predefined Picture Profiles in the RX100 V are as follows:

- **PP1:** Example setting using [Movie] gamma.
- **PP2:** Example setting using [Still] gamma.
- **PP3:** Example setting of natural color tone using the ITU709 gamma, a broadcast television standard. Use this profile when you won't be making extensive changes in post-processing, or when you need to match clips taken with other cameras; video taken using this profile is more likely to be compatible.
- **PP4:** Example setting of a color tone faithful to the [ITU709] standard, and thus will not require much adjustment of color tones in post-processing.
- **PP5:** Example setting using [Cine1] gamma. Gives you what Sony calls a "relaxed" color movie with soft contrast in dark areas, and emphasis on gradation in the highlights. That means improved results in high-contrast situations, such beach and snow scenes, or other bright sunny environments.

- **PP6:** Example setting using [Cine2] gamma. Similar to Cine1, but optimized for editing the full video signal with detail-filled highlights.
- **PP7:** Example setting using [S-Log2] gamma. Use this profile when you need the largest dynamic range and plan to adjust tones in post-processing. Use of an ISO setting of 1600 or higher is mandatory. The raw video captured using this profile will look dark and flat.

And here are the parameters you can adjust:

- **Black Level.** Sets the black level (-15 to +15). Black level is the level of brightness at which no light is emitted from a screen, resulting in a pure black screen. Adjustment of this parameter ensures that blacks are seen as black, and not a dark shade of gray.
- **Gamma.** Selects a gamma curve to adjust the relationship between the brightness (*luminance*) captured by a sensor and the brightness of the image as it's displayed on a monitor. As I've noted, this correction is needed to make what you see on a screen more closely resemble what the camera captured in real life. You can choose from nine different gamma curves.
- **Black Gamma.** Provides special correction for gamma in low-intensity areas, using Range and Level controls. This adjustment will make the video look more/less contrasty. Negative values make the darker parts of the image darker, but can lead to clipped blacks.
- **Knee.** Sets "knee point," which is the brightness level (*luma* in tech-talk) at which knee compression starts. It also allows adjusting the knee slope, or the *amount* of knee compression used. That prevents overexposure by limiting signals in high-intensity areas of the subject to the dynamic range of your camera. In short, a higher knee level produces more detail in the highlights; a lower knee level produces fewer details in the highlights. Too much compression may prevent exposure from reaching 100 percent.

- **Mode.** In Auto mode, the knee point and slope are set automatically; in Manual mode, they are set manually.
- **Auto Set.** When Auto is selected, values are automatically chosen by the camera for the maximum knee point, sensitivity, manual settings, knee point, and knee slope.
- **Color Mode.** Sets type and level of colors, from among Movie, Still, Cinema, Pro, ITU-709 Matrix, Black & White, and S-Gamut.
- **Saturation.** Sets the color saturation, from -32 to +32 values. This can be useful for reducing color in dark scenes that you want to appear low key, and help reduce noise levels in dark scenes.
- **Color Phase.** Sets the color phase (-7 to +7).
- **Color Depth.** Sets the color depth for each color phase.
- **Detail.** Sets parameters including Level, and Detail adjustments including Mode, Vertical/Horizontal Balance, B/W Balance, Limit, Crispning (sic), and Hi-Light Detail.
- **Copy.** Copies the settings of the picture profile to another picture profile number.
- **Reset.** Resets the picture profile to the default setting. You cannot reset all picture profile settings at once.
- **S-Log2** S-Log2 is a log gamma curve that is used when the video will be processed after shooting, and captures a much larger range of tones (as many as 14 stops!) than standard gamma curves. Indeed, the tones captured using S-Log2 can't be displayed in all their glory on a standard TV or monitor, which are generally adjusted for the broadcast television BT-709 standard. Instead, the unprocessed video will look darker and lower in contrast because all those tonal values have been squeezed into the BT-709 (also called REC-709) range.

Video signals normally encompass brightness levels from 0 percent to 109 percent (you read that right: modern video cameras can record detail in highlights that are actually brighter than was possible when the video age began; the old scale was retained, reminiscent of Nigel Tufnel's 11 setting on his amp). However, even the 109 percent provides too much of a limitation; cameras can capture detail in highlights that are even brighter than *that*. So, a log gamma curve (in this case one called S-Log2) is used to *compress* all that image detail to fit into the space allowed for conventional video signals. Post-processing in a video editor allows working with all that information and produces a finished video that contains the filmmaker's selection of tonal values in a form that can be displayed comfortably. The full dynamic range can be used to produce the finished movie. You might find that useful when exposing for highlights while avoiding blowing out the sky, or for capturing detail in shadows without losing mid tones and highlights.

The Picture Profile 7 (PP7) is already set up for S-Log2, and should be your choice if you want to work with that curve. I've oversimplified things a bit, because there are many other great things you can do with S-Log2, such as overexposing or "pushing" your video to reduce noise (but at the risk of losing some detail in brighter skin tones), and then output (called "grading") to produce an optimized final image.

I know this chapter doesn't tell you everything you need to know to take the next step in movie making with your RX100 V- camera, but my intent was to introduce you to enough of your Sony's capabilities to spur additional exploration of this exciting creative arena.

High Frame Rate Video

If half-speed or quarter-speed slow motion doesn't meet your needs for lethargic video, the HFR setting on your mode dial may be what you are looking for. It allows capturing video at much higher frame rates (up to 960 fps with NTSC systems or 1,000 fps with Pal Systems). When played back at 24/25 fps, the clips can be viewed in slow motion at up to 40X slower than normal rates. You can choose both the frame rate and playback rate to produce a range of slow-motion effects. To set up your camera for high frame rate video, just follow these steps.

1. **Switch to HFR mode.** Rotate the mode dial to the HFR position. The two HFR menu entries you'll need to access to set up the camera for slow motion cannot be accessed unless the RX100 V is set to HFR mode. If the Mode Dial Guide in the Setup 2 menu is set to On, you'll see a description of the HFR feature, and will need to press the center button to proceed. (See **Figure 10.5**, left.)
2. **Navigate to the Camera Settings 7 menu**, and highlight the High Frame Rate entry at the bottom of the listing. A screen like the one shown in **Figure 10.5**, bottom, appears.
3. **Choose exposure mode.** Highlight the exposure mode you want to use, choosing from Program, Aperture Priority, Shutter Priority, or Manual modes. Press the center button to confirm your choice. I listed the reasons for choosing each mode earlier in this chapter in the exposure mode section for conventional video. Keep in mind that you must use a shutter speed that's *faster* than your frame rate. In Shutter Priority or Manual modes, you cannot select a speed slower than 1/250th second at 240/250 fps; no slower than 1/500th second at 480/500 fps; and no slower than 1/1,000th second at 960/1000 fps.
4. **Adjust important settings.** Choose your ISO sensitivity, focus mode, focus area, and other settings as you would for

conventional video. Zoom to the focal length you want to use, and focus.

5. **Select HFR settings.** Navigate to the Camera Settings 2 menu and select Record Setting, Frame Rate, Priority Setting, and Record Timing. (See Figure 10.7.) I'll explain how to choose each of these in the next section.
6. **Enter standby mode.** To enter HFR Standby mode, press the center button. A green STBY notice will appear in the lower-left corner of the shooting screen. While that notice is shown, you will be unable to access menus or make any settings changes. To cancel standby mode, press the center button again.
7. **Capture your video.** While in standby mode, you can trigger recording by pressing the Movie button. When the button is pressed, the RX100 V will record and save either the 2 or 4 seconds that occur *after* you press the button (Start Trigger) or the 2 or 4 seconds leading *up to* the moment you pressed the button (End Trigger). I'll tell you more about those options and your other choices next.

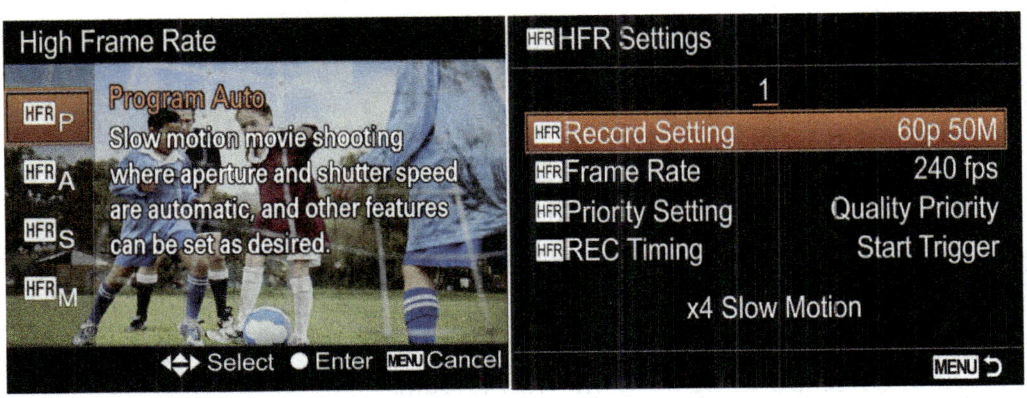

Figure 10.5

High Frame Rate exposure mode options.

The Record Setting, Frame Rate, Priority Setting, and Record Timing parameters control how and when your video is captured, and the degree of slow-motion effect. I'm going to explain each of these separately to help you understand how they work together.

Record Setting

This setting determines the *playback rate* for your finished high frame rate video. When this screen appears, you'll be given the choice of selecting 60p, 30p, or 24p playback. This setting is used with the frame rate to calculate the slow-motion effect, as I'll describe next.

Frame Rate

This setting determines the frame rate used by the camera when the video is captured. You can choose from 240 fps, 480 fps, and the top speed of 960 fps (when using NTSC video; with PAL systems the choices are 250/500/1000 fps). All three use a bit rate of 50 megabits per second, and use the XAVC S HD (1920 x 1080 pixel) video format to start. (The actual frame resolution will vary, depending on the Priority Setting you choose.)

The faster the frame rate, the greater the slow-motion effect at a given playback rate, as shown in **Table 10.5**. For example, if you set the Frame Rate to 240 fps and have selected a Record Setting of 24p, the resulting clip will play back at 24 fps, and will be 10X slower than the original action. Similarly, if your Frame Rate is 960 fps, and you play back at the 24 fps setting, your slow-motion video will be 40X slower.

It's easy to see where the numbers come from. With Quality Priority selected (as described next), the RX100 V will capture a 2-second clip. At 240 fps, you'll end up with 480 frames. When you play back those 480 frames at 24 fps, it will take 20 seconds to do so (480 divided by 24 equals 20). So, the original two seconds of motion will unfold 10X more slowly. Faster playback rates (30 fps or 60 fps) yield corresponding slow-motion effects.

Table 10.5 Slow Motion Effect

Record Setting/Frame Rate	240/250 fps	480/500 fps	960/1000 fps
24p	10X	20X	40X
30p/25p	8X/10X	16X/20X	32X/40X
60p/50p	4X/5X	8X/10X	16X/20X

Priority Setting

As you might expect, capturing 240-960 (or 250-1000) frames per second requires a lot of processing power, which in turn imposes some limitations on how much information you can collect in a given span of time. Your RX100 V gives you a choice of how that processing muscle is applied. You can choose to use it to collect the highest possible (feasible) image quality for a short period of time (2 seconds), or elect to record for a longer period of time (4 seconds), at a somewhat lower quality level.

Note that while the slices of time captured are two seconds and four seconds, the actual time required to write the video to your memory card (a red Recording bar appears on the screen) is much longer. The movie will be shown on the screen as it is saved, and the first time you see this it's easy to be fooled into thinking capture is still underway. Not so. You don't have to hold the camera steady during this process; capture has already finished.

This menu item lets you choose either Quality Priority or Shoot Time Priority, depending on whether you prefer a higher quality clip, or would rather record for a longer period of time. **Table 10.6** shows the capture resolution for both options at each of the available frame rates. Note that the camera automatically resamples the captured video and *converts it back to 1920 x 1080* (Full HD) for playback or editing, so you won't have to contend with viewing or processing oddball sizes like 1824 x 1026. The reduced capture resolution translates into reduced image quality after the conversion, however.

- **Quality Priority.** The RX100 V captures a two-second clip, using its highest quality level. Use this if you know that the event you want to capture will last two seconds or less, and you want the best possible image.
- **Shoot Time Priority.** A four-second clip is captured, but at a lower quality. Some events take longer to transpire, and you may need to use this setting to be sure you've captured all the action.

Table 10.6 HFR Movie Resolution

Priority/Frame Rate	240/250 fps	480/500 fps	960/1000 fps
Quality Priority (2 seconds)	1824 x 1026	1676 x 566	1136 x 384
Shoot Time Priority (4 seconds)	1676 x 566	1136 x 384	800 x 270

Note that the reduced resolution of each of the HFR formats results in "crop factor" from the smaller field of view. The net result is a telephoto effect that magnifies your image. **Figure 10.6** shows the actual cropped area captured at each of the Quality Priority/Shoot Time Priority settings.

The 240/250 fps Quality Priority setting, at 1824 x 1026 pixels is actually very close to Full HD resolution (1920 x 1080 pixels), and can be especially useful if you're mixing HD and HFR footage. You get only two seconds of capture, of course, but if you select the your action carefully, the slow motion video can be very effective, and merge smoothly with your conventional video.

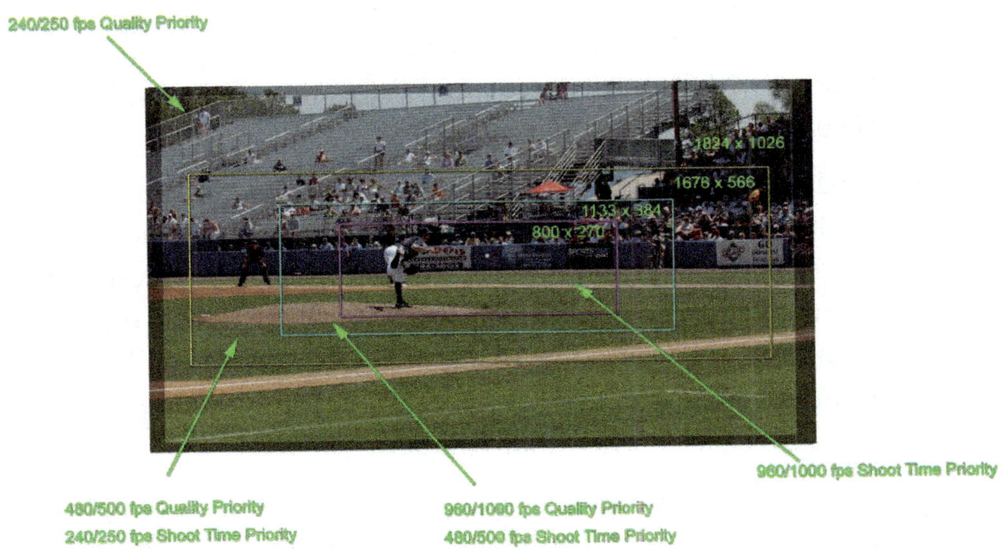

Figure 10.6

Effective crops at each of the Priority/Frame Rate settings.

Record Timing

You can decide *when* you want to record your video. You can capture the frames at the moment you press the center button, or wait, press the button, and capture the motion that happened up *until* you triggered the recording. Here's an easy to understand explanation:

- **Start Trigger.** The camera captures either 2 or 4 seconds of video, starting when you press the center button. Use this mode when the action is predictable and you think you can reliably capture the motion you want to record by pressing the button at the appropriate time.

  Say you were analyzing a friend's golf swing. The entire swing takes less than four seconds, so you could tell your friend to swing away, and start recording at that moment. The ensuing video would capture the movement completely. Or, perhaps you want slow-motion video of a baseball player's swing at a pitch. Start capture when you see the pitcher wind up to release the ball, and the swinging motion, along with the bat's contact with the ball (if you and the batter are lucky), will be recorded.

- **End Trigger.** In this mode, the camera captures motion continuously in its memory buffer *until* you press the button. Then, only the preceding two or four seconds of video that occurred prior to pressing the button will be stored on your memory card. You'd use this mode when the action is unpredictable: you know something is going to happen, but are not sure exactly when that will be.

  This mode is an excellent way of capturing bursts of lighting. Record continuously until you see a bolt strike, then press the button. The preceding two or four seconds showing the moments leading up to the burst, and the burst itself, will be stored on your memory card. (Unfortunately, if the lightning is far away from you, the thunder itself will arrive some time *after* the clip has concluded.) Or, perhaps you want slow-motion video of the final moments of a race. Start capture before the decisive moment, then press the button just after the winner crosses the finish line. The previous two or four seconds will be saved to your memory card as a slow motion clip.

Tips for Movie Making

I'm going to close out this introductory movie chapter with a general discussion of movie-making concepts that you need to understand as you move toward more polished video production. Once you have set up the camera for your video session and pressed the Movie button, you have done most of the technical work that's required of you for basic movie clips. Now your task is to use your skills at composition, lighting, scene selection, and, perhaps, directing actors, to make a compelling video production.

Here are some basic tips:

- **Keep things stable and on the level.** Camera shake's enough of a problem with still photography, but it becomes even more of a nuisance when you're shooting video. While the RX100 V's SteadyShot stabilization can help minimize this, neither can work miracles. Placing your camera on a tripod will work much better than trying to hand-hold it while shooting. One bit of really good news is that compared to pro dSLRs, the RX100 V can work very effectively on a lighter tripod, due to the camera's light weight. On windy days however, the extra mass of a heavy tripod is still valuable.
- **Use a shooting script.** A shooting script is nothing more than a coordinated plan that covers both audio and video and provides order and structure for your video. A detailed script will cover what types of shots you're going after, what dialogue you're going to use, audio effects, transitions, and graphics.
- **Plan with storyboards.** A storyboard is a series of panels providing visuals of what each scene should look like. While the ones produced by Hollywood are generally of very high quality, there's nothing that says drawing skills are important for this step. Stick figures work just fine if that's the best you

can do. The storyboard just helps you visualize locations, placement of actors/actresses, props, and furniture, and also helps everyone involved get an idea of what you're trying to show. It also helps show how you want to frame or compose a shot. You can even shoot a series of still photos and transform them into a "storyboard" if you want, such as in **Figure 10.7**.

Today's audience is used to fast-paced, short-scene storytelling. In order to produce interesting video for such viewers, it's important to view video storytelling as a kind of shorthand code for the more leisurely efforts print media offers. Audio and video should always be advancing the story. While it's okay to let the camera linger from time to time, it should only be for a compelling reason and only briefly.

It only takes a second or two for an establishing shot to impart the necessary information. For example, many of the scenes for a video documenting a model being photographed in a rock 'n' roll music setting might be close-ups and talking heads, but an establishing shot showing the studio where the video was captured helps set the scene.

- **Provide variety.** Provide variety too. Change camera angles and perspectives often and never leave a static scene on the screen for a long period of time. (You can record a static scene for a reasonably long period and then edit in other shots that cut away and back to the longer scene with close-ups that show each person talking.)
- **When editing, keep transitions basic!** I can't stress this one enough. Watch a television program or movie. The action "jumps" from one scene or person to the next. Fancy transitions that involve exotic "wipes," dissolves, or cross fades take too long for the average viewer and make your video ponderous.

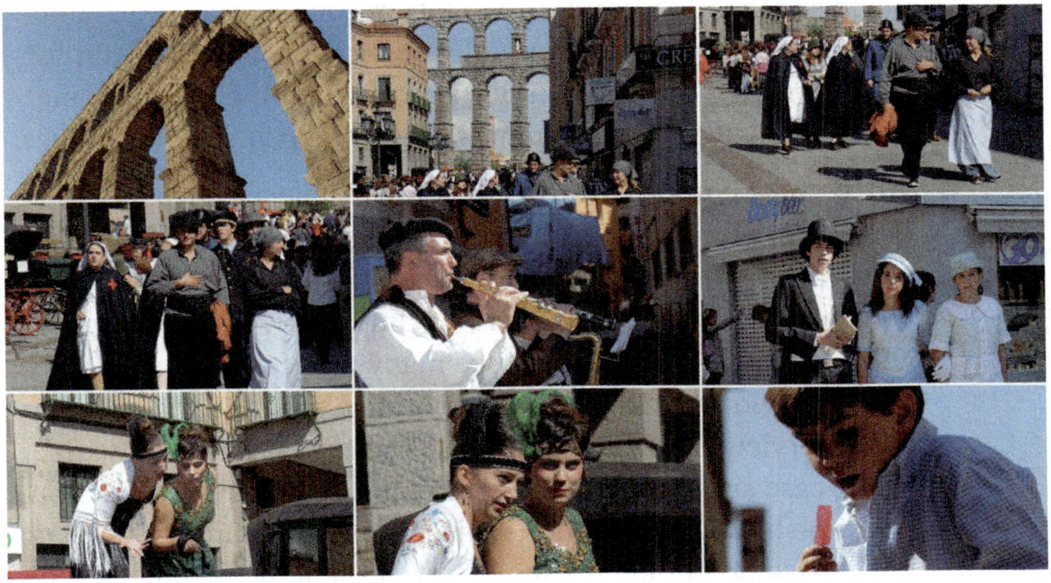

Figure 10.7

A storyboard is a series of simple sketches or photos to help visualize a segment of video.

Composition

In movie shooting, several factors restrict your composition, and impose requirements you just don't always have in still photography (although other rules of good composition do apply). Here are some of the key differences to keep in mind when composing movie frames:

- **Horizontal compositions only.** Some subjects, such as basketball players and tall buildings, just lend themselves to vertical compositions. But movies are generally shot and shown in horizontal format only. (Unless you're capturing a clip with your smartphone; I see many vertically oriented YouTube videos.) So if you're shooting a conventional video and interviewing a local basketball star, you can end up with a worst-case situation like the one shown in **Figure 10.8**. If you want to show how tall your subject is, it's often impractical to move back far enough to show him full-length. You really can't capture a vertical composition. Tricks like getting down on the floor and shooting up at your subject can exaggerate the perspective, but aren't a perfect solution.
- **Wasted space at the sides.** Moving in to frame the basketball player as outlined by the yellow box in **Figure 10.8** means that you're still forced to leave a lot of empty space on either side. (Of course, you can fill that space with other people and/or interesting stuff, but that defeats your intent of concentrating on your main subject.) So when faced with some types of subjects in a horizontal frame, you can be creative, or move in *really* tight. For example, if I was willing to give up the "height" aspect of my composition, I could have framed the shot as shown by the green box in the figure, and wasted less of the image area at either side.
- **Seamless (or seamed) transitions.** Unless you're telling a picture story with a photo essay, still pictures often stand alone. But with movies, each of your compositions must relate to the shot that preceded it, and the one that follows. It can be jarring to jump from a long shot to a tight close-up unless the director -- you -- is very creative. Another common error is the

"jump cut" in which successive shots vary only slightly in camera angle, making it appear that the main subject has "jumped" from one place to another. (Although everyone from French New Wave director Jean-Luc Goddard to Guy Ritchie -- Madonna's ex -- have used jump cuts effectively in their films.) The rule of thumb is to vary the camera angle by at least 30 degrees between shots to make it appear to be seamless. Unless you prefer that your images flaunt convention and appear to be "seamy."

- **The time dimension.** Unlike still photography, with motion pictures there's a lot more emphasis on using a series of images to build on each other to tell a story. Static shots where the camera is mounted on a tripod and everything is shot from the same distance are a recipe for dull videos. Watch a television program sometime and notice how often camera shots change distances and directions. Viewers are used to this variety and have come to expect it. Professional video productions are often done with multiple cameras shooting from different angles and positions. But many professional productions are shot with just one camera and careful planning, and you can do just fine with your RX100 V.

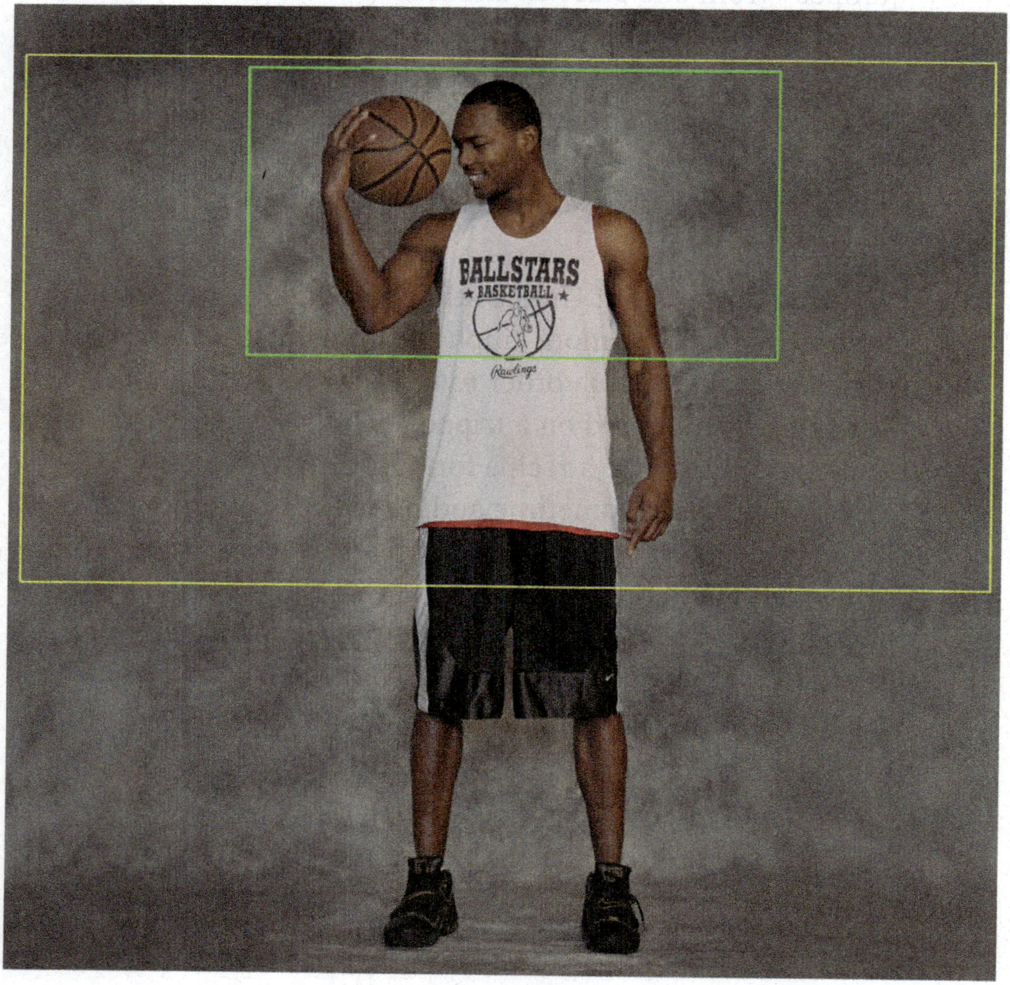

Figure 10.8

Movie shooting requires you to fit all your subjects into a horizontally oriented frame.

Here's a look at the different types of commonly used compositional tools:

- **Establishing shot.** Much like it sounds, this type of composition, as shown at top left in **Figure 10.9**, establishes the scene and tells the viewer where the action is taking place. Let's say you're shooting a video of your offspring's move to college; the establishing shot could be a wide shot of the campus with a sign welcoming you to the school in the foreground. Another example would be for a child's birthday party; the establishing shot could be the front of the house decorated with birthday signs and streamers or a shot of the dining room table decked out with party favors and a candle-covered birthday cake. In this case, I wanted to show the studio where the video was shot.

- **Medium shot.** This shot is composed from about waist to head room (some space above the subject's head). It's useful for providing variety from a series of close-ups and also makes for a useful first look at a speaker. (See **Figure 10.9**, top right.)
- **Close-up.** The close-up, usually described as "from shirt pocket to head room," provides a good composition for someone talking directly to the camera. Although it's common to have your talking head centered in the shot, that's not a requirement. In the middle left image in **Figure 10.9**, the subject was offset to the right. This would allow other images, especially graphics or titles, to be superimposed in the frame in a "real" (professional) production. But the compositional technique can be used with RX100 V videos, too, even if special effects are not going to be added.
- **Extreme close-up.** When I went through broadcast training, this shot was described as the "big talking face" shot and we were actively discouraged from employing it. Styles and tastes change over the years and now the big talking face is much more commonly used (maybe people are better looking these days?) and so this view may be appropriate. Just remember, the RX100 V is capable of shooting in high-definition video and you may be playing the video on a high-def TV; be careful that you use this composition on a face that can stand up to high definition. (See middle right, **Figure 10.9**.)
- **"Two" shot.** A two shot shows a pair of subjects in one frame. They can be side by side or one subject in the foreground and one in the background. This does not have to be a head-to-

ground composition. Subjects can be standing or seated. A "three shot" is the same principle except that three people are in the frame. (See **Figure 10.9**, lower left.)

- **Over-the-shoulder shot.** Long a composition of interview programs, the "over-the-shoulder shot" uses the rear of one person's head and shoulder to serve as a frame for the other person. This puts the viewer's perspective as that of the person facing away from the camera. (See **Figure 10.9**, lower right.)

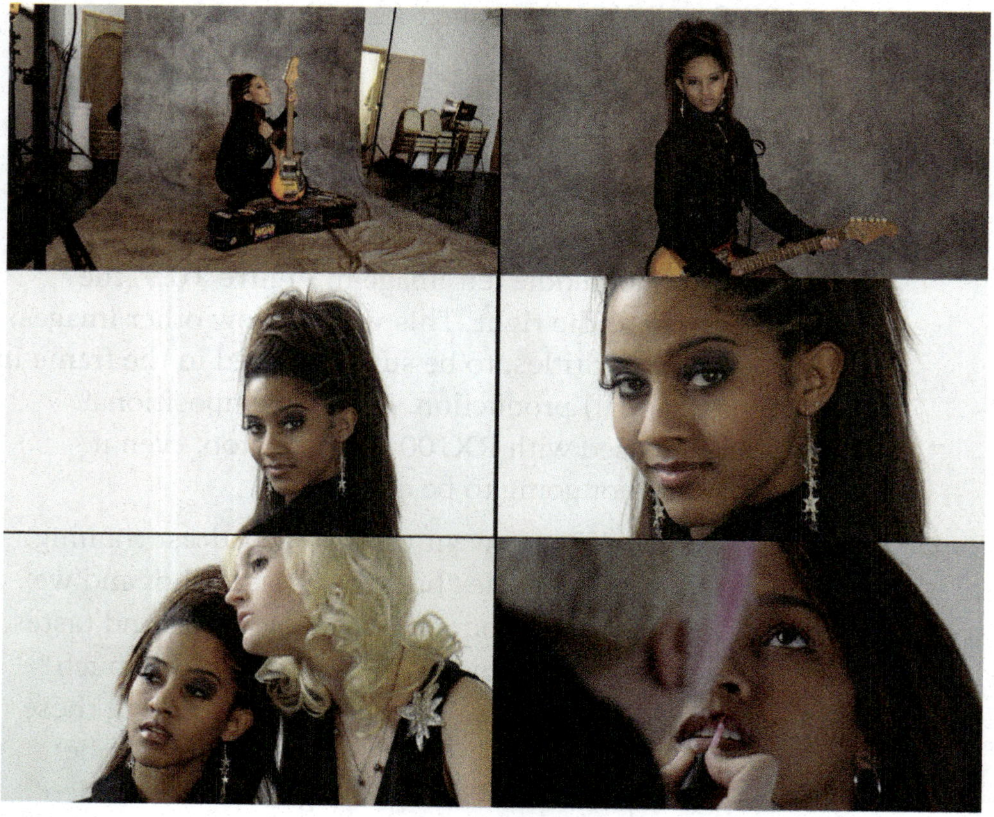

Figure 10.9

Establishing shot (upper left); Medium shot (upper right); Close-up (middle left); Extreme close-up (middle right); Two shot (lower left); Over-the-shoulder shot (lower right).

Lighting for Video

Much like in still photography, how you handle light pretty much can make or break your videography. Lighting for video can be more complicated than lighting for still photography, since both subject and camera movement are often part of the process.

Lighting for video presents several concerns. First off, you want enough illumination to create a useable video. Beyond that, you want to use light to help tell your story or increase drama. Let's take a better look at both.

Illumination

You can significantly improve the quality of your video by increasing the light falling in the scene. This is true indoors or out, by the way. While it may seem like sunlight is more than enough, it depends on how much contrast you're dealing with. If your subject is in shadow (which can help him from squinting) or wearing a ball cap, a video light can help make him look a lot better.

Lighting choices for amateur videographers are a lot better these days than they were a decade or two ago. An inexpensive incandescent video light, which will easily fit in a camera bag, can be found for $15 or $20. You can even get a good-quality LED video light for less than $100. Work lights sold at many home improvement stores can also serve as video lights since you can set the camera's white balance to correct for any color casts. You'll need to mount these lights on a tripod or other support, or, perhaps, to a bracket that fastens to the tripod socket on the bottom of the camera.

Much of the challenge depends upon whether you're just trying to add some fill light on your subject versus trying to boost the light on an entire scene. A small video light will do just fine for the former. It won't handle the latter. Fortunately, the versatility of the RX100 V comes in quite handy here. Since the camera shoots video in Auto ISO mode, it can compensate for lower lighting levels and still produce a decent image. For best results though, better lighting is necessary.

Creative Lighting

While ramping up the light intensity will produce better technical quality in your video, it won't necessarily improve the artistic quality of it. Whether we're outdoors or indoors, we're used to seeing light come from above. Videographers need to consider how they position their lights to provide even illumination while up high enough to angle shadows down low and out of sight of the camera.

When considering lighting for video, there are several factors. One is the quality of the light. It can either be hard (direct) light or soft (diffused) light. Hard light is good for showing detail, but it can also be very harsh and unforgiving. "Softening" the light, but diffusing it somehow, can reduce the intensity of the light but make for a kinder, gentler light as well.

While mixing light sources isn't always a good idea, one approach is to combine window light with supplemental lighting. Position your subject with the window to one side and bring in either a supplemental light or a reflector to the other side for reasonably even lighting.

Lighting Styles

Some lighting styles are more heavily used than others. Some forms are used for special effects, while others are designed to be invisible. At its most basic, lighting just illuminates the scene, but when used properly it can also create drama. Let's look at some types of lighting styles:

- **Three-point lighting.** This is a basic lighting setup for one person. A main light illuminates the strong side of a person's face, while a fill light lights up the other side. A third light is then positioned above and behind the subject to light the back of the head and shoulders. (See **Figure 10.10**, left.)
- **Flat lighting.** Use this type of lighting to provide illumination and nothing more. It calls for a variety of lights and diffusers set to raise the light level in a space enough for good video reproduction, but not to create a particular mood or emphasize

a particular scene or individual. With flat lighting, you're trying to create even lighting levels throughout the video space and minimize any shadows. Generally, the lights are placed up high and angled downward (or possibly pointed straight up to bounce off of a white ceiling). (See **Figure 10.10**, right.)

- **"Ghoul lighting."** This is the style of lighting used for old horror movies. The idea is to position the light down low, pointed upward. It's such an unnatural style of lighting that it makes its targets seem weird and ghoulish.
- **Outdoor lighting.** While shooting outdoors may seem easier because the sun provides more light, it also presents its own problems. As a general rule of thumb, keep the sun behind you when you're shooting video outdoors, except when shooting faces (anything from a medium shot and closer) since the viewer won't want to see a squinting subject. When shooting another human this way, put the sun behind her and use a video light to balance light levels between the foreground and background. If the sun is simply too bright, position the subject in the shade and use the video light for your main illumination. Using reflectors (white board panels or aluminum foil covered cardboard panels are cheap options) can also help balance light effectively.

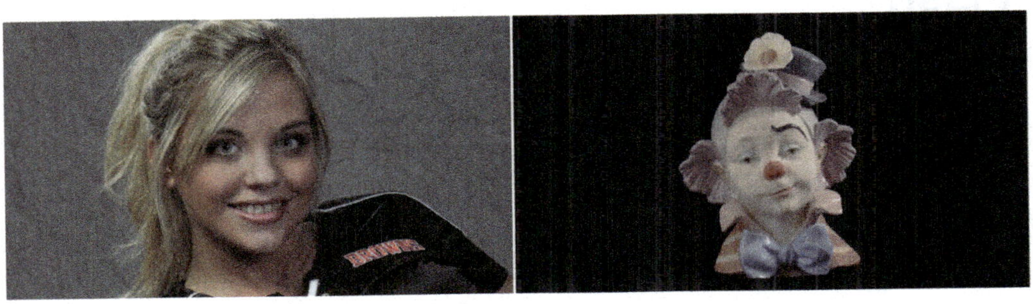

Figure 10.10

With three-point lighting (left) and flat lighting (right).

Chapter 11

Making Light Work for You

Successful photographers and artists have an intimate understanding of the importance of light in shaping an image. Rembrandt was a master of using light to create moods and reveal the character of his subjects. The late artist Thomas Kinkade's official tagline was "Painter of Light." Dean Collins, co-founder of Finelight Studios, revolutionized how a whole generation of photographers learned and used lighting. It's impossible to underestimate how the use of light adds to -- and how misuse can detract from -- your photographs.

As a Sony photographer, you must learn to be a painter and sculptor of light if you want to move from *taking* a picture to *making* a photograph. This chapter provides an introduction to using the two main types of illumination: *continuous* lighting (such as daylight, incandescent, or fluorescent sources) and the brief, but brilliant snippets of light we call *electronic flash.*

Continuous Illumination versus Electronic Flash

Continuous lighting is exactly what you might think: uninterrupted illumination that is available all the time during a shooting session. Daylight, moonlight, and the artificial lighting encountered both indoors and outdoors count as continuous light sources (although all of them can be "interrupted" by passing clouds, solar eclipses, a blown fuse, or simply by switching off a lamp). Indoor continuous illumination includes both the lights that are there already (such as incandescent lamps or overhead fluorescent lights indoors) and fixtures you supply yourself, including photoflood lamps or reflectors used to bounce existing light onto your subject.

The surge of light we call electronic flash is produced by a burst of photons generated by an electrical charge that is accumulated in a component called a *capacitor* and then directed through a glass tube containing xenon gas, which absorbs the energy and emits the brief flash. Electronic flash is notable because it can be much more intense than continuous lighting, lasts only a brief moment, and can be much more portable than supplementary incandescent sources. It's a light source you can carry with you and use anywhere.

Indeed, your Sony RX100 V comes with a built-in flash unit, shown elevated in **Figure 11.1**. Like all small flash tubes, this one is seriously underpowered. Sony says that with ISO Auto enabled, the flash range is 1.31 to 33.46 feet at the widest angle 24mm setting, and 1.31 to 21.33 feet at the 70mm setting. When you boost the ISO, the range increases because of greater sensor sensitivity, but you should be aware that at the greatest distances the ISO may be increased to ISO 1600 to 3200 and more visual noise will result.

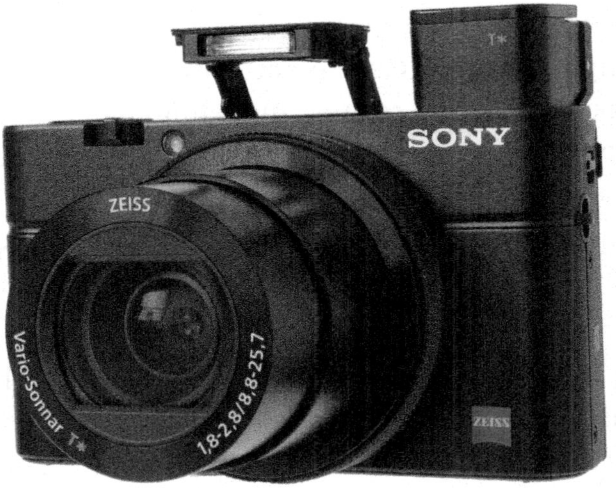

Figure 11.1

One form of light that's always available is the built-in pop-up flash on your RX100 V.

Since we do not usually want to shoot at very high ISO where digital noise can degrade image quality, the built-in flash is not ideal for all purposes. It's best reserved for fill-in flash to illuminate inky shadows in outdoor photography (where less power is required to achieve that effect), or for close-up photography in low light.

Before moving on to discussing your RX100 V's admittedly limited flash capabilities, let's review the advantages and disadvantages of each type of illumination. Here's a quick checklist of pros and cons:

- **Lighting preview -- Pro: continuous lighting.** With continuous lighting, such as incandescent lamps or daylight, you always know exactly what kind of lighting effect you're going to get. If you're using multiple lights, you can visualize how they will interact with each other. With electronic flash, the general effect you're going to see may be a mystery until you've built some experience.
- **Lighting preview -- Con: electronic flash.** The built-in flash does not provide any sort of "modeling light" function, so you have no way of knowing what your lighting effects will be until you take a test shot and review it.
- **Exposure calculation -- Pro: continuous lighting.** Your RX100 V has no problem calculating exposure for continuous lighting, because the lighting remains constant and can be measured through a sensor that interprets the light reaching the sensor. The amount of light available just before the exposure will, in almost all cases, be the same amount of light present when the shutter mechanism is opened to take the shot. The Spot metering mode can be used to measure brightness in the bright areas of the scene and the dark areas; if you have a bit of expertise in this technique, you'll know whether it would be useful to bounce some light into the shadow areas using a reflector panel accessory. You can also buy a hand-held light meter to measure the light falling onto the subject, instead of the light reflected by the subject.

- **Exposure calculation -- Con: electronic flash.** A flash unit provides no illumination until it actually fires so the exact exposure can't be measured by the RX100 V's exposure sensor before you take a photo. Instead, the light must be measured by metering the intensity of a pre-flash triggered an instant before the main flash, as it is reflected back to the camera and through the lens.
- **Evenness of illumination -- Pro/con: continuous lighting.** Of continuous light sources, daylight, in particular, provides illumination that tends to fill an image completely, lighting up the foreground, background, and your subject almost equally. A sunlit scene may have shadow areas too, of course, so you might need to use reflectors or fill-in light sources to even out the illumination. Barring objects that block large sections of your image from daylight, the light is spread fairly evenly. Indoors, however, continuous lighting is much less likely to be evenly distributed. The average living room, for example, has hot spots and dark corners. But on the plus side, you can *see* this uneven illumination and compensate with additional lamps.
- **Evenness of illumination -- Con: electronic flash.** Electronic flash units, like the continuous light provided by lamps, don't have the advantage of being located 93 million miles from the subject as the sun is. Because of this factor, they suffer from the effects of their proximity.

  The *inverse square law*, first applied to both gravity and light by Sir Isaac Newton, dictates that as a light source's distance increases from the subject, the amount of light reaching the subject falls off proportionately to the square of the distance. In plain English, that means that a flash or lamp that's 12 feet away from a subject provides only one-quarter as much illumination as a source that's 6 feet away (rather than half as much). (See **Figure 11.2**.) This translates into relatively shallow "depth-of-light." That's why your built-in flash can only be used at close distances.

- **Action stopping -- Pro: electronic flash.** When it comes to the ability to freeze moving objects in their tracks, the advantage goes to electronic flash. The brief duration of the emitted light serves as a very fast "shutter speed" when the flash is the main or only source of illumination for the photo. In other words, this effect is possible when shooting in a dark area without much if any lighting provided by ambient sources but assumes that subject is not beyond the range of the flash.

  In flash photography, your RX100 V's shutter speed (called sync speed in flash photography) with the camera's leaf shutter can be anything up to and including 1/2,000th second (faster speeds use the electronic shutter instead and flash is not possible), but when flash is the primary light source, the *effective* exposure time will be 1/1,000th to 1/50,000th second or less; this is the actual duration of the flash illumination. It's possible to freeze motion with flash of very short duration. The only fly in the ointment is that, if the ambient light is strong enough, it may produce a secondary "ghost" exposure, as I'll explain later in this chapter.

- **Action stopping -- Con: continuous lighting.** Action stopping with continuous light sources is completely dependent on the shutter speed you've dialed in on the camera. And the speeds available are dependent on the amount of light available and your camera's ISO sensitivity setting. Outdoors in daylight, there will probably be enough sunlight to let you shoot at 1/2,000th second and f/6.3 with a non-grainy ISO of 400. That's a fairly useful combination of settings if you're not using a super-telephoto with a small maximum aperture.

  But indoors, the reduced illumination quickly has you pushing your RX100 V to its limits. For example, if you're shooting indoor sports in a dark arena, there probably won't be enough available light to allow you to use a 1/2,000th second shutter speed unless you use a lens with an extremely wide aperture (such as f/1.8) or set a very high ISO where image quality can suffer. (In truth, the gym where I shoot indoor basketball allows me to do so at 1/500th second at f/4 using ISO 1600.) In many indoor sports situations, you may find yourself limited to a shutter speed of 1/500th second or slower.

- **Flexibility -- Pro: electronic flash.** The action-freezing power of electronic flash, at least for nearby subjects in a dark location, allows you to work without a tripod; that provides extra flexibility and speed when choosing angles and positions.
- **Flexibility -- Con: continuous lighting.** Because incandescent and fluorescent lamps are not as bright as electronic flash, the slower shutter speeds required (see "Action stopping," above) mean that you may have to use a tripod more often, especially when shooting portraits. The incandescent variety of continuous lighting gets hot, especially in the studio, and the side effects range from discomfort (for your human models) to disintegration (if you happen to be shooting perishable foods like ice cream).

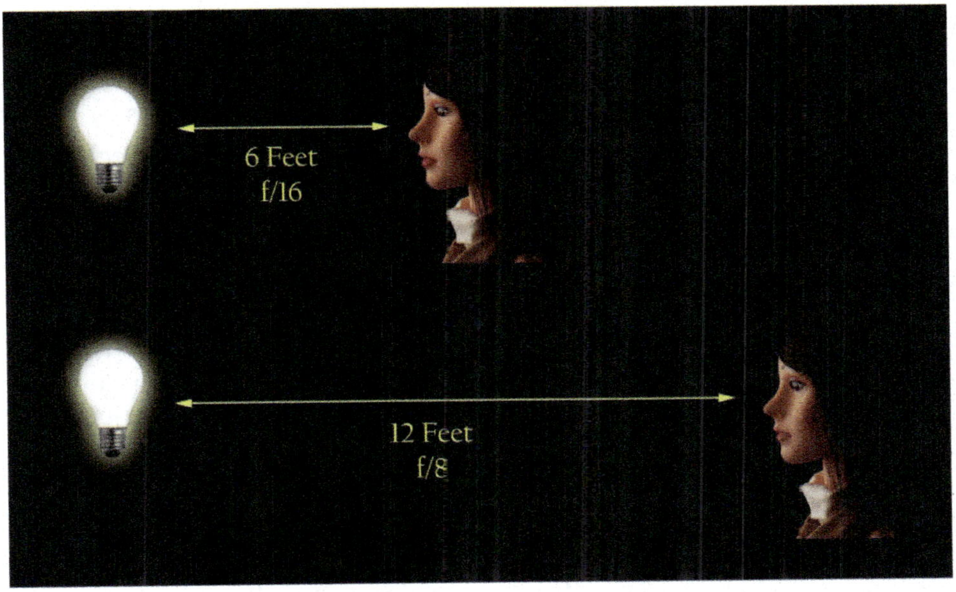

Figure 11.2

A light source that is twice as far away provides only one-quarter as much illumination.

Continuous Lighting Basics

While continuous lighting and its effects are generally much easier to visualize and use than electronic flash, there are some factors you need to take into account, particularly the color temperature of the light. (Color temperature concerns aren't exclusive to continuous light sources, of course, but the variations tend to be more extreme and less predictable compared to electronic flash.)

Color temperature, in practical terms, is how "bluish" or how "reddish" the light appears to the digital camera's sensor. Indoor illumination is often quite warm, comparatively, and appears reddish to the sensor. Daylight, in contrast, especially on an overcast day, seems much bluer to the sensor. Our eyes (our brains, actually) are quite adaptable to these variations, so white objects don't appear to have an orange tinge under a tungsten lamp or a blue tint on a cloudy day. Yet, these color temperature variations are real and the camera will record them unless you use an appropriate white balance setting.

It's important to be aware of the color temperature of the light when you want to get an accurate overall color balance (or *white balance*) -- either using the White Balance system's smarts or making manual settings, using your own knowledge and experience. Color temperature can be confusing, because of a seeming contradiction in how color temperatures are named.

We are all more familiar with the concept of ambient temperatures in the Arctic (low equaling cold) and at the equator (high or warm), but color temperature measurements (in degrees Kelvin) use the opposite approach. The *lower* numbers indicate warmer (reddish) light, while the higher numbers refer to cooler (bluer) light. It might not make sense to say that 3,400K is *warmer* than 6,000K, but that's the way it is. If it helps, think of a glowing red ember contrasted with a white-hot welder's torch, rather than fire and ice.

The confusion comes from physics. Scientists calculate color temperature from the light emitted by a mythical object called a black body radiator, which absorbs all the radiant energy that strikes it, and reflects none at all. Such a black body not only *absorbs* light perfectly, but it *emits* it perfectly when heated (and since nothing in the universe is perfect, that makes it mythical).

At a particular physical temperature, this imaginary object always emits light of the same wavelength or color. That makes it possible to define color temperature in terms of actual temperature in degrees on the Kelvin scale that scientists use. Incandescent light (from a light bulb that's not daylight balanced), for example, typically has a color temperature of 2,700K to 3,000K. If a room is lit only by candles, the color temperature will be in the 1,000K to 2,000K range. Outdoors in daylight however, the color temperature might range from 5,500K to 6,000K. Each type of illumination we use for photography has its own color temperature range -- with some cautions. The next sections will summarize everything you need to know about the qualities of these light sources.

Daylight

Daylight is produced by the sun, and so is moonlight (which is just reflected sunlight). Daylight is present, of course, even when you can't see the sun. When sunlight is direct, the illumination can be bright and harsh. If daylight is diffused by clouds, softened by bouncing off objects such as walls or your photo reflectors, or when filtered by shade, it can be much dimmer and less contrasty.

Daylight's color temperature can vary quite widely. It is highest (most blue) at noon when the sun is directly overhead, because the light is traveling through a minimum amount of the filtering layer we call the atmosphere. The color temperature at high noon may be around 5,500K to 6,000K. Earlier and later in the day, the sun is lower in the sky and the particles in the air provide a filtering effect that warms the illumination to about 4,500K on a sunny day. (If clouds completely cover the sun, the color temperature will be around 7,000K, slightly blue.) Starting an hour before dusk and for an hour after sunrise, the warm appearance of the sunlight is even visible to our eyes as shown in Figure 11.3; in such conditions, the color temperature may dip to around 4,500K and even to 3,200K.

Because you'll be taking so many photos in daylight, you'll want to learn how to use or compensate for the brightness and contrast of sunlight, as well as how to deal with its color temperature. I'll provide some hints later in this chapter.

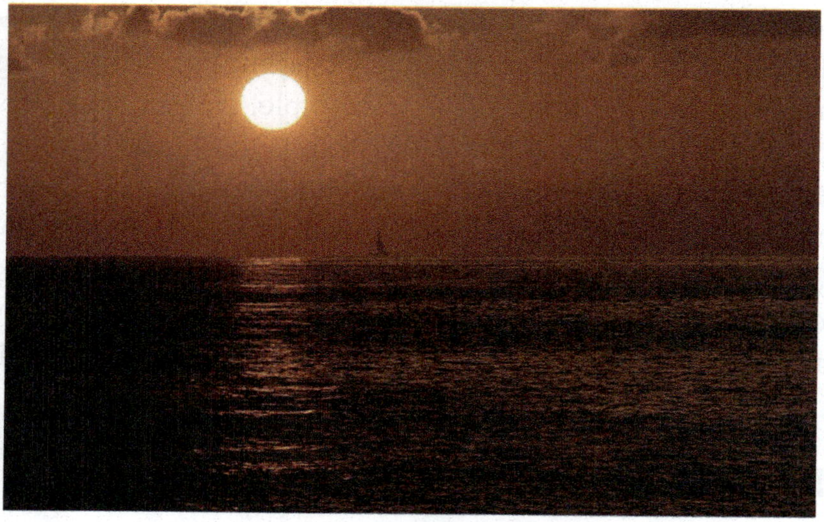

Figure 11.3

At dawn and dusk, the color temperature of the sunlight will dip to 4,500K or even to 3,200K, depending on the atmospheric conditions.

Incandescent/Tungsten Light

The term incandescent or tungsten illumination is usually applied to the direct descendents of Thomas Edison's original electric lamp. Such lights consist of a glass bulb that contains a vacuum, or is filled with a halogen gas, and contains a tungsten filament that is heated by an electrical current, producing photons and heat. Tungsten-halogen lamps are a variation on the basic light bulb, using a more rugged (and longer-lasting) filament that can be heated to a higher temperature; it's housed in a thicker glass or quartz envelope, and filled with iodine or bromine ("halogen") gases. The higher temperature allows tungsten-halogen (or quartz-halogen/quartz-iodine, depending on their construction) lamps to burn "hotter" and whiter. Used for many automobile headlamps today, they've also been popular for photographic illumination.

Although a tungsten flood lamp intended for photography isn't a perfect black body radiator, it's close enough that the color temperature of the light it emits can be precisely calculated (about 3,000K to 3,550K, depending on the type of lamp). With this type of lighting, there's little concern about color variation, at least, until you get very close to the end of the lamp's life. By comparison, the tungsten (incandescent) light bulbs intended for household use can vary in color temperature, and these days, many such bulbs are rated as "White" or "Daylight Balanced"; this indicates a modification that causes the light output to be bluer, closer to 5,500K to 6,000K, depending on the bulb.

The other qualities of this type of lighting, such as contrast, are dependent on the distance of the lamp from the subject, type of reflectors used, and other factors that I'll explain later in this chapter.

Fluorescent Light/Other Light Sources

Fluorescent light has some advantages in terms of illumination, but some disadvantages from a photographic standpoint. This type of lamp generates light through an electro-chemical reaction that emits most of its energy as visible light, rather than heat; that's why the bulbs don't get as hot. The type of light produced varies depending on the phosphor coatings and type of gas in the tube. So, the illumination produced by fluorescent tubes or bulbs can vary widely in its characteristics.

That's not great news for photographers. Different types of lamps have different "color temperatures" that can't be precisely measured in degrees Kelvin, because the light isn't produced by heating. Worse, fluorescent lamps have a discontinuous spectrum of light that can have some colors missing entirely. A particular type of tube can lack certain shades of red or other colors (see **Figure 11.4**), which is why fluorescent lamps and other alternative technologies such as sodium-vapor illumination can produce ghastly looking human skin tones. Their spectra can lack the reddish tones we associate with healthy skin and emphasize the blues and greens popular in horror movies.

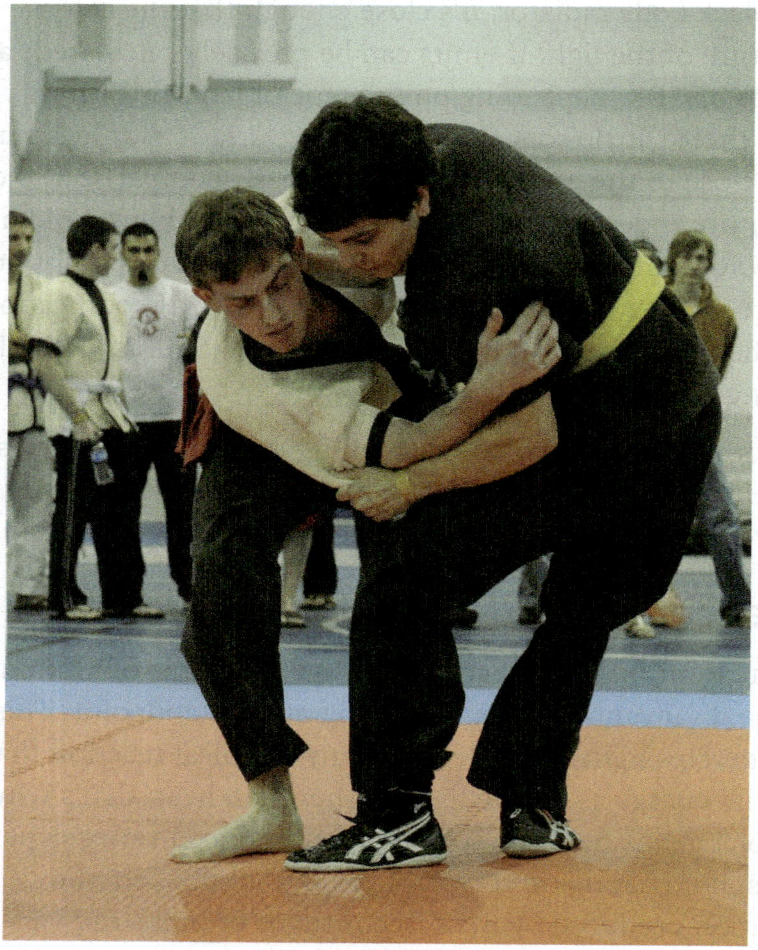

Figure 11.4
The fluorescent lighting in this huge indoor arena added a distinct greenish cast to the image.

Adjusting White Balance

I showed you how to adjust white balance in Chapter 7.

In most cases, however, the RX100 V will do a good job of calculating white balance for you, so Auto can be used as your choice most of the time. Use the preset values or set a custom white balance that matches the current shooting conditions when you need to. The only really problematic light sources are likely to be fluorescents. Vendors, such as GE and Sylvania, may actually provide a figure known as the *color rendering index* (or CRI), which is a measure of how accurately a particular light source represents standard colors, using a scale of 0 (some sodium-vapor lamps) to 100 (daylight and most incandescent lamps). Daylight fluorescents and deluxe cool white fluorescents might have a CRI of about 79 to 95, which is perfectly acceptable for most photographic applications. Warm white fluorescents might have a CRI of 55. White deluxe mercury vapor lights are less suitable with a CRI of 45, while low-pressure sodium lamps can vary from CRI 0 to 18.

Remember that if you shoot RAW format photos with the RX100 V, you can set any desired white balance for an image in the converter software whether you use the Photoshop, Photoshop Elements, or another image editor that supports the Sony RAW format. While color-balancing filters that fit on the front of the lens still exist (and require a clumsy adapter to be usable on the RX100 V), they are primarily useful for film cameras, because film's color balance can't be tweaked as extensively as that of a sensor.

Electronic Flash Basics

Electronic flash illumination is produced by a flash of photons generated by an electrical charge that is accumulated in a component called a *capacitor* and then directed through a glass tube containing xenon gas, which absorbs the energy and emits the brief flash. For the built-in flash furnished with the camera, the full burst of light lasts about 1/1,000th second, and provides enough illumination to shoot a nearby subject, unless you're using a wide aperture and/or a high ISO level as discussed earlier. As you can see, the built-in flash is relatively underpowered and not your best choice when photographing distant subjects.

The RX100 V's built-in flash is always available as required. There are several flash modes available in the Camera Settings 3 menu:

- **Flash Off.** The flash never fires; this may be useful in museums, concerts, or religious ceremonies where electronic flash would prove disruptive. (This option is not available in P, A, S, or M mode; if you do not want flash to fire, simply press it down into place.)
- **Auto Flash.** The flash fires as required, depending on lighting conditions. (Not available in P, A, S, or M mode because flash always fires in these modes if it's has been raised using the Flash switch.)
- **Fill-Flash.** When this option is set, the flash will always fire when using one of the two Auto modes or in SCN modes where flash is available. The camera balances the available illumination with flash to provide a balanced lighting effect. (See **Figure 11.5**.)
- **Slow Sync.** The RX100 V combines flash with slow shutter speeds; the nearby subject can be illuminated by flash, but during the longer shutter speed, there's enough time for the darker surroundings (lit by ambient light) to record on the sensor. (See **Figure 11.6**.)
- **Rear Sync.** Fires the flash at the end of the exposure time, after the ambient light exposure has been made, producing more satisfying photos of moving subjects when using a long exposure; light trails will be behind the "ghost" image, as illustrated in Figure **11.7**.

The built-in flash is a handy component because it is available as required, without the need to carry an external flash around with you constantly. This section explains how to use the flip-up flash. Start by pressing the flash button (on the center edge of the back of the camera) to the right towards the mode dial. Use the P, A, S, or M mode to ensure that all flash features will be available.

BOUNCE FLASH

Although the built-in flash doesn't have detents to allow variable angles, you can easily tilt it with the tip of your index finger while shooting to provide additional flexibility. For example, you can carefully angle the flash downward when shooting close-ups (perhaps with mixed results), or tilt it backward to bounce it off a ceiling or other diffusing surface. Of course, the light may not actually reach the subject; you would need to use a high ISO (to increase sensor sensitivity) for this technique to provide any effect. Fortunately, the RX100 V senses when the flash has been pointed upward, and automatically increases the ISO sensitivity to a more suitable level.

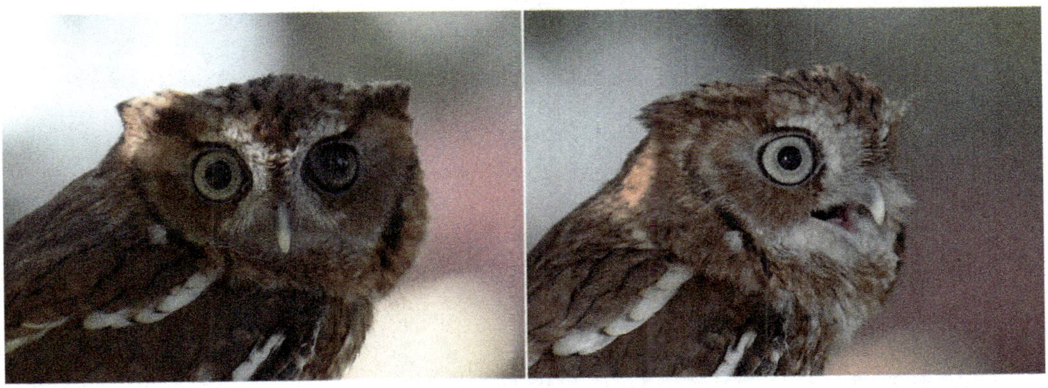

Figure 11.5

The owl (left) was in shadow. Fill-flash (right) brightened up the bird, while adding a little catch light to its eye.

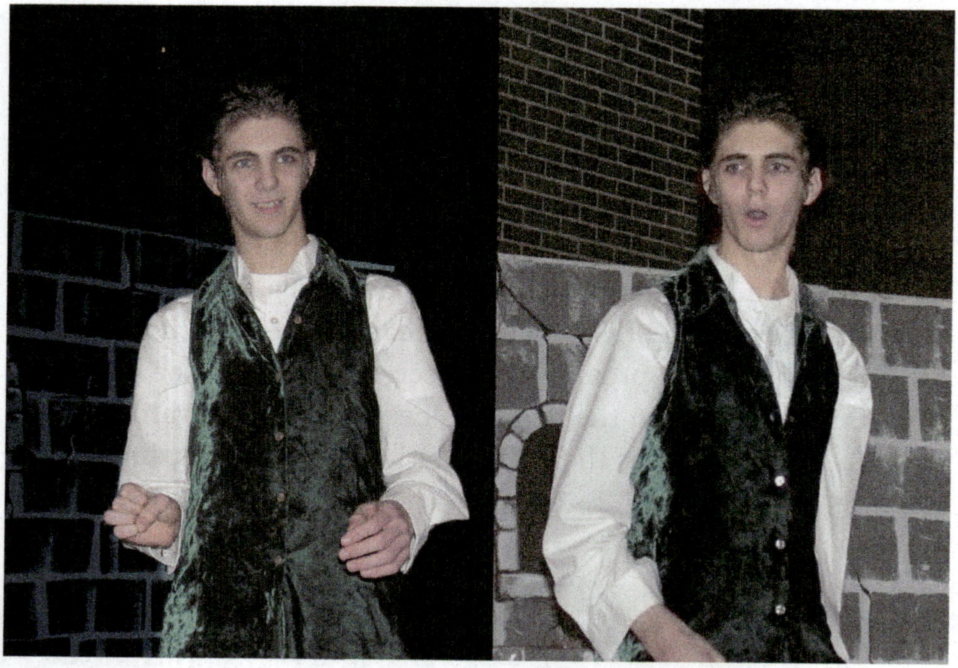

Figure 11.6
Slow sync uses longer shutter speeds to allow ambient light to fill in the background.

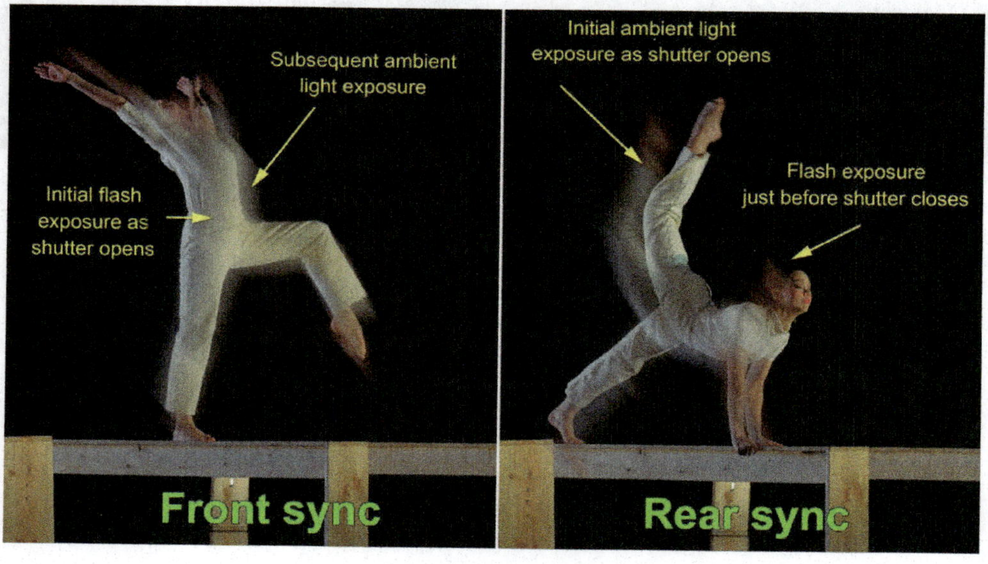

Figure 11.7
With front sync, the ambient light ghost image appears in front of a moving object. With rear sync, the ghost image trails behind the subject's motion.

Flash Exposure Compensation

It's important to keep in mind how the RX100 V's exposure compensation system works when you're using electronic flash. To activate exposure compensation for flash, visit the Flash Comp. item in the Camera Settings 3 menu and set the amount of plus or minus compensation you want. This function is not available when using Auto or SCN modes or Panorama mode. When you find that your flash photos are too dark even after you have set +3, then the flash simply cannot provide more power; you must move closer to the subject, or use a wider aperture, or set a higher ISO, or take all of these steps. Note too that when a subject is extremely close to the camera, even a -3 setting may not prevent an excessively bright image.

Flash exposure compensation affects only the amount of light emitted by the flash. If you want to adjust the brightness of the ambient light exposure, you would also need to use the conventional exposure compensation feature. In fact, you can use both features at the same time, to get a brighter subject and a darker background, or vice versa. Let's say you're taking a photo of a friend posing against a light-toned background such as a white cabana on a beach. A plus exposure compensation setting (perhaps +1 when using multi-segment metering) will ensure that the cabana won't be underexposed, while a -1/3 or -2/3 flash exposure compensation will ensure that shadows on your friend's face will be lightened by a very gentle burst of flash. This is an advanced technique that requires some experimentation but can be valuable when used with some expertise.

Red Eye Reduction

When using semi-automatic or manual exposure modes (or any SCN mode in which flash is used), red-eye reduction is available if Red Eye Reduction is On in the Camera Settings 3 menu (as described in Chapter 3). The flash will fire a burst before the photo is actually taken as you depress the shutter release button. That will theoretically cause your subjects' irises to contract (if they are looking toward the camera), thereby reducing the red-eye effect in your photograph. This option is not available when using Rear Sync.

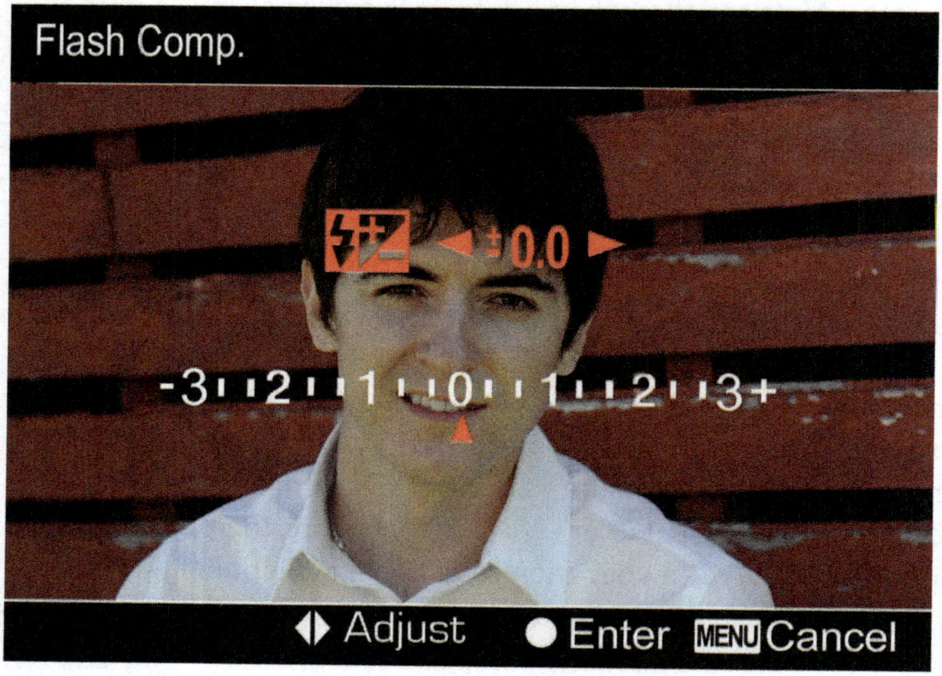

Figure 11.8

CPSIA information can be obtained
at www.ICGtesting.com
Printed in the USA
BVOW07s0726281217
503781BV00029B/115/P

9 781946 488053